THE NEW SHAKESPEARE

Designed to make Shakespeare's great plays available to all readers, the New Folger Library edition of Shakespeare's plays provides accurate texts in modern spelling and punctuation, as well as scene-by-scene action summaries, full explanatory notes, and notes recording the most significant departures from the early printed versions.

This collection of three of Shakespeare's greatest tragedies is based on the acclaimed individual Folger editions of the plays. In those editions, each play is prefaced by a brief introduction and followed by a "Modern Perspective" written by an expert on that particular play, along with many pictures clarifying Shakespeare's language. Each is also prefaced by a guide to reading Shakespeare's language and by accounts of his life and theater, and is followed by an annotated list of further readings.

Barbara A. Mowat is Director of Academic Programs at the Folger Shakespeare Library, Executive Editor of *Shakespeare Quarterly*, Chair of the Folger Institute, and author of *The Dramaturgy of Shakespeare's Romances* and of essays on Shakespeare's plays and on the editing of the plays.

Paul Werstine is Professor of English at King's College and the Graduate School of the University of Western Ontario, Canada. He is general editor of the New Variorum Shakespeare and author of many papers and articles on the printing and editing of Shakespeare's plays.

The Folger Shakespeare Library

The Folger Shakespeare Library in Washington, D.C., a privately funded research library dedicated to Shakespeare and the civilization of early modern Europe, was founded in 1932 by Henry Clay and Emily Jordan Folger. In addition to its role as the world's preeminent Shakespeare collection and its emergence as a leading center for Renaissance studies, the Folger Library offers a wide array of cultural and educational programs and services for the general public.

EDITORS

BARBARA A. MOWAT
Director of Academic Programs
Folger Shakespeare Library

PAUL WERSTINE
Professor of English
King's College and the University of Western Ontario

·THE NEW·
FOLGER LIBRARY SHAKESPEARE

THREE TRAGEDIES

ROMEO AND JULIET

HAMLET

MACBETH

BY WILLIAM SHAKESPEARE

EDITED BY BARBARA A. MOWAT
AND PAUL WERSTINE

WSP

WASHINGTON SQUARE PRESS

New York   London   Toronto   Sydney

WSP

A Washington Square Press Publication
1230 Avenue of the Americas, New York, NY 10020

Romeo and Juliet copyright © 1992 by The Folger Shakespeare Library
Hamlet copyright © 1992 by The Folger Shakespeare Library
Macbeth copyright © 1992 by The Folger Shakespeare Library

These titles were previously published individually by Washington Square Press

All rights reserved, including the right to reproduce this book or portions thereof in any form whatsoever. For information address Washington Square Press, 1230 Avenue of the Americas, New York, NY 10020

ISBN: 0-671-72261-1

First Washington Square Press printing February 2003

10 9 8 7 6 5 4 3

WASHINGTON SQUARE PRESS and colophon are registered trademarks of Simon & Schuster, Inc.

For information regarding special discounts for bulk purchases, please contact Simon & Schuster Special Sales at 1-800-456-6798 or business@simonandschuster.com

Cover design by Tom McKeveny
Cover art by Kinuko Y. Craft

Printed in the U.S.A.

From the Director of the Library

For over four decades, the Folger Library General Reader's Shakespeare provided accurate and accessible texts of the plays and poems to students, teachers, and millions of other interested readers. Today, in an age often impatient with the past, the passion for Shakespeare continues to grow. No author speaks more powerfully to the human condition, in all its variety, than this actor/playwright from a minor sixteenth-century English village.

Over the years vast changes have occurred in the way Shakespeare's works are edited, performed, studied, and taught. The New Folger Library Shakespeare replaces the earlier versions, bringing to bear the best and most current thinking concerning both the texts and their interpretation. Here is an edition which makes the plays and poems fully understandable for modern readers using uncompromising scholarship. Professors Barbara Mowat and Paul Werstine are uniquely qualified to produce this New Folger Shakespeare for a new generation of readers. The Library is grateful for the learning, clarity, and imagination they have brought to this ambitious project.

Werner Gundersheimer,
Director of the Folger Shakespeare Library
from 1984 to 2002

Acknowledgments

We are grateful to the Huntington and Newberry Libraries for fellowship support; to King's College for the grants it has provided to Paul Werstine; to the Social Sciences and Humanities Research Council of Canada, which provided him with a Research Time Stipend for 1990–91; to R. J. Shroyer of the University of Western Ontario for essential computer support; to the Folger Institute's Center for Shakespeare Studies for its fortuitous sponsorship of a workshop on "Shakespeare's Texts for Students and Teachers" (funded by the National Endowment for the Humanities and led by Richard Knowles of the University of Wisconsin), a workshop from which we learned an enormous amount about what is wanted by college and high-school teachers of Shakespeare today; to Alice Falk for her expert copyediting; and especially to Stephen Llano, our production editor at Washington Square Press, whose expertise and attention to detail are essential to this project.

Our biggest debt is to the Folger Shakespeare Library—to Werner Gundersheimer, Director of the Library from 1984 to 2002, who made possible our edition; to Deborah Curren-Aquino, who provides extensive editorial and production support; to Peggy O'Brien, former Director of Education at the Folger and now Director of Education Programs at the Corporation for Public Broadcasting, who gave us expert advice about the needs being expressed by Shakespeare teachers and students (and to Martha Christian and other "master teachers" who used our texts in manuscript in their classrooms); to Allan Shnerson and Mary Bloodworth for expert computer support;

to the staff of the Academic Programs Division, especially Rachel Kunkle (whose help is crucial), Mary Tonkinson, Kathleen Lynch, Carol Brobeck, Liz Pohland, Owen Williams, and Lisa Meyers; and, finally, to the generously supportive staff of the Library's Reading Room.

Barbara A. Mowat and Paul Werstine

Contents

An Introduction to the Texts of This Edition

In this collection of *Three Tragedies* we reprint the single-volume editions of plays edited by Mowat and Werstine and published by Washington Square Press in 1992. These single-volume editions are based directly upon early printed texts of the plays—*Romeo and Juliet* on the quarto printed in 1599; *Hamlet* on the quarto of 1604–5, with additional passages from the text first printed in the 1623 collection of Shakespeare's plays now known as the First Folio; and *Macbeth* on the 1623 First Folio printing. While the texts and explanatory notes are the same in this collection of *Three Tragedies* (except for formatting) as in the 1992 single-volume editions, the single-volume editions contain fuller discussions of the relation of our texts to the early printed versions, along with more extensive textual notes; an introduction to Shakespeare's language; information about Shakespeare, his theater, and the publication of his plays; a list of further readings; illustrations drawn from the Folger's holdings of rare books; and an essay about the play. Readers interested in such matters are encouraged to consult the 1992 editions. In the present volume we offer accurate texts in modern spelling, full explanatory notes, and scene-by-scene action summaries.

For the convenience of the reader, we have in our editions modernized the punctuation and the spelling of the early printed texts. Sometimes we go so far as to modernize certain old forms of words;

for example, when *a* means *he,* we change it to *he;* we change *mo* to *more,* *ye* to *you,* and *god buy to you* to *goodbye to you.* But we have not modernized forms of words that sound distinctly different from modern forms. For example, when the early printed texts read *sith* or *apricocks* or *porpentine,* we have not modernized to *since, apricots, porcupine.* When the forms *an, and,* or *and if* appear instead of the modern form *if,* we have reduced *and* to *an* but have not changed any of these forms to their modern equivalent, *if.* We also modernize and, where necessary, correct passages in foreign languages, unless an error in the early printed text can be reasonably explained as a joke.

Whenever we change the wording of the early printed text or add anything to its stage directions, we mark the change by enclosing it in superior half-brackets (⌐ ⌐). (In *Hamlet,* which we base on Q2 [the quarto of 1604–5], with variants and additional passages from F [the 1623 Folio text], we also use two other forms of brackets—pointed parentheses (⟨⟩) enclose all the words that are printed in F and not in Q2; square brackets ([]) mark off all the lines that are printed only in Q2 and not in F.) We want our readers to be immediately aware when we have intervened. (Only when we correct an obvious typographical error in the early printed text does the change not get marked.) Whenever we change the wording of an early printed text—as, for example, the 1604–5 quarto of *Hamlet*—we list the change in the textual notes that follow each play. In this edition, when we have simply corrected an obvious error, we do not list the change in the textual notes, nor do we list punctuation changes. (For more complete textual notes, the reader is advised to consult the single-volume editions of the plays.)

In our editions, we regularize a number of the proper names, as is the usual practice in editions of Shakespeare's plays. For example, although *Hamlet*'s queen of Denmark is called "Gertrard" or "Gertrad" in the 1604–5 quarto, in our edition she is always designated "Gertrude," her name in the 1623 printing of the play and the name that has become familiar to readers and playgoers. In addition, we expand the often severely abbreviated forms of names used as speech headings in early printed texts into the full names of the characters. We also silently regularize the speakers' names in speech headings, using only a single designation for each character, even though the early printed texts sometimes use a variety of designations.

Our editions differ from some earlier ones in trying to aid the reader in imagining the play as a performance rather than as a series of actual or novelistic events. Thus stage directions are written with reference to the stage. For example, in 2.3 of *Macbeth*, instead of providing a stage direction that says "The Porter opens the gate," as many editions do, this edition has "The Porter opens the door." There may have been doors on Shakespeare's stages for the Porter to open, but almost certainly there were no gates. Whenever it is reasonably certain, in our view, that a speech is accompanied by a particular action, we provide a stage direction describing the action. (Occasional exceptions to this rule occur when the action is so obvious that to add a stage direction would insult the reader). Stage directions for the entrance of characters in mid-scene are placed so that they immediately precede the characters' participation in the scene, even though these entrances may appear somewhat earlier in the early printed texts. We do not record these alterations in the position of stage directions in the textual notes. Latin stage directions (e.g., *Exeunt*) are translated into English (e.g., *They exit*).

In our editions, as well, we mark with a dash any change of address within a speech, unless a stage direction intervenes. When the *-ed* ending of a word is to be pronounced, we mark it with an accent. Like editors for the last two centuries, we print metrically linked lines in the following way:

BENVOLIO
  Good morrow, cousin.
ROMEO   Is the day so young?
               (*Romeo and Juliet* 1.1.163–64)

However, when there are a number of short verse-lines that can be linked in more than one way, we do not, with rare exceptions, indent any of them.

The Explanatory Notes

The notes that appear directly after each playtext are designed to provide readers with the help that they may need to enjoy the play. Whenever the meaning of a word in the text is not readily accessible in a good contemporary dictionary, we offer the meaning in a note. Sometimes we provide a note even when the relevant meaning is to be found in the dictionary but when the word has acquired since Shakespeare's time other potentially confusing meanings. In our notes, we try to offer modern synonyms for Shakespeare's words. We also try to indicate to the reader the connection between the word in the play and the modern synonym. For example, Shakespeare sometimes uses the word *head* to mean *source*, but, for modern readers, there may be no connection evident between these two words. We provide the connection by explaining Shakespeare's usage as follows: "**head:** fountain-head, source." On some occasions, a whole phrase or clause needs explanation. Then we rephrase in our own words the difficult passage, and add at the end synonyms for individual words in the passage. When scholars have been unable to determine the meaning of a word or phrase, we acknowledge the uncertainty.

The Tragedy of

ROMEO
AND
JULIET

Shakespeare's *Romeo and Juliet*

In *Romeo and Juliet*, Shakespeare creates a world of violence and generational conflict in which two young people fall in love and die because of that love. The story is rather extraordinary in that the normal problems faced by young lovers are here so very large. It is not simply that the families of Romeo and Juliet disapprove of the lovers' affection for each other; rather, the Montagues and the Capulets are on opposite sides in a blood feud and are trying to kill each other on the streets of Verona. Every time a member of one of the two families dies in the fight, his relatives demand the blood of his killer. Because of the feud, if Romeo is discovered with Juliet by her family, he will be killed. Once Romeo is banished, the only way that Juliet can avoid being married to someone else is to take a potion that apparently kills her, so that she is buried with the bodies of her slain relatives. In this violent, death-filled world, the movement of the story from love at first sight to the union of the lovers in death seems almost inevitable.

What is so striking about this play is that despite its extraordinary setting (one perhaps reflecting Elizabethan attitudes about hot-blooded Italians), it has become the quintessential story of young love. Because most young lovers feel that they have to overcome giant obstacles in order to be together, because they feel that they would rather die than be kept apart, and especially because the language that Shakespeare gives his young lovers is so exquisite, allowing them to say to each other just what we would all say to a lover if we only knew how, it is easy to respond to this play as if it were about all young lovers rather than about a particular couple in a very unusual world. (When the play was rewritten in the late seventeenth century as *The History and Fall of Caius Marius,* the violent setting became that of a particularly discordant period in classical Rome; when the play was rewritten in the twentieth century as *West Side Story,* the setting chosen was that of the violent world of New York street gangs.)

Characters in the Play

ROMEO
MONTAGUE, his father
LADY MONTAGUE, his mother
BENVOLIO, their kinsman
ABRAM, a Montague servingman
BALTHASAR, Romeo's servingman

JULIET
CAPULET, her father
LADY CAPULET, her mother
NURSE to Juliet
TYBALT, kinsman to the Capulets
PETRUCHIO, Tybalt's companion
Capulet's Cousin
SAMPSON ⎫
GREGORY ⎬ *servingmen*
PETER ⎭
Other Servingmen

ESCALUS, Prince of Verona
PARIS, the Prince's kinsman and Juliet's suitor
MERCUTIO, the Prince's kinsman and Romeo's friend
Paris' Page

FRIAR LAWRENCE
FRIAR JOHN
APOTHECARY
Three or four Citizens
Three Musicians
Three Watchmen

CHORUS

Attendants, Maskers, Torchbearers, a Boy with a drum,
  Gentlemen, Gentlewomen, Tybalt's Page, Servingmen

THE PROLOGUE

Two households, both alike in dignity
(In fair Verona, where we lay our scene),
From ancient grudge break to new mutiny,
Where civil blood makes civil hands unclean.
From forth the fatal loins of these two foes   5
A pair of star-crossed lovers take their life;
Whose misadventured piteous overthrows
Doth with their death bury their parents' strife.
The fearful passage of their death-marked love
And the continuance of their parents' rage,   10
Which, but their children's end, naught could remove,
Is now the two hours' traffic of our stage;
The which, if you with patient ears attend,
What here shall miss, our toil shall strive to mend.
                                ⌜*Chorus exits.*⌝

⌜ACT 1⌝

⌜Scene 1⌝

Enter Sampson and Gregory, with swords and bucklers,
of the house of Capulet.

SAMPSON Gregory, on my word we'll not carry coals.

GREGORY No, for then we should be colliers.

SAMPSON I mean, an we be in choler, we'll draw.

GREGORY Ay, while you live, draw your neck out of
collar.   5

SAMPSON I strike quickly, being moved.

GREGORY But thou art not quickly moved to strike.

SAMPSON A dog of the house of Montague moves me.

GREGORY To move is to stir, and to be valiant is to
stand. Therefore if thou art moved thou runn'st   10
away.

SAMPSON A dog of that house shall move me to stand. I
will take the wall of any man or maid of Montague's.

GREGORY That shows thee a weak slave, for the weak-
est goes to the wall.   15

SAMPSON 'Tis true, and therefore women, being the
weaker vessels, are ever thrust to the wall. Therefore I will push Montague's men from the wall and
thrust his maids to the wall.

GREGORY The quarrel is between our masters and us   20
their men.

SAMPSON 'Tis all one. I will show myself a tyrant.
When I have fought with the men, I will be civil
with the maids; I will cut off their heads.

9

GREGORY   The heads of the maids?   25

SAMPSON   Ay, the heads of the maids, or their maiden-
heads. Take it in what sense thou wilt.

GREGORY   They must take it ⌐in⌐ sense that feel it.

SAMPSON   Me they shall feel while I am able to stand,
and 'tis known I am a pretty piece of flesh.   30

GREGORY   'Tis well thou art not fish; if thou hadst, thou
hadst been poor-john. Draw thy tool. Here comes
of the house of Montagues.

Enter ⌐Abram with another Servingman.⌐

SAMPSON   My naked weapon is out. Quarrel, I will back
thee.   35

GREGORY   How? Turn thy back and run?

SAMPSON   Fear me not.

GREGORY   No, marry. I fear thee!

SAMPSON   Let us take the law of our sides; let them
begin.   40

GREGORY   I will frown as I pass by, and let them take it
as they list.

SAMPSON   Nay, as they dare. I will bite my thumb at
them, which is disgrace to them if they bear it.

⌐*He bites his thumb.*⌐

ABRAM   Do you bite your thumb at us, sir?   45

SAMPSON   I do bite my thumb, sir.

ABRAM   Do you bite your thumb at us, sir?

SAMPSON, ⌐*aside to Gregory*⌐   Is the law of our side if I
say "Ay"?

GREGORY, ⌐*aside to Sampson*⌐   No.   50

SAMPSON   No, sir, I do not bite my thumb at you, sir,
but I bite my thumb, sir.

GREGORY   Do you quarrel, sir?

ABRAM   Quarrel, sir? No, sir.

SAMPSON   But if you do, sir, I am for you. I serve as   55
good a man as you.

ABRAM   No better.

SAMPSON   Well, sir.

Enter Benvolio.

GREGORY, ⸢*aside to Sampson*⸣   Say "better"; here comes
  one of my master's kinsmen.   60

SAMPSON   Yes, better, sir.

ABRAM   You lie.

SAMPSON   Draw if you be men.—Gregory, remember
  thy washing blow.   *They fight.*

BENVOLIO   Part, fools!   ⸢*Drawing his sword.*⸣   65
  Put up your swords. You know not what you do.

Enter Tybalt, ⸢*drawing his sword.*⸣

TYBALT
  What, art thou drawn among these heartless hinds?
  Turn thee, Benvolio; look upon thy death.

BENVOLIO
  I do but keep the peace. Put up thy sword,
  Or manage it to part these men with me.   70

TYBALT
  What, drawn and talk of peace? I hate the word
  As I hate hell, all Montagues, and thee.
  Have at thee, coward!   ⸢*They fight.*⸣

Enter three or four Citizens with clubs or partisans.

⸢CITIZENS⸣
  Clubs, bills, and partisans! Strike! Beat them down!
  Down with the Capulets! Down with the Montagues!   75

Enter old Capulet in his gown, and his Wife.

CAPULET
  What noise is this? Give me my long sword, ho!

LADY CAPULET   A crutch, a crutch! Why call you for a
  sword?

Enter old Montague and his Wife.

CAPULET
My sword, I say. Old Montague is come
And flourishes his blade in spite of me.   80

MONTAGUE
Thou villain Capulet!—Hold me not; let me go.

LADY MONTAGUE
Thou shalt not stir one foot to seek a foe.

Enter Prince Escalus with his train.

PRINCE
Rebellious subjects, enemies to peace,
Profaners of this neighbor-stainèd steel—
Will they not hear?—What ho! You men, you beasts,   85
That quench the fire of your pernicious rage
With purple fountains issuing from your veins:
On pain of torture, from those bloody hands
Throw your mistempered weapons to the ground,
And hear the sentence of your movèd prince.   90
Three civil brawls bred of an airy word
By thee, old Capulet, and Montague,
Have thrice disturbed the quiet of our streets
And made Verona's ancient citizens
Cast by their grave-beseeming ornaments   95
To wield old partisans in hands as old,
Cankered with peace, to part your cankered hate.
If ever you disturb our streets again,
Your lives shall pay the forfeit of the peace.
For this time all the rest depart away.   100
You, Capulet, shall go along with me,
And, Montague, come you this afternoon
To know our farther pleasure in this case,
To old Free-town, our common judgment-place.
Once more, on pain of death, all men depart.   105

⌜*All but Montague, Lady Montague,
and Benvolio*⌝ *exit.*

MONTAGUE, ⌐*to Benvolio*⌐
    Who set this ancient quarrel new abroach?
    Speak, nephew, were you by when it began?
BENVOLIO
    Here were the servants of your adversary,
    And yours, close fighting ere I did approach.
    I drew to part them. In the instant came   110
    The fiery Tybalt with his sword prepared,
    Which, as he breathed defiance to my ears,
    He swung about his head and cut the winds
    Who, nothing hurt withal, hissed him in scorn.
    While we were interchanging thrusts and blows   115
    Came more and more and fought on part and part,
    Till the Prince came, who parted either part.
LADY MONTAGUE
    O, where is Romeo? Saw you him today?
    Right glad I am he was not at this fray.
BENVOLIO
    Madam, an hour before the worshiped sun   120
    Peered forth the golden window of the east,
    A troubled mind ⌐drove⌐ me to walk abroad,
    Where underneath the grove of sycamore
    That westward rooteth from this city side,
    So early walking did I see your son.   125
    Towards him I made, but he was 'ware of me
    And stole into the covert of the wood.
    I, measuring his affections by my own
    (Which then most sought where most might not be
        found,   130
    Being one too many by my weary self),
    Pursued my humor, not pursuing his,
    And gladly shunned who gladly fled from me.
MONTAGUE
    Many a morning hath he there been seen,
    With tears augmenting the fresh morning's dew,   135
    Adding to clouds more clouds with his deep sighs.

But all so soon as the all-cheering sun
Should in the farthest east begin to draw
The shady curtains from Aurora's bed,
Away from light steals home my heavy son   140
And private in his chamber pens himself,
Shuts up his windows, locks fair daylight out,
And makes himself an artificial night.
Black and portentous must this humor prove,
Unless good counsel may the cause remove.   145

BENVOLIO
My noble uncle, do you know the cause?

MONTAGUE
I neither know it nor can learn of him.

BENVOLIO
Have you importuned him by any means?

MONTAGUE
Both by myself and many other friends.
But he, ⌜his⌝ own affections' counselor,   150
Is to himself—I will not say how true,
But to himself so secret and so close,
So far from sounding and discovery,
As is the bud bit with an envious worm
Ere he can spread his sweet leaves to the air   155
Or dedicate his beauty to the same.
Could we but learn from whence his sorrows grow,
We would as willingly give cure as know.

Enter Romeo.

BENVOLIO
See where he comes. So please you, step aside.
I'll know his grievance or be much denied.   160

MONTAGUE
I would thou wert so happy by thy stay
To hear true shrift.—Come, madam, let's away.
⌜*Montague and Lady Montague*⌝ *exit.*

BENVOLIO
  Good morrow, cousin.
ROMEO   Is the day so young?
BENVOLIO
  But new struck nine.   165
ROMEO   Ay me, sad hours seem long.
  Was that my father that went hence so fast?
BENVOLIO
  It was. What sadness lengthens Romeo's hours?
ROMEO
  Not having that, which, having, makes them short.
BENVOLIO   In love?   170
ROMEO   Out—
BENVOLIO   Of love?
ROMEO
  Out of her favor where I am in love.
BENVOLIO
  Alas that love, so gentle in his view,
  Should be so tyrannous and rough in proof !   175
ROMEO
  Alas that love, whose view is muffled still,
  Should without eyes see pathways to his will!
  Where shall we dine?—O me! What fray was here?
  Yet tell me not, for I have heard it all.
  Here's much to do with hate, but more with love.   180
  Why then, O brawling love, O loving hate,
  O anything of nothing first ⌈create!⌉
  O heavy lightness, serious vanity,
  Misshapen chaos of ⌈well-seeming⌉ forms,
  Feather of lead, bright smoke, cold fire, sick health, 185
  Still-waking sleep that is not what it is!
  This love feel I, that feel no love in this.
  Dost thou not laugh?
BENVOLIO   No, coz, I rather weep.
ROMEO
  Good heart, at what?   190

BENVOLIO   At thy good heart's oppression.
ROMEO   Why, such is love's transgression.
  Griefs of mine own lie heavy in my breast,
  Which thou wilt propagate to have it pressed
  With more of thine. This love that thou hast shown   195
  Doth add more grief to too much of mine own.
  Love is a smoke made with the fume of sighs;
  Being purged, a fire sparkling in lovers' eyes;
  Being vexed, a sea nourished with loving tears.
  What is it else? A madness most discreet,   200
  A choking gall, and a preserving sweet.
  Farewell, my coz.
BENVOLIO   Soft, I will go along.
  An if you leave me so, you do me wrong.
ROMEO
  Tut, I have lost myself. I am not here.   205
  This is not Romeo. He's some other where.
BENVOLIO
  Tell me in sadness, who is that you love?
ROMEO   What, shall I groan and tell thee?
BENVOLIO
  Groan? Why, no. But sadly tell me who.
ROMEO
  A sick man in sadness makes his will—   210
  A word ill urged to one that is so ill.
  In sadness, cousin, I do love a woman.
BENVOLIO
  I aimed so near when I supposed you loved.
ROMEO
  A right good markman! And she's fair I love.
BENVOLIO
  A right fair mark, fair coz, is soonest hit.   215
ROMEO
  Well in that hit you miss. She'll not be hit
  With Cupid's arrow. She hath Dian's wit,
  And, in strong proof of chastity well armed,

From love's weak childish bow she lives uncharmed.
She will not stay the siege of loving terms,   220
Nor bide th' encounter of assailing eyes,
Nor ope her lap to saint-seducing gold.
O, she is rich in beauty, only poor
That, when she dies, with beauty dies her store.

BENVOLIO
Then she hath sworn that she will still live chaste?   225

ROMEO
She hath, and in that sparing ⌜makes⌝ huge waste;
For beauty, starved with her severity,
Cuts beauty off from all posterity.
She is too fair, too wise, wisely too fair,
To merit bliss by making me despair.   230
She hath forsworn to love, and in that vow
Do I live dead, that live to tell it now.

BENVOLIO
Be ruled by me. Forget to think of her.

ROMEO
O, teach me how I should forget to think !

BENVOLIO
By giving liberty unto thine eyes.   235
Examine other beauties.

ROMEO   'Tis the way
To call hers, exquisite, in question more.
These happy masks that kiss fair ladies' brows,
Being black, puts us in mind they hide the fair.   240
He that is strucken blind cannot forget
The precious treasure of his eyesight lost.
Show me a mistress that is passing fair;
What doth her beauty serve but as a note
Where I may read who passed that passing fair?   245
Farewell. Thou canst not teach me to forget.

BENVOLIO
I'll pay that doctrine or else die in debt.

                                        They exit.

⌈Scene 2⌉
Enter Capulet, County Paris, and ⌈*a Servingman.*⌉

CAPULET
But Montague is bound as well as I,
In penalty alike, and 'tis not hard, I think,
For men so old as we to keep the peace.

PARIS
Of honorable reckoning are you both,
And pity 'tis you lived at odds so long.   5
But now, my lord, what say you to my suit?

CAPULET
But saying o'er what I have said before.
My child is yet a stranger in the world.
She hath not seen the change of fourteen years.
Let two more summers wither in their pride   10
Ere we may think her ripe to be a bride.

PARIS
Younger than she are happy mothers made.

CAPULET
And too soon marred are those so early made.
Earth hath swallowed all my hopes but she;
She's the hopeful lady of my earth.   15
But woo her, gentle Paris, get her heart;
My will to her consent is but a part.
And, she agreed, within her scope of choice
Lies my consent and fair according voice.
This night I hold an old accustomed feast,   20
Whereto I have invited many a guest
Such as I love; and you among the store,
One more, most welcome, makes my number more.
At my poor house look to behold this night
Earth-treading stars that make dark heaven light. 25
Such comfort as do lusty young men feel
When well-appareled April on the heel
Of limping winter treads, even such delight

Among fresh fennel buds shall you this night
Inherit at my house. Hear all, all see,   30
And like her most whose merit most shall be;
Which, on more view of many, mine, being one,
May stand in number, though in reck'ning none.
Come go with me. ⌜*To Servingman, giving him a list.*⌝
                    Go, sirrah, trudge about   35
Through fair Verona, find those persons out
Whose names are written there, and to them say
My house and welcome on their pleasure stay.
                    ⌜*Capulet and Paris*⌝ *exit.*

SERVINGMAN   Find them out whose names are written
    here! It is written that the shoemaker should   40
    meddle with his yard and the tailor with his last, the
    fisher with his pencil and the painter with his nets.
    But I am sent to find those persons whose names
    are here writ, and can never find what names the
    writing person hath here writ. I must to the learned. 45
    In good time!

                    Enter Benvolio and Romeo.

BENVOLIO, ⌜*to Romeo*⌝
    Tut man, one fire burns out another's burning;
    One pain is lessened by another's anguish.
    Turn giddy, and be helped by backward turning.
    One desperate grief cures with another's languish.   50
    Take thou some new infection to thy eye,
    And the rank poison of the old will die.
ROMEO
    Your plantain leaf is excellent for that.
BENVOLIO
    For what, I pray thee?
ROMEO   For your broken shin.   55
BENVOLIO   Why Romeo, art thou mad?
ROMEO
    Not mad, but bound more than a madman is,

Shut up in prison, kept without my food,
Whipped and tormented, and—good e'en, good
fellow.   60

SERVINGMAN   God gi' good e'en. I pray, sir, can you
read?

ROMEO
Ay, mine own fortune in my misery.

SERVINGMAN   Perhaps you have learned it without
book. But I pray, can you read anything you see?   65

ROMEO
Ay, if I know the letters and the language.

SERVINGMAN   You say honestly. Rest you merry.

ROMEO   Stay, fellow. I can read.   *(He reads the letter.)*
Signior Martino and his wife and daughters,
County Anselme and his beauteous sisters,   70
The lady widow of Vitruvio,
Signior Placentio and his lovely nieces,
Mercutio and his brother Valentine,
Mine Uncle Capulet, his wife and daughters,
My fair niece Rosaline and Livia,   75
Signior Valentio and his cousin Tybalt,
Lucio and the lively Helena.
A fair assembly. Whither should they come?

SERVINGMAN   Up.

ROMEO   Whither? To supper?   80

SERVINGMAN   To our house.

ROMEO   Whose house?

SERVINGMAN   My master's.

ROMEO
Indeed I should have asked thee that before.

SERVINGMAN   Now I'll tell you without asking. My   85
master is the great rich Capulet, and, if you be not
of the house of Montagues, I pray come and crush a
cup of wine. Rest you merry.   ⌜*He exits.*⌝

BENVOLIO
At this same ancient feast of Capulet's

Sups the fair Rosaline whom thou so loves,   90
With all the admirèd beauties of Verona.
Go thither, and with unattainted eye
Compare her face with some that I shall show,
And I will make thee think thy swan a crow.

ROMEO
When the devout religion of mine eye   95
Maintains such falsehood, then turn tears to fire;
And these who, often drowned, could never die,
Transparent heretics, be burnt for liars.
One fairer than my love? The all-seeing sun
Ne'er saw her match since first the world begun.   100

BENVOLIO
Tut, you saw her fair, none else being by,
Herself poised with herself in either eye;
But in that crystal scales let there be weighed
Your lady's love against some other maid
That I will show you shining at this feast,   105
And she shall scant show well that now seems best.

ROMEO
I'll go along, no such sight to be shown,
But to rejoice in splendor of mine own.

⌜*They exit.*⌝

⌜Scene 3⌝
Enter ⌜*Lady Capulet*⌝ *and Nurse.*

LADY CAPULET
Nurse, where's my daughter? Call her forth to me.

NURSE
Now, by my maidenhead at twelve year old,
I bade her come.—What, lamb! What, ladybird!
God forbid. Where's this girl? What, Juliet!

Enter Juliet.

JULIET How now, who calls?   5
NURSE Your mother.
JULIET
  Madam, I am here. What is your will?
LADY CAPULET
  This is the matter.—Nurse, give leave awhile.
  We must talk in secret.—Nurse, come back again.
  I have remembered me, thou's hear our counsel.   10
  Thou knowest my daughter's of a pretty age.
NURSE
  Faith, I can tell her age unto ⌈an⌉ hour.
LADY CAPULET She's not fourteen.
NURSE I'll lay fourteen of my teeth (and yet, to my teen
    be it spoken, I have but four) she's not fourteen.   15
    How long is it now to Lammastide?
LADY CAPULET A fortnight and odd days.
NURSE
  Even or odd, of all days in the year,
  Come Lammas Eve at night shall she be fourteen.
  Susan and she (God rest all Christian souls!)   20
  Were of an age. Well, Susan is with God;
  She was too good for me. But, as I said,
  On Lammas Eve at night shall she be fourteen.
  That shall she. Marry, I remember it well.
  'Tis since the earthquake now eleven years,   25
  And she was weaned (I never shall forget it)
  Of all the days of the year, upon that day.
  For I had then laid wormwood to my dug,
  Sitting in the sun under the dovehouse wall.
  My lord and you were then at Mantua.   30
  Nay, I do bear a brain. But, as I said,
  When it did taste the wormwood on the nipple
  Of my dug and felt it bitter, pretty fool,
  To see it tetchy and fall out with ⌈the⌉ dug.
  "Shake," quoth the dovehouse. 'Twas no need, I   35
    trow,

To bid me trudge.
And since that time it is eleven years.
For then she could stand high-lone. Nay, by th'
   rood,   40
She could have run and waddled all about,
For even the day before, she broke her brow,
And then my husband (God be with his soul,
He was a merry man) took up the child.
"Yea," quoth he, "Dost thou fall upon thy face?   45
Thou wilt fall backward when thou hast more wit,
Wilt thou not, Jule?" And, by my holidam,
The pretty wretch left crying and said "Ay."
To see now how a jest shall come about!
I warrant, an I should live a thousand years,   50
I never should forget it. "Wilt thou not, Jule?"
   quoth he.
And, pretty fool, it stinted and said "Ay."

LADY CAPULET
  Enough of this. I pray thee, hold thy peace.

NURSE
  Yes, madam, yet I cannot choose but laugh   55
To think it should leave crying and say "Ay."
And yet, I warrant, it had upon its brow
A bump as big as a young cock'rel's stone,
A perilous knock, and it cried bitterly.
"Yea," quoth my husband. "Fall'st upon thy face?   60
Thou wilt fall backward when thou comest to age,
Wilt thou not, Jule?" It stinted and said "Ay."

JULIET
  And stint thou, too, I pray thee, Nurse, say I.

NURSE
  Peace. I have done. God mark thee to his grace,
Thou wast the prettiest babe that e'er I nursed.   65
An I might live to see thee married once,
I have my wish.

LADY CAPULET
  Marry, that "marry" is the very theme
  I came to talk of.—Tell me, daughter Juliet,
  How stands your ⌐disposition⌐ to be married?   70
JULIET
  It is an ⌐honor⌐ that I dream not of.
NURSE
  An ⌐honor?⌐ Were not I thine only nurse,
  I would say thou hadst sucked wisdom from thy
    teat.
LADY CAPULET
  Well, think of marriage now. Younger than you   75
  Here in Verona, ladies of esteem,
  Are made already mothers. By my count
  I was your mother much upon these years
  That you are now a maid. Thus, then, in brief:
  The valiant Paris seeks you for his love.   80
NURSE
  A man, young lady—lady, such a man
  As all the world—why, he's a man of wax.
LADY CAPULET
  Verona's summer hath not such a flower.
NURSE
  Nay, he's a flower, in faith, a very flower.
LADY CAPULET
  What say you? Can you love the gentleman?   85
  This night you shall behold him at our feast.
  Read o'er the volume of young Paris' face,
  And find delight writ there with beauty's pen.
  Examine every married lineament
  And see how one another lends content,   90
  And what obscured in this fair volume lies
  Find written in the margent of his eyes.
  This precious book of love, this unbound lover,
  To beautify him only lacks a cover.
  The fish lives in the sea, and 'tis much pride   95

For fair without the fair within to hide.
That book in many's eyes doth share the glory
That in gold clasps locks in the golden story.
So shall you share all that he doth possess
By having him, making yourself no less.   100

NURSE
No less? Nay, bigger. Women grow by men.

LADY CAPULET
Speak briefly. Can you like of Paris' love?

JULIET
I'll look to like, if looking liking move.
But no more deep will I endart mine eye
Than your consent gives strength to make ⌜it⌝ fly.   105

Enter ⌜Servingman.⌝

SERVINGMAN Madam, the guests are come, supper
served up, you called, my young lady asked for, the
Nurse cursed in the pantry, and everything in
extremity. I must hence to wait. I beseech you,
follow straight.   110

LADY CAPULET
We follow thee.   ⌜*Servingman exits.*⌝
                  Juliet, the County stays.

NURSE Go, girl, seek happy nights to happy days.
                                              They exit.

⌜Scene 4⌝
Enter Romeo, Mercutio, Benvolio, with five or six other
Maskers, Torchbearers, ⌜and a Boy with a drum.⌝

ROMEO
What, shall this speech be spoke for our excuse?
Or shall we on without apology?

BENVOLIO
The date is out of such prolixity.

We'll have no Cupid hoodwinked with a scarf,
Bearing a Tartar's painted bow of lath,   5
Scaring the ladies like a crowkeeper,
⌈Nor no without-book prologue, faintly spoke
After the prompter, for our entrance.⌉
But let them measure us by what they will.
We'll measure them a measure and be gone.   10

ROMEO
Give me a torch. I am not for this ambling.
Being but heavy I will bear the light.

MERCUTIO
Nay, gentle Romeo, we must have you dance.

ROMEO
Not I, believe me. You have dancing shoes
With nimble soles. I have a soul of lead   15
So stakes me to the ground I cannot move.

MERCUTIO
You are a lover. Borrow Cupid's wings
And soar with them above a common bound.

ROMEO
I am too sore enpiercèd with his shaft
To soar with his light feathers, and so bound   20
I cannot bound a pitch above dull woe.
Under love's heavy burden do I sink.

⌈MERCUTIO⌉
And to sink in it should you burden love—
Too great oppression for a tender thing.

ROMEO
Is love a tender thing? It is too rough,   25
Too rude, too boist'rous, and it pricks like thorn.

MERCUTIO
If love be rough with you, be rough with love.
Prick love for pricking, and you beat love down.—
Give me a case to put my visage in.—
A visor for a visor. What care I   30
What curious eye doth cote deformities?
Here are the beetle brows shall blush for me.

BENVOLIO
　Come, knock and enter, and no sooner in
　But every man betake him to his legs.

ROMEO
　A torch for me. Let wantons light of heart   35
　Tickle the senseless rushes with their heels,
　For I am proverbed with a grandsire phrase:
　I'll be a candle holder and look on;
　The game was ne'er so fair, and I am ⌜done.⌝

MERCUTIO
　Tut, dun's the mouse, the constable's own word.   40
　If thou art dun, we'll draw thee from the mire—
　Or (save ⌜your⌝ reverence) love—wherein thou
　　stickest
　Up to the ears. Come, we burn daylight, ho!

ROMEO
　Nay, that's not so.   45

MERCUTIO   I mean, sir, in delay
　We waste our lights; in vain, ⌜light⌝ lights by day.
　Take our good meaning, for our judgment sits
　Five times in that ere once in our ⌜five⌝ wits.

ROMEO
　And we mean well in going to this masque,   50
　But 'tis no wit to go.

MERCUTIO   Why, may one ask?

ROMEO
　I dreamt a dream tonight.

MERCUTIO   And so did I.

ROMEO
　Well, what was yours?   55

MERCUTIO   That dreamers often lie.

ROMEO
　In bed asleep while they do dream things true.

MERCUTIO
　O, then I see Queen Mab hath been with you.

She is the fairies' midwife, and she comes
In shape no bigger than an agate stone   60
On the forefinger of an alderman,
Drawn with a team of little ⌜atomi⌝
Over men's noses as they lie asleep.
Her wagon spokes made of long spinners' legs,
The cover of the wings of grasshoppers,   65
Her traces of the smallest spider web,
Her collars of the moonshine's wat'ry beams,
Her whip of cricket's bone, the lash of film,
Her wagoner a small gray-coated gnat,
Not half so big as a round little worm   70
Pricked from the lazy finger of a ⌜maid.⌝
Her chariot is an empty hazelnut,
Made by the joiner squirrel or old grub,
Time out o' mind the fairies' coachmakers.
And in this state she gallops night by night   75
Through lovers' brains, and then they dream of love;
On courtiers' knees, that dream on cur'sies straight;
O'er lawyers' fingers, who straight dream on fees;
O'er ladies' lips, who straight on kisses dream,
Which oft the angry Mab with blisters plagues   80
Because their ⌜breaths⌝ with sweetmeats tainted are.
Sometime she gallops o'er a courtier's nose,
And then dreams he of smelling out a suit.
And sometime comes she with a tithe-pig's tail,
Tickling a parson's nose as he lies asleep;   85
Then he dreams of another benefice.
Sometime she driveth o'er a soldier's neck,
And then dreams he of cutting foreign throats,
Of breaches, ambuscadoes, Spanish blades,
Of healths five fathom deep, and then anon   90
Drums in his ear, at which he starts and wakes
And, being thus frighted, swears a prayer or two
And sleeps again. This is that very Mab
That plats the manes of horses in the night

And bakes the ⌜elflocks⌝ in foul sluttish hairs,   95
Which once untangled much misfortune bodes.
This is the hag, when maids lie on their backs,
That presses them and learns them first to bear,
Making them women of good carriage.
This is she—   100
ROMEO   Peace, peace, Mercutio, peace.
Thou talk'st of nothing.
MERCUTIO   True, I talk of dreams,
Which are the children of an idle brain,
Begot of nothing but vain fantasy,   105
Which is as thin of substance as the air
And more inconstant than the wind, who woos
Even now the frozen bosom of the North
And, being angered, puffs away from thence,
Turning his side to the dew-dropping South.   110
BENVOLIO
This wind you talk of blows us from ourselves.
Supper is done, and we shall come too late.
ROMEO
I fear too early, for my mind misgives
Some consequence yet hanging in the stars
Shall bitterly begin his fearful date   115
With this night's revels, and expire the term
Of a despisèd life closed in my breast
By some vile forfeit of untimely death.
But he that hath the steerage of my course
Direct my ⌜sail.⌝ On, lusty gentlemen.   120
BENVOLIO   Strike, drum.

They march about the stage
and ⌜then withdraw to the side.⌝

⌜Scene 5⌝
Servingmen come forth with napkins.

⌜FIRST⌝ SERVINGMAN Where's Potpan that he helps not
to take away? He shift a trencher? He scrape a
trencher?

⌜SECOND⌝ SERVINGMAN When good manners shall lie
all in one or two men's hands, and they unwashed   5
too, 'tis a foul thing.

⌜FIRST⌝ SERVINGMAN Away with the joint stools, remove the court cupboard, look to the plate.—
Good thou, save me a piece of marchpane, and, as
thou loves me, let the porter let in Susan Grind-   10
stone and Nell.—Anthony and Potpan!

⌜THIRD⌝ SERVINGMAN Ay, boy, ready.

⌜FIRST⌝ SERVINGMAN You are looked for and called for,
asked for and sought for, in the great chamber.

⌜THIRD⌝ SERVINGMAN We cannot be here and there too.   15
Cheerly, boys! Be brisk awhile, and the longer liver
take all.   ⌜*They move aside.*⌝

Enter ⌜*Capulet and his household,*⌝ *all the guests and
gentlewomen to* ⌜*Romeo, Mercutio, Benvolio, and*⌝ *the
⌜other⌝ Maskers.*

CAPULET
Welcome, gentlemen. Ladies that have their toes
Unplagued with corns will walk ⌜a bout⌝ with
    you.—   20
Ah, my mistresses, which of you all
Will now deny to dance? She that makes dainty,
She, I'll swear, hath corns. Am I come near you
    now?—
Welcome, gentlemen. I have seen the day   25
That I have worn a visor and could tell
A whispering tale in a fair lady's ear,
Such as would please. 'Tis gone, 'tis gone, 'tis gone.

You are welcome, gentlemen.—Come, musicians,
   play.   *Music plays and they dance.*   30
A hall, a hall, give room!—And foot it, girls.—
More light, you knaves, and turn the tables up,
And quench the fire; the room is grown too hot.—
Ah, sirrah, this unlooked-for sport comes well.—
Nay, sit, nay, sit, good cousin Capulet,   35
For you and I are past our dancing days.
How long is 't now since last yourself and I
Were in a mask?
CAPULET'S COUSIN By 'r Lady, thirty years.
CAPULET
  What, man, 'tis not so much, 'tis not so much.   40
  'Tis since the nuptial of ⌜Lucentio,⌝
  Come Pentecost as quickly as it will,
  Some five and twenty years, and then we masked.
CAPULET'S COUSIN
  'Tis more, 'tis more. His son is elder, sir.
  His son is thirty.   45
CAPULET   Will you tell me that?
  His son was but a ward two years ago.
ROMEO, ⌜*to a Servingman*⌝
  What lady's that which doth enrich the hand
  Of yonder knight?
SERVINGMAN I know not, sir.   50
ROMEO
  O, she doth teach the torches to burn bright!
  It seems she hangs upon the cheek of night
  As a rich jewel in an Ethiop's ear—
  Beauty too rich for use, for earth too dear.
  So shows a snowy dove trooping with crows   55
  As yonder lady o'er her fellows shows.
  The measure done, I'll watch her place of stand
  And, touching hers, make blessèd my rude hand.
  Did my heart love till now? Forswear it, sight,
  For I ne'er saw true beauty till this night.   60

TYBALT
  This, by his voice, should be a Montague.—
  Fetch me my rapier, boy.   ⌐*Page exits.*⌐
                    What, dares the slave
  Come hither covered with an antic face
  To fleer and scorn at our solemnity?   65
  Now, by the stock and honor of my kin,
  To strike him dead I hold it not a sin.

CAPULET
  Why, how now, kinsman? Wherefore storm you so?

TYBALT
  Uncle, this is a Montague, our foe,
  A villain that is hither come in spite   70
  To scorn at our solemnity this night.

CAPULET
  Young Romeo is it?

TYBALT   'Tis he, that villain Romeo.

CAPULET
  Content thee, gentle coz. Let him alone.
  He bears him like a portly gentleman,   75
  And, to say truth, Verona brags of him
  To be a virtuous and well-governed youth.
  I would not for the wealth of all this town
  Here in my house do him disparagement.
  Therefore be patient. Take no note of him.   80
  It is my will, the which if thou respect,
  Show a fair presence and put off these frowns,
  An ill-beseeming semblance for a feast.

TYBALT
  It fits when such a villain is a guest.
  I'll not endure him.   85

CAPULET   He shall be endured.
  What, goodman boy? I say he shall. Go to.
  Am I the master here or you? Go to.
  You'll not endure him! God shall mend my soul,

You'll make a mutiny among my guests,   90
You will set cock-a-hoop, you'll be the man!

TYBALT
Why, uncle, 'tis a shame.

CAPULET   Go to, go to.
You are a saucy boy. Is 't so indeed?
This trick may chance to scathe you. I know what.   95
You must contrary me. Marry, 'tis time—
Well said, my hearts.—You are a princox, go.
Be quiet, or—More light, more light!—for shame,
I'll make you quiet.—What, cheerly, my hearts!

TYBALT
Patience perforce with willful choler meeting   100
Makes my flesh tremble in their different greeting.
I will withdraw, but this intrusion shall,
Now seeming sweet, convert to bitt'rest gall.

                                        He exits.

ROMEO, ⌜*taking Juliet's hand*⌝
If I profane with my unworthiest hand
This holy shrine, the gentle sin is this: 105
My lips, two blushing pilgrims, ready stand
To smooth that rough touch with a tender kiss.

JULIET
Good pilgrim, you do wrong your hand too much,
Which mannerly devotion shows in this;
For saints have hands that pilgrims' hands do touch,   110
And palm to palm is holy palmers' kiss.

ROMEO
Have not saints lips, and holy palmers too?

JULIET
Ay, pilgrim, lips that they must use in prayer.

ROMEO
O then, dear saint, let lips do what hands do.
They pray: grant thou, lest faith turn to despair.   115

JULIET
Saints do not move, though grant for prayers' sake.

ROMEO
Then move not while my prayer's effect I take.
⌜*He kisses her.*⌝
Thus from my lips, by thine, my sin is purged.

JULIET
Then have my lips the sin that they have took.

ROMEO
Sin from my lips? O trespass sweetly urged!   120
Give me my sin again.   ⌜*He kisses her.*⌝

JULIET   You kiss by th' book.

NURSE
Madam, your mother craves a word with you.
⌜*Juliet moves toward her mother.*⌝

ROMEO
What is her mother?

NURSE   Marry, bachelor,   125
Her mother is the lady of the house,
And a good lady, and a wise and virtuous.
I nursed her daughter that you talked withal.
I tell you, he that can lay hold of her
Shall have the chinks.   ⌜*Nurse moves away.*⌝   130

ROMEO, ⌜*aside*⌝   Is she a Capulet?
O dear account! My life is my foe's debt.

BENVOLIO
Away, begone. The sport is at the best.

ROMEO
Ay, so I fear. The more is my unrest.

CAPULET
Nay, gentlemen, prepare not to be gone.   135
We have a trifling foolish banquet towards.—
Is it e'en so? Why then, I thank you all.
I thank you, honest gentlemen. Good night.—
More torches here.—Come on then, let's to bed.—
Ah, sirrah, by my fay, it waxes late.   140
I'll to my rest.
⌜*All but Juliet and the Nurse begin to exit.*⌝

JULIET
  Come hither, Nurse. What is yond gentleman?
NURSE
  The son and heir of old Tiberio.
JULIET
  What's he that now is going out of door?
NURSE
  Marry, that, I think, be young Petruchio.   145
JULIET
  What's he that follows here, that would not dance?
NURSE   I know not.
JULIET
  Go ask his name. ⌜*The Nurse goes.*⌝ If he be marrièd,
  My grave is like to be my wedding bed.
NURSE, ⌜*returning*⌝
  His name is Romeo, and a Montague,   150
  The only son of your great enemy.
JULIET
  My only love sprung from my only hate!
  Too early seen unknown, and known too late!
  Prodigious birth of love it is to me
  That I must love a loathèd enemy.   155
NURSE
  What's this? What's this?
JULIET   A rhyme I learned even now
  Of one I danced withal.
                    One calls within "Juliet."
NURSE   Anon, anon.
  Come, let's away. The strangers all are gone.   160
                    They exit.

⌐*Enter*⌐ *Chorus.*

Now old desire doth in his deathbed lie,
And young affection gapes to be his heir.
That fair for which love groaned for and would die,
With tender Juliet ⌐matched,⌐ is now not fair.
Now Romeo is beloved and loves again,   5
Alike bewitchèd by the charm of looks,
But to his foe supposed he must complain,
And she steal love's sweet bait from fearful hooks.
Being held a foe, he may not have access
To breathe such vows as lovers use to swear,   10
And she as much in love, her means much less
To meet her new belovèd anywhere.
But passion lends them power, time means, to meet,
Temp'ring extremities with extreme sweet.

⌐*Chorus exits.*⌐

⌐Scene 1⌐
Enter Romeo alone.

ROMEO
    Can I go forward when my heart is here?
    Turn back, dull earth, and find thy center out.

⌐*He withdraws.*⌐

Enter Benvolio with Mercutio.

BENVOLIO
  Romeo, my cousin Romeo, Romeo!
MERCUTIO   He is wise
  And, on my life, hath stol'n him home to bed.   5
BENVOLIO
  He ran this way and leapt this orchard wall.
  Call, good Mercutio.
⌜MERCUTIO⌝   Nay, I'll conjure too.
  Romeo! Humors! Madman! Passion! Lover!
  Appear thou in the likeness of a sigh.   10
  Speak but one rhyme and I am satisfied.
  Cry but "Ay me," ⌜pronounce⌝ but "love" and
    ⌜"dove."⌝
  Speak to my gossip Venus one fair word,
  One nickname for her purblind son and ⌜heir,⌝   15
  Young Abraham Cupid, he that shot so ⌜trim⌝
  When King Cophetua loved the beggar maid.—
  He heareth not, he stirreth not, he moveth not.
  The ape is dead, and I must conjure him.—
  I conjure thee by Rosaline's bright eyes,   20
  By her high forehead, and her scarlet lip,
  By her fine foot, straight leg, and quivering thigh,
  And the demesnes that there adjacent lie,
  That in thy likeness thou appear to us.
BENVOLIO
  An if he hear thee, thou wilt anger him.   25
MERCUTIO
  This cannot anger him. 'Twould anger him
  To raise a spirit in his mistress' circle
  Of some strange nature, letting it there stand
  Till she had laid it and conjured it down.
  That were some spite. My invocation   30
  Is fair and honest. In his mistress' name,
  I conjure only but to raise up him.
BENVOLIO
  Come, he hath hid himself among these trees

To be consorted with the humorous night.
Blind is his love and best befits the dark.   35

MERCUTIO
If love be blind, love cannot hit the mark.
Now will he sit under a medlar tree
And wish his mistress were that kind of fruit
As maids call medlars when they laugh alone.—
O Romeo, that she were, O, that she were   40
An open-⌜arse,⌝ thou a pop'rin pear.
Romeo, good night. I'll to my truckle bed;
This field-bed is too cold for me to sleep.—
Come, shall we go?

BENVOLIO   Go, then, for 'tis in vain   45
To seek him here that means not to be found.
                                        ⌜*They*⌝ *exit.*

                        ⌜Scene 2⌝
                ⌜*Romeo comes forward.*⌝

ROMEO
He jests at scars that never felt a wound.

                ⌜*Enter Juliet above.*⌝

But soft, what light through yonder window breaks?
It is the East, and Juliet is the sun.
Arise, fair sun, and kill the envious moon,
Who is already sick and pale with grief   5
That thou, her maid, art far more fair than she.
Be not her maid since she is envious.
Her vestal livery is but sick and green,
And none but fools do wear it. Cast it off.
It is my lady. O, it is my love!   10
O, that she knew she were!
She speaks, yet she says nothing. What of that?
Her eye discourses; I will answer it.

I am too bold. 'Tis not to me she speaks.
Two of the fairest stars in all the heaven,   15
Having some business, ⌈do⌉ entreat her eyes
To twinkle in their spheres till they return.
What if her eyes were there, they in her head?
The brightness of her cheek would shame those
    stars   20
As daylight doth a lamp; her eye in heaven
Would through the airy region stream so bright
That birds would sing and think it were not night.
See how she leans her cheek upon her hand.
O, that I were a glove upon that hand,   25
That I might touch that cheek!
JULIET   Ay me.
ROMEO, ⌈*aside*⌉   She speaks.
O, speak again, bright angel, for thou art
As glorious to this night, being o'er my head,   30
As is a wingèd messenger of heaven
Unto the white-upturnèd wond'ring eyes
Of mortals that fall back to gaze on him
When he bestrides the lazy puffing clouds
And sails upon the bosom of the air.   35
JULIET
O Romeo, Romeo, wherefore art thou Romeo?
Deny thy father and refuse thy name,
Or, if thou wilt not, be but sworn my love,
And I'll no longer be a Capulet.
ROMEO, ⌈*aside*⌉
Shall I hear more, or shall I speak at this?   40
JULIET
'Tis but thy name that is my enemy.
Thou art thyself, though not a Montague.
What's Montague? It is nor hand, nor foot,
Nor arm, nor face, ⌈nor any other part⌉
Belonging to a man. O, be some other name!   45
What's in a name? That which we call a rose

By any other word would smell as sweet.
So Romeo would, were he not Romeo called,
Retain that dear perfection which he owes
Without that title. Romeo, doff thy name,   50
And, for thy name, which is no part of thee,
Take all myself.

ROMEO   I take thee at thy word.
Call me but love, and I'll be new baptized.
Henceforth I never will be Romeo.   55

JULIET
What man art thou that, thus bescreened in night,
So stumblest on my counsel?

ROMEO   By a name
I know not how to tell thee who I am.
My name, dear saint, is hateful to myself   60
Because it is an enemy to thee.
Had I it written, I would tear the word.

JULIET
My ears have yet not drunk a hundred words
Of thy tongue's uttering, yet I know the sound.
Art thou not Romeo, and a Montague?   65

ROMEO
Neither, fair maid, if either thee dislike.

JULIET
How camest thou hither, tell me, and wherefore?
The orchard walls are high and hard to climb,
And the place death, considering who thou art,
If any of my kinsmen find thee here.   70

ROMEO
With love's light wings did I o'erperch these walls,
For stony limits cannot hold love out,
And what love can do, that dares love attempt.
Therefore thy kinsmen are no stop to me.

JULIET
If they do see thee, they will murder thee.   75

ROMEO
 Alack, there lies more peril in thine eye
 Than twenty of their swords. Look thou but sweet,
 And I am proof against their enmity.
JULIET
 I would not for the world they saw thee here.
ROMEO
 I have night's cloak to hide me from their eyes,   80
 And, but thou love me, let them find me here.
 My life were better ended by their hate
 Than death proroguèd, wanting of thy love.
JULIET
 By whose direction found'st thou out this place?
ROMEO
 By love, that first did prompt me to inquire.   85
 He lent me counsel, and I lent him eyes.
 I am no pilot; yet, wert thou as far
 As that vast shore ⌐washed⌐ with the farthest sea,
 I should adventure for such merchandise.
JULIET
 Thou knowest the mask of night is on my face,   90
 Else would a maiden blush bepaint my cheek
 For that which thou hast heard me speak tonight.
 Fain would I dwell on form; fain, fain deny
 What I have spoke. But farewell compliment.
 Dost thou love me? I know thou wilt say "Ay,"   95
 And I will take thy word. Yet, if thou swear'st,
 Thou mayst prove false. At lovers' perjuries,
 They say, Jove laughs. O gentle Romeo,
 If thou dost love, pronounce it faithfully.
 Or, if thou thinkest I am too quickly won,   100
 I'll frown and be perverse and say thee nay,
 So thou wilt woo, but else not for the world.
 In truth, fair Montague, I am too fond,
 And therefore thou mayst think my ⌐havior⌐ light.
 But trust me, gentleman, I'll prove more true   105

Than those that have ⌜more⌝ coying to be strange.
I should have been more strange, I must confess,
But that thou overheard'st ere I was ware
My true-love passion. Therefore pardon me,
And not impute this yielding to light love,   110
Which the dark night hath so discoverèd.

ROMEO
Lady, by yonder blessed moon I vow,
That tips with silver all these fruit-tree tops—

JULIET
O, swear not by the moon, th' inconstant moon,
That monthly changes in her ⌜circled⌝ orb,   115
Lest that thy love prove likewise variable.

ROMEO
What shall I swear by?

JULIET   Do not swear at all.
Or, if thou wilt, swear by thy gracious self,
Which is the god of my idolatry,   120
And I'll believe thee.

ROMEO   If my heart's dear love—

JULIET
Well, do not swear. Although I joy in thee,
I have no joy of this contract tonight.
It is too rash, too unadvised, too sudden,   125
Too like the lightning, which doth cease to be
Ere one can say "It lightens." Sweet, good night.
This bud of love, by summer's ripening breath,
May prove a beauteous flower when next we meet.
Good night, good night. As sweet repose and rest   130
Come to thy heart as that within my breast.

ROMEO
O, wilt thou leave me so unsatisfied?

JULIET
What satisfaction canst thou have tonight?

ROMEO
Th' exchange of thy love's faithful vow for mine.

JULIET
   I gave thee mine before thou didst request it,   135
   And yet I would it were to give again.

ROMEO
   Wouldst thou withdraw it? For what purpose, love?

JULIET
   But to be frank and give it thee again.
   And yet I wish but for the thing I have.
   My bounty is as boundless as the sea,   140
   My love as deep. The more I give to thee,
   The more I have, for both are infinite.
                    ⌐*Nurse calls from within.*¬
   I hear some noise within. Dear love, adieu.—
   Anon, good nurse.—Sweet Montague, be true.
   Stay but a little; I will come again.   ⌐*She exits.*¬ 145

ROMEO
   O blessèd, blessèd night! I am afeard,
   Being in night, all this is but a dream,
   Too flattering sweet to be substantial.

             ⌐*Reenter Juliet above.*¬

JULIET
   Three words, dear Romeo, and good night indeed.
   If that thy bent of love be honorable,   150
   Thy purpose marriage, send me word tomorrow,
   By one that I'll procure to come to thee,
   Where and what time thou wilt perform the rite,
   And all my fortunes at thy foot I'll lay
   And follow thee my ⌐lord¬ throughout the world.   155
⌐NURSE *within*¬   Madam.

JULIET
   I come anon.—But if thou meanest not well,
   I do beseech thee—
⌐NURSE *within*¬   Madam.
JULIET   By and by, I come.—   160
   To cease thy strife and leave me to my grief.
   Tomorrow will I send.

ROMEO   So thrive my soul—
JULIET   A thousand times good night.   ⌈*She exits.*⌉
ROMEO
  A thousand times the worse to want thy light.   165
  Love goes toward love as schoolboys from their
    books,
  But love from love, toward school with heavy looks.
                                        ⌈*Going.*⌉

Enter Juliet ⌈*above*⌉ *again.*

JULIET
  Hist, Romeo, hist! O, for a falc'ner's voice
  To lure this tassel-gentle back again!   170
  Bondage is hoarse and may not speak aloud,
  Else would I tear the cave where Echo lies
  And make her airy tongue more hoarse than ⌈mine⌉
  With repetition of "My Romeo!"
ROMEO
  It is my soul that calls upon my name.   175
  How silver-sweet sound lovers' tongues by night,
  Like softest music to attending ears.
JULIET
  Romeo.
ROMEO   My ⌈dear.⌉
JULIET   What o'clock tomorrow   180
  Shall I send to thee?
ROMEO   By the hour of nine.
JULIET
  I will not fail. 'Tis twenty year till then.
  I have forgot why I did call thee back.
ROMEO
  Let me stand here till thou remember it.   185
JULIET
  I shall forget, to have thee still stand there,
  Rememb'ring how I love thy company.

ROMEO
   And I'll still stay, to have thee still forget,
   Forgetting any other home but this.

JULIET
   'Tis almost morning. I would have thee gone,   190
   And yet no farther than a wanton's bird,
   That lets it hop a little from his hand,
   Like a poor prisoner in his twisted gyves,
   And with a silken thread plucks it back again,
   So loving-jealous of his liberty.   195

ROMEO
   I would I were thy bird.

JULIET   Sweet, so would I.
   Yet I should kill thee with much cherishing.
   Good night, good night. Parting is such sweet
      sorrow   200
   That I shall say "Good night" till it be morrow.
                                    ⌈*She exits.*⌉

⌈ROMEO⌉
   Sleep dwell upon thine eyes, peace in thy breast.
   Would I were sleep and peace so sweet to rest.
   Hence will I to my ghostly friar's close cell,
   His help to crave, and my dear hap to tell.   205
                                    He exits.

                    ⌈Scene 3⌉
   Enter Friar ⌈Lawrence⌉ alone with a basket.

FRIAR LAWRENCE
   The gray-eyed morn smiles on the frowning night,
   ⌈Check'ring⌉ the eastern clouds with streaks of light,
   And fleckled darkness like a drunkard reels
   From forth day's path and Titan's ⌈fiery⌉ wheels.
   Now, ere the sun advance his burning eye,   5
   The day to cheer and night's dank dew to dry,

I must upfill this osier cage of ours
With baleful weeds and precious-juicèd flowers.
The earth that's nature's mother is her tomb;
What is her burying grave, that is her womb;　10
And from her womb children of divers kind
We sucking on her natural bosom find,
Many for many virtues excellent,
None but for some, and yet all different.
O, mickle is the powerful grace that lies　15
In plants, herbs, stones, and their true qualities.
For naught so vile that on the earth doth live
But to the earth some special good doth give;
Nor aught so good but, strained from that fair use,
Revolts from true birth, stumbling on abuse.　20
Virtue itself turns vice, being misapplied,
And vice sometime by action dignified.

Enter Romeo.

Within the infant rind of this weak flower
Poison hath residence and medicine power:
For this, being smelt, with that part cheers each　25
　part;
Being tasted, stays all senses with the heart.
Two such opposèd kings encamp them still
In man as well as herbs—grace and rude will;
And where the worser is predominant,　30
Full soon the canker death eats up that plant.

ROMEO
Good morrow, Father.

FRIAR LAWRENCE　　　　　Benedicite.
What early tongue so sweet saluteth me?
Young son, it argues a distempered head　35
So soon to bid "Good morrow" to thy bed.
Care keeps his watch in every old man's eye,
And, where care lodges, sleep will never lie;
But where unbruisèd youth with unstuffed brain

Doth couch his limbs, there golden sleep doth   40
  reign.
Therefore thy earliness doth me assure
Thou art uproused with some distemp'rature,
Or, if not so, then here I hit it right:
Our Romeo hath not been in bed tonight.   45

ROMEO
That last is true. The sweeter rest was mine.

FRIAR LAWRENCE
God pardon sin! Wast thou with Rosaline?

ROMEO
With Rosaline, my ghostly Father? No.
I have forgot that name and that name's woe.

FRIAR LAWRENCE
That's my good son. But where hast thou been   50
  then?

ROMEO
I'll tell thee ere thou ask it me again.
I have been feasting with mine enemy,
Where on a sudden one hath wounded me
That's by me wounded. Both our remedies   55
Within thy help and holy physic lies.
I bear no hatred, blessèd man, for, lo,
My intercession likewise steads my foe.

FRIAR LAWRENCE
Be plain, good son, and homely in thy drift.
Riddling confession finds but riddling shrift.   60

ROMEO
Then plainly know my heart's dear love is set
On the fair daughter of rich Capulet.
As mine on hers, so hers is set on mine,
And all combined, save what thou must combine
By holy marriage. When and where and how   65
We met, we wooed, and made exchange of vow
I'll tell thee as we pass, but this I pray,
That thou consent to marry us today.

FRIAR LAWRENCE
  Holy Saint Francis, what a change is here!
  Is Rosaline, that thou didst love so dear,   70
  So soon forsaken? Young men's love then lies
  Not truly in their hearts, but in their eyes.
  Jesu Maria, what a deal of brine
  Hath washed thy sallow cheeks for Rosaline!
  How much salt water thrown away in waste   75
  To season love, that of it doth not taste!
  The sun not yet thy sighs from heaven clears,
  Thy old groans yet ringing in mine ancient ears.
  Lo, here upon thy cheek the stain doth sit
  Of an old tear that is not washed off yet.   80
  If e'er thou wast thyself, and these woes thine,
  Thou and these woes were all for Rosaline.
  And art thou changed? Pronounce this sentence
    then:
  Women may fall when there's no strength in men.   85
ROMEO
  Thou chid'st me oft for loving Rosaline.
FRIAR LAWRENCE
  For doting, not for loving, pupil mine.
ROMEO
  And bad'st me bury love.
FRIAR LAWRENCE   Not in a grave,
  To lay one in another out to have.   90
ROMEO
  I pray thee, chide me not. Her I love now
  Doth grace for grace and love for love allow.
  The other did not so.
FRIAR LAWRENCE   O, she knew well
  Thy love did read by rote, that could not spell.   95
  But come, young waverer, come, go with me.
  In one respect I'll thy assistant be,
  For this alliance may so happy prove
  To turn your households' rancor to pure love.

ROMEO
  O, let us hence. I stand on sudden haste.   100
FRIAR LAWRENCE
  Wisely and slow. They stumble that run fast.
                                    They exit.

                    ⌜Scene 4⌝
              Enter Benvolio and Mercutio.

MERCUTIO
  Where the devil should this Romeo be?
  Came he not home tonight?
BENVOLIO
  Not to his father's. I spoke with his man.
MERCUTIO
  Why, that same pale hard-hearted wench, that
    Rosaline,   5
  Torments him so that he will sure run mad.
BENVOLIO
  Tybalt, the kinsman to old Capulet,
  Hath sent a letter to his father's house.
MERCUTIO A challenge, on my life.
BENVOLIO Romeo will answer it.   10
MERCUTIO Any man that can write may answer a letter.
BENVOLIO Nay, he will answer the letter's master, how
  he dares, being dared.
MERCUTIO Alas, poor Romeo, he is already dead,
  stabbed with a white wench's black eye, run   15
  through the ear with a love-song, the very pin of his
  heart cleft with the blind bow-boy's butt shaft. And
  is he a man to encounter Tybalt?
⌜**BENVOLIO**⌝ Why, what is Tybalt?
MERCUTIO More than prince of cats. O, he's the coura-   20
  geous captain of compliments. He fights as you sing
  prick-song, keeps time, distance, and proportion.

He rests his minim rests, one, two, and the third in
your bosom—the very butcher of a silk button, a
duelist, a duelist, a gentleman of the very first house 25
of the first and second cause. Ah, the immortal
passado, the *punto reverso,* the *hay!*

BENVOLIO The what?

MERCUTIO The pox of such antic, lisping, affecting
⌜phantasimes,⌝ these new tuners of accent: "By 30
Jesu, a very good blade! A very tall man! A very good
whore!" Why, is not this a lamentable thing, grand-
• sire, that we should be thus afflicted with these
strange flies, these fashion-mongers, these ⌜"pardon-me" 's,⌝ who stand so much on the new form 35
that they cannot sit at ease on the old bench? O their
bones, their bones!

Enter Romeo.

BENVOLIO Here comes Romeo, here comes Romeo.

MERCUTIO Without his roe, like a dried herring. O
flesh, flesh, how art thou fishified? Now is he for the 40
numbers that Petrarch flowed in. Laura to his lady
was a kitchen wench (marry, she had a better love
to berhyme her), Dido a dowdy, Cleopatra a gypsy,
Helen and Hero hildings and harlots, Thisbe a gray
eye or so, but not to the purpose.—Signior Romeo, 45
bonjour. There's a French salutation to your French
slop. You gave us the counterfeit fairly last night.

ROMEO Good morrow to you both. What counterfeit
did I give you?

MERCUTIO The slip, sir, the slip. Can you not conceive? 50

ROMEO Pardon, good Mercutio, my business was
great, and in such a case as mine a man may strain
courtesy.

MERCUTIO That's as much as to say such a case as
yours constrains a man to bow in the hams. 55

ROMEO Meaning, to curtsy.

MERCUTIO   Thou hast most kindly hit it.

ROMEO   A most courteous exposition.

MERCUTIO   Nay, I am the very pink of courtesy.

ROMEO   "Pink" for flower.   60

MERCUTIO   Right.

ROMEO   Why, then is my pump well flowered.

MERCUTIO   Sure wit, follow me this jest now till thou
hast worn out thy pump, that when the single sole
of it is worn, the jest may remain, after the wearing,   65
solely singular.

ROMEO   O single-soled jest, solely singular for the
singleness.

MERCUTIO   Come between us, good Benvolio. My wits
faints.   70

ROMEO   Switch and spurs, switch and spurs, or I'll cry
a match.

MERCUTIO   Nay, if our wits run the wild-goose chase, I
am done, for thou hast more of the wild goose in
one of thy wits than, I am sure, I have in my whole   75
five. Was I with you there for the goose?

ROMEO   Thou wast never with me for anything when
thou wast not there for the goose.

MERCUTIO   I will bite thee by the ear for that jest.

ROMEO   Nay, good goose, bite not.   80

MERCUTIO   Thy wit is a very bitter sweeting; it is a most
sharp sauce.

ROMEO   And is it not, then, well served into a sweet
goose?

MERCUTIO   O, here's a wit of cheveril that stretches   85
from an inch narrow to an ell broad.

ROMEO   I stretch it out for that word "broad," which
added to the goose, proves thee far and wide a
broad goose.

MERCUTIO   Why, is not this better now than groaning   90
for love? Now art thou sociable, now art thou
Romeo, now art thou what thou art, by art as well as

by nature. For this driveling love is like a great
natural that runs lolling up and down to hide his
bauble in a hole.   95

BENVOLIO   Stop there, stop there.

MERCUTIO   Thou desirest me to stop in my tale against
the hair.

BENVOLIO   Thou wouldst else have made thy tale large.

MERCUTIO   O, thou art deceived. I would have made it 100
short, for I was come to the whole depth of my tale
and meant indeed to occupy the argument no
longer.

Enter Nurse and her man ⌐Peter.⌐

ROMEO   Here's goodly gear. A sail, a sail!

MERCUTIO   Two, two—a shirt and a smock.   105

NURSE   Peter.

PETER   Anon.

NURSE   My fan, Peter.

MERCUTIO   Good Peter, to hide her face, for her fan's
the fairer face.   110

NURSE   God you good morrow, gentlemen.

MERCUTIO   God you good e'en, fair gentlewoman.

NURSE   Is it good e'en?

MERCUTIO   'Tis no less, I tell you, for the bawdy hand of
the dial is now upon the prick of noon.   115

NURSE   Out upon you! What a man are you? .

ROMEO   One, gentlewoman, that God hath made, himself to mar.

NURSE   By my troth, it is well said: "for himself to
mar," quoth he? Gentlemen, can any of you tell me 120
where I may find the young Romeo?

ROMEO   I can tell you, but young Romeo will be older
when you have found him than he was when you
sought him. I am the youngest of that name, for
fault of a worse.   125

NURSE   You say well.

MERCUTIO Yea, is the worst well? Very well took, i'
faith, wisely, wisely.

NURSE If you be he, sir, I desire some confidence with
you.   130

BENVOLIO She will indite him to some supper.

MERCUTIO A bawd, a bawd, a bawd. So ho!

ROMEO What hast thou found?

MERCUTIO No hare, sir, unless a hare, sir, in a Lenten
pie, that is something stale and hoar ere it be spent.   135
⌈*Singing.*⌉   *An old hare hoar,*
                          And an old hare hoar,
                             Is very good meat in Lent.
                          But a hare that is hoar
                             Is too much for a score   140
                                When it hoars ere it be spent.
Romeo, will you come to your father's? We'll to
dinner thither.

ROMEO I will follow you.

MERCUTIO Farewell, ancient lady. Farewell, lady, lady,   145
lady.   ⌈*Mercutio and Benvolio*⌉ *exit.*

NURSE I pray you, sir, what saucy merchant was this
that was so full of his ropery?

ROMEO A gentleman, Nurse, that loves to hear himself
talk and will speak more in a minute than he will   150
stand to in a month.

NURSE An he speak anything against me, I'll take him
down, an he were lustier than he is, and twenty
such jacks. An if I cannot, I'll find those that shall.
Scurvy knave, I am none of his flirt-gills; I am none   155
of his skains-mates. ⌈*To Peter.*⌉ And thou must stand
by too and suffer every knave to use me at his
pleasure.

PETER I saw no man use you at his pleasure. If I had,
my weapon should quickly have been out. I war-   160
rant you, I dare draw as soon as another man, if I
see occasion in a good quarrel, and the law on my
side.

NURSE Now, afore God, I am so vexed that every part
about me quivers. Scurvy knave! ⌜*To Romeo.*⌝ Pray 165
you, sir, a word. And, as I told you, my young lady
bid me inquire you out. What she bid me say, I will
keep to myself. But first let me tell you, if you
should lead her in a fool's paradise, as they say, it
were a very gross kind of behavior, as they say. For 170
the gentlewoman is young; and therefore, if you
should deal double with her, truly it were an ill
thing to be offered to any gentlewoman, and very
weak dealing.

ROMEO Nurse, commend me to thy lady and mistress. 175
I protest unto thee—

NURSE Good heart, and i' faith I will tell her as much.
Lord, Lord, she will be a joyful woman.

ROMEO What wilt thou tell her, Nurse? Thou dost not
mark me. 180

NURSE I will tell her, sir, that you do protest, which, as
I take it, is a gentlemanlike offer.

ROMEO Bid her devise
Some means to come to shrift this afternoon,
And there she shall at Friar Lawrence' cell 185
Be shrived and married. Here is for thy pains.
⌜*Offering her money.*⌝

NURSE No, truly, sir, not a penny.

ROMEO Go to, I say you shall.

NURSE
This afternoon, sir? Well, she shall be there.

ROMEO
And stay, good Nurse, behind the abbey wall. 190
Within this hour my man shall be with thee
And bring thee cords made like a tackled stair,
Which to the high topgallant of my joy
Must be my convoy in the secret night.
Farewell. Be trusty, and I'll quit thy pains. 195
Farewell. Commend me to thy mistress.

NURSE
  Now, God in heaven bless thee! Hark you, sir.
ROMEO   What sayst thou, my dear Nurse?
NURSE
  Is your man secret? Did you ne'er hear say
  "Two may keep counsel, putting one away"?   200
ROMEO
  Warrant thee, my man's as true as steel.
NURSE   Well, sir, my mistress is the sweetest lady. Lord,
  Lord, when 'twas a little prating thing—O, there is
  a nobleman in town, one Paris, that would fain lay
  knife aboard, but she, good soul, had as lief see a   205
  toad, a very toad, as see him. I anger her sometimes
  and tell her that Paris is the properer man, but I'll
  warrant you, when I say so, she looks as pale as any
  clout in the versal world. Doth not rosemary and
  Romeo begin both with a letter?   210
ROMEO   Ay, Nurse, what of that? Both with an *R*.
NURSE   Ah, mocker, that's the ⌜dog's⌝ name. *R* is for
  the—No, I know it begins with some other letter,
  and she hath the prettiest sententious of it, of you
  and rosemary, that it would do you good to hear it.   215
ROMEO   Commend me to thy lady.
NURSE   Ay, a thousand times.—Peter.
PETER   Anon.
NURSE   Before and apace.
                              ⌜*They*⌝ *exit.*

                      ⌜Scene 5⌝
                    Enter Juliet.

JULIET
  The clock struck nine when I did send the Nurse.
  In half an hour she promised to return.
  Perchance she cannot meet him. That's not so.
  O, she is lame! Love's heralds should be thoughts,
  Which ten times faster glides than the sun's beams,   5

Driving back shadows over louring hills.
Therefore do nimble-pinioned doves draw Love,
And therefore hath the wind-swift Cupid wings.
Now is the sun upon the highmost hill
Of this day's journey, and from nine till twelve   10
Is ⌜three⌝ long hours, yet she is not come.
Had she affections and warm youthful blood,
She would be as swift in motion as a ball;
My words would bandy her to my sweet love,
And his to me.   15
But old folks, many feign as they were dead,
Unwieldy, slow, heavy, and pale as lead.

Enter Nurse ⌜and Peter.⌝

O God, she comes!—O, honey Nurse, what news?
Hast thou met with him? Send thy man away.
NURSE   Peter, stay at the gate.   ⌜*Peter exits.*⌝ 20
JULIET
Now, good sweet Nurse—O Lord, why lookest thou
    sad?
Though news be sad, yet tell them merrily.
If good, thou shamest the music of sweet news
By playing it to me with so sour a face.   25
NURSE
I am aweary. Give me leave awhile.
Fie, how my bones ache! What a jaunt have I!
JULIET
I would thou hadst my bones, and I thy news.
Nay, come, I pray thee, speak. Good, good Nurse,
    speak.   30
NURSE
Jesu, what haste! Can you not stay awhile?
Do you not see that I am out of breath?
JULIET
How art thou out of breath, when thou hast breath
To say to me that thou art out of breath?
The excuse that thou dost make in this delay   35

Is longer than the tale thou dost excuse.
Is thy news good or bad? Answer to that.
Say either, and I'll stay the circumstance.
Let me be satisfied; is 't good or bad?

NURSE Well, you have made a simple choice. You know   40
not how to choose a man. Romeo? No, not he.
Though his face be better than any man's, yet his leg
excels all men's, and for a hand and a foot and a
body, though they be not to be talked on, yet they
are past compare. He is not the flower of courtesy,   45
but I'll warrant him as gentle as a lamb. Go thy
ways, wench. Serve God. What, have you dined at
home?

JULIET
No, no. But all this did I know before.
What says he of our marriage? What of that?   50

NURSE
Lord, how my head aches! What a head have I!
It beats as it would fall in twenty pieces.
My back o' t' other side! Ah, my back, my back!
Beshrew your heart for sending me about
To catch my death with jaunting up and down.   55

JULIET
I' faith, I am sorry that thou art not well.
Sweet, sweet, sweet Nurse, tell me, what says my
    love?

NURSE Your love says, like an honest gentleman, and a
courteous, and a kind, and a handsome, and, I   60
warrant, a virtuous—Where is your mother?

JULIET
Where is my mother? Why, she is within.
Where should she be? How oddly thou repliest:
"Your love says, like an honest gentleman,
Where is your mother?"   65

NURSE   O God's lady dear,
Are you so hot? Marry, come up, I trow.

Is this the poultice for my aching bones?
Henceforward do your messages yourself.

JULIET
Here's such a coil. Come, what says Romeo?   70

NURSE
Have you got leave to go to shrift today?

JULIET I have.

NURSE
Then hie you hence to Friar Lawrence' cell.
There stays a husband to make you a wife.
Now comes the wanton blood up in your cheeks;   75
They'll be in scarlet straight at any news.
Hie you to church. I must another way,
To fetch a ladder by the which your love
Must climb a bird's nest soon when it is dark.
I am the drudge and toil in your delight,   80
But you shall bear the burden soon at night.
Go. I'll to dinner. Hie you to the cell.

JULIET
Hie to high fortune! Honest Nurse, farewell.
                                        They exit.

⌜Scene 6⌝
Enter Friar ⌜*Lawrence*⌝ *and Romeo.*

FRIAR LAWRENCE
So smile the heavens upon this holy act
That after-hours with sorrow chide us not.

ROMEO
Amen, amen. But come what sorrow can,
It cannot countervail the exchange of joy
That one short minute gives me in her sight.   5
Do thou but close our hands with holy words,
Then love-devouring death do what he dare,
It is enough I may but call her mine.

FRIAR LAWRENCE
These violent delights have violent ends

And in their triumph die, like fire and powder, 10
Which, as they kiss, consume. The sweetest honey
Is loathsome in his own deliciousness
And in the taste confounds the appetite.
Therefore love moderately. Long love doth so.
Too swift arrives as tardy as too slow. 15

Enter Juliet.

Here comes the lady. O, so light a foot
Will ne'er wear out the everlasting flint.
A lover may bestride the gossamers
That idles in the wanton summer air,
And yet not fall, so light is vanity. 20

JULIET
Good even to my ghostly confessor.

FRIAR LAWRENCE
Romeo shall thank thee, daughter, for us both.

JULIET
As much to him, else is his thanks too much.

ROMEO
Ah, Juliet, if the measure of thy joy
Be heaped like mine, and that thy skill be more 25
To blazon it, then sweeten with thy breath
This neighbor air, and let rich ⌜music's⌝ tongue
Unfold the imagined happiness that both
Receive in either by this dear encounter.

JULIET
Conceit, more rich in matter than in words, 30
Brags of his substance, not of ornament.
They are but beggars that can count their worth,
But my true love is grown to such excess
I cannot sum up sum of half my wealth.

FRIAR LAWRENCE
Come, come with me, and we will make short work, 35
For, by your leaves, you shall not stay alone
Till Holy Church incorporate two in one.

⌜*They exit.*⌝

⌜ACT 3⌝

⌜Scene 1⌝

Enter Mercutio, Benvolio, and ⌜their⌝ men.

BENVOLIO
  I pray thee, good Mercutio, let's retire.
  The day is hot, the Capels ⌜are⌝ abroad,
  And if we meet we shall not 'scape a brawl,
  For now, these hot days, is the mad blood stirring.

MERCUTIO Thou art like one of these fellows that, when   5
  he enters the confines of a tavern, claps me his
  sword upon the table and says "God send me no
  need of thee" and, by the operation of the second
  cup, draws him on the drawer when indeed there is
  no need.   10

BENVOLIO Am I like such a fellow?

MERCUTIO Come, come, thou art as hot a jack in thy
  mood as any in Italy, and as soon moved to be
  moody, and as soon moody to be moved.

BENVOLIO And what to?   15

MERCUTIO Nay, an there were two such, we should
  have none shortly, for one would kill the other.
  Thou—why, thou wilt quarrel with a man that
  hath a hair more or a hair less in his beard than
  thou hast. Thou wilt quarrel with a man for crack-   20
  ing nuts, having no other reason but because thou
  hast hazel eyes. What eye but such an eye would spy
  out such a quarrel? Thy head is as full of quarrels as

60

an egg is full of meat, and yet thy head hath been
beaten as addle as an egg for quarreling. Thou hast   25
quarreled with a man for coughing in the street
because he hath wakened thy dog that hath lain
asleep in the sun. Didst thou not fall out with a tailor
for wearing his new doublet before Easter? With
another, for tying his new shoes with old ribbon?   30
And yet thou wilt tutor me from quarreling?

BENVOLIO   An I were so apt to quarrel as thou art, any
man should buy the fee simple of my life for an
hour and a quarter.

MERCUTIO   The fee simple? O simple!   35

Enter Tybalt, Petruchio, and others.

BENVOLIO   By my head, here comes the Capulets.

MERCUTIO   By my heel, I care not.

TYBALT, ⌈*to his companions*⌉
Follow me close, for I will speak to them.—
Gentlemen, good e'en. A word with one of you.

MERCUTIO   And but one word with one of us? Couple it   40
with something. Make it a word and a blow.

TYBALT   You shall find me apt enough to that, sir, an
you will give me occasion.

MERCUTIO   Could you not take some occasion without
giving?   45

TYBALT   Mercutio, thou consortest with Romeo.

MERCUTIO   Consort? What, dost thou make us minstrels? An thou make minstrels of us, look to hear
nothing but discords. Here's my fiddlestick; here's
that shall make you dance. Zounds, consort!   50

BENVOLIO
We talk here in the public haunt of men.
Either withdraw unto some private place,
Or reason coldly of your grievances,
Or else depart. Here all eyes gaze on us.

MERCUTIO
   Men's eyes were made to look, and let them gaze. 55
   I will not budge for no man's pleasure, I.

         Enter Romeo.

TYBALT
   Well, peace be with you, sir. Here comes my man.
MERCUTIO
   But I'll be hanged, sir, if he wear your livery.
   Marry, go before to field, he'll be your follower.
   Your Worship in that sense may call him "man." 60
TYBALT
   Romeo, the love I bear thee can afford
   No better term than this: thou art a villain.
ROMEO
   Tybalt, the reason that I have to love thee
   Doth much excuse the appertaining rage
   To such a greeting. Villain am I none. 65
   Therefore farewell. I see thou knowest me not.
TYBALT
   Boy, this shall not excuse the injuries
   That thou hast done me. Therefore turn and draw.
ROMEO
   I do protest I never injured thee
   But love thee better than thou canst devise 70
   Till thou shalt know the reason of my love.
   And so, good Capulet, which name I tender
   As dearly as mine own, be satisfied.
MERCUTIO
   O calm, dishonorable, vile submission!
   Alla stoccato carries it away.   ⌜*He draws.*⌝ 75
   Tybalt, you ratcatcher, will you walk?
TYBALT   What wouldst thou have with me?
MERCUTIO   Good king of cats, nothing but one of your
     nine lives, that I mean to make bold withal, and, as
     you shall use me hereafter, dry-beat the rest of the 80

eight. Will you pluck your sword out of his pilcher
by the ears? Make haste, lest mine be about your
ears ere it be out.

TYBALT   I am for you.   ⌜*He draws.*⌝

ROMEO
   Gentle Mercutio, put thy rapier up.   85

MERCUTIO   Come, sir, your *passado*.   ⌜*They fight.*⌝

ROMEO
   Draw, Benvolio, beat down their weapons.
                                           ⌜*Romeo draws.*⌝
   Gentlemen, for shame forbear this outrage!
   Tybalt! Mercutio! The Prince expressly hath
   Forbid this bandying in Verona streets.   90
   Hold, Tybalt! Good Mercutio!
          ⌜*Romeo attempts to beat down their rapiers.*
                         Tybalt stabs Mercutio.⌝

⌜PETRUCHIO⌝   Away, Tybalt!
          ⌜*Tybalt, Petruchio, and their followers exit.*⌝

MERCUTIO   I am hurt.
   A plague o' both houses! I am sped.
   Is he gone and hath nothing?   95

BENVOLIO   What, art thou hurt?

MERCUTIO
   Ay, ay, a scratch, a scratch. Marry, 'tis enough.
   Where is my page?—Go, villain, fetch a surgeon.
                                           ⌜*Page exits.*⌝

ROMEO
   Courage, man, the hurt cannot be much.

MERCUTIO   No, 'tis not so deep as a well, nor so wide as 100
   a church door, but 'tis enough. 'Twill serve. Ask for
   me tomorrow, and you shall find me a grave man. I
   am peppered, I warrant, for this world. A plague o'
   both your houses! Zounds, a dog, a rat, a mouse, a
   cat, to scratch a man to death! A braggart, a rogue, a 105
   villain that fights by the book of arithmetic! Why the
   devil came you between us? I was hurt under your
   arm.

ROMEO   I thought all for the best.
MERCUTIO
  Help me into some house, Benvolio,   110
  Or I shall faint. A plague o' both your houses!
  They have made worms' meat of me.
  I have it, and soundly, too. Your houses!
                ⌜*All but Romeo*⌝ *exit.*

ROMEO
  This gentleman, the Prince's near ally,
  My very friend, hath got this mortal hurt   115
  In my behalf. My reputation stained
  With Tybalt's slander—Tybalt, that an hour
  Hath been my cousin! O sweet Juliet,
  Thy beauty hath made me effeminate
  And in my temper softened valor's steel.   120

          Enter Benvolio.

BENVOLIO
  O Romeo, Romeo, brave Mercutio is dead.
  That gallant spirit hath aspired the clouds,
  Which too untimely here did scorn the earth.
ROMEO
  This day's black fate on more days doth depend.
  This but begins the woe others must end.   125

          ⌜*Enter Tybalt.*⌝

BENVOLIO
  Here comes the furious Tybalt back again.
ROMEO
  ⌜Alive⌝ in triumph, and Mercutio slain!
  Away to heaven, respective lenity,
  And ⌜fire-eyed⌝ fury be my conduct now.—
  Now, Tybalt, take the "villain" back again   130
  That late thou gavest me, for Mercutio's soul
  Is but a little way above our heads,
  Staying for thine to keep him company.
  Either thou or I, or both, must go with him.

TYBALT
　　Thou, wretched boy, that didst consort him here,   135
　　Shalt with him hence.
ROMEO　　　　　　　　　This shall determine that.
　　　　　　　　　　　　　　They fight. Tybalt falls.

BENVOLIO
　　Romeo, away, begone!
　　The citizens are up, and Tybalt slain.
　　Stand not amazed. The Prince will doom thee death   140
　　If thou art taken. Hence, be gone, away.
ROMEO
　　O, I am Fortune's fool!
BENVOLIO　　　　　　　　Why dost thou stay?
　　　　　　　　　　　　　　Romeo exits.

　　　　　　　Enter Citizens.

CITIZEN
　　Which way ran he that killed Mercutio?
　　Tybalt, that murderer, which way ran he?   145
BENVOLIO
　　There lies that Tybalt.
CITIZEN, ⌜*to Tybalt*⌝　　　Up, sir, go with me.
　　I charge thee in the Prince's name, obey.

Enter Prince, old Montague, Capulet, their Wives and all.

PRINCE
　　Where are the vile beginners of this fray?
BENVOLIO
　　O noble Prince, I can discover all   150
　　The unlucky manage of this fatal brawl.
　　There lies the man, slain by young Romeo,
　　That slew thy kinsman, brave Mercutio.
LADY CAPULET
　　Tybalt, my cousin, O my brother's child!
　　O Prince! O cousin! Husband! O, the blood is spilled   155
　　Of my dear kinsman! Prince, as thou art true,

For blood of ours, shed blood of Montague.
O cousin, cousin!

PRINCE
Benvolio, who began this bloody fray?

BENVOLIO
Tybalt, here slain, whom Romeo's hand did slay.   160
Romeo, that spoke him fair, bid him bethink
How nice the quarrel was, and urged withal
Your high displeasure. All this utterèd
With gentle breath, calm look, knees humbly bowed
Could not take truce with the unruly spleen   165
Of Tybalt, deaf to peace, but that he tilts
With piercing steel at bold Mercutio's breast,
Who, all as hot, turns deadly point to point
And, with a martial scorn, with one hand beats
Cold death aside and with the other sends   170
It back to Tybalt, whose dexterity
Retorts it. Romeo he cries aloud
"Hold, friends! Friends, part!" and swifter than his
    tongue
His ⌈agile⌉ arm beats down their fatal points,   175
And 'twixt them rushes; underneath whose arm
An 'envious thrust from Tybalt hit the life
Of stout Mercutio, and then Tybalt fled.
But by and by comes back to Romeo,
Who had but newly entertained revenge,   180
And to 't they go like lightning, for, ere I
Could draw to part them, was stout Tybalt slain,
And, as he fell, did Romeo turn and fly.
This is the truth, or let Benvolio die.

LADY CAPULET
He is a kinsman to the Montague.   185
Affection makes him false; he speaks not true.
Some twenty of them fought in this black strife,
And all those twenty could but kill one life.
I beg for justice, which thou, Prince, must give.
Romeo slew Tybalt; Romeo must not live.   190

PRINCE
  Romeo slew him; he slew Mercutio.
  Who now the price of his dear blood doth owe?
⌜MONTAGUE⌝
  Not Romeo, Prince; he was Mercutio's friend.
  His fault concludes but what the law should end,
  The life of Tybalt.   195
PRINCE   And for that offense
  Immediately we do exile him hence.
  I have an interest in your hearts' proceeding:
  My blood for your rude brawls doth lie a-bleeding.
  But I'll amerce you with so strong a fine   200
  That you shall all repent the loss of mine.
  ⌜I⌝ will be deaf to pleading and excuses.
  Nor tears nor prayers shall purchase out abuses.
  Therefore use none. Let Romeo hence in haste,
  Else, when he is found, that hour is his last.   205
  Bear hence this body and attend our will.
  Mercy but murders, pardoning those that kill.
                    ⌜*They*⌝ *exit,* ⌜*the Capulet men*
                    bearing off Tybalt's body.⌝

⌜Scene 2⌝
Enter Juliet alone.

JULIET
  Gallop apace, you fiery-footed steeds,
  Towards Phoebus' lodging. Such a wagoner
  As Phaeton would whip you to the west
  And bring in cloudy night immediately.
  Spread thy close curtain, love-performing night,   5
  That runaways' eyes may wink, and Romeo
  Leap to these arms, untalked of and unseen.
  Lovers can see to do their amorous rites
  By their own beauties, or, if love be blind,

It best agrees with night. Come, civil night,   10
Thou sober-suited matron all in black,
And learn me how to lose a winning match
Played for a pair of stainless maidenhoods.
Hood my unmanned blood, bating in my cheeks,
With thy black mantle till strange love grow bold,   15
Think true love acted simple modesty.
Come, night. Come, Romeo. Come, thou day in
    night,
For thou wilt lie upon the wings of night
Whiter than new snow upon a raven's back.   20
Come, gentle night; come, loving black-browed
    night,
Give me my Romeo, and when I shall die,
Take him and cut him out in little stars,
And he will make the face of heaven so fine   25
That all the world will be in love with night
And pay no worship to the garish sun.
O, I have bought the mansion of a love
But not possessed it, and, though I am sold,
Not yet enjoyed. So tedious is this day   30
As is the night before some festival
To an impatient child that hath new robes
And may not wear them.

Enter Nurse with cords.

                        O, here comes my nurse,
And she brings news, and every tongue that speaks   35
But Romeo's name speaks heavenly eloquence.—
Now, Nurse, what news? What hast thou there? The
    cords
That Romeo bid thee fetch?
NURSE   Ay, ay, the cords.   40
                    ⌜*Dropping the rope ladder.*⌝

JULIET
Ay me, what news? Why dost thou wring thy hands?

NURSE
Ah weraday, he's dead, he's dead, he's dead!
We are undone, lady, we are undone.
Alack the day, he's gone, he's killed, he's dead.

JULIET
Can heaven be so envious?   45

NURSE   Romeo can,
Though heaven cannot. O Romeo, Romeo,
Whoever would have thought it? Romeo!

JULIET
What devil art thou that dost torment me thus?
This torture should be roared in dismal hell.   50
Hath Romeo slain himself? Say thou but "Ay,"
And that bare vowel "I" shall poison more
Than the death-darting eye of cockatrice.
I am not I if there be such an "I,"
Or those eyes ⌈shut⌉ that makes thee answer "Ay."   55
If he be slain, say "Ay," or if not, "No."
Brief sounds determine my weal or woe.

NURSE
I saw the wound. I saw it with mine eyes
(God save the mark!) here on his manly breast—
A piteous corse, a bloody piteous corse,   60
Pale, pale as ashes, all bedaubed in blood,
All in gore blood. I swoonèd at the sight.

JULIET
O break, my heart, poor bankrout, break at once!
To prison, eyes; ne'er look on liberty.
Vile earth to earth resign; end motion here,   65
And thou and Romeo press one heavy bier.

NURSE
O Tybalt, Tybalt, the best friend I had!
O courteous Tybalt, honest gentleman,
That ever I should live to see thee dead!

JULIET
What storm is this that blows so contrary?   70

Is Romeo slaughtered and is Tybalt dead?
My dearest cousin, and my dearer lord?
Then, dreadful trumpet, sound the general doom,
For who is living if those two are gone?

NURSE
Tybalt is gone and Romeo banishèd.   75
Romeo that killed him—he is banishèd.

JULIET
O God, did Romeo's hand shed Tybalt's blood?

⌜NURSE⌝
It did, it did, alas the day, it did.

⌜JULIET⌝
O serpent heart hid with a flow'ring face!
Did ever dragon keep so fair a cave?   80
Beautiful tyrant, fiend angelical!
Dove-feathered raven, wolvish-ravening lamb!
Despisèd substance of divinest show!
Just opposite to what thou justly seem'st,
A ⌜damnèd⌝ saint, an honorable villain.   85
O nature, what hadst thou to do in hell
When thou didst bower the spirit of a fiend
In mortal paradise of such sweet flesh?
Was ever book containing such vile matter
So fairly bound? O, that deceit should dwell   90
In such a gorgeous palace!

NURSE   There's no trust,
No faith, no honesty in men. All perjured,
All forsworn, all naught, all dissemblers.
Ah, where's my man? Give me some aqua vitae.   95
These griefs, these woes, these sorrows make me
   old.
Shame come to Romeo!

JULIET   Blistered be thy tongue
For such a wish! He was not born to shame.   100
Upon his brow shame is ashamed to sit,
For 'tis a throne where honor may be crowned

Sole monarch of the universal earth.
O, what a beast was I to chide at him!

NURSE
Will you speak well of him that killed your cousin? 105

JULIET
Shall I speak ill of him that is my husband?
Ah, poor my lord, what tongue shall smooth thy
   name
When I, thy three-hours wife, have mangled it?
But wherefore, villain, didst thou kill my cousin? 110
That villain cousin would have killed my husband.
Back, foolish tears, back to your native spring;
Your tributary drops belong to woe,
Which you, mistaking, offer up to joy.
My husband lives, that Tybalt would have slain, 115
And Tybalt's dead, that would have slain my
   husband.
All this is comfort. Wherefore weep I then?
Some word there was, worser than Tybalt's death,
That murdered me. I would forget it fain, 120
But, O, it presses to my memory
Like damnèd guilty deeds to sinners' minds:
"Tybalt is dead and Romeo banishèd."
That "banishèd," that one word "banishèd,"
Hath slain ten thousand Tybalts. Tybalt's death 125
Was woe enough if it had ended there;
Or, if sour woe delights in fellowship
And needly will be ranked with other griefs,
Why followed not, when she said "Tybalt's dead,"
"Thy father" or "thy mother," nay, or both, 130
Which modern lamentation might have moved?
But with a rearward following Tybalt's death,
"Romeo is banishèd." To speak that word
Is father, mother, Tybalt, Romeo, Juliet,
All slain, all dead. "Romeo is banishèd." 135
There is no end, no limit, measure, bound,

In that word's death. No words can that woe sound.
Where is my father and my mother, Nurse?

NURSE
Weeping and wailing over Tybalt's corse.
Will you go to them? I will bring you thither.   140

JULIET
Wash they his wounds with tears? Mine shall be
　　spent,
When theirs are dry, for Romeo's banishment.—
Take up those cords.
　　　　　　⌜*The Nurse picks up the rope ladder.*⌝
　　　　　　　　　Poor ropes, you are beguiled,   145
Both you and I, for Romeo is exiled.
He made you for a highway to my bed,
But I, a maid, die maiden-widowèd.
Come, cords—come, Nurse. I'll to my wedding bed,
And death, not Romeo, take my maidenhead!   150

NURSE
Hie to your chamber. I'll find Romeo
To comfort you. I wot well where he is.
Hark you, your Romeo will be here at night.
I'll to him. He is hid at Lawrence' cell.

JULIET
O, find him!　　　　　　⌜*Giving the Nurse a ring.*⌝ 155
　　　　Give this ring to my true knight
And bid him come to take his last farewell.
　　　　　　　　　　　　　⌜*They*⌝ *exit.*

　　　　　　⌜Scene 3⌝
　　　Enter Friar ⌜*Lawrence.*⌝

FRIAR LAWRENCE
Romeo, come forth; come forth, thou fearful man.
Affliction is enamored of thy parts,
And thou art wedded to calamity.

⌈*Enter Romeo.*⌉

ROMEO
  Father, what news? What is the Prince's doom?
  What sorrow craves acquaintance at my hand   5
  That I yet know not?
FRIAR LAWRENCE   Too familiar
  Is my dear son with such sour company.
  I bring thee tidings of the Prince's doom.
ROMEO
  What less than doomsday is the Prince's doom?   10
FRIAR LAWRENCE
  A gentler judgment vanished from his lips:
  Not body's death, but body's banishment.
ROMEO
  Ha, banishment? Be merciful, say "death,"
  For exile hath more terror in his look,
  Much more than death. Do not say "banishment."   15
FRIAR LAWRENCE
  Here from Verona art thou banishèd.
  Be patient, for the world is broad and wide.
ROMEO
  There is no world without Verona walls
  But purgatory, torture, hell itself.
  Hence "banishèd" is "banished from the world,"   20
  And world's exile is death. Then "banishèd"
  Is death mistermed. Calling death "banishèd,"
  Thou cutt'st my head off with a golden ax
  And smilest upon the stroke that murders me.
FRIAR LAWRENCE
  O deadly sin, O rude unthankfulness!   25
  Thy fault our law calls death, but the kind Prince,
  Taking thy part, hath rushed aside the law
  And turned that black word "death" to
    "banishment."
  This is dear mercy, and thou seest it not.   30

ROMEO
    'Tis torture and not mercy. Heaven is here
    Where Juliet lives, and every cat and dog
    And little mouse, every unworthy thing,
    Live here in heaven and may look on her,
    But Romeo may not. More validity,   35
    More honorable state, more courtship lives
    In carrion flies than Romeo. They may seize
    On the white wonder of dear Juliet's hand
    And steal immortal blessing from her lips,
    Who even in pure and vestal modesty   40
    Still blush, as thinking their own kisses sin;
    But Romeo may not; he is banishèd.
    Flies may do this, but I from this must fly.
    They are free men, but I am banishèd.
    And sayest thou yet that exile is not death?   45
    Hadst thou no poison mixed, no sharp-ground
        knife,
    No sudden mean of death, though ne'er so mean,
    But "banishèd" to kill me? "Banishèd"?
    O Friar, the damnèd use that word in hell.   50
    Howling attends it. How hast thou the heart,
    Being a divine, a ghostly confessor,
    A sin absolver, and my friend professed,
    To mangle me with that word "banishèd"?

FRIAR LAWRENCE
    ⌈Thou⌉ fond mad man, hear me a little speak.   55

ROMEO
    O, thou wilt speak again of banishment.

FRIAR LAWRENCE
    I'll give thee armor to keep off that word,
    Adversity's sweet milk, philosophy,
    To comfort thee, though thou art banishèd.

ROMEO
    Yet "banishèd"? Hang up philosophy.   60
    Unless philosophy can make a Juliet,

Displant a town, reverse a prince's doom,
It helps not, it prevails not. Talk no more.

FRIAR LAWRENCE
O, then I see that ⌜madmen⌝ have no ears.

ROMEO
How should they when that wise men have no eyes?   65

FRIAR LAWRENCE
Let me dispute with thee of thy estate.

ROMEO
Thou canst not speak of that thou dost not feel.
Wert thou as young as I, Juliet thy love,
An hour but married, Tybalt murderèd,
Doting like me, and like me banishèd,   70
Then mightst thou speak, then mightst thou tear thy
    hair
And fall upon the ground as I do now,
                    ⌜*Romeo throws himself down.*⌝
Taking the measure of an unmade grave.
                            Knock ⌜*within.*⌝

FRIAR LAWRENCE
Arise. One knocks. Good Romeo, hide thyself.   75

ROMEO
Not I, unless the breath of heartsick groans,
Mistlike, enfold me from the search of eyes.
                                    Knock.

FRIAR LAWRENCE
Hark, how they knock!—Who's there?—Romeo,
    arise.
Thou wilt be taken.—Stay awhile.—Stand up.   80
                                    Knock.
Run to my study.—By and by.—God's will,
What simpleness is this?—I come, I come.
                                    Knock.
Who knocks so hard? Whence come you? What's
    your will?

NURSE, ⌈*within*⌉
    Let me come in, and you shall know my errand.   85
    I come from Lady Juliet.
FRIAR LAWRENCE, ⌈*admitting the Nurse*⌉
                Welcome then.

          ⌈*Enter Nurse.*⌉

NURSE
    O holy Friar, O, tell me, holy Friar,
    Where's my lady's lord? Where's Romeo?
FRIAR LAWRENCE
    There on the ground, with his own tears made   90
        drunk.
NURSE
    O, he is even in my mistress' case,
    Just in her case. O woeful sympathy!
    Piteous predicament! Even so lies she,
    Blubb'ring and weeping, weeping and blubb'ring.—   95
    Stand up, stand up. Stand an you be a man.
    For Juliet's sake, for her sake, rise and stand.
    Why should you fall into so deep an O?
ROMEO   Nurse.
NURSE
    Ah sir, ah sir, death's the end of all.   100
ROMEO, ⌈*rising up*⌉
    Spakest thou of Juliet? How is it with her?
    Doth not she think me an old murderer,
    Now I have stained the childhood of our joy
    With blood removed but little from her own?
    Where is she? And how doth she? And what says   105
    My concealed lady to our canceled love?
NURSE
    O, she says nothing, sir, but weeps and weeps,
    And now falls on her bed, and then starts up,
    And "Tybalt" calls, and then on Romeo cries,
    And then down falls again.   110

ROMEO   As if that name,
  Shot from the deadly level of a gun,
  Did murder her, as that name's cursèd hand
  Murdered her kinsman.—O, tell me, Friar, tell me,
  In what vile part of this anatomy   115
  Doth my name lodge? Tell me, that I may sack
  The hateful mansion.   ⌜*He draws his dagger.*⌝
FRIAR LAWRENCE   Hold thy desperate hand!
  Art thou a man? Thy form cries out thou art.
  Thy tears are womanish; thy wild acts ⌜denote⌝   120
  The unreasonable fury of a beast.
  Unseemly woman in a seeming man,
  And ill-beseeming beast in seeming both!
  Thou hast amazed me. By my holy order,
  I thought thy disposition better tempered.   125
  Hast thou slain Tybalt? Wilt thou slay thyself,
  And slay thy lady that in thy life ⌜lives,⌝
  By doing damnèd hate upon thyself?
  Why railest thou on thy birth, the heaven, and earth,
  Since birth and heaven and earth, all three do meet   130
  In thee at once, which thou at once wouldst lose?
  Fie, fie, thou shamest thy shape, thy love, thy wit,
  Which, like a usurer, abound'st in all
  And usest none in that true use indeed
  Which should bedeck thy shape, thy love, thy wit.   135
  Thy noble shape is but a form of wax,
  Digressing from the valor of a man;
  Thy dear love sworn but hollow perjury,
  Killing that love which thou hast vowed to cherish;
  Thy wit, that ornament to shape and love,   140
  Misshapen in the conduct of them both,
  Like powder in a skilless soldier's flask,
  Is set afire by thine own ignorance,
  And thou dismembered with thine own defense.
  What, rouse thee, man! Thy Juliet is alive,   145
  For whose dear sake thou wast but lately dead:

There art thou happy. Tybalt would kill thee,
But thou slewest Tybalt: there art thou happy.
The law that threatened death becomes thy friend
And turns it to exile: there art thou happy.   150
A pack of blessings light upon thy back;
Happiness courts thee in her best array;
But, like a ⌐misbehaved⌐ and sullen wench,
Thou ⌐pouts upon⌐ thy fortune and thy love.
Take heed, take heed, for such die miserable.   155
Go, get thee to thy love, as was decreed.
Ascend her chamber. Hence and comfort her.
But look thou stay not till the watch be set,
For then thou canst not pass to Mantua,
Where thou shalt live till we can find a time   160
To blaze your marriage, reconcile your friends,
Beg pardon of the Prince, and call thee back
With twenty hundred thousand times more joy
Than thou went'st forth in lamentation.—
Go before, Nurse. Commend me to thy lady,   165
And bid her hasten all the house to bed,
Which heavy sorrow makes them apt unto.
Romeo is coming.

NURSE
O Lord, I could have stayed here all the night
To hear good counsel. O, what learning is!—   170
My lord, I'll tell my lady you will come.

ROMEO
Do so, and bid my sweet prepare to chide.

NURSE
Here, sir, a ring she bid me give you, sir.
                         ⌐*Nurse gives Romeo a ring.*⌐
Hie you, make haste, for it grows very late.
                                        ⌐*She exits.*⌐

ROMEO
How well my comfort is revived by this!   175

FRIAR LAWRENCE
Go hence, good night—and here stands all your
    state:
Either be gone before the watch be set
Or by the break of day ⌜disguised⌝ from hence.
Sojourn in Mantua. I'll find out your man,   180
And he shall signify from time to time
Every good hap to you that chances here.
Give me thy hand. 'Tis late. Farewell. Good night.

ROMEO
But that a joy past joy calls out on me,
It were a grief so brief to part with thee.   185
Farewell.

They exit.

⌜Scene 4⌝
Enter old Capulet, his Wife, and Paris.

CAPULET
Things have fallen out, sir, so unluckily
That we have had no time to move our daughter.
Look you, she loved her kinsman Tybalt dearly,
And so did I. Well, we were born to die.
'Tis very late. She'll not come down tonight.   5
I promise you, but for your company,
I would have been abed an hour ago.

PARIS
These times of woe afford no times to woo.—
Madam, good night. Commend me to your
    daughter.   10

LADY CAPULET
I will, and know her mind early tomorrow.
Tonight she's mewed up to her heaviness.

CAPULET
Sir Paris, I will make a desperate tender
Of my child's love. I think she will ⌜be⌝ ruled

In all respects by me. Nay, more, I doubt it not.— 15
Wife, go you to her ere you go to bed.
Acquaint her here of my son Paris' love,
And bid her—mark you me?—on Wednesday
    next—
But soft, what day is this? 20

PARIS   Monday, my lord.

CAPULET
Monday, ha ha! Well, Wednesday is too soon.
O' Thursday let it be.—O' Thursday, tell her,
She shall be married to this noble earl.—
Will you be ready? Do you like this haste? 25
⌜We'll⌝ keep no great ado: a friend or two.
For hark you, Tybalt being slain so late,
It may be thought we held him carelessly,
Being our kinsman, if we revel much.
Therefore we'll have some half a dozen friends, 30
And there an end. But what say you to Thursday?

PARIS
My lord, I would that Thursday were tomorrow.

CAPULET
Well, get you gone. O' Thursday be it, then.
⌜*To Lady Capulet.*⌝ Go you to Juliet ere you go to bed.
Prepare her, wife, against this wedding day.— 35
Farewell, my lord.—Light to my chamber, ho!—
Afore me, it is so very late that we
May call it early by and by.—Good night.

                                        They exit.

                        ⌜Scene 5⌝
                Enter Romeo and Juliet aloft.

JULIET
Wilt thou be gone? It is not yet near day.
It was the nightingale, and not the lark,
That pierced the fearful hollow of thine ear.

Nightly she sings on yond pomegranate tree.
Believe me, love, it was the nightingale.   5

ROMEO
  It was the lark, the herald of the morn,
  No nightingale. Look, love, what envious streaks
  Do lace the severing clouds in yonder east.
  Night's candles are burnt out, and jocund day
  Stands tiptoe on the misty mountain-tops.   10
  I must be gone and live, or stay and die.

JULIET
  Yond light is not daylight, I know it, I.
  It is some meteor that the sun ⌐exhaled⌐
  To be to thee this night a torchbearer
  And light thee on thy way to Mantua.   15
  Therefore stay yet. Thou need'st not to be gone.

ROMEO
  Let me be ta'en; let me be put to death.
  I am content, so thou wilt have it so.
  I'll say yon gray is not the morning's eye;
  'Tis but the pale reflex of Cynthia's brow.   20
  Nor that is not the lark whose notes do beat
  The vaulty heaven so high above our heads.
  I have more care to stay than will to go.
  Come death and welcome. Juliet wills it so.
  How is 't, my soul? Let's talk. It is not day.   25

JULIET
  It is, it is. Hie hence, begone, away!
  It is the lark that sings so out of tune,
  Straining harsh discords and unpleasing sharps.
  Some say the lark makes sweet division.
  This doth not so, for she divideth us.   30
  Some say the lark and loathèd toad ⌐changed⌐ eyes.
  O, now I would they had changed voices too,
  Since arm from arm that voice doth us affray,
  Hunting thee hence with hunt's-up to the day.
  O, now begone. More light and light it grows.   35

ROMEO
　More light and light, more dark and dark our woes.

　　　　　　　　Enter Nurse.

NURSE　Madam.
JULIET　Nurse?
NURSE
　Your lady mother is coming to your chamber.
　The day is broke; be wary; look about.　⌜*She exits.*⌝　40
JULIET
　Then, window, let day in, and let life out.
ROMEO
　Farewell, farewell. One kiss and I'll descend.
　　　　　⌜*They kiss, and Romeo descends.*⌝
JULIET
　Art thou gone so? Love, lord, ay husband, friend!
　I must hear from thee every day in the hour,
　For in a minute there are many days.　　　　　45
　O, by this count I shall be much in years
　Ere I again behold my Romeo.
ROMEO　Farewell.
　I will omit no opportunity
　That may convey my greetings, love, to thee.　　50
JULIET
　O, think'st thou we shall ever meet again?
ROMEO
　I doubt it not; and all these woes shall serve
　For sweet discourses in our times to come.
⌜JULIET⌝
　O God, I have an ill-divining soul!
　Methinks I see thee, now thou art so low,　　　5⸱
　As one dead in the bottom of a tomb.
　Either my eyesight fails or thou lookest pale.
ROMEO
　And trust me, love, in my eye so do you.
　Dry sorrow drinks our blood. Adieu, adieu.　*He exits.*

JULIET
O Fortune, Fortune, all men call thee fickle. 60
If thou art fickle, what dost thou with him
That is renowned for faith? Be fickle, Fortune,
For then I hope thou wilt not keep him long,
But send him back.

Enter ⌜Lady Capulet.⌝

LADY CAPULET   Ho, daughter, are you up? 65
JULIET
Who is 't that calls? It is my lady mother.
Is she not down so late or up so early?
What unaccustomed cause procures her hither?
                              ⌜*Juliet descends.*⌝

LADY CAPULET
Why, how now, Juliet?
JULIET   Madam, I am not well. 70
LADY CAPULET
Evermore weeping for your cousin's death?
What, wilt thou wash him from his grave with tears?
An if thou couldst, thou couldst not make him live.
Therefore have done. Some grief shows much of
   love, 75
But much of grief shows still some want of wit.
JULIET
Yet let me weep for such a feeling loss.
LADY CAPULET
So shall you feel the loss, but not the friend
Which you weep for.
JULIET   Feeling so the loss, 80
I cannot choose but ever weep the friend.
LADY CAPULET
Well, girl, thou weep'st not so much for his death
As that the villain lives which slaughtered him.
JULIET
What villain, madam?

LADY CAPULET   That same villain, Romeo.   85
JULIET, ⌜*aside*⌝
    Villain and he be many miles asunder.—
    God pardon ⌜him.⌝ I do with all my heart,
    And yet no man like he doth grieve my heart.
LADY CAPULET
    That is because the traitor murderer lives.
JULIET
    Ay, madam, from the reach of these my hands.   90
    Would none but I might venge my cousin's death!
LADY CAPULET
    We will have vengeance for it, fear thou not.
    Then weep no more. I'll send to one in Mantua,
    Where that same banished runagate doth live,
    Shall give him such an unaccustomed dram   95
    That he shall soon keep Tybalt company.
    And then, I hope, thou wilt be satisfied.
JULIET
    Indeed, I never shall be satisfied
    With Romeo till I behold him—dead—
    Is my poor heart, so for a kinsman vexed.   100
    Madam, if you could find out but a man
    To bear a poison, I would temper it,
    That Romeo should, upon receipt thereof,
    Soon sleep in quiet. O, how my heart abhors
    To hear him named and cannot come to him   105
    To wreak the love I bore my cousin
    Upon his body that hath slaughtered him.
LADY CAPULET
    Find thou the means, and I'll find such a man.
    But now I'll tell thee joyful tidings, girl.
JULIET
    And joy comes well in such a needy time.   110
    What are they, beseech your ladyship?
LADY CAPULET
    Well, well, thou hast a careful father, child,

One who, to put thee from thy heaviness,
Hath sorted out a sudden day of joy
That thou expects not, nor I looked not for.   115

JULIET
  Madam, in happy time! What day is that?

LADY CAPULET
  Marry, my child, early next Thursday morn
  The gallant, young, and noble gentleman,
  The County Paris, at Saint Peter's Church
  Shall happily make thee there a joyful bride.   120

JULIET
  Now, by Saint Peter's Church, and Peter too,
  He shall not make me there a joyful bride!
  I wonder at this haste, that I must wed
  Ere he that should be husband comes to woo.
  I pray you, tell my lord and father, madam,   125
  I will not marry yet, and when I do I swear
  It shall be Romeo, whom you know I hate,
  Rather than Paris. These are news indeed!

LADY CAPULET
  Here comes your father. Tell him so yourself,
  And see how he will take it at your hands.   130

                    Enter Capulet and Nurse.

CAPULET
  When the sun sets, the earth doth drizzle dew,
  But for the sunset of my brother's son
  It rains downright.
  How now, a conduit, girl? What, still in tears?
  Evermore show'ring? In one little body   135
  Thou counterfeits a bark, a sea, a wind.
  For still thy eyes, which I may call the sea,
  Do ebb and flow with tears; the bark thy body is,
  Sailing in this salt flood; the winds thy sighs,
  Who, raging with thy tears and they with them,   140
  Without a sudden calm, will overset

Thy tempest-tossèd body.—How now, wife?
Have you delivered to her our decree?

LADY CAPULET
Ay, sir, but she will none, she ⌜gives⌝ you thanks.
I would the fool were married to her grave.   145

CAPULET
Soft, take me with you, take me with you, wife.
How, will she none? Doth she not give us thanks?
Is she not proud? Doth she not count her blessed,
Unworthy as she is, that we have wrought
So worthy a gentleman to be her bride?   150

JULIET
Not proud you have, but thankful that you have.
Proud can I never be of what I hate,
But thankful even for hate that is meant love.

CAPULET
How, how, how, how? Chopped logic? What is this?
"Proud," and "I thank you," and "I thank you not,"   155
And yet "not proud"? Mistress minion you,
Thank me no thankings, nor proud me no prouds,
But fettle your fine joints 'gainst Thursday next
To go with Paris to Saint Peter's Church,
Or I will drag thee on a hurdle thither.   160
Out, you green-sickness carrion! Out, you baggage!
You tallow face!

LADY CAPULET   Fie, fie, what, are you mad?

JULIET, ⌜*kneeling*⌝
Good father, I beseech you on my knees,
Hear me with patience but to speak a word.   165

CAPULET
Hang thee, young baggage, disobedient wretch!
I tell thee what: get thee to church o' Thursday,
Or never after look me in the face.
Speak not; reply not; do not answer me.
My fingers itch.—Wife, we scarce thought us   170
   blessed

That God had lent us but this only child,
But now I see this one is one too much,
And that we have a curse in having her.
Out on her, hilding.   175
NURSE   God in heaven bless her!
  You are to blame, my lord, to rate her so.
CAPULET
  And why, my Lady Wisdom? Hold your tongue.
  Good Prudence, smatter with your gossips, go.
NURSE
  I speak no treason.   180
⌜CAPULET⌝   O, God 'i' g' eden!
⌜NURSE⌝
  May not one speak?
CAPULET   Peace, you mumbling fool!
  Utter your gravity o'er a gossip's bowl,
  For here we need it not.   185
LADY CAPULET
  You are too hot.
CAPULET   God's bread, it makes me mad.
  Day, night, hour, tide, time, work, play,
  Alone, in company, still my care hath been
  To have her matched. And having now provided   190
  A gentleman of noble parentage,
  Of fair demesnes, youthful, and nobly ⌜ligned,⌝
  Stuffed, as they say, with honorable parts,
  Proportioned as one's thought would wish a man—
  And then to have a wretched puling fool,   195
  A whining mammet, in her fortune's tender,
  To answer "I'll not wed. I cannot love.
  I am too young. I pray you, pardon me."
  But, an you will not wed, I'll pardon you!
  Graze where you will, you shall not house with me.   200
  Look to 't; think on 't. I do not use to jest.
  Thursday is near. Lay hand on heart; advise.
  An you be mine, I'll give you to my friend.

An you be not, hang, beg, starve, die in the streets,
For, by my soul, I'll ne'er acknowledge thee,   205
Nor what is mine shall never do thee good.
Trust to 't; bethink you. I'll not be forsworn.

He exits.

JULIET
Is there no pity sitting in the clouds
That sees into the bottom of my grief?—
O sweet my mother, cast me not away.   210
Delay this marriage for a month, a week,
Or, if you do not, make the bridal bed
In that dim monument where Tybalt lies.

LADY CAPULET
Talk not to me, for I'll not speak a word.
Do as thou wilt, for I have done with thee.   215

She exits.

JULIET, ⌜*rising*⌝
O God! O Nurse, how shall this be prevented?
My husband is on earth, my faith in heaven.
How shall that faith return again to earth
Unless that husband send it me from heaven
By leaving earth? Comfort me; counsel me.—   220
Alack, alack, that heaven should practice stratagems
Upon so soft a subject as myself.—
What sayst thou? Hast thou not a word of joy?
Some comfort, Nurse.

NURSE   Faith, here it is.   225
Romeo is banished, and all the world to nothing
That he dares ne'er come back to challenge you,
Or, if he do, it needs must be by stealth.
Then, since the case so stands as now it doth,
I think it best you married with the County.   230
O, he's a lovely gentleman!
Romeo's a dishclout to him. An eagle, madam,
Hath not so green, so quick, so fair an eye
As Paris hath. Beshrew my very heart,

I think you are happy in this second match,   235
For it excels your first, or, if it did not,
Your first is dead, or 'twere as good he were
As living here and you no use of him.

NURSE

Speak'st thou from thy heart?

NURSE

And from my soul too, else beshrew them both.   240

JULIET   Amen.

NURSE   What?

JULIET

Well, thou hast comforted me marvelous much.
Go in and tell my lady I am gone,
Having displeased my father, to Lawrence' cell   245
To make confession and to be absolved.

NURSE

Marry, I will; and this is wisely done.   ⌜*She exits.*⌝

JULIET

Ancient damnation, O most wicked fiend!
Is it more sin to wish me thus forsworn
Or to dispraise my lord with that same tongue   250
Which she hath praised him with above compare
So many thousand times? Go, counselor.
Thou and my bosom henceforth shall be twain.
I'll to the Friar to know his remedy.
If all else fail, myself have power to die.   255

                                    She exits.

⌜ACT 4⌝

⌜Scene 1⌝
Enter Friar ⌜Lawrence⌝ and County Paris.

FRIAR LAWRENCE
  On Thursday, sir? The time is very short.
PARIS
  My father Capulet will have it so,
  And I am nothing slow to slack his haste.
FRIAR LAWRENCE
  You say you do not know the lady's mind?
  Uneven is the course. I like it not.   5
PARIS
  Immoderately she weeps for Tybalt's death,
  And therefore have I little talk of love,
  For Venus smiles not in a house of tears.
  Now, sir, her father counts it dangerous
  That she do give her sorrow so much sway,   10
  And in his wisdom hastes our marriage
  To stop the inundation of her tears,
  Which, too much minded by herself alone,
  May be put from her by society.
  Now do you know the reason of this haste.   15
FRIAR LAWRENCE, ⌜*aside*⌝
  I would I knew not why it should be slowed.—
  Look, sir, here comes the lady toward my cell.

Enter Juliet.

90

PARIS
  Happily met, my lady and my wife.
JULIET
  That may be, sir, when I may be a wife.
PARIS
  That "may be" must be, love, on Thursday next.   20
JULIET
  What must be shall be.
FRIAR LAWRENCE   That's a certain text.
PARIS
  Come you to make confession to this father?
JULIET
  To answer that, I should confess to you.
PARIS
  Do not deny to him that you love me.   25
JULIET
  I will confess to you that I love him.
PARIS
  So will you, I am sure, that you love me.
JULIET
  If I do so, it will be of more price,
  Being spoke behind your back, than to your face.
PARIS
  Poor soul, thy face is much abused with tears.   30
JULIET
  The tears have got small victory by that,
  For it was bad enough before their spite.
PARIS
  Thou wrong'st it more than tears with that report.
JULIET
  That is no slander, sir, which is a truth,
  And what I spake, I spake it to my face.   35
PARIS
  Thy face is mine, and thou hast slandered it.
JULIET
  It may be so, for it is not mine own.—

Are you at leisure, holy Father, now,
Or shall I come to you at evening Mass?

FRIAR LAWRENCE
My leisure serves me, pensive daughter, now.— 40
My lord, we must entreat the time alone.

PARIS
God shield I should disturb devotion!—
Juliet, on Thursday early will I rouse you.
Till then, adieu, and keep this holy kiss. *He exits.*

JULIET
O, shut the door, and when thou hast done so, 45
Come weep with me, past hope, past care, past help.

FRIAR LAWRENCE
O Juliet, I already know thy grief.
It strains me past the compass of my wits.
I hear thou must, and nothing may prorogue it,
On Thursday next be married to this County. 50

JULIET
Tell me not, Friar, that thou hearest of this,
Unless thou tell me how I may prevent it.
If in thy wisdom thou canst give no help,
Do thou but call my resolution wise,
And with this knife I'll help it presently. 55
⌜*She shows him her knife.*⌝
God joined my heart and Romeo's, thou our hands;
And ere this hand, by thee to Romeo's sealed,
Shall be the label to another deed,
Or my true heart with treacherous revolt
Turn to another, this shall slay them both. 60
Therefore out of thy long-experienced time
Give me some present counsel, or, behold,
'Twixt my extremes and me this bloody knife
Shall play the umpire, arbitrating that
Which the commission of thy years and art 65
Could to no issue of true honor bring.
Be not so long to speak. I long to die
If what thou speak'st speak not of remedy.

FRIAR LAWRENCE
  Hold, daughter, I do spy a kind of hope,
  Which craves as desperate an execution   70
  As that is desperate which we would prevent.
  If, rather than to marry County Paris,
  Thou hast the strength of will to ⌜slay⌝ thyself,
  Then is it likely thou wilt undertake
  A thing like death to chide away this shame,   75
  That cop'st with death himself to 'scape from it;
  And if thou darest, I'll give thee remedy.

JULIET
  O, bid me leap, rather than marry Paris,
  From off the battlements of any tower,
  Or walk in thievish ways, or bid me lurk   80
  Where serpents are. Chain me with roaring bears,
  Or hide me nightly in a charnel house,
  O'ercovered quite with dead men's rattling bones,
  With reeky shanks and yellow ⌜chapless⌝ skulls.
  Or bid me go into a new-made grave   85
  And hide me with a dead man in his ⌜shroud⌝
  (Things that to hear them told have made me
    tremble),
  And I will do it without fear or doubt,
  To live an unstained wife to my sweet love.   90

FRIAR LAWRENCE
  Hold, then. Go home; be merry; give consent
  To marry Paris. Wednesday is tomorrow.
  Tomorrow night look that thou lie alone;
  Let not the Nurse lie with thee in thy chamber.
                       ⌜*Holding out a vial.*⌝
  Take thou this vial, being then in bed,   95
  And this distilling liquor drink thou off;
  When presently through all thy veins shall run
  A cold and drowsy humor; for no pulse
  Shall keep his native progress, but surcease.
  No warmth, no ⌜breath⌝ shall testify thou livest.   100

The roses in thy lips and cheeks shall fade
To ⌜paly⌝ ashes, thy eyes' windows fall
Like death when he shuts up the day of life.
Each part, deprived of supple government,
Shall, stiff and stark and cold, appear like death,   105
And in this borrowed likeness of shrunk death
Thou shalt continue two and forty hours
And then awake as from a pleasant sleep.
Now, when the bridegroom in the morning comes
To rouse thee from thy bed, there art thou dead.   110
Then, as the manner of our country is,
⌜In⌝ thy best robes uncovered on the bier
Thou ⌜shalt⌝ be borne to that same ancient vault
Where all the kindred of the Capulets lie.
In the meantime, against thou shalt awake,   115
Shall Romeo by my letters know our drift,
And hither shall he come, and he and I
Will watch thy ⌜waking,⌝ and that very night
Shall Romeo bear thee hence to Mantua.
And this shall free thee from this present shame,   120
If no inconstant toy nor womanish fear
Abate thy valor in the acting it.

JULIET
Give me, give me! O, tell not me of fear!

FRIAR LAWRENCE, ⌜*giving Juliet the vial*⌝
Hold, get you gone. Be strong and prosperous
In this resolve. I'll send a friar with speed   125
To Mantua with my letters to thy lord.

JULIET
Love give me strength, and strength shall help
  afford.
Farewell, dear Father.
                    ⌜*They*⌝ *exit* ⌜*in different directions.*⌝

⌜Scene 2⌝
Enter Father Capulet, Mother, Nurse, and Servingmen,
two or three.

CAPULET
So many guests invite as here are writ.
⌜*One or two of the Servingmen exit*
with Capulet's list.⌝
Sirrah, go hire me twenty cunning cooks.

SERVINGMAN You shall have none ill, sir, for I'll try if
they can lick their fingers.

CAPULET How canst thou try them so?   5

SERVINGMAN Marry, sir, 'tis an ill cook that cannot lick
his own fingers. Therefore he that cannot lick his
fingers goes not with me.

CAPULET Go, begone.   ⌜*Servingman exits.*⌝
We shall be much unfurnished for this time.—   10
What, is my daughter gone to Friar Lawrence?

NURSE Ay, forsooth.

CAPULET
Well, he may chance to do some good on her.
A peevish ⌜self-willed⌝ harlotry it is.

Enter Juliet.

NURSE
See where she comes from shrift with merry look.   15

CAPULET
How now, my headstrong, where have you been
    gadding?

JULIET
Where I have learned me to repent the sin
Of disobedient opposition
To you and your behests, and am enjoined   20
By holy Lawrence to fall prostrate here   ⌜*Kneeling.*⌝
To beg your pardon. Pardon, I beseech you.
Henceforward I am ever ruled by you.

CAPULET
Send for the County. Go tell him of this.
I'll have this knot knit up tomorrow morning.   25

JULIET
I met the youthful lord at Lawrence' cell
And gave him what becomèd love I might,
Not stepping o'er the bounds of modesty.

CAPULET
Why, I am glad on 't. This is well. Stand up.
⌜*Juliet rises.*⌝
This is as 't should be.—Let me see the County.   30
Ay, marry, go, I say, and fetch him hither.—
Now, afore God, this reverend holy friar,
All our whole city is much bound to him.

JULIET
Nurse, will you go with me into my closet
To help me sort such needful ornaments   35
As you think fit to furnish me tomorrow?

LADY CAPULET
No, not till Thursday. There is time enough.

CAPULET
Go, Nurse. Go with her. We'll to church tomorrow.
⌜*Juliet and the Nurse*⌝ *exit.*

LADY CAPULET
We shall be short in our provision.
'Tis now near night.   40

CAPULET   Tush, I will stir about,
And all things shall be well, I warrant thee, wife.
Go thou to Juliet. Help to deck up her.
I'll not to bed tonight. Let me alone.
I'll play the housewife for this once.—What ho!—   45
They are all forth. Well, I will walk myself
To County Paris, to prepare up him
Against tomorrow. My heart is wondrous light
Since this same wayward girl is so reclaimed.
⌜*They*⌝ *exit.*

⌜Scene 3⌝
Enter Juliet and Nurse.

JULIET
Ay, those attires are best. But, gentle Nurse,
I pray thee leave me to myself tonight,
For I have need of many orisons
To move the heavens to smile upon my state,
Which, well thou knowest, is cross and full of sin.   5

Enter ⌜Lady Capulet.⌝

LADY CAPULET
What, are you busy, ho? Need you my help?
JULIET
No, madam, we have culled such necessaries
As are behooveful for our state tomorrow.
So please you, let me now be left alone,
And let the Nurse this night sit up with you,   10
For I am sure you have your hands full all
In this so sudden business.
LADY CAPULET   Good night.
Get thee to bed and rest, for thou hast need.
                    ⌜*Lady Capulet and the Nurse*⌝ *exit.*

JULIET
Farewell.—God knows when we shall meet again.   15
I have a faint cold fear thrills through my veins
That almost freezes up the heat of life.
I'll call them back again to comfort me.—
Nurse!—What should she do here?
My dismal scene I needs must act alone.   20
Come, vial.   ⌜*She takes out the vial.*⌝
What if this mixture do not work at all?
Shall I be married then tomorrow morning?
                    ⌜*She takes out her knife
                    and puts it down beside her.*⌝
No, no, this shall forbid it. Lie thou there.
What if it be a poison which the Friar   25

Subtly hath ministered to have me dead,
Lest in this marriage he should be dishonored
Because he married me before to Romeo?
I fear it is. And yet methinks it should not,
For he hath still been tried a holy man.   30
How if, when I am laid into the tomb,
I wake before the time that Romeo
Come to redeem me? There's a fearful point.
Shall I not then be stifled in the vault,
To whose foul mouth no healthsome air breathes in,   35
And there die strangled ere my Romeo comes?
Or, if I live, is it not very like
The horrible conceit of death and night,
Together with the terror of the place—
As in a vault, an ancient receptacle   40
Where for this many hundred years the bones
Of all my buried ancestors are packed;
Where bloody Tybalt, yet but green in earth,
Lies fest'ring in his shroud; where, as they say,
At some hours in the night spirits resort—   45
Alack, alack, is it not like that I,
So early waking, what with loathsome smells,
And shrieks like mandrakes torn out of the earth,
That living mortals, hearing them, run mad—
O, if I ⌈wake,⌉ shall I not be distraught,   50
Environèd with all these hideous fears,
And madly play with my forefathers' joints,
And pluck the mangled Tybalt from his shroud,
And, in this rage, with some great kinsman's bone,
As with a club, dash out my desp'rate brains?   55
O look, methinks I see my cousin's ghost
Seeking out Romeo that did spit his body
Upon a rapier's point! Stay, Tybalt, stay!
Romeo, Romeo, Romeo! Here's drink. I drink to
   thee.   ⌈*She drinks and falls upon her bed*   6
                        within the curtains.⌉

⌈Scene 4⌉
Enter ⌈*Lady Capulet*⌉ *and Nurse.*

LADY CAPULET
  Hold, take these keys, and fetch more spices, Nurse.
NURSE
  They call for dates and quinces in the pastry.

Enter old Capulet.

CAPULET
  Come, stir, stir, stir! The second cock hath crowed.
  The curfew bell hath rung. 'Tis three o'clock.—
  Look to the baked meats, good Angelica.   5
  Spare not for cost.
NURSE   Go, you cot-quean, go,
  Get you to bed. Faith, you'll be sick tomorrow
  For this night's watching.
CAPULET
  No, not a whit. What, I have watched ere now   10
  All night for lesser cause, and ne'er been sick.
LADY CAPULET
  Ay, you have been a mouse-hunt in your time,
  But I will watch you from such watching now.
                Lady ⌈*Capulet*⌉ *and Nurse exit.*
CAPULET
  A jealous hood, a jealous hood!

Enter three or four ⌈*Servingmen*⌉ *with spits and logs
              and baskets.*

                          Now fellow,   15
  What is there?
⌈FIRST SERVINGMAN⌉
  Things for the cook, sir, but I know not what.
CAPULET
  Make haste, make haste.   ⌈*First Servingman exits.*⌉
                Sirrah, fetch drier logs.
  Call Peter. He will show thee where they are.   20

⌜SECOND SERVINGMAN⌝
 I have a head, sir, that will find out logs
 And never trouble Peter for the matter.

CAPULET
 Mass, and well said. A merry whoreson, ha!
 Thou shalt be loggerhead.
      ⌜*Second Servingman exits.*⌝
      Good ⌜faith,⌝ 'tis day.   25
 The County will be here with music straight,
           Play music.
 For so he said he would. I hear him near.—
 Nurse!—Wife! What ho!—What, Nurse, I say!

     Enter Nurse.

 Go waken Juliet. Go and trim her up.
 I'll go and chat with Paris. Hie, make haste, 30
 Make haste. The bridegroom he is come already.
 Make haste, I say.
          ⌜*He exits.*⌝

     ⌜Scene 5⌝

NURSE, ⌜*approaching the bed*⌝
 Mistress! What, mistress! Juliet!—Fast, I warrant
  her, she.—
 Why, lamb, why, lady! Fie, you slugabed!
 Why, love, I say! Madam! Sweetheart! Why, bride!—
 What, not a word?—You take your pennyworths 5
  now.
 Sleep for a week, for the next night, I warrant,
 The County Paris hath set up his rest
 That you shall rest but little.—God forgive me,
 Marry, and amen! How sound is she asleep! 10
 I needs must wake her.—Madam, madam, madam!
 Ay, let the County take you in your bed,

He'll fright you up, i' faith.—Will it not be?
　　　　　　　⌈*She opens the bed's curtains.*⌉
What, dressed, and in your clothes, and down
　　again?　　　　　　　　　　　　　　　　15
I must needs wake you. Lady, lady, lady!—
Alas, alas! Help, help! My lady's dead.—
O, weraday, that ever I was born!—
Some aqua vitae, ho!—My lord! My lady!

　　　　　⌈*Enter Lady Capulet.*⌉

LADY CAPULET
　What noise is here?　　　　　　　　　　　20
NURSE　　　　　　　O lamentable day!
LADY CAPULET
　What is the matter?
NURSE　　　　　　　Look, look!—O heavy day!
LADY CAPULET
　O me! O me! My child, my only life.
　Revive, look up, or I will die with thee.　　25
　Help, help! Call help.

　　　　　Enter ⌈*Capulet.*⌉

CAPULET
　For shame, bring Juliet forth. Her lord is come.
NURSE
　She's dead, deceased. She's dead, alack the day!
LADY CAPULET
　Alack the day, she's dead, she's dead, she's dead.
CAPULET
　Ha, let me see her! Out, alas, she's cold.　　30
　Her blood is settled, and her joints are stiff.
　Life and these lips have long been separated.
　Death lies on her like an untimely frost
　Upon the sweetest flower of all the field.
NURSE
　O lamentable day!　　　　　　　　　　　35

LADY CAPULET   O woeful time!

CAPULET

Death, that hath ta'en her hence to make me wail,
Ties up my tongue and will not let me speak.

*Enter Friar ⌐Lawrence⌐ and the County ⌐Paris, with
Musicians.⌐*

FRIAR LAWRENCE

Come, is the bride ready to go to church?

CAPULET

Ready to go, but never to return.—   40
O son, the night before thy wedding day
Hath death lain with thy wife. There she lies,
Flower as she was, deflowerèd by him.
Death is my son-in-law; death is my heir.
My daughter he hath wedded. I will die   45
And leave him all. Life, living, all is death's.

PARIS

Have I thought ⌐long⌐ to see this morning's face,
And doth it give me such a sight as this?

LADY CAPULET

Accursed, unhappy, wretched, hateful day!
Most miserable hour that e'er time saw   50
In lasting labor of his pilgrimage!
But one, poor one, one poor and loving child,
But one thing to rejoice and solace in,
And cruel death hath catched it from my sight!

NURSE

O woe, O woeful, woeful, woeful day!   55
Most lamentable day, most woeful day
That ever, ever I did yet behold!
O day, O day, O day, O hateful day!
Never was seen so black a day as this!
O woeful day, O woeful day!   60

PARIS

Beguiled, divorcèd, wrongèd, spited, slain!

Most detestable death, by thee beguiled,
By cruel, cruel thee quite overthrown!
O love! O life! Not life, but love in death!

CAPULET
Despised, distressèd, hated, martyred, killed!   65
Uncomfortable time, why cam'st thou now
To murder, murder our solemnity?
O child! O child! My soul and not my child!
Dead art thou! Alack, my child is dead,
And with my child my joys are burièd.   70

FRIAR LAWRENCE
Peace, ho, for shame! Confusion's ⌐cure⌐ lives not
In these confusions. Heaven and yourself
Had part in this fair maid. Now heaven hath all,
And all the better is it for the maid.
Your part in her you could not keep from death,   75
But heaven keeps his part in eternal life.
The most you sought was her promotion,
For 'twas your heaven she should be advanced;
And weep you now, seeing she is advanced
Above the clouds, as high as heaven itself?   80
O, in this love you love your child so ill
That you run mad, seeing that she is well.
She's not well married that lives married long,
But she's best married that dies married young.
Dry up your tears, and stick your rosemary   85
On this fair corse, and, as the custom is,
And in her best array, bear her to church,
For though ⌐fond⌐ nature bids us all lament,
Yet nature's tears are reason's merriment.

CAPULET
All things that we ordainèd festival   90
Turn from their office to black funeral:
Our instruments to melancholy bells,
Our wedding cheer to a sad burial feast,
Our solemn hymns to sullen dirges change,

Our bridal flowers serve for a buried corse,   95
And all things change them to the contrary.
FRIAR LAWRENCE
  Sir, go you in, and, madam, go with him,
  And go, Sir Paris. Everyone prepare
  To follow this fair corse unto her grave.
  The heavens do lour upon you for some ill.   100
  Move them no more by crossing their high will.
                    ⌈*All but the Nurse and the Musicians*⌉ *exit.*
⌈FIRST MUSICIAN⌉
  Faith, we may put up our pipes and be gone.
NURSE
  Honest good fellows, ah, put up, put up,
  For, well you know, this is a pitiful case.
⌈FIRST MUSICIAN⌉
  Ay, ⌈by⌉ my troth, the case may be amended.   105
                              ⌈*Nurse*⌉ *exits.*

                    Enter ⌈*Peter.*⌉

PETER Musicians, O musicians, "Heart's ease,"
    "Heart's ease." O, an you will have me live, play
    "Heart's ease."
⌈FIRST MUSICIAN⌉ Why "Heart's ease"?
PETER O musicians, because my heart itself plays "My   110
    heart is full." O, play me some merry dump to
    comfort me.
⌈FIRST MUSICIAN⌉ Not a dump, we. 'Tis no time to play
    now.
PETER You will not then?   115
⌈FIRST MUSICIAN⌉ No.
PETER I will then give it you soundly.
⌈FIRST MUSICIAN⌉ What will you give us?
PETER No money, on my faith, but the gleek. I will give
    you the minstrel.   120
⌈FIRST MUSICIAN⌉ Then will I give you the serving-
    creature.

PETER   Then will I lay the serving-creature's dagger on
your pate. I will carry no crochets. I'll *re* you, I'll *fa*
you. Do you note me?   125

⌐FIRST MUSICIAN⌐   An you *re* us and *fa* us, you note us.

SECOND ⌐MUSICIAN⌐   Pray you, put up your dagger and
put out your wit.

⌐PETER⌐   Then have at you with my wit. I will dry-beat
you with an iron wit, and put up my iron dagger. 130
Answer me like men.

    ⌐*Sings.*⌐   *When griping griefs the heart doth wound*
        ⌐*And doleful dumps the mind oppress,*⌐
        Then music with her silver sound—

Why "silver sound"? Why "music with her silver 135
sound"? What say you, Simon Catling?

⌐FIRST MUSICIAN⌐   Marry, sir, because silver hath a
sweet sound.

PETER   Prates.—What say you, Hugh Rebeck?

SECOND ⌐MUSICIAN⌐   I say "silver sound" because musi- 140
cians sound for silver.

PETER   Prates too.—What say you, James Soundpost?

THIRD ⌐MUSICIAN⌐   Faith, I know not what to say.

PETER   O, I cry you mercy. You are the singer. I will say
for you. It is "music with her silver sound" because 145
musicians have no gold for sounding:

    ⌐*Sings.*⌐   *Then music with her silver sound*
        With speedy help doth lend redress.

                                        He exits.

⌐FIRST MUSICIAN⌐   What a pestilent knave is this same!

SECOND ⌐MUSICIAN⌐   Hang him, Jack. Come, we'll in 150
here, tarry for the mourners, and stay dinner.

                                    ⌐*They*⌐ *exit.*

⌜ACT 5⌝

⌜Scene 1⌝
Enter Romeo.

ROMEO
  If I may trust the flattering truth of sleep,
  My dreams presage some joyful news at hand.
  My bosom's ⌜lord⌝ sits lightly in his throne,
  And all this day an unaccustomed spirit
  Lifts me above the ground with cheerful thoughts.   5
  I dreamt my lady came and found me dead
  (Strange dream that gives a dead man leave to
      think!)
  And breathed such life with kisses in my lips
  That I revived and was an emperor.   10
  Ah me, how sweet is love itself possessed
  When but love's shadows are so rich in joy!

  Enter Romeo's man ⌜Balthasar, in riding boots.⌝

  News from Verona!—How now, Balthasar?
  Dost thou not bring me letters from the Friar?
  How doth my lady? Is my father well?   15
  How doth my Juliet? That I ask again,
  For nothing can be ill if she be well.
BALTHASAR
  Then she is well and nothing can be ill.
  Her body sleeps in Capels' monument,
  And her immortal part with angels lives.   20

106

I saw her laid low in her kindred's vault
And presently took post to tell it you.
O, pardon me for bringing these ill news,
Since you did leave it for my office, sir.

ROMEO
Is it e'en so?—Then I ⌐defy⌐ you, stars!—   25
Thou knowest my lodging. Get me ink and paper,
And hire post-horses. I will hence tonight.

BALTHASAR
I do beseech you, sir, have patience.
Your looks are pale and wild and do import
Some misadventure.   30

ROMEO   Tush, thou art deceived.
Leave me, and do the thing I bid thee do.
Hast thou no letters to me from the Friar?

BALTHASAR
No, my good lord.

ROMEO   No matter. Get thee gone,   35
And hire those horses. I'll be with thee straight.
                              ⌐*Balthasar*⌐ *exits.*
Well, Juliet, I will lie with thee tonight.
Let's see for means. O mischief, thou art swift
To enter in the thoughts of desperate men.
I do remember an apothecary   40
(And hereabouts he dwells) which late I noted
In tattered weeds, with overwhelming brows,
Culling of simples. Meager were his looks.
Sharp misery had worn him to the bones.
And in his needy shop a tortoise hung,   45
An alligator stuffed, and other skins
Of ill-shaped fishes; and about his shelves,
A beggarly account of empty boxes,
Green earthen pots, bladders, and musty seeds,
Remnants of packthread, and old cakes of roses   50
Were thinly scattered to make up a show.
Noting this penury, to myself I said

"An if a man did need a poison now,
Whose sale is present death in Mantua,
Here lives a caitiff wretch would sell it him."   55
O, this same thought did but forerun my need,
And this same needy man must sell it me.
As I remember, this should be the house.
Being holiday, the beggar's shop is shut.—
What ho, Apothecary!   60

⌜*Enter Apothecary.*⌝

APOTHECARY   Who calls so loud?
ROMEO
  Come hither, man. I see that thou art poor.
                              ⌜*He offers money.*⌝
  Hold, there is forty ducats. Let me have
  A dram of poison, such soon-speeding gear
  As will disperse itself through all the veins,   65
  That the life-weary taker may fall dead,
  And that the trunk may be discharged of breath
  As violently as hasty powder fired
  Doth hurry from the fatal cannon's womb.
APOTHECARY
  Such mortal drugs I have, but Mantua's law   70
  Is death to any he that utters them.
ROMEO
  Art thou so bare and full of wretchedness,
  And fearest to die? Famine is in thy cheeks,
  Need and oppression starveth in thy eyes,
  Contempt and beggary hangs upon thy back.   75
  The world is not thy friend, nor the world's law.
  The world affords no law to make thee rich.
  Then be not poor, but break it, and take this.
APOTHECARY
  My poverty, but not my will, consents.
ROMEO
  I ⌜pay⌝ thy poverty and not thy will.   80

APOTHECARY, ⌈*giving him the poison*⌉
　Put this in any liquid thing you will
　And drink it off, and if you had the strength
　Of twenty men, it would dispatch you straight.
ROMEO, ⌈*handing him the money*⌉
　There is thy gold, worse poison to men's souls,
　Doing more murder in this loathsome world　　　　85
　Than these poor compounds that thou mayst not
　　sell.
　I sell thee poison; thou hast sold me none.
　Farewell, buy food, and get thyself in flesh.
　　　　　　　　　　　　⌈*Apothecary exits.*⌉
　Come, cordial and not poison, go with me　　　　90
　To Juliet's grave, for there must I use thee.
　　　　　　　　　　　　　　⌈*He exits.*⌉

⌈Scene 2⌉
Enter Friar John.

FRIAR JOHN
　Holy Franciscan Friar, brother, ho!.

　　　　　Enter ⌈*Friar*⌉ *Lawrence.*

FRIAR LAWRENCE
　This same should be the voice of Friar John.—
　Welcome from Mantua. What says Romeo?
　Or, if his mind be writ, give me his letter.
FRIAR JOHN
　Going to find a barefoot brother out,　　　　　5
　One of our order, to associate me,
　Here in this city visiting the sick,
　And finding him, the searchers of the town,
　Suspecting that we both were in a house
　Where the infectious pestilence did reign,　　　10
　Sealed up the doors and would not let us forth,
　So that my speed to Mantua there was stayed.

FRIAR LAWRENCE
  Who bare my letter, then, to Romeo?
FRIAR JOHN
  I could not send it (here it is again)
                      ⌜*Returning the letter.*⌝
  Nor get a messenger to bring it thee,   15
  So fearful were they of infection.
FRIAR LAWRENCE
  Unhappy fortune! By my brotherhood,
  The letter was not nice but full of charge,
  Of dear import, and the neglecting it
  May do much danger. Friar John, go hence.   20
  Get me an iron crow and bring it straight
  Unto my cell.
FRIAR JOHN
  Brother, I'll go and bring it thee.   *He exits.*
FRIAR LAWRENCE
  Now must I to the monument alone.
  Within this three hours will fair Juliet wake.   25
  She will beshrew me much that Romeo
  Hath had no notice of these accidents.
  But I will write again to Mantua,
  And keep her at my cell till Romeo come.
  Poor living corse, closed in a dead man's tomb!   30
                                      He exits.

⌜Scene 3⌝
Enter Paris and his Page.

PARIS
  Give me thy torch, boy. Hence and stand aloof.
  Yet put it out, for I would not be seen.
  Under yond ⌜yew⌝ trees lay thee all along,
  Holding thy ear close to the hollow ground.
  So shall no foot upon the churchyard tread   5
  (Being loose, unfirm, with digging up of graves)

But thou shalt hear it. Whistle then to me
As signal that thou hearest something approach.
Give me those flowers. Do as I bid thee. Go.

PAGE, ⌜*aside*⌝
I am almost afraid to stand alone   10
Here in the churchyard. Yet I will adventure.
                              ⌜*He moves away from Paris.*⌝

PARIS, ⌜*scattering flowers*⌝
Sweet flower, with flowers thy bridal bed I strew
(O woe, thy canopy is dust and stones!)
Which with sweet water nightly I will dew,
Or, wanting that, with tears distilled by moans.   15
The obsequies that I for thee will keep
Nightly shall be to strew thy grave and weep.
                              ⌜*Page*⌝ *whistles.*
The boy gives warning something doth approach.
What cursèd foot wanders this way tonight,
To cross my obsequies and true love's rite?   20
What, with a torch? Muffle me, night, awhile.
                              ⌜*He steps aside.*⌝

Enter Romeo and ⌜*Balthasar.*⌝

ROMEO
Give me that mattock and the wrenching iron.
Hold, take this letter. Early in the morning
See thou deliver it to my lord and father.
Give me the light. Upon thy life I charge thee,   25
Whate'er thou hearest or seest, stand all aloof
And do not interrupt me in my course.
Why I descend into this bed of death
Is partly to behold my lady's face,
But chiefly to take thence from her dead finger   30
A precious ring, a ring that I must use
In dear employment. Therefore hence, begone.
But, if thou, jealous, dost return to pry
In what I farther shall intend to do,

By heaven, I will tear thee joint by joint   35
And strew this hungry churchyard with thy limbs.
The time and my intents are savage-wild,
More fierce and more inexorable far
Than empty tigers or the roaring sea.

⌜BALTHASAR⌝
I will be gone, sir, and not trouble you.   40

ROMEO
So shalt thou show me friendship. Take thou that.
                    ⌜*Giving money.*⌝
Live and be prosperous, and farewell, good fellow.

⌜BALTHASAR, *aside*⌝
For all this same, I'll hide me hereabout.
His looks I fear, and his intents I doubt.
                    ⌜*He steps aside.*⌝

ROMEO, ⌜*beginning to force open the tomb*⌝
Thou detestable maw, thou womb of death,   45
Gorged with the dearest morsel of the earth,
Thus I enforce thy rotten jaws to open,
And in despite I'll cram thee with more food.

PARIS
This is that banished haughty Montague
That murdered my love's cousin, with which grief   50
It is supposèd the fair creature died,
And here is come to do some villainous shame
To the dead bodies. I will apprehend him.
                    ⌜*Stepping forward.*⌝
Stop thy unhallowed toil, vile Montague.
Can vengeance be pursued further than death?   55
Condemnèd villain, I do apprehend thee.
Obey and go with me, for thou must die.

ROMEO
I must indeed, and therefore came I hither.
Good gentle youth, tempt not a desp'rate man.
Fly hence and leave me. Think upon these gone.   60
Let them affright thee. I beseech thee, youth,

Put not another sin upon my head
By urging me to fury. O, begone!
By heaven, I love thee better than myself,
For I come hither armed against myself.   65
Stay not, begone, live, and hereafter say
A madman's mercy bid thee run away.

PARIS
I do defy thy ⌜commination⌝
And apprehend thee for a felon here.

ROMEO
Wilt thou provoke me? Then have at thee, boy!   70
                              ⌜*They draw and fight.*⌝

⌜PAGE⌝
O Lord, they fight! I will go call the watch.
                              ⌜*He exits.*⌝

PARIS
O, I am slain! If thou be merciful,
Open the tomb; lay me with Juliet.   ⌜*He dies.*⌝

ROMEO
In faith, I will.—Let me peruse this face.
Mercutio's kinsman, noble County Paris!   75
What said my man when my betossèd soul
Did not attend him as we rode? I think
He told me Paris should have married Juliet.
Said he not so? Or did I dream it so?
Or am I mad, hearing him talk of Juliet,   80
To think it was so?—O, give me thy hand,
One writ with me in sour misfortune's book!
I'll bury thee in a triumphant grave.—
                              ⌜*He opens the tomb.*⌝
A grave? O, no. A lantern, slaughtered youth,
For here lies Juliet, and her beauty makes   85
This vault a feasting presence full of light.—
Death, lie thou there, by a dead man interred.
                              ⌜*Laying Paris in the tomb.*⌝
How oft when men are at the point of death

Have they been merry, which their keepers call
A light'ning before death! O, how may I　　　　　90
Call this a light'ning?—O my love, my wife,
Death, that hath sucked the honey of thy breath,
Hath had no power yet upon thy beauty.
Thou art not conquered. Beauty's ensign yet
Is crimson in thy lips and in thy cheeks,　　　　95
And death's pale flag is not advancèd there.—
Tybalt, liest thou there in thy bloody sheet?
O, what more favor can I do to thee
Than with that hand that cut thy youth in twain
To sunder his that was thine enemy?　　　　　100
Forgive me, cousin.—Ah, dear Juliet,
Why art thou yet so fair? Shall I believe
That unsubstantial death is amorous,
And that the lean abhorrèd monster keeps
Thee here in dark to be his paramour?　　　　105
For fear of that I still will stay with thee
And never from this ⌜palace⌝ of dim night
Depart again. Here, here will I remain
With worms that are thy chambermaids. O, here
Will I set up my everlasting rest　　　　　110
And shake the yoke of inauspìcious stars
From this world-wearied flesh! Eyes, look your last.
Arms, take your last embrace. And, lips, O, you
The doors of breath, seal with a righteous kiss
A dateless bargain to engrossing death.　　　　115
　　　　　　　　　　　⌜*Kissing Juliet.*⌝
Come, bitter conduct, come, unsavory guide!
Thou desperate pilot, now at once run on
The dashing rocks thy seasick weary bark!
Here's to my love. ⌜*Drinking.*⌝ O true apothecary,
Thy drugs are quick. Thus with a kiss I die.　　120
　　　　　　　　　　　　⌜*He dies.*⌝

Enter Friar ⌜*Lawrence*⌝ *with lantern, crow, and spade.*

FRIAR LAWRENCE
   Saint Francis be my speed! How oft tonight
   Have my old feet stumbled at graves!—Who's there?
⌜BALTHASAR⌝
   Here's one, a friend, and one that knows you well.
FRIAR LAWRENCE
   Bliss be upon you. Tell me, good my friend,
   What torch is yond that vainly lends his light   125
   To grubs and eyeless skulls? As I discern,
   It burneth in the Capels' monument.
⌜BALTHASAR⌝
   It doth so, holy sir, and there's my master,
   One that you love.
FRIAR LAWRENCE   Who is it?   130
⌜BALTHASAR⌝   Romeo.
FRIAR LAWRENCE
   How long hath he been there?
⌜BALTHASAR⌝   Full half an hour.
FRIAR LAWRENCE
   Go with me to the vault.
⌜BALTHASAR⌝   I dare not, sir.   135
   My master knows not but I am gone hence,
   And fearfully did menace me with death
   If I did stay to look on his intents.
FRIAR LAWRENCE
   Stay, then. I'll go alone. Fear comes upon me.
   O, much I fear some ill unthrifty thing.   140
⌜BALTHASAR⌝
   As I did sleep under this ⌜yew⌝ tree here,
   I dreamt my master and another fought,
   And that my master slew him.
FRIAR LAWRENCE, ⌜*moving toward the tomb*⌝
                        Romeo!—
   Alack, alack, what blood is this which stains   145
   The stony entrance of this sepulcher?
   What mean these masterless and gory swords

To lie discolored by this place of peace?
Romeo! O, pale! Who else? What, Paris too?
And steeped in blood? Ah, what an unkind hour   150
Is guilty of this lamentable chance!
The lady stirs.

JULIET
O comfortable Friar, where is my lord?
I do remember well where I should be,
And there I am. Where is my Romeo?   155

FRIAR LAWRENCE
I hear some noise.—Lady, come from that nest
Of death, contagion, and unnatural sleep.
A greater power than we can contradict
Hath thwarted our intents. Come, come away.
Thy husband in thy bosom there lies dead,   160
And Paris, too. Come, I'll dispose of thee
Among a sisterhood of holy nuns.
Stay not to question, for the watch is coming.
Come, go, good Juliet. I dare no longer stay.

JULIET
Go, get thee hence, for I will not away.   165
                                        He exits.
What's here? A cup closed in my true love's hand?
Poison, I see, hath been his timeless end.—
O churl, drunk all, and left no friendly drop
To help me after! I will kiss thy lips.
Haply some poison yet doth hang on them,   170
To make me die with a restorative. ⌜*She kisses him.*⌝
Thy lips are warm!

              Enter ⌜*Paris's Page*⌝ *and Watch.*

⌜FIRST⌝ WATCH Lead, boy. Which way?
JULIET
Yea, noise? Then I'll be brief. O, happy dagger,
This is thy sheath. There rust, and let me die.   175
    ⌜*She takes Romeo's dagger, stabs herself, and dies.*⌝

⌜PAGE⌝
  This is the place, there where the torch doth burn.
⌜FIRST⌝ WATCH
  The ground is bloody.—Search about the
    churchyard.
  Go, some of you; whoe'er you find, attach.
                  ⌜*Some Watchmen exit.*⌝
  Pitiful sight! Here lies the County slain,   180
  And Juliet bleeding, warm, and newly dead,
  Who here hath lain this two days burièd.—
  Go, tell the Prince. Run to the Capulets.
  Raise up the Montagues. Some others search.
                     ⌜*Others exit.*⌝
  We see the ground whereon these woes do lie,   185
  But the true ground of all these piteous woes
  We cannot without circumstance descry.

    Enter ⌜*Watchmen with*⌝ *Romeo's man* ⌜*Balthasar.*⌝

⌜SECOND⌝ WATCH
  Here's Romeo's man. We found him in the
    churchyard.
⌜FIRST⌝ WATCH
  Hold him in safety till the Prince come hither.   190

    Enter Friar ⌜*Lawrence*⌝ *and another Watchman.*

THIRD WATCH
  Here is a friar that trembles, sighs, and weeps.
  We took this mattock and this spade from him
  As he was coming from this churchyard's side.
⌜FIRST⌝ WATCH
  A great suspicion. Stay the Friar too.

    Enter the Prince ⌜*with Attendants.*⌝

PRINCE
  What misadventure is so early up   195
  That calls our person from our morning rest?

Enter ⌜Capulet and Lady Capulet.⌝

CAPULET
  What should it be that is so ⌜shrieked⌝ abroad?
LADY CAPULET
  O, the people in the street cry "Romeo,"
  Some "Juliet," and some "Paris," and all run
  With open outcry toward our monument.   200
PRINCE
  What fear is this which startles in ⌜our⌝ ears?
⌜FIRST⌝ WATCH
  Sovereign, here lies the County Paris slain,
  And Romeo dead, and Juliet, dead before,
  Warm and new killed.
PRINCE
  Search, seek, and know how this foul murder   205
    comes.
⌜FIRST⌝ WATCH
  Here is a friar, and ⌜slaughtered⌝ Romeo's man,
  With instruments upon them fit to open
  These dead men's tombs.
CAPULET
  O heavens! O wife, look how our daughter bleeds!   210
  This dagger hath mista'en, for, lo, his house
  Is empty on the back of Montague,
  And it mis-sheathèd in my daughter's bosom.
LADY CAPULET
  O me, this sight of death is as a bell
  That warns my old age to a sepulcher.   215

Enter Montague.

PRINCE
  Come Montague, for thou art early up
  To see thy son and heir now ⌜early⌝ down.
MONTAGUE
  Alas, my liege, my wife is dead tonight.

Grief of my son's exile hath stopped her breath.
What further woe conspires against mine age? 220
PRINCE Look, and thou shalt see.
MONTAGUE, ⌜*seeing Romeo dead*⌝
O thou untaught! What manners is in this,
To press before thy father to a grave?
PRINCE
Seal up the mouth of outrage for awhile,
Till we can clear these ambiguities 225
And know their spring, their head, their true
    descent,
And then will I be general of your woes
And lead you even to death. Meantime forbear,
And let mischance be slave to patience.— 230
Bring forth the parties of suspicion.
FRIAR LAWRENCE
I am the greatest, able to do least,
Yet most suspected, as the time and place
Doth make against me, of this direful murder.
And here I stand, both to impeach and purge 235
Myself condemnèd and myself excused.
PRINCE
Then say at once what thou dost know in this.
FRIAR LAWRENCE
I will be brief, for my short date of breath
Is not so long as is a tedious tale.
Romeo, there dead, was husband to that Juliet, 240
And she, there dead, ⌜that⌝ Romeo's faithful wife.
I married them, and their stol'n marriage day
Was Tybalt's doomsday, whose untimely death
Banished the new-made bridegroom from this city,
For whom, and not for Tybalt, Juliet pined. 245
You, to remove that siege of grief from her,
Betrothed and would have married her perforce
To County Paris. Then comes she to me,
And with wild looks bid me devise some mean

To rid her from this second marriage, 250
Or in my cell there would she kill herself.
Then gave I her (so tutored by my art)
A sleeping potion, which so took effect
As I intended, for it wrought on her
The form of death. Meantime I writ to Romeo 255
That he should hither come as this dire night
To help to take her from her borrowed grave,
Being the time the potion's force should cease.
But he which bore my letter, Friar John,
Was stayed by accident, and yesternight 260
Returned my letter back. Then all alone
At the prefixèd hour of her waking
Came I to take her from her kindred's vault,
Meaning to keep her closely at my cell
Till I conveniently could send to Romeo. 265
But when I came, some minute ere the time
Of her awakening, here untimely lay
The noble Paris and true Romeo dead.
She wakes, and I entreated her come forth
And bear this work of heaven with patience. 270
But then a noise did scare me from the tomb,
And she, too desperate, would not go with me
But, as it seems, did violence on herself.
All this I know, and to the marriage
Her nurse is privy. And if aught in this 275
Miscarried by my fault, let my old life
Be sacrificed some hour before his time
Unto the rigor of severest law.

PRINCE
We still have known thee for a holy man.—
Where's Romeo's man? What can he say to this? 280

BALTHASAR
I brought my master news of Juliet's death,
And then in post he came from Mantua
To this same place, to this same monument.

This letter he early bid me give his father
And threatened me with death, going in the vault,   285
If I departed not and left him there.

PRINCE
Give me the letter. I will look on it.—
                        ⌜*He takes Romeo's letter.*⌝
Where is the County's page, that raised the
    watch?—
Sirrah, what made your master in this place?   290

PAGE
He came with flowers to strew his lady's grave
And bid me stand aloof, and so I did.
Anon comes one with light to ope the tomb,
And by and by my master drew on him,
And then I ran away to call the watch.   295

PRINCE
This letter doth make good the Friar's words,
Their course of love, the tidings of her death;
And here he writes that he did buy a poison
Of a poor 'pothecary, and therewithal
Came to this vault to die and lie with Juliet.   300
Where be these enemies?—Capulet, Montague,
See what a scourge is laid upon your hate,
That heaven finds means to kill your joys with love,
And I, for winking at your discords too,
Have lost a brace of kinsmen. All are punished.   305

CAPULET
O brother Montague, give me thy hand.
This is my daughter's jointure, for no more
Can I demand.

MONTAGUE   But I can give thee more,
For I will ray her statue in pure gold,   310
That whiles Verona by that name is known,
There shall no figure at such rate be set
As that of true and faithful Juliet.

CAPULET
    As rich shall Romeo's by his lady's lie,
    Poor sacrifices of our enmity.   315
PRINCE
    A glooming peace this morning with it brings.
    The sun for sorrow will not show his head.
    Go hence to have more talk of these sad things.
    Some shall be pardoned, and some punishèd.
    For never was a story of more woe   320
    Than this of Juliet and her Romeo.

                        ⌐*All exit.*¬

Explanatory Notes

Prologue

0 SD. **Chorus:** a character who addresses the audience, commenting on the action (Here this commentary is in the form of a sonnet.)

1. **dignity:** social position

3. **mutiny:** riot

4. **civil:** of citizens; also (ironically here) civilized

5–6. **From . . . life:** i.e., from the loins of these warring families were born two ill-fated lovers   **star-crossed:** thwarted by fate through the influence of the stars

7. **misadventured:** unlucky

11. **but:** except for

12. **two . . . stage:** i.e., the subject of our two-hour performance

1.1 A street fight breaks out between the Montagues and the Capulets, which is broken up by the ruler of Verona, Prince Escalus. He threatens the Montagues and Capulets with death if they fight again.

A melancholy Romeo enters and is questioned by his cousin Benvolio, who learns that the cause of Romeo's sadness is unrequited love.

0 SD. **bucklers:** small shields

1. **carry coals:** i.e., suffer humiliation patiently

2. **colliers:** carriers of coal

3. **an . . . draw:** if we are angry, we will **draw** our swords

5. **collar:** i.e., the hangman's noose

6. **moved:** provoked

12. **stand:** i.e., stand one's ground

13. **take the wall:** i.e., walk close to **the wall** (forcing others into the middle of the street)

123

15. **goes to the wall:** proverbial for "is shoved aside"

16–17. **women ... vessels:** biblical: 1 Peter 3.7 (Here begins a series of sexual puns on "thrust," "heads," "stand," "tool," "weapon.")

20–21. **The quarrel ... men:** i.e., the maids are not involved

22. **one:** the same

23. **civil:** gentle, humane

27. **what sense:** whatever meaning

28. **They ... sense:** i.e., the women must be the ones who feel what I do to them

32. **poor-john:** dried, salted fish, of poor quality; **tool:** sword

37. **Fear:** mistrust

38. **marry:** i.e., indeed; **fear:** am afraid of

39. **take ... sides:** have the law on our side

42. **list:** please

43. **bite my thumb:** a gesture of defiance

64. **washing:** slashing with great force

67. **heartless hinds:** cowardly servants

70. **manage:** use

73. **Have at thee:** i.e., on guard!

73 SD. **partisans:** long-handled bladed weapons

74. **Clubs, bills:** a rallying cry to apprentices, who carried heavy staffs or **clubs**, and watchmen, who carried long-handled weapons or **bills**

76. **long sword:** heavy, old-fashioned weapon

80. **spite:** defiance

84. **Profaners ... steel:** i.e., you who put weapons to degrading use by shedding your neighbors' blood

89. **mistempered:** (1) tempered (hardened) for bad purposes; (2) ill-tempered, angry

90. **movèd:** angry

95. **grave-beseeming:** appropriately sober

97. **Cankered ... cankered:** rusted ... virulent

99. **forfeit of the peace:** penalty for disturbing **the peace**

103. **our:** The prince uses the royal "we."

104. **common:** public

106. **set ... new abroach:** i.e., stirred up the quarrel anew (literally, started it flowing again)

114. **Who:** i.e., the winds; **withal:** with it, i.e., with the sword

116. **on ... part:** on one side and on the other

117. **either part:** both sides

122. **abroad:** out of doors

124. **That ... side:** that grows on the west side of the city

126. **made:** went; **'ware:** aware

128. **affections:** desires

129–30. **Which ... found:** i.e., which wanted most to find a place to be alone

132. **Pursued ... his:** followed my own inclination by not questioning him about his

133. **who:** one who

137. **all so soon:** just as soon

139. **Aurora:** goddess of the dawn

140. **heavy:** sorrowful

144. **humor:** state of mind

148. **importuned:** questioned (accent on second syllable)

151. **Is ... true:** i.e., is perhaps not being true or faithful to himself

152. **close:** synonymous with **secret**

153. **sounding:** being sounded or searched into

154. **envious:** malicious

155. **he:** i.e., it; **his:** its

160. **his grievance:** the cause of his distress

161. **happy:** fortunate

162. **shrift:** confession

163. **morrow:** morning

174. **view:** appearance

175. **in proof:** in our experience of it

176. **love . . . still:** Cupid, god of love, is often pictured with his eyes blindfolded.　**still:** always

177. **his will:** his purposes

182. **create:** created

183. **vanity:** foolishness

184. **well-seeming:** attractive in appearance

186. **Still-waking:** always wakeful

189. **coz:** cousin

193–95. **Griefs . . . thine:** i.e., you increase the weight of grief in my breast by adding your own griefs to it (The words "propagate," "breast," and "pressed" lend Romeo's words a sexual implication, as if the "new griefs" are bred upon his existing griefs.)

198. **Being purged:** i.e., love, being purged, is

200. **discreet:** judicious

203. **Soft:** i.e., wait

204. **An if:** if

207. **in sadness:** seriously

215. **fair mark:** target plainly in sight

217. **Dian's wit:** the wisdom of Diana, goddess of chastity, who was opposed to love and marriage

218. **proof:** i.e., well-tested armor

219. **uncharmed:** i.e., not subject to (love's) spell

224. **with . . . store:** Beauty dies when she does, and so does **beauty's store**, the reserve of beauty that has been deposited with her so that she may bestow it upon her offspring.

225. **still:** always

226. **sparing:** refusal to marry

229. **fair . . . fair:** beautiful . . . just

231. **forsworn to:** sworn not to

238. **To . . . more:** i.e., to force me to dwell even more upon her exquisite beauty

243. **a mistress:** any woman; **passing:** surpassingly

244. **but as a note:** except as a marginal note

245. **who:** i.e., Rosaline; **passed:** surpassed

247. **I'll . . . debt:** i.e., I undertake to teach you to forget or die trying to meet that obligation

1.2 In conversation with Capulet, Count Paris declares his wish to marry Juliet. Capulet invites him to a party that night.

Capulet gives a servant the guest list for the party and orders him off to issue invitations. The servant cannot read the list and asks for help from Romeo and Benvolio. When they find out that Rosaline, on whom Romeo dotes, is invited to the party, they decide to go too.

0 SD. **County:** Count
1. **bound:** under bond to keep the peace
4. **reckoning:** reputation
7. **o'er:** over again
15. **hopeful lady of my earth:** perhaps, the only surviving child of my body, and thus my only heir **earth:** body; or, land and possessions
18. **agreed:** i.e., consenting
18–19. **within . . . voice:** i.e., I will consent to her marrying only someone she has chosen herself **fair:** favorable **according:** assenting
20. **accustomed:** customary
22–23. **and . . . more:** i.e., Capulet invites and welcomes Paris to be one more guest among the great many already invited **store:** abundance
26. **lusty:** vigorous
29. **fennel:** herb believed to inspire passion
30. **Inherit:** receive
32–33. **Which . . . none:** i.e., when you gaze upon the women present, you may find my daughter to be merely one of the crowd
35. **sirrah:** term of address to a social inferior
41. **meddle:** busy himself; **yard:** yardstick; **last:** model of the foot

42. **pencil:** artist's paintbrush
48. **another's:** i.e., of another pain
50. **another's:** i.e., another grief's
52. **rank:** virulent
53. **Your plantain leaf:** a **leaf** used to staunch bleeding (**Your** is impersonal, meaning "the" or "a.")
55. **your broken shin:** a cut **shin**
57. **bound:** physically restrained
59. **e'en:** evening (i.e., afternoon)
61. **God . . . e'en:** God give you good even
64–65. **without book:** by memorizing what you have heard
67. **Rest you merry:** i.e., good-bye
87. **crush:** i.e., drink
89. **ancient:** traditional
92. **unattainted:** impartial
97. **these:** i.e., my eyes
101. **fair:** i.e., to be beautiful
102. **poised:** weighed
103. **scales:** i.e., Romeo's eyes (**Scales** is treated as a singular noun.)
106. **scant:** scarcely
108. **mine own:** i.e., my love, Rosaline

1.3 Lady Capulet informs Juliet of Paris's marriage proposal and praises him extravagantly. Juliet says that she has not even dreamed of marrying, but that she will consider Paris as a possible husband if her parents wish her to.

3. **What:** an interjection, here perhaps suggesting impatience; **ladybird:** sweetheart
8. **give leave:** i.e., excuse us
10. **thou's:** thou shalt
14. **teen:** suffering
16. **Lammastide:** August 1 is Lammas Day. Lammas-

tide (i.e., Lammas time) may refer either to that day or to the time around it. **Lammas Eve** is July 31.

17. **odd:** a few

28. **wormwood:** a bitter-tasting plant; **dug:** breast

33. **fool:** term of endearment

34. **fall out with:** become irritated with

35. **"Shake"** . . . **dovehouse:** i.e., the dovehouse shook with the earthquake   **quoth:** said

39. **high-lone:** i.e., by herself

40. **rood:** cross

42. **even:** just; **broke her brow:** cut her forehead

47. **holidam:** perhaps the Nurse's confusion of "holy dame" (Mary), and "halidom" (holiness)

53. **stinted:** quit (crying)

58. **stone:** testicle

70. **disposition:** liking

73–74. **thy teat:** the nipple at which you nursed

78. **much . . . years:** i.e., at about the same age

82. **man of wax:** the ideal form of a man such as an artist might fashion in wax

87. **Read o'er the volume:** Here begins a very affected description of Paris as if he were a beautiful but unbound book in need of a cover (binding).

89. **married lineament:** perfectly matched feature

90. **content:** (1) pleasure (for the viewer); (2) substance (as in the contents of a book)

92. **margent:** margin, where obscure passages are explained

95. **pride:** splendid sight

96. **fair without . . . within:** the beautiful outside to hide the beauty within

97–98. **That book . . . story:** In the opinion of many, a beautifully bound book shares **the glory** that belongs to **the story** printed on its pages.

108–9. **in extremity:** urgent

110. **straight:** immediately

1.4 Romeo and Benvolio are going to the Capulets' party with their friend Mercutio and others, wearing the disguises customarily donned by "maskers." Romeo is anxious because of an ominous dream. Mercutio mocks him with a speech about a dream-giving queen of fairies.

0 SD. **Maskers:** participants in an impromptu masquerade of their own devising (They wear masks and fancy clothes, and offer to dance.)

1. **this speech:** i.e., an apology to their host for intruding

2. **on:** i.e., go forward with our masquerade

3. **The . . . prolixity:** such wordiness is out-of-date

4–8. **We'll . . . entrance:** i.e., we will not preface our dancing with speeches given by someone dressed up as Cupid or with a timidly spoken prologue **Tartar's . . . bow:** an Oriental, lip-shaped **bow without-book:** memorized

10. **measure . . . measure:** i.e., give them a dance

12. **heavy:** sad

16. **So:** i.e., that so

18. **bound:** (1) leap; (2) limit

19. **sore:** sorely, painfully

21. **bound a pitch:** i.e., leap to any height

23. **should you:** you would

28. **Prick . . . down:** i.e., wound love for wounding you and you thus defeat it (with a suggestion that "pricking" may satisfy desire and thus deflate it)

30. **for a visor:** for a face that is itself a mask

31. **cote:** observe

34. **betake . . . legs:** i.e., dance

35. **wantons:** playful persons

37. **I . . . phrase:** i.e., I am the subject of the following old sayings

38. **I'll . . . on:** Proverb: "He that worst may must hold the candle."

39. The . . . done: Proverb: "When game is best it is time to leave."

40. dun's . . . word: Proverb: "Dun's the mouse" (i.e., "Be still"), a fitting motto for a constable on night watch **dun:** gray-brown

41. dun: a play on **done** (with a reference to the game called "Dun the horse is in the mire")

42. save your reverence: a request to be excused for mentioning an indecent word, in this case "love," which, for Mercutio, is equivalent to "mire"

44. we burn daylight: i.e., we waste time (Romeo takes him literally and objects, presumably because it is evening. So in lines 46–47 Mercutio explains his sense: using up torchlight in delay is as wasteful as using lights in daytime.)

48. good: proper

49. in that: i.e., in our meaning; **wits:** senses

51. wit: wisdom

53. tonight: last night

60. agate stone: quartz crystal set in a ring

62. with: by; **atomi:** minute creatures, atoms

64. spinners: spiders

65. cover of: cover made **of**

66. traces: harness straps

67. collars: part of the harness

68. film: fine thread, filament

69. wagoner: driver

72–74. These lines are printed by many editors between lines 63 and 64.

73. joiner: cabinetmaker; **grub:** grubworm

75. in this state: in this ceremonial splendor

77. on cur'sies: of curtsies ("On" means "of" in lines 78 and 79 as well.); **straight:** immediately

81. sweetmeats: candies or candied fruit

83. smelling out a suit: i.e., finding someone who will pay him to present a petition to the king

84. **tithe-pig:** a pig due to the church as part of one's tithe

89. **breaches:** gaps in fortifications; **ambuscadoes:** ambushes; **Spanish blades:** swords of Toledo steel

90. **healths:** toasts; **anon:** straightway

91. **Drums:** i.e., dreams of drums

94. **plats:** plaits, braids

95. **bakes the elflocks in:** i.e., mats, tangles

96. **misfortune bodes:** i.e., the elves avenge themselves for the undoing of their work

98. **learns:** teaches

105. **vain fantasy:** insubstantial imagination

110. **his:** its

113. **misgives:** is apprehensive that

115. **his fearful date:** its dreadful term

116. **expire:** cause to end

118. **forfeit:** what must be given up by the debtor at the end of the **term** of a loan he cannot pay

120. **lusty:** lively

121. **drum:** drummer

121 SD. Even though the Maskers seem not to exit, the entrance of the Servingmen indicates that the scene changes to a room in Capulet's house.

1.5 Capulet welcomes the disguised Romeo and his friends. Romeo, watching the dance, is caught by the beauty of Juliet. Overhearing Romeo ask about her, Tybalt recognizes Romeo's voice and is enraged at Romeo's intrusion.

Romeo then meets Juliet, and they fall in love. Not until they are separated do they discover that they belong to enemy houses.

2. **take away:** i.e., **take away** the dirty dishes

7. **joint stools: stools** made of joined parts

8. **court cupboard:** sideboard; **plate:** utensils

9. **marchpane:** marzipan

16. **longer liver:** survivor (proverbial)

19. **walk a bout:** i.e., dance a round

22. **makes dainty:** coyly refuses (to dance)

23–24. **Am . . . now?:** i.e., have I hit close to home?

31. **A hall:** i.e., clear the hall for dancing

32. **turn . . . up:** i.e., remove the boards and trestles

35. **cousin:** kinsman

39. **By 'r Lady:** an oath, "by our Lady"

47. **ward:** one under the care of a guardian

57. **measure done:** dance ended; **her . . . stand:** where she stands

58. **rude:** roughly formed

61. **should be:** must be

64. **antic face:** grotesque or fantastic mask

65. **fleer:** sneer; **solemnity:** festivity

70. **in spite:** out of malice

75. **portly:** stately

80. **patient:** calm

82. **fair presence:** gentle manner

83. **ill-beseeming semblance:** unsuitable way to appear

87. **goodman:** a man below the rank of gentleman; **Go to:** an expression of anger

89. **God . . . soul:** i.e., God save me

91. **You . . . cock-a-hoop:** i.e., you will be reckless; **you'll . . . man:** i.e., you will take charge

94. **saucy:** insolent

97. Capulet begins to intersperse his rebuke of Tybalt with comments to his guests (**my hearts**) and servants. **princox:** insolent boy

100. **Patience perforce:** i.e., enforced calmness; **willful choler:** obstinate anger

104. The fourteen lines of dialogue that begin with line 104 have the structure and rhyme scheme of a sonnet.

109. **Which . . . this:** i.e., your hand shows seemly (**mannerly**) devotion in touching mine

111. **palmers:** pilgrims returning with palm branches from the Holy Land

116. **move:** initiate (blessings or favors)

117. **move not:** keep still

122. **You kiss by th' book:** perhaps, you speak as if well-read in the language of kissing

128. **withal:** with

130. **the chinks:** plenty of coin (money)

132. **dear:** costly; **foe's debt:** owed to a foe, i.e., Juliet

133. **The . . . best:** alluding to the proverb Romeo cited at 1.4.39

136. **banquet:** a light meal; or, dessert; **towards:** i.e., about to be served

140. **fay:** faith

Chorus

0 SD. Again the Chorus's speech is in the form of a sonnet.

2. **gapes:** desires eagerly

3. **fair:** i.e., fair one (Rosaline)

4. **matched:** compared

5. **again:** in return

6. **Alike bewitchèd:** just as bewitched as Juliet is

7. **complain:** plead for favor

8. **fearful:** frightening

9. **held:** considered; **access:** i.e., **access** to Juliet

10. **use:** are accustomed

13. **time means: time** (lends them) **means**

14. **Temp'ring . . . sweet:** mixing great difficulties (**extremities**) with great pleasure (**extreme sweet**)

2.1   Romeo finds himself so in love with Juliet that he cannot leave her. He scales a wall and enters Capulet's garden. Meanwhile Benvolio and Mercutio look for him in vain.

2. **earth:** body (which is **dull** [i.e., slow] because it is moving away from what attracts it, its **center**)

6. **orchard:** garden

8. **conjure:** raise up a spirit by invoking its proper name (In line 9 Mercutio tries out a variety of names for Romeo.)

10. **likeness:** form (Sighs and rhyming were traditionally associated with lovers.)

14. **gossip:** familiar acquaintance; **fair:** flattering

16. **Abraham:** i.e., old (as the biblical **Abraham**); or, cheating (An "**Abraham** man" was a confidence man.); **trim:** accurately

17. **King . . . maid:** alluding to a ballad

19. **ape:** i.e., a trained ape who plays dead

23. **demesnes:** regions

24. **in thy likeness:** in your own form

27. **raise:** conjure up in a magic **circle** (Mercutio's rather explicit sexual meaning is carried in the words "raise," "mistress' circle," "stand," and "laid.")

30. **were some spite:** would be some injury

34. **consorted:** in league; **humorous:** moody

36. **mark:** target

37. **medlar:** a fruit, also called **open-arse**

41. **pop'rin:** a pear from Poperinghe, in Flanders

42. **truckle bed:** i.e., trundle **bed**

2.2 From Capulet's garden Romeo overhears Juliet express her love for him. When he answers her, they acknowledge their love and their desire to be married.

1. The scene now moves into Capulet's garden. Though the action is continuous, editors mark a new scene because of the change in location.

3–9. **It is . . . wear it:** In this elaborate comparison, Romeo plays first with the idea of **the sun** (Juliet) in a contest with **the moon** (equated with Diana, goddess of the moon). As the sun rises, the moon begins to look pale. The image then shifts toward Diana's role as goddess of chastity. Juliet is the **maid** of Diana as long as Juliet is a virgin. **vestal livery:** clothing worn by Diana's maidens   **sick and green:** perhaps a reference to green-sickness, a form of anemia thought to afflict girls in puberty, making them pale

17. **spheres:** In Ptolemaic astronomy, the planets (here called **stars**) were carried in their orbits around the earth in crystalline spheres.

22. **stream:** issue a stream of light

33. **him:** the angel

36. **wherefore:** why

38. **be but:** only be

41. **but:** only

42. **Thou ... Montague:** i.e., you would still be yourself even if you were not called Montague

43. **nor ... nor:** neither ... nor

49. **owes:** owns

51. **for:** in return for

54. **Call me but:** only call me; **new baptized:** given a new Christian name

56. **bescreened:** i.e., concealed

57. **counsel:** secrets

66. **thee dislike:** displeases you

69. **death:** i.e., mortally dangerous

71. **o'erperch:** fly over

73. **And ... attempt:** love dares to attempt whatever it is possible for love to do

74. **stop:** obstacle

78. **proof:** invulnerably armed

81. **but:** unless

83. **proroguèd:** deferred; **wanting of:** lacking

92. **For:** because of

93. **Fain ... form:** I would gladly follow the proper formalities.

94. **compliment:** observance of ceremony

102. **So:** so that; **else:** otherwise

103. **too fond:** too much in love

104. **havior light:** behavior immodest

106. **coying:** affectation of shyness; **strange:** distant, apparently reluctant

110. **light:** unchaste or frivolous

111. **discoverèd:** revealed

115. **orb:** sphere (See note to line 17.)

124. **contract:** accented on the second syllable

125. **unadvised:** ill-considered

136. **were:** i.e., were in my possession

138. **frank:** lavish

139. **but:** only

148. **substantial:** real, not dreamt

150. **thy bent of love:** the intention of your **love**

155. **thee my lord:** i.e., you as **my lord**

160. **By and by:** immediately

161. **strife:** striving, efforts

165. **want:** lack

166. **from:** i.e., go away from

168. **But . . . school:** i.e., **but love** goes away **from love as schoolboys** go **toward school**; **heavy:** gloomy

170. **tassel-gentle:** tercel-gentle, a male falcon

171. **Bondage is hoarse:** i.e., still under her father's rule, Juliet must keep her desires secret and whisper (hoarsely)

172. **Echo:** Shunned by her lover, Narcissus, the mythological Echo dwindled to a mere voice and lived in caves, condemned to repeat what others spoke.

177. **attending:** listening (French *attendre*)

179. **My dear:** This is the reading of the Fourth Quarto of 1622. The Second Quarto's "My Neece" (niece) is an obvious error, and the First Quarto's "Madame" is no better, since "Madam" is the term the Nurse, not Romeo, uses to address Juliet. Many editors use "My nyas," the term for a young hawk.

183. **year:** i.e., years
191. **wanton:** a spoiled child
193. **gyves:** leg chains
195. **his:** its
201. **morrow:** morning
204. **ghostly:** spiritual; **close:** secluded
205. **hap:** good fortune

2.3 Determined to marry Juliet, Romeo hurries to Friar Lawrence. The Friar agrees to marry them, expressing the hope that the marriage may end the feud between their families.

3. **fleckled:** light-splotched
4. **From forth:** out of the way of; **Titan:** the sun god (the Titan Helios) whose chariot is the sun
7. **osier cage:** i.e., basket made of willow twigs
10. **What . . . womb:** i.e., the **grave** in which she buries her dead is also **her womb**
11. **divers kind:** various kinds
13. **virtues:** powers
14. **None . . . some:** i.e., none is totally lacking in some powers (This idea is expanded in lines 17–18 below.)
15. **mickle:** great; **grace:** capacity to heal
18. **to the earth:** i.e., to humankind
19. **but:** i.e., but that; **strained:** perverted
20. **Revolts . . . birth:** i.e., it **revolts** from its nature
22. **by . . . dignified:** i.e., acquires worth through a good **action**
25–26. **with . . . part:** i.e., with the sense of smell enlivens every **part** of the body
27. **stays:** stops
29. **rude will:** violent inclinations, desires
31. **canker:** cankerworm
33. **Benedicite:** bless you (This five-syllable word is accented on the first, third, and fifth syllables.)

35. **argues:** indicates; **distempered:** disturbed
37. **his:** its
43. **distemp'rature:** disturbance of the mind
55. **Both our remedies:** the cure for both of us
56. **physic:** medicine
58. **My intercession . . . foe:** my petition is in aid of my enemy (Juliet) as well as of myself
59. **homely in thy drift:** straightforward in your meaning
60. **shrift:** absolution
64. **save:** except
67. **pass:** move along
73. **deal of brine:** quantity of salt water (tears)
76. **season:** preserve; flavor
77. **The . . . clears:** i.e., the clouds of your sighs have not yet been dispersed by (this morning's) sun
83. **sentence:** truism, cliché
85. **may fall:** i.e., may be excused for acting immorally (This cliché assumes that men are morally stronger than women.)
86. **chid'st:** chided, scolded
88. **bad'st me:** bade me, told me to
91. **Her I love now:** i.e., the one **I now love**
95. **read by rote:** recite from memory; **spell:** read
97. **In one respect:** i.e., because of one consideration
100. **stand on:** i.e., insist on

2.4 Mercutio and Benvolio meet the newly enthusiastic Romeo in the street. Romeo defeats Mercutio in a battle of wits. The Nurse finds Romeo, and he gives her a message for Juliet: meet me at Friar Lawrence's cell this afternoon, and we will there be married.

1. **should:** can
3. **his man:** Romeo's servant
8. **his:** Romeo's

10. **answer it:** accept the challenge

12. **how:** i.e., by saying how

16. **pin:** bull's-eye

17. **blind . . . butt shaft:** Cupid's unbarbed arrow

20. **prince of cats:** Tybalt is the Prince of Cats in *Reynard the Fox.*

21. **compliments:** i.e., fencing etiquette

22. **prick-song:** a written counterpoint to a simple melody

23. **rests:** pauses (in music and fencing); **minim:** a musical note, in ancient music the shortest

25. **first house:** i.e., best fencing school

26. **first . . . cause:** causes demanding satisfaction according to the code of dueling

27. **passado:** a step forward with a thrust; **punto reverso:** backhanded thrust; **hay:** successful thrust (*ai*, Italian for "thou hast [it]")

29–30. **affecting phantasimes:** pretentious fops

30. **new tuners of accent:** fashionable phrasemakers

31. **tall:** brave

35. **stand . . . on:** insist upon; **form:** (1) fashion; (2) bench

39. **Without his roe:** (1) without the first syllable of his name (so that nothing is left of him but a lover's sigh: "O me"); (2) without his "dear" (A **roe** is a small deer.); (3) sexually spent

41. **numbers:** verses; **Petrarch:** fourteenth-century Italian poet, who wrote sonnets to an idealized lady, Laura; **to:** in comparison to

43–44. **Dido . . . Cleopatra . . . Helen . . . Hero . . . Thisbe:** legendary and fictional romantic heroines

46–47. **French slop:** baggy trousers

47. **counterfeit:** i.e., slip (**Slip** [line 50] was a term for a counterfeit coin.)

50. **conceive:** understand

52. **strain:** act in violation of

59. **pink:** (1) perfect example; (2) a flower; (3) a decorative eyelet on a shoe

62. **my . . . flowered:** my shoe well pinked (decorated)

67–68. **O . . . singleness:** feeble joke, unique in its weakness   **solely singular:** unique (the only sole left)

71. **Switch and spurs:** Romeo calls on Mercutio to urge on his wit as if it were a horse.

71–72. **cry a match:** declare myself the winner

73. **wild-goose chase:** a race in which the rider in the lead chooses the course

76. **Was . . . goose?:** i.e., have I scored a victory over you by talking of **the goose**?

78. **for the goose:** as a fool

81. **sweeting:** a sweet-flavored apple

85. **cheveril:** kid leather, which stretches easily

86. **ell:** about 45 inches

94. **natural:** idiot

95. **bauble:** (1) jester's baton; (2) penis (Possible sexual puns continue with the words "hole," "tale," "hair," "large," "short," "whole," "depth," and "occupy.")

97–98. **against the hair:** i.e., against my wishes

104. **goodly gear:** attractive stuff

105. **a shirt and a smock:** i.e., a man and a woman (A shirt was a man's undergarment, a smock a woman's.)

112. **e'en:** i.e., afternoon

115. **dial:** clock; **prick:** point; penis

116. **Out upon you:** expression of annoyance; **What:** what sort of

119. **By my troth:** truly (a mild oath)

125. **fault:** lack

127. **took:** understood

129. **confidence:** Nurse's mistake for "conference"

131. **indite:** a deliberate "mistake" for "invite"

132. **bawd:** procuress (The word also had the dialect meaning "hare."); **So ho:** hunter's cry

134–35. **Lenten pie:** i.e., a **pie** that should contain no meat

135. **something:** somewhat; **hoar:** musty (with a pun on "whore"); **ere it be spent:** before it's used up

140. **for a score:** i.e., to pay for

141. **hoars:** turns moldy, hoary

147. **saucy merchant:** insolent fellow

148. **ropery:** perhaps, indecent talk (Mercutio's puns); or, perhaps, roguery

151. **stand to:** i.e., defend

153. **lustier:** more vigorous

154. **jacks:** rascals

155. **flirt-gills:** flirting women

156. **skains-mates:** meaning unknown

157. **suffer:** allow

167. **inquire you out:** find you

169. **in:** i.e., into

174. **weak:** despicable

175. **commend me:** offer my greetings

180. **mark me:** listen to me

184. **shrift:** confession

192. **tackled stair:** rope ladder

193. **topgallant:** summit (literally, the platform atop a mast on a ship)

194. **convoy:** means of conveyance

195. **quit:** reward

200. **counsel:** i.e., a secret

203. **prating:** chattering

204–5. **would . . . aboard:** i.e., is eager to claim her

205. **had as lief:** i.e., would just as happily

209. **clout:** rag; **versal:** i.e., universal

210. **a letter:** i.e., the same **letter**

212. **that's . . . dog's name:** because the letter *R* may be sounded as a growl

214. **sententious:** the Nurse's mistake for "sentence," i.e., clever saying; **of it:** about it

219. **apace:** quickly

2.5 Juliet waits impatiently for the Nurse to return. Her impatience grows when the Nurse returns but is slow to deliver Romeo's message. Finally Juliet learns that if she wants to marry Romeo, she need only go to Friar Lawrence's cell that afternoon.

   6. **louring:** darkly threatening

   7. **Therefore . . . Love:** i.e., this is why Love (i.e., Venus, goddess of love) is often represented in a chariot drawn by quick-winged **doves**

  12. **affections:** feelings, emotions

  16. **feign as:** act as if

  23. **them:** i.e., news (often treated as a plural)

  26. **Give me leave:** i.e., leave me alone

  27. **jaunt:** tiring journey

  31. **stay:** wait

  35. **in:** i.e., with respect to

  38. **stay the circumstance:** wait for the details

  40. **simple:** foolish

  44. **on:** about

  45. **flower:** best example

  53. **o' t' other:** on the other

  54. **Beshrew:** curse (here, much milder)

  59. **honest:** honorable

  66. **God's lady:** the Virgin Mary

  67. **hot:** impatient; **Marry, come up, I trow:** an expression of irritation

  70. **coil:** fuss

  73. **hie you:** hurry

  75. **wanton:** uncontrollable, rebellious

  76. **They'll . . . straight:** they turn red immediately

  79. **climb a bird's nest:** i.e., **climb** up to your bedroom

  81. **bear the burden:** (1) do your own work; (2) **bear** the weight of your lover; **soon at night:** i.e., tonight

2.6 Juliet meets Romeo at Friar Lawrence's cell. After expressing their mutual love, they exit with the Friar to be married.

3. **But . . . can:** i.e., no matter **what sorrow** comes
4. **countervail:** i.e., outweigh
6. **Do thou but close:** if you will only join
10. **powder:** gunpowder
12. **his:** its
13. **confounds:** destroys
15. **Too swift:** i.e., that which goes too fast
18. **gossamers:** cobwebs
19. **idles:** move idly; **wanton:** playful
20. **light:** insubstantial
21. **confessor:** accented on the first and third syllables
24. **measure:** quantity
25. **that:** i.e., if; **more:** greater
26. **blazon:** describe; proclaim
28. **Unfold:** reveal
29. **in either:** in each other; **by:** by means of
30. **Conceit:** understanding
31. **Brags . . . his:** boasts of its
32. **but:** only; **count:** enumerate
34. **sum up sum:** calculate the total
36. **by your leaves:** i.e., begging your pardon
37. **Till . . . one:** i.e., until I, on behalf of the church, make you a married couple

3.1 Mercutio and Benvolio encounter Tybalt on the street. As soon as Romeo arrives, Tybalt tries to provoke him to fight. When Romeo refuses, Mercutio answers Tybalt's challenge. They duel and Mercutio is fatally wounded. Romeo then avenges Mercutio's death by killing Tybalt in a duel. Benvolio tries to persuade the Prince to excuse Romeo's slaying of Tybalt; however, the Capulets demand that Romeo pay with his life; the Prince instead banishes Romeo from Verona.

2. **Capels:** Capulets

6. **claps me:** i.e., **claps** (just as **draws him** [line 9] is Mercutio's way of saying "**draws** his sword")

8–9. **by . . . cup:** i.e., by the time his second drink has had an effect on him

9. **drawer:** waiter

13–14. **as soon moved . . . moved:** i.e., as soon provoked to be angry and as irritable

16. **an:** if; **two:** Mercutio deliberately misconstrues Benvolio's "to" as "two."

24. **meat:** food

24–25. **hath . . . quarreling:** has **been beaten** into the state of a rotten **egg** (i.e., has been made addle-headed) as a consequence of your **quarreling**

29. **doublet:** close-fitting jacket

31. **tutor me from:** teach me to avoid

33. **fee simple:** title to full ownership

35. **simple:** foolish

46. **consortest:** associate

47. **Consort:** play music with (A **consort** is a company of musicians. Mercutio links musicians to **minstrels**, who were classed with vagabonds.)

49. **fiddlestick:** probably his rapier

50. **Zounds:** i.e., by Christ's wounds, a strong oath

51. **haunt:** meeting place

58. **your livery:** the uniform of your servants

59. **field:** i.e., place for a duel

64–65. **appertaining rage / To:** rage appropriate in response to

70. **devise:** think out, imagine

71. **of:** i.e., for

72. **tender:** regard

75. **Alla stoccato:** literally, "at the thrust," presumably Mercutio's derisive nickname for Tybalt, the fencing expert; **carries it away:** i.e., wins (because Romeo refuses to fight)

76. **ratcatcher:** "prince of cats" (See note to 2.4.20.)
79. **withal:** with
80. **use:** treat; **dry-beat:** thrash
81. **pilcher:** A "pilch" is, literally, a leather garment; here, a scabbard.
86. **passado:** a fencing step forward with a thrust
90. **bandying:** fighting
94. **sped:** done for, destroyed
95. **hath nothing:** i.e., has suffered no wound
98. **villain:** i.e., villein, servant
103. **peppered:** finished off, destroyed
106. **book of arithmetic:** i.e., the fencing manual
112. **worms' meat:** food for worms
114. **near ally:** close relative
115. **very:** true, sincere
118. **cousin:** i.e., kinsman by marriage
120. **in my temper softened valor's steel:** i.e., has made my disposition soft **temper:** temperament (with a glancing reference to the hardening or tempering of steel)
121. **brave:** splendid
122. **aspired:** risen up to
123. **untimely:** prematurely
124. **on more . . . depend:** waits in suspense on the future
125. **others:** future days
128. **respective lenity:** considerate mercifulness
129. **conduct:** guide
131. **late:** recently
139. **up:** i.e., up in arms
140. **amazed:** astounded; **doom thee death:** condemn you to **death**
142. **fool:** plaything
150. **discover:** reveal
151. **manage:** course
161. **fair:** politely; **bethink:** reflect upon
162. **nice:** trivial, trifling; **withal:** in addition

165. **take truce with:** placate; **spleen:** i.e., anger
166. **tilts:** strikes
172. **Retorts it:** sends it back again
177. **envious:** malicious
178. **stout:** valiant
180. **entertained:** contemplated
186. **Affection:** i.e., inclination toward them
192. **his dear blood:** i.e., Mercutio's **blood**
194. **concludes but:** only **concludes**; **should end: should** have ended
198. **I:** The Prince switches from the royal "we" of line 197 to express a personal, rather than merely official, interest in the feud.
199. **My blood:** i.e., my kinsman (Mercutio)
200. **amerce:** punish
203. **Nor tears:** i.e., neither **tears**; **purchase out:** i.e., buy impunity for
206. **attend:** pay attention to, heed

3.2   Juliet longs for Romeo to come to her. The Nurse arrives with the news that Romeo has killed Tybalt and has been banished. Juliet at first feels grief for the loss of her cousin Tybalt and verbally attacks Romeo, but then renounces these feelings and devotes herself to grief for Romeo's banishment. The Nurse promises to bring Romeo to Juliet that night.

1–2. **Gallop . . . lodging:** addressed to the horses of Phoebus, the sun god, urging speed
2. **wagoner:** charioteer
3. **Phaeton:** the son of Phoebus, allowed to drive the chariot of the sun but unable to control the horses
5. **close curtain:** i.e., curtain of secrecy
6. **runaways:** perhaps, vagabonds; **wink:** i.e., shut, close
9. **By:** i.e., by the light of

10. **civil:** i.e., soberly dressed

12. **learn:** teach

14–15. **Hood ... mantle:** i.e., cover my blushes with your dark cloak (The language is from falconry. An untamed [**unmanned**] falcon beat its wings [**bating**] unless its head was covered with a black **hood**.)

15. **strange:** unfamiliar

16. **Think:** i.e., and think

23. **I:** often changed by editors to "he"

28. **mansion:** dwelling place

33 SD. **cords:** i.e., the rope ladder

42. **weraday:** welladay, an expression of sorrow

45. **envious:** malicious

52. **"I":** pronounced the same as **ay,** which means "yes"

53. **cockatrice:** a mythical serpent (with the head, wings, and feet of a cock) whose look could kill

55. **those eyes:** i.e., Romeo's **eyes**

57. **weal:** well-being, happiness

59. **God save the mark:** a superstitious expression

60. **corse:** i.e., corpse

62. **gore:** clotted

63. **bankrout:** i.e., bankrupt

65. **Vile ... resign:** i.e., let my body (itself, according to the Bible, originally made from dust or **vile earth**) be committed to the **earth**

66. **press ... bier:** i.e., weigh down a single **bier**

73. **dreadful ... doom:** i.e., let the **trumpet** be blown to announce the Last Judgment

79. **hid with:** hidden by

80. **keep:** dwell in

82. **wolvish-ravening:** i.e., wolfishly devouring

83. **show:** appearance

84. **Just:** exact; **justly:** truly

87. **bower:** i.e., give a dwelling to

94. **naught:** evil; **dissemblers:** deceivers

95. **aqua vitae:** strong drink, usually brandy

107. **poor my lord:** i.e., **my poor lord**

110. **wherefore:** why

113. **Your ... woe:** i.e., tears are properly the tribute (i.e., tax) paid to sorrow

131. **Which ... moved:** i.e., which might have provoked ordinary mourning **modern:** everyday

132. **a rearward:** the rearguard of a marching army (Juliet has been comparing the Nurse's speech to an army: see **ranked** [line 128]. In the first rank or vanguard is the statement "Tybalt's dead"; behind it, in the rear, is "Romeo is banishèd.")

136. **bound:** boundary

137. **that word's death:** i.e., the death expressed by the word **banishèd**; **sound:** (1) express; (2) measure (i.e., by taking soundings to determine its depth)

145. **you are beguiled:** your hopes are cheated

151. **Hie:** hurry

152. **wot:** know

3.3 Friar Lawrence tells Romeo that his punishment for killing Tybalt is banishment, not death. Romeo responds that death is preferable to banishment from Juliet. When the Nurse enters and tells Romeo that Juliet is grief-stricken, Romeo attempts suicide. Friar Lawrence then says that Romeo may spend the night with Juliet and leave for exile in Mantua next morning. The Friar promises that Balthasar will bring Romeo news of Verona and suggests that Romeo can expect in time that the Prince may relent and allow him to return to Verona.

2. **Affliction ... parts:** i.e., it is as if disaster were in love with your attractive qualities

4. **doom:** sentence, judgment

5. **craves acquaintance at my hand:** is anxious to meet me (literally, to shake hands with me)

11. **vanished:** disappeared (a reference to words as mere breath that vanish as soon as spoken)

14. **his:** its

17. **patient:** calm

18. **without:** outside

21. **world's exile:** exile from the world

22. **mistermed:** misnamed

26. **Thy fault . . . death:** i.e., your crime is punishable by **death** under our **law**

27. **part:** side; **rushed aside:** shoved aside

36. **courtship:** status as a courtier

40. **vestal:** i.e., virginal

41. **Still:** always; **their own kisses:** i.e., the **kisses** each lip gives the other

48. **mean:** means; **mean:** sordid

51. **attends:** accompanies

53. **professed:** self-proclaimed

55. **fond:** foolish

60. **Yet:** still

62. **Displant:** uproot

65. **when that:** when

66. **dispute:** reason; **of:** about; **estate:** condition

70. **Doting:** in love

81. **By and by:** soon (addressed to the person knocking)

82. **simpleness:** foolishness

92. **even:** exactly; **case:** plight

93. **woeful sympathy:** i.e., harmony (between Romeo and Juliet) in their grief

106. **My concealed lady:** i.e., she who is secretly my wife (**concealed** accented on the first syllable); **canceled:** annulled (because of his banishment)

109. **on Romeo cries:** i.e., calls Romeo's name

112. **level:** aim

116. **sack:** destroy by plundering and pillaging

122. **Unseemly:** improper (even for a woman); **seeming:** apparent

123. **ill-beseeming . . . both:** i.e., unnatural animal in appearing to be both a woman and a man

125. **tempered:** adjusted

129. **railest . . . on:** heap scorn upon, revile

132–44. **thou shamest . . . defense:** In these lines the Friar shows, in turn, how Romeo is shaming his form as a man, his love for Juliet, and his intelligence (**wit**). Like a **usurer** (one who, contrary to the morality of the time, lent money to get interest), Romeo has an abundance of wealth (his **shape**, **love**, and **wit**) but does not use any of it properly.

133. **Which:** who

136. **but . . . wax:** no better than a **wax** figure

137. **Digressing from:** if it swerves away from

138. **dear love sworn:** **love** you have **sworn** is **dear**

139. **Killing:** in that it kills

141. **conduct:** management

142. **powder:** gunpowder; **flask:** powder **flask**

144. **thou dismembered . . . defense:** i.e., you are blown to pieces by your own weapons

146. **thou . . . dead:** i.e., you were just now willing to die

147. **happy:** fortunate; **would:** wanted to

150. **exile:** accent on the second syllable

154. **fortune:** i.e., good **fortune**

155. **such:** i.e., such ungrateful persons

156. **decreed:** decided

158. **look:** i.e., **look** that, be sure that; **watch:** guards stationed at the city gates

159. **pass:** i.e., leave Verona

161. **blaze:** make public; **friends:** relatives (the warring Capulets and Montagues)

165. **Commend:** i.e., offer my respects

167. **apt unto:** inclined to do

176–77. **here stands all your state:** your condition depends on the following

180. **find out your man:** search out your servant
181–82. **signify . . . to you:** i.e., let you know every piece of good fortune
185. **brief:** quickly

3.4 Paris again approaches Capulet about marrying Juliet. Capulet, saying that Juliet will do as she is told, promises Paris that she will marry him in three days.

1. **fallen out:** happened
2. **move our daughter:** i.e., persuade Juliet
6. **but:** except
12. **mewed up to:** shut up with (The term is from falconry and means "caged."); **heaviness:** grief
13. **desperate tender:** bold (or risky) offer
17. **son:** future son-in-law
18. **mark you me?:** i.e., do you hear?
26. **We'll . . . ado:** i.e., we won't make much of a fuss
27. **late:** recently
28. **held him carelessly:** i.e., esteemed him little
35. **against:** in preparation for
37. **Afore me:** a mild oath

3.5 Romeo and Juliet separate at the first light of day. Just after Romeo has descended from Juliet's room, her mother comes to announce that Juliet must marry Paris. When Juliet refuses, her father becomes enraged and vows to put her out on the streets if she will not accept Paris as her husband. The Nurse recommends that Juliet forget the banished Romeo and regard Paris as a more desirable husband. Juliet is secretly outraged at the Nurse's advice and decides to seek Friar Lawrence's help.

0 SD. **aloft:** i.e., in the gallery above the stage
3. **fearful:** anxious
7. **envious:** malicious

9. **Night's candles:** i.e., the stars

13. **exhaled:** drew up as a gas (A **meteor** was thought to be a fiery gas drawn up by the **sun**.)

18. **so thou:** i.e., if you

19. **the morning's eye:** See 2.3.1, where the morn is "gray-eyed."

20. **reflex of Cynthia's brow:** i.e., the moon's reflection **Cynthia:** goddess of the moon

23. **care, will:** desire

28. **sharps:** discordant notes (above the true pitch)

29. **division:** a rapid, melodious passage of music

33. **affray:** frighten

34. **hunt's-up:** i.e., an early morning song

46. **by this count:** according to this calculation; **much in years:** i.e., very old

54. **ill-divining:** prophetic of evil

55. **Methinks:** I think

59. **Dry . . . blood:** i.e., we are pale with grief (Sorrow is represented as thirsty because it was believed that each sorrowful sigh consumed a drop of blood from the heart.)

60. **fickle:** inconstant, changeable

62. **faith:** constancy

67. **not down:** not yet in bed

68. **procures:** i.e., brings

76. **shows . . . wit:** always manifests a lack of intelligence

77. **feeling:** strongly felt

88. **grieve:** (1) incense with anger; (2) afflict with longing (From here to line 107, Juliet's words say what her mother expects her to say of a hated Montague but also say what Juliet truly feels about Romeo.)

90. **reach:** (1) grasp; (2) touch

91. **Would:** I wish that

94. **runagate:** runaway, fugitive

95. **dram:** a small draught (here, of poison)

99. **—dead—:** By suspending this word between dashes,

editions since Alexander Pope's (1725) have been able to show Juliet's double meaning. She may be read to say "till I behold him dead," or to say "dead is my poor heart."

100. **kinsman:** (1) Tybalt; (2) Romeo

101. **find out but:** only **find out**

102. **temper:** (1) mix; (2) dilute and thereby turn it from poison into a sleeping potion

106. **wreak:** (1) avenge; (2) bestow

107. **his body that:** the **body** of the man who

112. **careful:** full of care (for you)

113. **heaviness:** i.e., grief

114. **sorted out:** selected; **sudden day:** i.e., a **day** that is about to come soon

116. **in happy time:** i.e., how opportune

134. **conduit:** fountain

136. **counterfeits:** imitates; **bark:** small sailboat

141. **Without a sudden calm:** i.e., unless suddenly there's **a calm; overset:** capsize

144. **but . . . thanks:** i.e., she refuses any part in it, saying "No, thank you"

146. **Soft:** i.e., wait a moment; **take me with you:** i.e., let me understand you

148. **count her:** regard herself as

149. **wrought:** produced

150. **bride:** i.e., bridegroom

151. **proud you:** i.e., **proud** that **you**

153. **for hate . . . love:** i.e., for what I **hate** when it is intended as **love**

154. **Chopped logic:** quibbling

156. **minion:** darling (here, a contemptuous term)

158. **fettle:** prepare; **'gainst:** in preparation for

160. **hurdle:** a wooden frame on which criminals were drawn through the streets to execution

161. **green-sickness:** a form of anemia thought to affect girls in puberty, making them pale; **carrion:** a term

of contempt (literally, dead flesh); **baggage:** good-for-nothing woman

162. **tallow:** animal fat used in candles (another reference to Juliet's pale face)

175. **hilding:** good-for-nothing

177. **to blame:** blameworthy, deserving rebuke; **rate:** berate, scold

179. **smatter:** chatter

181. **God 'i' g' eden:** exclamation of annoyance (literally, God give you good evening)

184. **gravity:** serious remarks (said contemptuously)

187. **God's bread:** i.e., the sacrament of communion (a strong oath)

188. **tide:** season

189. **still:** always, constantly

192. **demesnes:** property; **nobly ligned:** i.e., noble by lineal descent, by birth

193. **parts:** qualities

195. **puling:** feebly wailing

196. **mammet:** doll; **in her fortune's tender:** i.e., when she is offered (tendered) good fortune

201. **do not use:** am not accustomed

202. **advise:** ponder, consider

207. **bethink you:** reflect seriously; **I'll not be forsworn:** i.e., I'll not take back my words

217. **on earth:** i.e., alive

220. **By leaving earth:** by dying (She has vowed to be his wife until death parts them.)

221–22. **practice stratagems / Upon:** set traps for

226. **all the world to nothing:** i.e., I would bet **all** against **nothing**

227. **challenge:** claim

232. **dishclout:** dishrag

233. **quick:** lively

237–38. **'twere . . . him:** i.e., he is as good as dead since you live here (rather than with him) and have **no use of him**

240. **both:** i.e., heart and soul

241. **Amen:** Juliet's "Amen" transforms the Nurse's **beshrew** into a solemn curse.

246. **absolved:** forgiven (be given absolution)

248. **Ancient damnation:** old damned one

249. **thus forsworn:** i.e., to break my marriage vows to Romeo

251. **above compare:** beyond comparison

253. **bosom:** i.e., secrets; **twain:** separate

255. **myself:** I

4.1   Paris is talking with Friar Lawrence about the coming wedding when Juliet arrives. After Paris leaves, she threatens suicide if Friar Lawrence cannot save her from marrying Paris. Friar Lawrence gives her a potion that will make her appear as if dead the morning of the wedding. He assures her that when she awakes in the vault, Romeo will be there to take her away.

2. **father:** i.e., prospective father-in-law

3. **nothing . . . haste:** perhaps, not in the least hesitant myself, lest I slow him down

7. **talk of:** conversation about

8. **Venus:** goddess of love

10. **That . . . sway:** i.e., that she lets her sorrow master her

11. **marriage:** pronounced as a three-syllable word

13–14. **Which . . . society:** i.e., her tears, to which she is too much disposed (**minded**) when she is alone, may be driven away by company (**society**)

18. **Happily:** fortunately

24. **I should confess:** i.e., I would be confessing

28. **price:** value

33. **report:** statement

40. **pensive:** sorrowful, sad

41. **entreat:** ask for

42. **shield:** prevent that

43. **rouse you:** awaken you (with music, as was customary on the wedding day)

46. **past care:** past being taken **care** of; **past** any concern for taking **care** of myself (Many texts follow the First Quarto and print "past cure.")

48. **strains . . . wits:** forces me beyond the limits of my ingenuity

49. **prorogue:** postpone

54. **Do thou but call:** only **call**

57–58. **sealed . . . label . . . deed:** A **label** was a strip of parchment that attached a seal to a **deed.** **deed:** a legal document or contract

60. **this:** i.e., the knife; **both:** hand and heart

62. **present counsel:** immediate advice

63. **extremes:** extreme difficulties

65. **commission:** authority; **art:** learning

66. **issue . . . honor:** i.e., honorable conclusion

69. **Hold:** stop, wait

70. **craves . . . execution:** demands as reckless action

71. **As . . . desperate:** as that action is unbearable

74. **is it:** i.e., **it is**

76. **That . . . it:** i.e., you who would meet **death** itself in order to escape this shame

80. **thievish ways:** roads infested with thieves

82. **charnel house: house** for storing the bones of the dead

83. **O'ercovered quite:** entirely covered up

84. **reeky:** reeking; **chapless:** jawless

86. **hide me:** i.e., **hide**

95. **being then:** once you are

96. **distilling:** (1) distilled; (2) infusing (the body); **liquor:** liquid

99. **native:** natural; **surcease:** cease

102. **paly:** pale

104. **supple government:** flexibility
105. **stark:** rigid
112. **uncovered:** bare-faced
115. **against:** in preparation for the time at which
116. **drift:** purpose
121. **inconstant toy:** whim that interferes with your firmness of purpose
122. **Abate:** lessen
127–28. **help afford:** provide **help**

4.2 Capulet energetically directs preparations for Juliet's wedding. When she returns from Friar Lawrence and pretends to have learned obedience, Capulet is so delighted that he moves the wedding up to the next day and goes off to tell Paris the new date.

0 SD. **Servingmen, two or three:** i.e., two or three servingmen
2. **cunning:** skilled
3. **none ill:** no incompetent ones; **try:** test (to see)
6–7. **'tis . . . fingers:** proverbial
10. **unfurnished:** unprovided
14. **peevish:** obstinate; **harlotry:** good-for-nothing (often—but probably not here—with reference to a harlot, or whore); **it:** i.e., she
18. **learned me:** i.e., **learned**
25. **this knot:** the marriage of Juliet and Paris
27. **becomèd:** fitting, becoming
29. **on 't:** of it
33. **bound:** obliged
34. **closet:** private room
35–36. **sort . . . furnish me:** select **such** clothes as **you think** suitable for me to wear
48. **Against:** in preparation for

4.3 Juliet sends the Nurse away for the night. After facing her terror at the prospect of awaking in her family's burial vault, Juliet drinks the potion that Friar Lawrence has given her.

1. **those attires:** this apparel
4. **state:** condition
5. **cross:** full of contradictions
7. **culled:** chosen
7–8. **necessaries . . . behooveful:** i.e., necessary and useful things
8. **state:** display
26. **Subtly:** craftily; **ministered:** provided
29. **should not:** i.e., **should not** be
30. **still been tried:** always been proved to be
36. **strangled:** suffocated
37. **like:** i.e., likely that
38. **conceit of:** thoughts (or images) of
40. **As:** i.e., as being
43. **green in earth:** freshly interred in the vault
48. **mandrakes:** plants whose forked roots make them resemble the human body, and which were thought to shriek when torn out of the ground
49. **That:** i.e., so that
54. **rage:** madness; **great kinsman:** e.g., great-grandfather or great-uncle
57. **spit:** impale
58. **Stay:** wait

4.4 The Capulets and the Nurse stay up all night to get ready for the wedding. Capulet, hearing Paris approach with musicians, orders the Nurse to awaken Juliet.

2. **pastry:** room where pastry is made
3. **second cock hath crowed:** i.e., it is after 3 A.M. (Conventionally, the cock crowed first at midnight, then at 3 A.M., and then one hour before daybreak.)
5. **baked meats:** meat pies

7. **cot-quean:** i.e., a man who meddles in women's kitchen tasks (Some editors assign this speech to Lady Capulet on the grounds that the Nurse would not be free to speak to Capulet in this way.)

9. **For:** because of; **watching:** staying awake

12. **mouse-hunt:** i.e., chaser of women (literally, a mouse-hunter like a cat or weasel)

13. **watch . . . watching:** keep you in sight in order to prevent you from "mouse-hunting"

14. **jealous hood:** i.e., probably, jealous woman (otherwise unexplained)

23. **Mass:** i.e., by the **Mass**; **whoreson:** literally, whore's son, but here only a kind of familiar address

24. **loggerhead:** blockhead

26. **straight:** straightway, immediately

29. **trim:** dress

4.5 The Nurse finds Juliet in the deathlike trance caused by the Friar's potion and announces Juliet's death. Juliet's parents and Paris join the Nurse in lamentation. Friar Lawrence interrupts them and begins to arrange Juliet's funeral. The scene closes with an exchange of wordplay between Capulet's servant Peter and Paris's musicians.

1. **Fast:** i.e., **fast** asleep

5. **pennyworths:** little bits (of sleep)

8. **set up his rest:** firmly decided (with a sexual implication for which the Nurse then asks forgiveness, only to introduce further sexual implications with "take" [line 12] and "fright you up" [line 13])

10. **Marry:** by the Virgin Mary

13. **Will . . . be?:** i.e., won't you wake up

18. **weraday:** exclamation of sorrow

19. **aqua vitae:** strong drink, usually brandy

23. **heavy:** sorrowful

30. **Out, alas:** expressions of sorrow

43. **deflowerèd by him:** i.e., sexually visited by Death
46. **living:** livelihood
47. **thought long to see:** i.e., long looked forward to seeing (From this line to the Friar's interruption at line 71, four characters each have a half-dozen lines of laments over Juliet's "death." It has been suggested that the four ought to deliver their lines simultaneously, as may just possibly be indicated by this stage direction in the First Quarto: "All at once cry out and wring their hands.")
49. **unhappy:** disastrous
51. **lasting:** everlasting
54. **catched:** snatched
61. **Beguiled:** disappointed, cheated
66. **Uncomfortable:** causing discomfort
67. **solemnity:** festival (Juliet's wedding)
71. **Confusion:** ruin
72. **confusions:** outbursts, commotions
73. **Had part:** i.e., each had a share
77. **her promotion:** her material advancement
81. **ill:** badly
82. **she is well:** i.e., she is happy in heaven ("She is well" was a phrase indicating that someone had died.)
85. **rosemary:** an aromatic plant, symbol of remembrance (associated with both funerals and weddings)
88. **fond:** foolish
89. **reason's merriment:** i.e., cause for **reason's** rejoicing
90. **ordainèd festival:** planned to be festive
91. **office:** function
93. **cheer:** food and drink
94. **sullen dirges:** mournful funeral songs
100. **lour:** frown
101. **Move:** provoke
102. **put up:** i.e., **put** away
104. **case:** event

105. **the case may be amended:** (1) the situation might be improved; (2) the **case** in which I keep my instrument might be mended

106. **"Heart's ease":** the name of a popular song

110–11. **"My heart is full":** part of a line from a popular song

111. **merry dump:** a contradiction in terms, since a **dump** is a sad song

119. **gleek:** jest, jeer

119–20. **give you the minstrel:** call **you** a **minstrel**

124. **carry no crochets:** i.e., tolerate none of your whims (**Crochets** also meant quarter notes.); **re, fa:** names of musical notes

125. **note:** pay attention to

128. **put out:** display

129. **have at you:** i.e., I'll attack you

132–34. **When griping . . . sound:** from a song by Richard Edwardes published in 1576   **griping:** distressing   **dumps:** low spirits

136. **Catling:** a small catgut string for a fiddle

139. **Prates:** i.e., he just chatters; **Rebeck:** a fiddle

141. **sound:** play

142. **Soundpost:** a peg of wood fixed underneath the bridge of a violin or fiddle

144. **cry you mercy:** i.e., beg your pardon; **say:** i.e., speak, because you can only sing

148. **lend redress:** make amends

149. **this same:** i.e., this man (Peter)

151. **tarry:** wait; **stay:** i.e., stay for

5.1 Romeo's man, Balthasar, arrives in Mantua with news of Juliet's death. Romeo sends him to hire horses for their immediate return to Verona. Romeo then buys poison so that he can join Juliet in death in the Capulets' burial vault.

1. **trust . . . sleep:** depend on the illusory hopes provided by dreams, as if they were true

2. **at hand:** soon

3. **bosom's . . . throne:** i.e., perhaps, love sits lightly in my heart; or, perhaps, my heart sits lightly in my breast

7. **gives . . . leave:** permits

12. **shadows:** i.e., images, dreams

22. **presently took post:** immediately departed on a post-horse (See line 27.)

24. **office:** duty

27. **post-horses:** horses kept at inns for the use of travelers

28. **patience:** self-control

29. **import:** portend, forebode

38. **for means:** by what **means**

40. **apothecary:** druggist

41. **late:** recently

42. **weeds:** clothes; **overwhelming:** jutting

43. **Culling of simples:** selecting medicinal herbs

45–47. **tortoise . . . fishes:** Other writings of the period suggest that apothecaries decorated their shops with the remains of alligators and such things.

50. **of roses:** made of compressed rose petals

54. **Whose . . . Mantua:** i.e., the sale of which in Mantua is penalized by immediate execution

55. **caitiff:** miserable

63. **ducats:** valuable gold coins

64. **dram:** a small draught; **soon-speeding gear:** quick-working stuff

66. **That:** i.e., so that

67. **trunk:** body

70. **mortal:** deadly

71. **any he:** i.e., anyone; **utters:** sells

74. **Need and oppression:** i.e., oppressive **need**

75. **Contempt and beggary:** i.e., contemptible **beggary**

77. **affords:** provides
90. **cordial:** invigorating drink

5.2 Friar John enters, bringing with him the letter that he was to have delivered to Romeo. He tells why he was unable to deliver the letter. Friar Lawrence anxiously goes to the tomb to be there when Juliet comes out of her trance.

2. **This same:** i.e., this
5. **Going:** i.e., I going; **a barefoot brother:** i.e., another Franciscan friar
6. **associate:** accompany
7. **Here:** i.e., who was here
8. **finding:** i.e., I finding; **searchers:** i.e., officials
10. **pestilence:** plague
12. **speed:** i.e., journey
13. **bare:** i.e., bore, carried
17. **my brotherhood:** my vocation as friar
18. **nice:** trivial; **charge:** importance
19. **dear:** precious; dire, costly
21. **crow:** crowbar
27. **accidents:** events, happenings

5.3 Paris visits Juliet's tomb and, when Romeo arrives, challenges him. Romeo and Paris fight and Paris is killed. Romeo then takes poison, dying as he kisses Juliet. As Friar Lawrence enters the tomb, Juliet awakes to find Romeo lying dead. Frightened by a noise, the Friar flees the tomb. Juliet kills herself with Romeo's dagger. Alerted by Paris's page, the watch arrives and finds the bodies. Then the Prince, the Capulets, and Montague arrive. Friar Lawrence gives an account of the marriage of Romeo and Juliet, whose deaths lead Montague and Capulet to declare that their hostility is at an end.

1. **aloof:** at a distance
2. **it:** i.e., the torch
3. **lay thee all along:** i.e., stretch out
11. **adventure:** venture, take the risk
14. **sweet:** scented; **dew:** dampen
15. **wanting:** lacking
20. **cross:** impede, thwart
21. **Muffle:** wrap up and thereby hide
22. **wrenching iron:** i.e., crowbar
25. **charge:** command
27. **course:** proceedings
32. **dear:** important
33. **jealous:** suspicious
39. **empty:** hungry
43. **For all this same:** i.e., **all** the **same**
44. **fear:** distrust; **doubt:** suspect
45. **detestable:** accented on the first and third syllables; **maw, womb:** stomach
48. **in despite:** maliciously (because the stomach-tomb is already **gorged**)
52. **villainous shame:** i.e., shameful villainy
68. **commination:** threat (This word, first adopted into an edition of *Romeo and Juliet* by G. W. Williams, is in the Church of England's *Book of Common Prayer*, in "A Commination Against Sinners.")
71. **watch:** watchmen, guards
78. **should have:** was to have
83. **triumphant:** glorious
84. **lantern:** a turret with many windows
86. **feasting presence:** chamber where a monarch would entertain
90. **light'ning:** sudden lifting of the spirits
94. **ensign:** military flag or banner
97. **sheet:** shroud
98. **more:** greater
100. **his:** i.e., Romeo's

106. **still:** always

110. **set ... rest:** venture everything (from the card game primero); also, rest here forever

114–15. **seal ... death:** The legal language that begins with **seal** is carried through in **bargain** (contract) and **engrossing** (monopolizing, buying up in quantity).

116. **conduct:** guide

117. **pilot:** i.e., **pilot** of a sailing vessel (**bark**) (Romeo here addresses himself.)

121. **be my speed:** i.e., help me

140. **ill unthrifty:** evil and unlucky

150. **unkind:** (1) unnatural; (2) cruel

151. **lamentable:** accented on the first and third syllables

153. **comfortable:** comfort-bringing

167. **timeless:** (1) untimely, premature; (2) eternal

168. **churl:** selfish one, miser

171. **with a restorative:** i.e., with Romeo's kiss, which should be for her like a restorative medicine

174. **happy:** fortunate

179. **attach:** arrest

185. **ground:** earth; **woes:** i.e., the corpses

186. **ground:** cause; **woes:** sorrows

187. **circumstance:** details; **descry:** discover

190. **in safety:** i.e., securely

194. **great:** i.e., cause for **great**

196. **our person:** The Prince uses the royal "we."

201. **startles:** i.e., sounds startlingly

205. **know:** learn

211. **mista'en:** mistaken (its proper place); **his house:** its sheath

215. **warns:** summons

223. **press:** hurry, thrust yourself forward

224. **outrage:** outcry

226. **spring:** source; **head:** fountainhead, source

230. **let ... patience:** i.e., let calmness master your misfortunes

231. **parties of suspicion:** i.e., suspicious parties

232. **greatest:** i.e., most suspicious

234. **make:** i.e., provide evidence

235–36. **impeach ... excused:** i.e., accuse myself of that for which I should be condemned and clear myself of that of which I should be found innocent

238. **date of breath:** lifetime

242. **stol'n:** secret

247. **perforce:** under compulsion

252. **art:** i.e., skill in medicine

256. **as this:** i.e., this

262. **prefixèd:** predetermined

264. **closely:** secretly

272. **desperate:** in despair

275. **is privy:** knows the secret

277. **some ... time:** i.e., an **hour** or so before its **time** (to end)

279. **still:** always

282. **in post:** in haste

284. **he ... father:** i.e., he instructed me to give **his father early** this morning

285. **going:** i.e., as he was **going**

288. **that raised:** i.e., who alerted

290. **what made your master:** i.e., what was **your master** doing

299. **therewithal:** i.e., with the poison

303. **your joys:** i.e., your children

304. **winking at:** closing my eyes to

307. **jointure:** the present given the bride by the groom's family

310. **ray:** i.e., array, dress (**Ray** is the reading of the Second Quarto; the alternative and more familiar reading, "raise," is found in the Fourth Quarto and the Folio. But Montague is evidently promising to gold-plate the fig-

ure of Juliet that would customarily lie on top of her tomb or sarcophagus. Compare the "gilded monuments" of Shakespeare's Sonnet 55.)

311. **whiles:** as long as
312. **figure:** statue; **at . . . set:** be valued as greatly
314. **Romeo's:** i.e., **Romeo's** statue

Textual Notes

The reading of the present text appears to the left of the square bracket. The earliest sources of readings not in **Q2,** the quarto of 1599 (upon which this text is based, except for 1.2.55–1.3.37, which are based on the 1597 quarto, from which Q2 apparently copied this passage), are indicated as follows: **Q1** is the quarto of 1597; **Q3** is that of 1609; **Q4** is that of 1622; and **F** is the Shakespeare First Folio of 1623, in which *Romeo and Juliet* is a slightly edited reprint of Q3. **Ed.** is an earlier editor of Shakespeare, from the editor of the Second Folio of 1632 to the present. **SD** means stage direction; **SP** means speech prefix.

1.1. 28. in] Q1; *omit* Q2   33. SD *Enter . . . Servingman.*] this ed.; *Enter two other seruing men.* Q2   74. SP CITIZENS] Ed.; *Offi.* Q2   122. drove] Q3 (draue); driue Q2   150. his] Q3; is Q2   182. create] Q1; created Q2   184. well-seeming] Q4; welseeing Q2   226. makes] Q4; make Q2
1.2. 0. SD *a Servingman*] Ed.; *the Clowne* Q2   38. SD *Capulet . . . exit.*] Ed.; *Exit.* Q2   75. *and*] Q1; *omit* Q2   84. thee] Q1; you Q2
1.3. 0. SD *Lady Capulet*] Ed.; *Capulets wife* Q1, Q2   12. an] Q2; a Q1   34. the] Q2; *omit* Q1   70. disposition] Ed.; dispositions Q2   71, 72. honor] Q1; houre Q2   105. it] Q1; *omit* Q2   105. SD *Servingman*] F; *Seruing.* Q2

169

1.4   7–8. Q1; *omit* Q2   23. SP MERCUTIO] Q4; *Horatio*
Q2   39. done] Q1; dum Q2   42. your] F; you Q2   47.
light] Ed.; lights Q2   49. five 2] Ed.; fine Q2   62. atomi]
Q1; ottamie Q2   71. maid] Q1; man Q2   81. breaths] Q1
(breathes); breath Q2   86. he dreams] *stet* Q2   95.
elflocks] Q1; Elklocks Q2   120. sail] Q1; sute Q2

1.5.   0. SD *napkins*] F; *Napkins.* | *Enter* Romeo. Q2   1,
7, 13. SP FIRST SERVINGMAN] Ed.; *Ser.* Q2   4. SP SECOND
SERVINGMAN] Ed.; 1. Q2   12. SP THIRD SERVINGMAN] Ed.; 2.
Q2   15. SP THIRD SERVINGMAN] Ed.; 3. Q2   17. SD
They . . . aside.] this ed.; *Exeunt.* Q2   18, 40, 46. SP CAP-
ULET] Q1; 1. *Capu.* Q2   19. a bout] Ed.; about Q2   39, 44.
SP CAPULET'S COUSIN] Ed.; 2 *Capu.* Q2   41. Lucentio] Q1;
Lucientio Q2 ˙106. pilgrims, ready] Q1; pilgrims did
readie Q2

2. Chor.   4. matched] Q3; match Q2

2.1   8. SP MERCUTIO] Q1; *omit* Q2   9. Romeo] Q1; *Mer.*
Romeo Q2   12. pronounce] Q1; prouaunt Q2   13. "dove"]
Q1; day Q2   15. heir] Q1; her Q2   16. trim] Q1; true Q2
36. SP MERCUTIO] Q3; *Mar.* Q2   41. open-arse] Ed.; open,
or Q2   46. SD *They exit.*] Q4; *Exit.* Q2

2.2.   16. do] Q1; to Q2   44. nor any other part] Q1;
omit Q2   45. Belonging . . . name] Ed.; O be some other
name | Belonging to a man Q2   48. were] Q3; wene Q2
88. washed] Q1; washeth Q2   104. havior] Q1; behauior
Q2   106. more] Q1; *omit* Q2   115. circled] Q1; circle Q2
155. lord] Q1; L. Q2   159–60. Madam . . . come] Ed.; (by
and by I come) Madam. Q2   173. mine] Q1; *omit* Q2
179. dear] Q4; Neece Q2   202. SP ROMEO] Q1; *Iu.* Q2
203. Would] Q4; *Ro.* Would Q2   203. rest.] Q1; rest | The
grey eyde morne smiles on the frowning night, | Check-
ring the Easterne Clouds with streaks of light, | And dark-
nesse fleckted like a drunkard reeles, | From forth daies
pathway, made by *Tytans* wheeles. Q2

2.3.   2. Check'ring] Q2 2.2.203 (above); Checking Q2
2.3.2   4. fiery] Q1; burning Q2

2.4. 19. SP BENVOLIO] Q1; *Ro.* Q2   30. phantasimes] Ed.; phantacies Q2   34–35. "pardon-me" 's] Q1; pardons mees Q2   212. dog's name. *R*] Q3; dog, name *R.* Q2   219. SD *They exit.*] Q1 *(Ex. omnes.); Exit.* Q2

2.5 7. Love] F; loue Q2   11. three] Q3; there Q2   15. And] Q4; *M.* And Q2

2.6. 27. music's] Q4; musicke Q2

3.1. 2. are] Q1; *omit* Q2   91. SD *Romeo. . . Mercutio.*] this ed.; *omit* Q2; *Tibalt vnder Romeos arme thrusts Mercutio, in and flyes.* Q1   92. SP PETRUCHIO] Ed.; *omit* Q2, *which sets this speech as a* SD   113. SD *All . . . exit.*] Ed.; *Exit.* Q2   127. Alive] Q1; He gan Q2   129. fire-eyed] Q1; fier and Q2   175. agile] Q1; aged Q2   193. SP MONTAGUE] Q4; *Capu.* Q2   202. I] Q1; It Q2   207. SD *They . . . body.*] this ed.; *Exit.* Q2

3.2. 1. SP JULIET] Q1; *omit* Q2   9. By] Q4; And by Q2   55. shut] Ed.; shot Q2   57. determine my] Q2 *stet*; determine of my F   78. SP NURSE] Q1; *omit* Q2   79. SP JULIET] Q1; *Nur.* Q2   80. Did] Ed.; *Iu.* Did Q2   82. Dove-feathered] Ed.; Rauenous doue-featherd Q2   85. damnèd] Q4; dimme Q2   157. SD *They exit.*] Q1; *Exit.* Q2

3.3. 0. SD *Enter . . . Lawrence.*] Ed.; *Enter Frier and* Romeo. Q2   41–46. sin. . . . Hadst] Ed.; sin. | This may flyes do, when I from this must flie, | And sayest thou yet, that exile is not death? | But *Romeo* may not, he is banished. | Flies may do this, but I from this must flie: | They are freemen, but I am banished. | Hadst Q2   55. Thou] Q1; Then Q2   64. madmen] Q1; mad man Q2   71. mightst] Q1; mightest Q2   74. SD *Knock within.*] Ed.; *Enter Nurse, and knocke.* Q2   77. SD *Knock.*] Q4; *They knocke.* Q2   80. SD *Knock.*] F; *Slud knock.* Q2   85. SP NURSE, *within*] Ed.; *Enter Nurse.* | *Nur.* Q2   120. denote] Q1; deuote Q2   127. lives] Ed.; lies Q2   153. misbehaved] Q1; mishaued Q2   154. pouts upon] Q4; puts vp Q2   179. disguised] Q3; disguise Q2

3.4. 14. be] Q1; me Q2   26. We'll] Q1; Well Q2

3.5. 13. exhaled] Ed.; exhale Q2   19. the] the the Q2
31. changed] Ed.; change Q2   36. SD *Enter Nurse.*] Ed.;
Enter Madame and Nurse. Q2   54. SP JULIET] Q1; *Ro.* Q2
64. SD *Enter Lady Capulet.*] Ed.; *Enter Mother.* Q2   87.
him] Q4; *omit* Q2   144. gives] Q3; giue Q2   181. SP CAP-
ULET O] Q1; Father O Q2   182. SP NURSE] Q4; *omit* Q2
192. ligned] Ed.; liand Q2

4.1. 73. slay] Q1; stay Q2   79. off] Q2 (of)   84. chap-
less] Q1; chapels Q2   86. shroud] Q4; *omit* Q2   100.
breath] Q1; breast Q2   102. paly] Q4; many Q2   112. In]
Q3; Is Q2   112–13. bier | Thou] Ed.; Beere, | Be borne to
buriall in thy kindreds graue: | Thou Q2   113. shalt] Q3;
shall Q2   118. waking] Q3; walking Q2   129. SD *They . . .
directions.*] this ed.; *Exit.* Q2

4.2. 3, 6. SP SERVINGMAN] Ed.; *Ser.* Q2   14. self-willed]
Q3; selfewield Q2   27. becomèd] Q4; becomd Q2   38.
SD *Juliet . . . exit.*] Q1; *Exeunt.* Q2   49. SD *They exit.*] Q1;
Exit. Q2

4.3. 5. SD *Lady Capulet*] Ed.; *Mother* Q2   14. SD
Lady . . . exit.] Ed.; *Exeunt.* Q2   50. wake] Q4; walke Q2
60. SD *She . . . curtains.*] this ed.; *omit* Q2; *She fals vpon
her bed within the Curtaines.* Q1

4.4. 0. SD *Lady Capulet*] Ed.; *Lady of the house* Q2   13.
SD *Lady Capulet*] Ed.; *Lady* Q2   17. SP FIRST SERVINGMAN]
Ed.; *Fel.* Q2   21. SP SECOND SERVINGMAN] Ed.; *Fel.* Q2   25.
faith] Q4; father Q2

4.5. 26. SD *Capulet*] Ed.; *Father* Q2   43. deflowerèd]
Ed.; deflowred Q2   47. long] Q1; loue Q2   71. cure] Ed.;
care Q2   88. fond] Ed.; some Q2   101. SD *All . . . exit.*]
Ed.; *Fxeunt manet.* Q2   102. SP FIRST MUSICIAN] Ed.; *Musi.*
Q2   105. SP FIRST MUSICIAN] Ed.; *Fid.* Q2   105. by] Q1;
my Q2   105. SD *Nurse exits.*] Q1; *Exit omnes.* Q2   105.
SD *Peter*] Q4; *Will Kemp* Q2   109. SP FIRST MUSICIAN] Ed.;
Fidler. Q2   113. SP FIRST MUSICIAN] Ed.; *Minstrels.* Q2
116, 118, 126, 137. SP FIRST MUSICIAN] Ed.; *Minst.* Q2
121. SP FIRST MUSICIAN] Ed.; *Minstrel.* Q2   127, 140. SP

SECOND MUSICIAN] Ed.; 2. *M.* Q2   129. SP PETER] Q4; *omit*
Q2   129. wit. I] Q4; wit. | *Peter* I Q2   133. *And . . . op-
press*] Q1; *omit* Q2   143. SP THIRD MUSICIAN] Ed.; 3. *M.* Q2
149. SP FIRST MUSICIAN] Ed.; *Min.* Q2   150. SP SECOND MU-
SICIAN] Ed.; *M.* 2. Q2   151. SD *They exit.*] Q1; *Exit.* Q2

    5.1.   3. lord] Q1; *L.* Q2   12. SD *Balthasar in riding
boots*] this ed.; *Balthasar his man booted* Q1; *omit* Q2   16.
Juliet] Q1; Lady Juliet Q2   18, 28, 34. SP BALTHASAR] Q1;
Man. Q2   25. defy] Q1; denie Q2   70, 79, 81. SP APOTHE-
CARY] Q1; *Poti.* Q2   80. pay] Q1; pray Q2   91. SD *He
exits.*] Ed.; *Exeunt.* Q2

    5.2.   0. SD Q2 *adds "to Frier* Lawrence"

    5.3.   3, 141. yew] Q1 (Ew, 3); young Q2   17. SD *Page
whistles.*] Ed.; *Whistle Boy.* Q2   21. SD *Balthasar*] Q1;
Peter Q2   40, 43. SP BALTHASAR] Q1 *(Balt.)*; *Peter* Q2   45.
SD *beginning to force open the tomb*] Ed.; *Romeo opens the
tombe.* Q1; *omit* Q2   68. commination] Ed.; commiration
Q2   70. SD *They draw and fight.*] *They fight.* Q1; *omit* Q2
71. SP PAGE] Ed.; *Boy* Q1; *omit* Q2, *which sets this speech
as a stage direction*   102. Shall] Ed.; I will beleeue | Shall
Q2   107. palace] Q3; pallat Q2   108. Depart again. Here]
Q4; Depart againe, come lye thou in my arme, | Heer's to
thy health, where ere thou tumblest in. | O true Appothe-
carie! | Thy drugs are quicke. Thus with a kisse I die. | De-
part againe, here Q2   123, 128, 131, 133, 135, 141. SP
BALTHASAR] Q4; *Man.* Q2   172. SD *Paris's Page*] Ed.; *Boy*
Q2   173, 177, 202, 207. SP FIRST WATCH] Ed.; *Watch* Q2
176. SP PAGE] Ed.; *Watch boy* Q2   188. SP SECOND] Ed.;
omit Q2   190, 194. SP FIRST] Ed.; *Chief.* Q2   194. too.]
too too. Q2   196. SD *Capulet and Lady Capulet*] Ed.;
Capels Q2   197. shrieked] Ed.; shrike Q2   201. our] Ed.;
your Q2   207. slaughtered] Q3; Slaughter Q2   209. SD
tombs.] Tombes. *Enter Capulet and his wife.* Q2   213.
mis-sheathèd] missheathd Q2   217. early] Q1; earling Q2
241. that] Q1; thats Q2   291. SP PAGE] F; *Boy* Q2

The Tragedy of

HAMLET,
Prince of Denmark

Shakespeare's *Hamlet*

Hamlet is the most popular of Shakespeare's plays for
readers and theater audiences, and it is also one of the
most puzzling. Many questions about the play continue to
fascinate readers and playgoers, making *Hamlet* not only
a revenge tragedy but also very much a mystery. What is
this Ghost that appears to Hamlet? Is it Hamlet's murdered father returned from the everlasting fire to demand
justice upon his murderer? Is it a "goblin damned"—that
is, a demon bent on claiming Hamlet's soul by tempting
him to assassinate his king? Or is the Ghost "a spirit of
health," an angelic messenger revealing to Hamlet that
the young man's mission in life is to cleanse the kingdom
of Denmark of its corrupt king?

And what happens to Hamlet after the Ghost commands that the throne of Denmark be cleansed? Does
Hamlet actually go mad, becoming unhinged by the accu-
sation that his uncle murdered his father or by the ugly
picture the Ghost paints of Hamlet's lustful mother? Or
does Hamlet merely pretend to be mad, pretend so well
that he makes us wonder if we can tell the difference between sanity and madness? Why is he so hostile to
women, both to his mother and to the woman whom he
once courted and whom he claims to have loved dearly?
Why does he wait so long to confirm the guilt of the king
after the Ghost has accused the king of murder? And once
he is convinced that the king is a murderer, why does
Hamlet not act immediately?

And what about Gertrude? Was she unfaithful to her
husband during his lifetime? Was she complicit in his
murder? What does she come to believe about Hamlet's
madness? And about her new husband?

Beyond such questions about the play and its characters lie deeper issues about the rightness of revenge, about how to achieve an ethical life, and about how to live in a world where tears of sorrow, loving smiles, and friendly words are all suspect because all are "actions that a man might *play.*" Hamlet's world is bleak and cold because almost no one and nothing can be trusted. But his world, and Hamlet himself, continue to draw us to them, speaking to every generation of its own problems and its own yearnings. It is a play that seems particularly pertinent today—just as it has seemed particularly pertinent to any number of generations before us.

Characters in the Play

THE GHOST

HAMLET, Prince of Denmark, son of the late King Hamlet and Queen Gertrude

QUEEN GERTRUDE, widow of King Hamlet, now married to Claudius

KING CLAUDIUS, brother to the late King Hamlet

OPHELIA

LAERTES, her brother

POLONIUS, father of Ophelia and Laertes, councillor to King Claudius

REYNALDO, servant to Polonius

HORATIO, Hamlet's friend and confidant

VOLTEMAND
CORNELIUS
ROSENCRANTZ
GUILDENSTERN } *courtiers at the Danish court*
OSRIC
Gentlemen
A Lord

FRANCISCO
BARNARDO } *Danish soldiers*
MARCELLUS

FORTINBRAS, Prince of Norway

A Captain in Fortinbras's army

Ambassadors to Denmark from England

Players who take the roles of Prologue, Player King, Player Queen, and Lucianus in *The Murder of Gonzago*

179

Two Messengers
Sailors
Gravedigger
Gravedigger's companion
Doctor of Divinity

Attendants, Lords, Guards, Musicians, Laertes's Followers, Soldiers, Officers

⟨ACT 1⟩

⟨Scene 1⟩
Enter Barnardo and Francisco, two sentinels.

BARNARDO   Who's there?

FRANCISCO
Nay, answer me. Stand and unfold yourself.

BARNARDO   Long live the King!

FRANCISCO   Barnardo.

BARNARDO   He.   5

FRANCISCO
You come most carefully upon your hour.

BARNARDO
'Tis now struck twelve. Get thee to bed, Francisco.

FRANCISCO
For this relief much thanks. 'Tis bitter cold,
And I am sick at heart.

BARNARDO   Have you had quiet guard?   10

FRANCISCO   Not a mouse stirring.

BARNARDO   Well, good night.
If you do meet Horatio and Marcellus,
The rivals of my watch, bid them make haste.

Enter Horatio and Marcellus.

FRANCISCO
I think I hear them.—Stand ho! Who is there?   15

HORATIO   Friends to this ground.

MARCELLUS   And liegemen to the Dane.

FRANCISCO   Give you good night.

MARCELLUS
O farewell, honest ⟨soldier.⟩ Who hath relieved
  you?   20

FRANCISCO
Barnardo hath my place. Give you good night.
                                            Francisco exits.

MARCELLUS   Holla, Barnardo.

BARNARDO   Say, what, is Horatio there?

HORATIO   A piece of him.

BARNARDO
Welcome, Horatio.—Welcome, good Marcellus.   25

HORATIO
What, has this thing appeared again tonight?

BARNARDO   I have seen nothing.

MARCELLUS
Horatio says 'tis but our fantasy
And will not let belief take hold of him
Touching this dreaded sight twice seen of us.   30
Therefore I have entreated him along
With us to watch the minutes of this night,
That, if again this apparition come,
He may approve our eyes and speak to it.

HORATIO
Tush, tush, 'twill not appear.   35

BARNARDO   Sit down awhile,
And let us once again assail your ears,
That are so fortified against our story,
What we have two nights seen.

HORATIO   Well, sit we down,   40
And let us hear Barnardo speak of this.

BARNARDO   Last night of all,
When yond same star that's westward from the pole
Had made his course t' illume that part of heaven
Where now it burns, Marcellus and myself,   45
The bell then beating one—

Enter Ghost.

MARCELLUS
  Peace, break thee off ! Look where it comes again.
BARNARDO
  In the same figure like the King that's dead.
MARCELLUS, ⌈*to Horatio*⌉
  Thou art a scholar. Speak to it, Horatio.
BARNARDO
  Looks he not like the King? Mark it, Horatio.   50
HORATIO
  Most like. It ⟨harrows⟩ me with fear and wonder.
BARNARDO
  It would be spoke to.
MARCELLUS   Speak to it, Horatio.
HORATIO
  What art thou that usurp'st this time of night,
  Together with that fair and warlike form   55
  In which the majesty of buried Denmark
  Did sometimes march? By heaven, I charge thee,
     speak.
MARCELLUS
  It is offended.
BARNARDO   See, it stalks away.   60
HORATIO
  Stay! speak! speak! I charge thee, speak!
                              Ghost exits.
MARCELLUS   'Tis gone and will not answer.
BARNARDO
  How now, Horatio, you tremble and look pale.
  Is not this something more than fantasy?
  What think you on 't?   65
HORATIO
  Before my God, I might not this believe
  Without the sensible and true avouch
  Of mine own eyes.

MARCELLUS   Is it not like the King?
HORATIO   As thou art to thyself.   70
    Such was the very armor he had on
    When he the ambitious Norway combated.
    So frowned he once when, in an angry parle,
    He smote the sledded ⌜Polacks⌝ on the ice.
    'Tis strange.   75

MARCELLUS
    Thus twice before, and jump at this dead hour,
    With martial stalk hath he gone by our watch.

HORATIO
    In what particular thought to work I know not,
    But in the gross and scope of mine opinion
    This bodes some strange eruption to our state.   80

MARCELLUS
    Good now, sit down, and tell me, he that knows,
    Why this same strict and most observant watch
    So nightly toils the subject of the land,
    And ⟨why⟩ such daily ⟨cast⟩ of brazen cannon
    And foreign mart for implements of war,   85
    Why such impress of shipwrights, whose sore task
    Does not divide the Sunday from the week.
    What might be toward that this sweaty haste
    Doth make the night joint laborer with the day?
    Who is 't that can inform me?   90

HORATIO   That can I.
    At least the whisper goes so: our last king,
    Whose image even but now appeared to us,
    Was, as you know, by Fortinbras of Norway,
    Thereto pricked on by a most emulate pride,   95
    Dared to the combat; in which our valiant Hamlet
    (For so this side of our known world esteemed him)
    Did slay this Fortinbras, who by a sealed compact,
    Well ratified by law and heraldry,
    Did forfeit, with his life, all ⟨those⟩ his lands   100
    Which he stood seized of, to the conqueror.

Against the which a moiety competent
Was gagèd by our king, which had ⟨returned⟩
To the inheritance of Fortinbras
Had he been vanquisher; as, by the same comart   105
And carriage of the article ⌈designed,⌉
His fell to Hamlet. Now, sir, young Fortinbras,
Of unimprovèd mettle hot and full,
Hath in the skirts of Norway here and there
Sharked up a list of lawless resolutes   110
For food and diet to some enterprise
That hath a stomach in 't; which is no other
(As it doth well appear unto our state)
But to recover of us, by strong hand
And terms compulsatory, those foresaid lands   115
So by his father lost. And this, I take it,
Is the main motive of our preparations,
The source of this our watch, and the chief head
Of this posthaste and rummage in the land.

⌈BARNARDO
I think it be no other but e'en so.   120
Well may it sort that this portentous figure
Comes armèd through our watch so like the king
That was and is the question of these wars.

HORATIO
A mote it is to trouble the mind's eye.
In the most high and palmy state of Rome,   125
A little ere the mightiest Julius fell,
The graves stood tenantless, and the sheeted dead
Did squeak and gibber in the Roman streets;
As stars with trains of fire and dews of blood,
Disasters in the sun; and the moist star,   130
Upon whose influence Neptune's empire stands,
Was sick almost to doomsday with eclipse.
And even the like precurse of ⌈feared⌉ events,
As harbingers preceding still the fates
And prologue to the omen coming on,   135

Have heaven and earth together demonstrated
Unto our climatures and countrymen.]

Enter Ghost.

But soft, behold! Lo, where it comes again!
I'll cross it though it blast me.—Stay, illusion!
                              It spreads his arms.
If thou hast any sound or use of voice,   140
Speak to me.
If there be any good thing to be done
That may to thee do ease and grace to me,
Speak to me.
If thou art privy to thy country's fate,   145
Which happily foreknowing may avoid,
O, speak!
Or if thou hast uphoarded in thy life
Extorted treasure in the womb of earth,
For which, they say, ⟨you⟩ spirits oft walk in death,   150
Speak of it.   *The cock crows.*
          Stay and speak!—Stop it, Marcellus.
MARCELLUS
Shall I strike it with my partisan?
HORATIO   Do, if it will not stand.
BARNARDO   'Tis here.   155
HORATIO   'Tis here.
                                  ⟨*Ghost exits.*⟩
MARCELLUS   'Tis gone.
We do it wrong, being so majestical,
To offer it the show of violence,
For it is as the air, invulnerable,   160
And our vain blows malicious mockery.
BARNARDO
It was about to speak when the cock crew.
HORATIO
And then it started like a guilty thing
Upon a fearful summons. I have heard

The cock, that is the trumpet to the morn,   165
Doth with his lofty and shrill-sounding throat
Awake the god of day, and at his warning,
Whether in sea or fire, in earth or air,
Th' extravagant and erring spirit hies
To his confine, and of the truth herein   170
This present object made probation.
MARCELLUS
  It faded on the crowing of the cock.
  Some say that ever 'gainst that season comes
  Wherein our Savior's birth is celebrated,
  This bird of dawning singeth all night long;   175
  And then, they say, no spirit dare stir abroad,
  The nights are wholesome; then no planets strike,
  No fairy takes, nor witch hath power to charm,
  So hallowed and so gracious is that time.
HORATIO
  So have I heard and do in part believe it.   180
  But look, the morn in russet mantle clad
  Walks o'er the dew of yon high eastward hill.
  Break we our watch up, and by my advice
  Let us impart what we have seen tonight
  Unto young Hamlet; for, upon my life,   185
  This spirit, dumb to us, will speak to him.
  Do you consent we shall acquaint him with it
  As needful in our loves, fitting our duty?
MARCELLUS
  Let's do 't, I pray, and I this morning know
  Where we shall find him most convenient.   190
                                        They exit.

⟨Scene 2⟩

Flourish. Enter Claudius, King of Denmark, Gertrude the
Queen, ⌈the⌉ Council, as Polonius, and his son Laertes,
Hamlet, with others, ⌈among them Voltemand and
Cornelius.⌉

KING

Though yet of Hamlet our dear brother's death
The memory be green, and that it us befitted
To bear our hearts in grief, and our whole kingdom
To be contracted in one brow of woe,
Yet so far hath discretion fought with nature   5
That we with wisest sorrow think on him
Together with remembrance of ourselves.
Therefore our sometime sister, now our queen,
Th' imperial jointress to this warlike state,
Have we (as 'twere with a defeated joy,   10
With an auspicious and a dropping eye,
With mirth in funeral and with dirge in marriage,
In equal scale weighing delight and dole)
Taken to wife. Nor have we herein barred
Your better wisdoms, which have freely gone   15
With this affair along. For all, our thanks.
Now follows that you know. Young Fortinbras,
Holding a weak supposal of our worth
Or thinking by our late dear brother's death
Our state to be disjoint and out of frame,   20
Colleaguèd with this dream of his advantage,
He hath not failed to pester us with message
Importing the surrender of those lands
Lost by his father, with all bonds of law,
To our most valiant brother—so much for him.   25
Now for ourself and for this time of meeting.
Thus much the business is: we have here writ
To Norway, uncle of young Fortinbras,
Who, impotent and bedrid, scarcely hears

Of this his nephew's purpose, to suppress　　　30
His further gait herein, in that the levies,
The lists, and full proportions are all made
Out of his subject; and we here dispatch
You, good Cornelius, and you, Voltemand,
For bearers of this greeting to old Norway,　　　35
Giving to you no further personal power
To business with the King more than the scope
Of these dilated articles allow.
⌜*Giving them a paper.*⌝
Farewell, and let your haste commend your duty.
CORNELIUS/VOLTEMAND
In that and all things will we show our duty.　　　40
KING
We doubt it nothing. Heartily farewell.
〈*Voltemand and Cornelius exit.*〉
And now, Laertes, what's the news with you?
You told us of some suit. What is 't, Laertes?
You cannot speak of reason to the Dane
And lose your voice. What wouldst thou beg,　　　45
　　Laertes,
That shall not be my offer, not thy asking?
The head is not more native to the heart,
The hand more instrumental to the mouth,
Than is the throne of Denmark to thy father.　　　50
What wouldst thou have, Laertes?
LAERTES　　　　　　　　　　My dread lord,
Your leave and favor to return to France,
From whence though willingly I came to Denmark
To show my duty in your coronation,　　　55
Yet now I must confess, that duty done,
My thoughts and wishes bend again toward France
And bow them to your gracious leave and pardon.
KING
Have you your father's leave? What says Polonius?

POLONIUS

    Hath, my lord, [wrung from me my slow leave   60
    By laborsome petition, and at last
    Upon his will I sealed my hard consent.]
    I do beseech you give him leave to go.

KING

    Take thy fair hour, Laertes. Time be thine,
    And thy best graces spend it at thy will.—   65
    But now, my cousin Hamlet and my son—

HAMLET, ⌐*aside*¬

    A little more than kin and less than kind.

KING

    How is it that the clouds still hang on you?

HAMLET

    Not so, my lord; I am too much in the sun.

QUEEN

    Good Hamlet, cast thy nighted color off,   70
    And let thine eye look like a friend on Denmark.
    Do not forever with thy vailèd lids
    Seek for thy noble father in the dust.
    Thou know'st 'tis common; all that lives must die,
    Passing through nature to eternity.   75

HAMLET

    Ay, madam, it is common.

QUEEN   If it be,
    Why seems it so particular with thee?

HAMLET

    "Seems," madam? Nay, it is. I know not "seems."
    'Tis not alone my inky cloak, ⟨good⟩ mother,   80
    Nor customary suits of solemn black,
    Nor windy suspiration of forced breath,
    No, nor the fruitful river in the eye,
    Nor the dejected havior of the visage,
    Together with all forms, moods, ⌐shapes¬ of grief,   85
    That can ⟨denote⟩ me truly. These indeed "seem,"
    For they are actions that a man might play;

But I have that within which passes show,
These but the trappings and the suits of woe.
KING
'Tis sweet and commendable in your nature,   90
   Hamlet,
To give these mourning duties to your father.
But you must know your father lost a father,
That father lost, lost his, and the survivor bound
In filial obligation for some term   95
To do obsequious sorrow. But to persever
In obstinate condolement is a course
Of impious stubbornness. 'Tis unmanly grief.
It shows a will most incorrect to heaven,
A heart unfortified, ⟨a⟩ mind impatient,   100
An understanding simple and unschooled.
For what we know must be and is as common
As any the most vulgar thing to sense,
Why should we in our peevish opposition
Take it to heart? Fie, 'tis a fault to heaven,   105
A fault against the dead, a fault to nature,
To reason most absurd, whose common theme
Is death of fathers, and who still hath cried,
From the first corse till he that died today,
"This must be so." We pray you, throw to earth   110
This unprevailing woe and think of us
As of a father; for let the world take note,
You are the most immediate to our throne,
And with no less nobility of love
Than that which dearest father bears his son   115
Do I impart toward you. For your intent
In going back to school in Wittenberg,
It is most retrograde to our desire,
And we beseech you, bend you to remain
Here in the cheer and comfort of our eye,   120
Our chiefest courtier, cousin, and our son.

QUEEN
    Let not thy mother lose her prayers, Hamlet.
    I pray thee, stay with us. Go not to Wittenberg.
HAMLET
    I shall in all my best obey you, madam.
KING
    Why, 'tis a loving and a fair reply.   125
    Be as ourself in Denmark.—Madam, come.
    This gentle and unforced accord of Hamlet
    Sits smiling to my heart, in grace whereof
    No jocund health that Denmark drinks today
    But the great cannon to the clouds shall tell,   130
    And the King's rouse the heaven shall bruit again,
    Respeaking earthly thunder. Come away.
                        Flourish. All but Hamlet exit.

HAMLET
    O, that this too, too sullied flesh would melt,
    Thaw, and resolve itself into a dew,
    Or that the Everlasting had not fixed   135
    His canon 'gainst ⟨self-slaughter!⟩ O God, God,
    How ⟨weary,⟩ stale, flat, and unprofitable
    Seem to me all the uses of this world!
    Fie on 't, ah fie! 'Tis an unweeded garden
    That grows to seed. Things rank and gross in nature   140
    Possess it merely. That it should come ⟨to this:⟩
    But two months dead—nay, not so much, not two.
    So excellent a king, that was to this
    Hyperion to a satyr; so loving to my mother
    That he might not beteem the winds of heaven   145
    Visit her face too roughly. Heaven and earth,
    Must I remember? Why, she ⟨would⟩ hang on him
    As if increase of appetite had grown
    By what it fed on. And yet, within a month
    (Let me not think on 't; frailty, thy name is woman!), 150
    A little month, or ere those shoes were old
    With which she followed my poor father's body,

Like Niobe, all tears—why she, ⟨even she⟩
(O God, a beast that wants discourse of reason
Would have mourned longer!), married with my   155
  uncle,
My father's brother, but no more like my father
Than I to Hercules. Within a month,
Ere yet the salt of most unrighteous tears
Had left the flushing in her gallèd eyes,   160
She married. O, most wicked speed, to post
With such dexterity to incestuous sheets!
It is not, nor it cannot come to good.
But break, my heart, for I must hold my tongue.

Enter Horatio, Marcellus, and Barnardo.

HORATIO   Hail to your lordship.   165
HAMLET   I am glad to see you well.
  Horatio—or I do forget myself!
HORATIO
  The same, my lord, and your poor servant ever.
HAMLET
  Sir, my good friend. I'll change that name with you.
  And what make you from Wittenberg, Horatio?—   170
  Marcellus?
MARCELLUS   My good lord.
HAMLET
  I am very glad to see you. ⌜*To Barnardo.*⌝ Good
    even, sir.—
  But what, in faith, make you from Wittenberg?   175
HORATIO
  A truant disposition, good my lord.
HAMLET
  I would not hear your enemy say so,
  Nor shall you do my ear that violence
  To make it truster of your own report
  Against yourself. I know you are no truant.   180
  But what is your affair in Elsinore?
  We'll teach you to drink ⟨deep⟩ ere you depart.

HORATIO
　My lord, I came to see your father's funeral.
HAMLET
　I prithee, do not mock me, fellow student.
　I think it was to ⟨see⟩ my mother's wedding.　　　　185
HORATIO
　Indeed, my lord, it followed hard upon.
HAMLET
　Thrift, thrift, Horatio. The funeral baked meats
　Did coldly furnish forth the marriage tables.
　Would I had met my dearest foe in heaven
　Or ever I had seen that day, Horatio!　　　　190
　My father—methinks I see my father.
HORATIO
　Where, my lord?
HAMLET　　　　　　　In my mind's eye, Horatio.
HORATIO
　I saw him once. He was a goodly king.
HAMLET
　He was a man. Take him for all in all,　　　　195
　I shall not look upon his like again.
HORATIO
　My lord, I think I saw him yesternight.
HAMLET　　Saw who?
HORATIO
　My lord, the King your father.
HAMLET　　　　　　　　　　　The King my father?　　200
HORATIO
　Season your admiration for a while
　With an attent ear, till I may deliver
　Upon the witness of these gentlemen
　This marvel to you.
HAMLET　　　　　　　For God's love, let me hear!　　20⁵
HORATIO
　Two nights together had these gentlemen,
　Marcellus and Barnardo, on their watch,

In the dead waste and middle of the night,
Been thus encountered: a figure like your father,
Armèd at point exactly, cap-à-pie,   210
Appears before them and with solemn march
Goes slow and stately by them. Thrice he walked
By their oppressed and fear-surprisèd eyes
Within his truncheon's length, whilst they, distilled
Almost to jelly with the act of fear,   215
Stand dumb and speak not to him. This to me
In dreadful secrecy impart they did,
And I with them the third night kept the watch,
⌜Where, as⌝ they had delivered, both in time,
Form of the thing (each word made true and good),   220
The apparition comes. I knew your father;
These hands are not more like.

HAMLET   But where was this?

MARCELLUS
My lord, upon the platform where we watch.

HAMLET
Did you not speak to it?   225

HORATIO   My lord, I did,
But answer made it none. Yet once methought
It lifted up its head and did address
Itself to motion, like as it would speak;
But even then the morning cock crew loud,   230
And at the sound it shrunk in haste away
And vanished from our sight.

HAMLET   'Tis very strange.

HORATIO
As I do live, my honored lord, 'tis true.
And we did think it writ down in our duty   235
To let you know of it.

HAMLET   Indeed, sirs, but this troubles me.
Hold you the watch tonight?

ALL   We do, my lord.

HAMLET
Armed, say you?   240

ALL	Armed, my lord.
HAMLET	From top to toe?
ALL	My lord, from head to foot.
HAMLET	Then saw you not his face?

HORATIO
  O, yes, my lord, he wore his beaver up.   245

HAMLET   What, looked he frowningly?

HORATIO
  A countenance more in sorrow than in anger.

HAMLET   Pale or red?

HORATIO
  Nay, very pale.

HAMLET   And fixed his eyes upon you?   250

HORATIO
  Most constantly.

HAMLET   I would I had been there.

HORATIO   It would have much amazed you.

HAMLET   Very like. Stayed it long?

HORATIO
  While one with moderate haste might tell a   255
    hundred.

BARNARDO/MARCELLUS   Longer, longer.

HORATIO
  Not when I saw 't.

HAMLET   His beard was grizzled, no?

HORATIO
  It was as I have seen it in his life,   260
  A sable silvered.

HAMLET   I will watch ⌈tonight.⌉
  Perchance 'twill walk again.

HORATIO   I warrant it will.

HAMLET
  If it assume my noble father's person,   265
  I'll speak to it, though hell itself should gape
  And bid me hold my peace. I pray you all,
  If you have hitherto concealed this sight,

Let it be tenable in your silence still;
And whatsomever else shall hap tonight,   270
Give it an understanding but no tongue.
I will requite your loves. So fare you well.
Upon the platform, 'twixt eleven and twelve,
I'll visit you.
ALL   Our duty to your Honor.   275

HAMLET
Your loves, as mine to you. Farewell.
                              ⌐*All but Hamlet*⌐ *exit.*
My father's spirit—in arms! All is not well.
I doubt some foul play. Would the night were come!
Till then, sit still, my soul. ⟨Foul⟩ deeds will rise,
Though all the earth o'erwhelm them, to men's   280
   eyes.

                                        He exits.

                    ⟨Scene 3⟩
         Enter Laertes and Ophelia, his sister.

LAERTES
My necessaries are embarked. Farewell.
And, sister, as the winds give benefit
And convey ⟨is⟩ assistant, do not sleep,
But let me hear from you.
OPHELIA   Do you doubt that?   5
LAERTES
For Hamlet, and the trifling of his favor,
Hold it a fashion and a toy in blood,
A violet in the youth of primy nature,
Forward, not permanent, sweet, not lasting,
The perfume and suppliance of a minute,   10
No more.
OPHELIA   No more but so?
LAERTES   Think it no more.

For nature, crescent, does not grow alone
In thews and ⟨bulk,⟩ but, as this temple waxes,   15
The inward service of the mind and soul
Grows wide withal. Perhaps he loves you now,
And now no soil nor cautel doth besmirch
The virtue of his will; but you must fear,
His greatness weighed, his will is not his own,   20
⟨For he himself is subject to his birth.⟩
He may not, as unvalued persons do,
Carve for himself, for on his choice depends
The safety and ⌜the⌝ health of this whole state.
And therefore must his choice be circumscribed   25
Unto the voice and yielding of that body
Whereof he is the head. Then, if he says he loves
    you,
It fits your wisdom so far to believe it
As he in his particular act and place   30
May give his saying deed, which is no further
Than the main voice of Denmark goes withal.
Then weigh what loss your honor may sustain
If with too credent ear you list his songs
Or lose your heart or your chaste treasure open   35
To his unmastered importunity.
Fear it, Ophelia; fear it, my dear sister,
And keep you in the rear of your affection,
Out of the shot and danger of desire.
The chariest maid is prodigal enough   40
If she unmask her beauty to the moon.
Virtue itself 'scapes not calumnious strokes.
The canker galls the infants of the spring
Too oft before their buttons be disclosed,
And, in the morn and liquid dew of youth,   45
Contagious blastments are most imminent.
Be wary, then; best safety lies in fear.
Youth to itself rebels, though none else near.

OPHELIA
    I shall the effect of this good lesson keep

As watchman to my heart. But, good my brother, 50
Do not, as some ungracious pastors do,
Show me the steep and thorny way to heaven,
Whiles, ⟨like⟩ a puffed and reckless libertine,
Himself the primrose path of dalliance treads
And recks not his own rede. 55

LAERTES   O, fear me not.

Enter Polonius.

I stay too long. But here my father comes.
A double blessing is a double grace.
Occasion smiles upon a second leave.

POLONIUS
Yet here, Laertes? Aboard, aboard, for shame! 60
The wind sits in the shoulder of your sail,
And you are stayed for. There, my blessing with
    thee.
And these few precepts in thy memory
Look thou character. Give thy thoughts no tongue, 65
Nor any unproportioned thought his act.
Be thou familiar, but by no means vulgar.
Those friends thou hast, and their adoption tried,
Grapple them unto thy soul with hoops of steel,
But do not dull thy palm with entertainment 70
Of each new-hatched, unfledged courage. Beware
Of entrance to a quarrel, but, being in,
Bear 't that th' opposèd may beware of thee.
Give every man thy ear, but few thy voice.
Take each man's censure, but reserve thy judgment. 75
Costly thy habit as thy purse can buy,
But not expressed in fancy (rich, not gaudy),
For the apparel oft proclaims the man,
And they in France of the best rank and station
⟨Are⟩ of a most select and generous chief in that. 80
Neither a borrower nor a lender ⟨be,⟩
For ⟨loan⟩ oft loses both itself and friend,

And borrowing ⟨dulls the⟩ edge of husbandry.
This above all: to thine own self be true,
And it must follow, as the night the day,   85
Thou canst not then be false to any man.
Farewell. My blessing season this in thee.

LAERTES
Most humbly do I take my leave, my lord.

POLONIUS
The time invests you. Go, your servants tend.

LAERTES
Farewell, Ophelia, and remember well   90
What I have said to you.

OPHELIA   'Tis in my memory locked,
And you yourself shall keep the key of it.

LAERTES   Farewell.   *Laertes exits.*

POLONIUS
What is 't, Ophelia, he hath said to you?   95

OPHELIA
So please you, something touching the Lord
    Hamlet.

POLONIUS   Marry, well bethought.
'Tis told me he hath very oft of late
Given private time to you, and you yourself   100
Have of your audience been most free and
    bounteous.
If it be so (as so 'tis put on me,
And that in way of caution), I must tell you
You do not understand yourself so clearly   105
As it behooves my daughter and your honor.
What is between you? Give me up the truth.

OPHELIA
He hath, my lord, of late made many tenders
Of his affection to me.

POLONIUS
Affection, puh! You speak like a green girl   110
Unsifted in such perilous circumstance.
Do you believe his "tenders," as you call them?

OPHELIA
　I do not know, my lord, what I should think.
POLONIUS
　Marry, I will teach you. Think yourself a baby
　That you have ta'en these tenders for true pay,　　　115
　Which are not sterling. Tender yourself more dearly,
　Or (not to crack the wind of the poor phrase,
　⌜Running⌝ it thus) you'll tender me a fool.
OPHELIA
　My lord, he hath importuned me with love
　In honorable fashion—　　　120
POLONIUS
　Ay, "fashion" you may call it. Go to, go to!
OPHELIA
　And hath given countenance to his speech, my lord,
　With almost all the holy vows of heaven.
POLONIUS
　Ay, ⟨springes⟩ to catch woodcocks. I do know,
　When the blood burns, how prodigal the soul　　　125
　Lends the tongue vows. These blazes, daughter,
　Giving more light than heat, extinct in both
　Even in their promise as it is a-making,
　You must not take for fire. From this time
　Be something scanter of your maiden presence.　　　130
　Set your entreatments at a higher rate
　Than a command to parle. For Lord Hamlet,
　Believe so much in him that he is young,
　And with a larger ⟨tether⟩ may he walk
　Than may be given you. In few, Ophelia,　　　135
　Do not believe his vows, for they are brokers,
　Not of that dye which their investments show,
　But mere ⟨implorators⟩ of unholy suits,
　Breathing like sanctified and pious ⌜bawds⌝
　The better to ⟨beguile.⟩ This is for all:　　　140
　I would not, in plain terms, from this time forth
　Have you so slander any moment leisure

As to give words or talk with the Lord Hamlet.
Look to 't, I charge you. Come your ways.
OPHELIA   I shall obey, my lord.   145

They exit.

Scene 4
Enter Hamlet, Horatio, and Marcellus.

HAMLET
The air bites shrewdly; it is very cold.
HORATIO
It is ⟨a⟩ nipping and an eager air.
HAMLET   What hour now?
HORATIO   I think it lacks of twelve.
MARCELLUS   No, it is struck.   5
HORATIO
Indeed, I heard it not. It then draws near the season
Wherein the spirit held his wont to walk.
            A flourish of trumpets and two pieces goes off.
What does this mean, my lord?
HAMLET
The King doth wake tonight and takes his rouse,
Keeps wassail, and the swagg'ring upspring reels;   10
And, as he drains his draughts of Rhenish down,
The kettledrum and trumpet thus bray out
The triumph of his pledge.
HORATIO   Is it a custom?
HAMLET   Ay, marry, is 't,   15
But, to my mind, though I am native here
And to the manner born, it is a custom
More honored in the breach than the observance.
[This heavy-headed revel east and west
Makes us traduced and taxed of other nations.   20
They clepe us drunkards and with swinish phrase
Soil our addition. And, indeed, it takes

From our achievements, though performed at
　　height,
The pith and marrow of our attribute.　　　　　　25
So oft it chances in particular men
That for some vicious mole of nature in them,
As in their birth (wherein they are not guilty,
Since nature cannot choose his origin),
By ⌜the⌝ o'ergrowth of some complexion　　　　　30
(Oft breaking down the pales and forts of reason),
Or by some habit that too much o'erleavens
The form of plausive manners—that these men,
Carrying, I say, the stamp of one defect,
Being nature's livery or fortune's star,　　　　　35
His virtues else, be they as pure as grace,
As infinite as man may undergo,
Shall in the general censure take corruption
From that particular fault. The dram of ⌜evil⌝
Doth all the noble substance of a doubt　　　　　40
To his own scandal.]

Enter Ghost.

HORATIO　　　　　　　　Look, my lord, it comes.
IIAMLET
Angels and ministers of grace, defend us!
Be thou a spirit of health or goblin damned,
Bring with thee airs from heaven or blasts from　45
　　hell,
Be thy intents wicked or charitable,
Thou com'st in such a questionable shape
That I will speak to thee. I'll call thee "Hamlet,"
"King," "Father," "Royal Dane." O, answer me!　50
Let me not burst in ignorance, but tell
Why thy canonized bones, hearsèd in death,
Have burst their cerements; why the sepulcher,
Wherein we saw thee quietly interred,
Hath oped his ponderous and marble jaws　　　55

To cast thee up again. What may this mean
That thou, dead corse, again in complete steel,
Revisits thus the glimpses of the moon,
Making night hideous, and we fools of nature
So horridly to shake our disposition   60
With thoughts beyond the reaches of our souls?
Say, why is this? Wherefore? What should we do?
⟨*Ghost*⟩ *beckons.*

HORATIO
It beckons you to go away with it
As if it some impartment did desire
To you alone.   65

MARCELLUS   Look with what courteous action
It waves you to a more removèd ground.
But do not go with it.

HORATIO   No, by no means.

HAMLET
It will not speak. Then I will follow it.   70

HORATIO
Do not, my lord.

HAMLET   Why, what should be the fear?
I do not set my life at a pin's fee.
And for my soul, what can it do to that,
Being a thing immortal as itself?   75
It waves me forth again. I'll follow it.

HORATIO
What if it tempt you toward the flood, my lord?
Or to the dreadful summit of the cliff
That beetles o'er his base into the sea,
And there assume some other horrible form   80
Which might deprive your sovereignty of reason
And draw you into madness? Think of it.
[The very place puts toys of desperation,
Without more motive, into every brain
That looks so many fathoms to the sea   85
And hears it roar beneath.]

HAMLET
  It waves me still.—Go on, I'll follow thee.
MARCELLUS
  You shall not go, my lord. ⌜*They hold back Hamlet.*⌝
HAMLET   Hold off your hands.
HORATIO
  Be ruled. You shall not go.   90
HAMLET   My fate cries out
  And makes each petty arture in this body
  As hardy as the Nemean lion's nerve.
  Still am I called. Unhand me, gentlemen.
  By heaven, I'll make a ghost of him that lets me!   95
  I say, away!—Go on. I'll follow thee.
                              Ghost and Hamlet exit.
HORATIO
  He waxes desperate with imagination.
MARCELLUS
  Let's follow. 'Tis not fit thus to obey him.
HORATIO
  Have after. To what issue will this come?
MARCELLUS
  Something is rotten in the state of Denmark.   100
HORATIO
  Heaven will direct it.
MARCELLUS   Nay, let's follow him.
                                        They exit.

⌜Scene 5⌝
Enter Ghost and Hamlet.

HAMLET
  Whither wilt thou lead me? Speak. I'll go no
    further.
GHOST
  Mark me.

HAMLET   I will.

GHOST   My hour is almost come   5
  When I to sulf'rous and tormenting flames
  Must render up myself.

HAMLET   Alas, poor ghost!

GHOST
  Pity me not, but lend thy serious hearing
  To what I shall unfold.   10

HAMLET   Speak. I am bound to hear.

GHOST
  So art thou to revenge, when thou shalt hear.

HAMLET   What?

GHOST   I am thy father's spirit,
  Doomed for a certain term to walk the night   15
  And for the day confined to fast in fires
  Till the foul crimes done in my days of nature
  Are burnt and purged away. But that I am forbid
  To tell the secrets of my prison house,
  I could a tale unfold whose lightest word   20
  Would harrow up thy soul, freeze thy young blood,
  Make thy two eyes, like stars, start from their
    spheres,
  Thy knotted and combinèd locks to part,
  And each particular hair to stand an end,   25
  Like quills upon the fearful porpentine.
  But this eternal blazon must not be
  To ears of flesh and blood. List, list, O list!
  If thou didst ever thy dear father love—

HAMLET   O God!   30

GHOST
  Revenge his foul and most unnatural murder.

HAMLET   Murder?

GHOST
  Murder most foul, as in the best it is,
  But this most foul, strange, and unnatural.

HAMLET
  Haste me to know 't, that I, with wings as swift   3[5]

As meditation or the thoughts of love,
May sweep to my revenge.
GHOST   I find thee apt;
And duller shouldst thou be than the fat weed
That roots itself in ease on Lethe wharf,   40
Wouldst thou not stir in this. Now, Hamlet, hear.
'Tis given out that, sleeping in my orchard,
A serpent stung me. So the whole ear of Denmark
Is by a forgèd process of my death
Rankly abused. But know, thou noble youth,   45
The serpent that did sting thy father's life
Now wears his crown.
HAMLET   O, my prophetic soul! My uncle!
GHOST
Ay, that incestuous, that adulterate beast,
With witchcraft of his ⌜wit,⌝ with traitorous gifts—   50
O wicked wit and gifts, that have the power
So to seduce!—won to his shameful lust
The will of my most seeming-virtuous queen.
O Hamlet, what ⟨a⟩ falling off was there!
From me, whose love was of that dignity   55
That it went hand in hand even with the vow
I made to her in marriage, and to decline
Upon a wretch whose natural gifts were poor
To those of mine.
But virtue, as it never will be moved,   60
Though lewdness court it in a shape of heaven,
So, ⟨lust,⟩ though to a radiant angel linked,
Will ⟨sate⟩ itself in a celestial bed
And prey on garbage.
But soft, methinks I scent the morning air.   65
Brief let me be. Sleeping within my orchard,
My custom always of the afternoon,
Upon my secure hour thy uncle stole,
With juice of cursèd hebona in a vial,
And in the porches of my ears did pour   70

The leprous distilment, whose effect
Holds such an enmity with blood of man
That swift as quicksilver it courses through
The natural gates and alleys of the body,
And with a sudden vigor it doth ⟨posset⟩   75
And curd, like eager droppings into milk,
The thin and wholesome blood. So did it mine,
And a most instant tetter barked about,
Most lazar-like, with vile and loathsome crust
All my smooth body.   80
Thus was I, sleeping, by a brother's hand
Of life, of crown, of queen at once dispatched,
Cut off, even in the blossoms of my sin,
Unhouseled, disappointed, unaneled,
No reck'ning made, but sent to my account   85
With all my imperfections on my head.
O horrible, O horrible, most horrible!
If thou hast nature in thee, bear it not.
Let not the royal bed of Denmark be
A couch for luxury and damnèd incest.   90
But, howsomever thou pursues this act,
Taint not thy mind, nor let thy soul contrive
Against thy mother aught. Leave her to heaven
And to those thorns that in her bosom lodge
To prick and sting her. Fare thee well at once.   95
The glowworm shows the matin to be near
And 'gins to pale his uneffectual fire.
Adieu, adieu, adieu. Remember me.   ⟨*He exits.*⟩

HAMLET
O all you host of heaven! O earth! What else?
And shall I couple hell? O fie! Hold, hold, my heart,   100
And you, my sinews, grow not instant old,
But bear me ⟨stiffly⟩ up. Remember thee?
Ay, thou poor ghost, whiles memory holds a seat
In this distracted globe. Remember thee?
Yea, from the table of my memory   105

I'll wipe away all trivial, fond records,
All saws of books, all forms, all pressures past,
That youth and observation copied there,
And thy commandment all alone shall live
Within the book and volume of my brain,   110
Unmixed with baser matter. Yes, by heaven!
O most pernicious woman!
O villain, villain, smiling, damnèd villain!
My tables—meet it is I set it down
That one may smile and smile and be a villain.   115
At least I am sure it may be so in Denmark.

                                   ⌈*He writes.*⌉

So, uncle, there you are. Now to my word.
It is "adieu, adieu, remember me."
I have sworn 't.

                 Enter Horatio and Marcellus.

HORATIO   My lord, my lord!   120
MARCELLUS   Lord Hamlet.
HORATIO   Heavens secure him!
HAMLET   So be it.
MARCELLUS   Illo, ho, ho, my lord!
HAMLET   Hillo, ho, ho, boy! Come, ⟨bird,⟩ come!   125
MARCELLUS
How is 't, my noble lord?
HORATIO   What news, my lord?
HAMLET   O, wonderful!
HORATIO
Good my lord, tell it.
HAMLET   No, you will reveal it.   130
HORATIO
Not I, my lord, by heaven.
MARCELLUS   Nor I, my lord.
HAMLET
How say you, then? Would heart of man once think
    it?
But you'll be secret?   135

HORATIO/MARCELLUS Ay, by heaven, ⟨my lord.⟩
HAMLET
  There's never a villain dwelling in all Denmark
  But he's an arrant knave.
HORATIO
  There needs no ghost, my lord, come from the grave
  To tell us this.   140
HAMLET   Why, right, you are in the right.
  And so, without more circumstance at all,
  I hold it fit that we shake hands and part,
  You, as your business and desire shall point you
  (For every man hath business and desire,   145
  Such as it is), and for my own poor part,
  I will go pray.
HORATIO
  These are but wild and whirling words, my lord.
HAMLET
  I am sorry they offend you, heartily;
  Yes, faith, heartily.   150
HORATIO   There's no offense, my lord.
HAMLET
  Yes, by Saint Patrick, but there is, Horatio,
  And much offense, too. Touching this vision here,
  It is an honest ghost—that let me tell you.
  For your desire to know what is between us,   155
  O'ermaster 't as you may. And now, good friends,
  As you are friends, scholars, and soldiers,
  Give me one poor request.
HORATIO What is 't, my lord? We will.
HAMLET
  Never make known what you have seen tonight.   160
HORATIO/MARCELLUS My lord, we will not.
HAMLET Nay, but swear 't.
HORATIO In faith, my lord, not I.
MARCELLUS Nor I, my lord, in faith.
HAMLET
  Upon my sword.   16⟨5⟩

MARCELLUS   We have sworn, my lord, already.
HAMLET   Indeed, upon my sword, indeed.
GHOST *cries under the stage*   Swear.
HAMLET
  Ha, ha, boy, sayst thou so? Art thou there,
    truepenny?   170
  Come on, you hear this fellow in the cellarage.
  Consent to swear.
HORATIO   Propose the oath, my lord.
HAMLET
  Never to speak of this that you have seen,
  Swear by my sword.   175
GHOST, ⌈*beneath*⌉   Swear.
HAMLET
  Hic et ubique? Then we'll shift our ground.
  Come hither, gentlemen,
  And lay your hands again upon my sword.
  Swear by my sword   180
  Never to speak of this that you have heard.
GHOST, ⌈*beneath*⌉   Swear by his sword.
HAMLET
  Well said, old mole. Canst work i' th' earth so fast?
  A worthy pioner! Once more remove, good friends.
HORATIO
  O day and night, but this is wondrous strange.   185
HAMLET
  And therefore as a stranger give it welcome.
  There are more things in heaven and earth, Horatio,
  Than are dreamt of in your philosophy. But come.
  Here, as before, never, so help you mercy,
  How strange or odd some'er I bear myself   190
  (As I perchance hereafter shall think meet
  To put an antic disposition on)
  That you, at such times seeing me, never shall,
  With arms encumbered thus, or this headshake,
  Or by pronouncing of some doubtful phrase,   195

As "Well, well, we know," or "We could an if we
would,"
Or "If we list to speak," or "There be an if they
might,"
Or such ambiguous giving-out, to note   200
That you know aught of me—this do swear,
So grace and mercy at your most need help you.
GHOST, ⌜*beneath*⌝ Swear.
HAMLET
Rest, rest, perturbèd spirit.—So, gentlemen,
With all my love I do commend me to you,   205
And what so poor a man as Hamlet is
May do t' express his love and friending to you,
God willing, shall not lack. Let us go in together,
And still your fingers on your lips, I pray.
The time is out of joint. O cursèd spite   210
That ever I was born to set it right!
Nay, come, let's go together.

                                            They exit.

⟨ACT 2⟩

⌜Scene 1⌝
Enter old Polonius with his man ⟨Reynaldo.⟩

POLONIUS
Give him this money and these notes, Reynaldo.

REYNALDO I will, my lord.

POLONIUS
You shall do marvelous wisely, good Reynaldo,
Before you visit him, to make inquire
Of his behavior.   5

REYNALDO   My lord, I did intend it.

POLONIUS
Marry, well said, very well said. Look you, sir,
Inquire me first what Danskers are in Paris;
And how, and who, what means, and where they
    keep,   10
What company, at what expense; and finding
By this encompassment and drift of question
That they do know my son, come you more nearer
Than your particular demands will touch it.
Take you, as 'twere, some distant knowledge of him,   15
As thus: "I know his father and his friends
And, in part, him." Do you mark this, Reynaldo?

REYNALDO Ay, very well, my lord.

POLONIUS
"And, in part, him, but," you may say, "not well.

213

But if 't be he I mean, he's very wild, 20
Addicted so and so." And there put on him
What forgeries you please—marry, none so rank
As may dishonor him, take heed of that,
But, sir, such wanton, wild, and usual slips
As are companions noted and most known 25
To youth and liberty.

REYNALDO   As gaming, my lord.

POLONIUS   Ay, or drinking, fencing, swearing,
Quarreling, drabbing—you may go so far.

REYNALDO   My lord, that would dishonor him. 30

POLONIUS
Faith, ⟨no,⟩ as you may season it in the charge.
You must not put another scandal on him
That he is open to incontinency;
That's not my meaning. But breathe his faults so
    quaintly 35
That they may seem the taints of liberty,
The flash and outbreak of a fiery mind,
A savageness in unreclaimèd blood,
Of general assault.

REYNALDO   But, my good lord— 40

POLONIUS   Wherefore should you do this?

REYNALDO   Ay, my lord, I would know that.

POLONIUS   Marry, sir, here's my drift,
And I believe it is a fetch of wit.
You, laying these slight sullies on my son, 45
As 'twere a thing a little soiled ⟨i' th'⟩ working,
Mark you, your party in converse, him you would
    sound,
Having ever seen in the prenominate crimes
The youth you breathe of guilty, be assured 50
He closes with you in this consequence:
"Good sir," or so, or "friend," or "gentleman,"
According to the phrase or the addition
Of man and country—

REYNALDO   Very good, my lord.   55

POLONIUS And then, sir, does he this, he does—what
    was I about to say? By the Mass, I was about to say
    something. Where did I leave?

REYNALDO At "closes in the consequence," ⟨at "friend,
    or so, and gentleman."⟩   60

POLONIUS

  At "closes in the consequence"—ay, marry—
  He closes thus: "I know the gentleman.
  I saw him yesterday," or "th' other day"
  (Or then, or then, with such or such), "and as you
     say,   65
  There was he gaming, there ⟨o'ertook⟩ in 's rouse,
  There falling out at tennis"; or perchance
  "I saw him enter such a house of sale"—
  Videlicet, a brothel—or so forth. See you now
  Your bait of falsehood take this carp of truth;   70
  And thus do we of wisdom and of reach,
  With windlasses and with assays of bias,
  By indirections find directions out.
  So by my former lecture and advice
  Shall you my son. You have me, have you not?   75

REYNALDO ·

  My lord, I have.

POLONIUS   God be wi' you. Fare you well.

REYNALDO Good my lord.

POLONIUS

  Observe his inclination in yourself.

REYNALDO I shall, my lord.   80

POLONIUS And let him ply his music.

REYNALDO Well, my lord.

POLONIUS

  Farewell.   *Reynaldo exits.*

                    Enter Ophelia.

    How now, Ophelia, what's the matter?

OPHELIA
O, my lord, my lord, I have been so affrighted! 85
POLONIUS With what, i' th' name of God?
OPHELIA
My lord, as I was sewing in my closet,
Lord Hamlet, with his doublet all unbraced,
No hat upon his head, his stockings fouled,
Ungartered, and down-gyvèd to his ankle, 90
Pale as his shirt, his knees knocking each other,
And with a look so piteous in purport
As if he had been loosèd out of hell
To speak of horrors—he comes before me.
POLONIUS
Mad for thy love? 95
OPHELIA   My lord, I do not know,
But truly I do fear it.
POLONIUS   What said he?
OPHELIA
He took me by the wrist and held me hard.
Then goes he to the length of all his arm, 100
And, with his other hand thus o'er his brow,
He falls to such perusal of my face
As he would draw it. Long stayed he so.
At last, a little shaking of mine arm,
And thrice his head thus waving up and down, 105
He raised a sigh so piteous and profound
As it did seem to shatter all his bulk
And end his being. That done, he lets me go,
And, with his head over his shoulder turned,
He seemed to find his way without his eyes, 110
For out o' doors he went without their helps
And to the last bended their light on me.
POLONIUS
Come, go with me. I will go seek the King.
This is the very ecstasy of love,
Whose violent property fordoes itself 115

And leads the will to desperate undertakings
As oft as any passions under heaven
That does afflict our natures. I am sorry.
What, have you given him any hard words of late?

OPHELIA
No, my good lord, but as you did command   120
I did repel his letters and denied
His access to me.

POLONIUS   That hath made him mad.
I am sorry that with better heed and judgment
I had not coted him. I feared he did but trifle   125
And meant to wrack thee. But beshrew my jealousy!
By heaven, it is as proper to our age
To cast beyond ourselves in our opinions
As it is common for the younger sort
To lack discretion. Come, go we to the King.   130
This must be known, which, being kept close, might
     move
More grief to hide than hate to utter love.
Come.

                              They exit.

                    ⟨Scene 2⟩
Flourish. Enter King and Queen, Rosencrantz and
     Guildenstern ⌐and Attendants.⌐

KING
Welcome, dear Rosencrantz and Guildenstern.
Moreover that we much did long to see you,
The need we have to use you did provoke
Our hasty sending. Something have you heard
Of Hamlet's transformation, so call it,   5
Sith nor th' exterior nor the inward man
Resembles that it was. What it should be,
More than his father's death, that thus hath put him

So much from th' understanding of himself
I cannot dream of. I entreat you both   10
That, being of so young days brought up with him
And sith so neighbored to his youth and havior,
That you vouchsafe your rest here in our court
Some little time, so by your companies
To draw him on to pleasures, and to gather   15
So much as from occasion you may glean,
[Whether aught to us unknown afflicts him thus]
That, opened, lies within our remedy.

QUEEN
Good gentlemen, he hath much talked of you,
And sure I am two men there is not living   20
To whom he more adheres. If it will please you
To show us so much gentry and goodwill
As to expend your time with us awhile
For the supply and profit of our hope,
Your visitation shall receive such thanks   25
As fits a king's remembrance.

ROSENCRANTZ   Both your Majesties
Might, by the sovereign power you have of us,
Put your dread pleasures more into command
Than to entreaty.   30

GUILDENSTERN   But we both obey,
And here give up ourselves in the full bent
To lay our service freely at your feet,
To be commanded.

KING
Thanks, Rosencrantz and gentle Guildenstern.   35

QUEEN
Thanks, Guildenstern and gentle Rosencrantz.
And I beseech you instantly to visit
My too much changèd son. Go, some of you,
And bring these gentlemen where Hamlet is.

GUILDENSTERN
Heavens make our presence and our practices   40
Pleasant and helpful to him!

QUEEN   Ay, amen!
                    Rosencrantz and Guildenstern exit
                              ⌜*with some Attendants.*⌝

                       Enter Polonius.

POLONIUS
  Th' ambassadors from Norway, my good lord,
  Are joyfully returned.
KING
  Thou still hast been the father of good news.   45
POLONIUS
  Have I, my lord? I assure my good liege
  I hold my duty as I hold my soul,
  Both to my God and to my gracious king,
  And I do think, or else this brain of mine
  Hunts not the trail of policy so sure   50
  As it hath used to do, that I have found
  The very cause of Hamlet's lunacy.
KING
  O, speak of that! That do I long to hear.
POLONIUS
  Give first admittance to th' ambassadors.
  My news shall be the fruit to that great feast.   55
KING
  Thyself do grace to them and bring them in.
                              ⌜*Polonius exits.*⌝
  He tells me, my dear Gertrude, he hath found
  The head and source of all your son's distemper.
QUEEN
  I doubt it is no other but the main—
  His father's death and our ⟨o'erhasty⟩ marriage.   60
KING
  Well, we shall sift him.

  Enter Ambassadors ⟨*Voltemand and Cornelius* ⌜*with*⌝
                      Polonius.⟩

Welcome, my good friends.
Say, Voltemand, what from our brother Norway?

VOLTEMAND
Most fair return of greetings and desires.
Upon our first, he sent out to suppress   65
His nephew's levies, which to him appeared
To be a preparation 'gainst the Polack,
But, better looked into, he truly found
It was against your Highness. Whereat, grieved
That so his sickness, age, and impotence   70
Was falsely borne in hand, sends out arrests
On Fortinbras, which he, in brief, obeys,
Receives rebuke from Norway, and, in fine,
Makes vow before his uncle never more
To give th' assay of arms against your Majesty.   75
Whereon old Norway, overcome with joy,
Gives him three-score thousand crowns in annual
    fee
And his commission to employ those soldiers,
So levied as before, against the Polack,   80
With an entreaty, herein further shown,
                                ⌜*He gives a paper.*⌝
That it might please you to give quiet pass
Through your dominions for this enterprise,
On such regards of safety and allowance
As therein are set down.   85

KING   It likes us well,
And, at our more considered time, we'll read,
Answer, and think upon this business.
Meantime, we thank you for your well-took labor.
Go to your rest. At night we'll feast together.   90
Most welcome home!
                    ⌜*Voltemand and Cornelius*⌝ *exit.*

POLONIUS   This business is well ended.
My liege, and madam, to expostulate
What majesty should be, what duty is,

Why day is day, night night, and time is time   95
Were nothing but to waste night, day, and time.
Therefore, ⟨since⟩ brevity is the soul of wit,
And tediousness the limbs and outward flourishes,
I will be brief. Your noble son is mad.
"Mad" call I it, for, to define true madness,   100
What is 't but to be nothing else but mad?
But let that go.
QUEEN   More matter with less art.
POLONIUS
Madam, I swear I use no art at all.
That he's mad, 'tis true; 'tis true 'tis pity,   105
And pity 'tis 'tis true—a foolish figure,
But farewell it, for I will use no art.
Mad let us grant him then, and now remains
That we find out the cause of this effect,
Or, rather say, the cause of this defect,   110
For this effect defective comes by cause.
Thus it remains, and the remainder thus.
Perpend.
I have a daughter (have while she is mine)
Who, in her duty and obedience, mark,   115
Hath given me this. Now gather and surmise.
      ⌐He reads.⌐ *To the celestial, and my soul's idol, the*
      most beautified Ophelia—
      That's an ill phrase, a vile phrase; "beautified" is a
      vile phrase. But you shall hear. Thus: ⌐He reads.⌐ 120
      In her excellent white bosom, these, etc.—
QUEEN   Came this from Hamlet to her?
POLONIUS
Good madam, stay awhile. I will be faithful.
⌐He reads the⌐ *letter.*
            Doubt thou the stars are fire,
                Doubt that the sun doth move,   125
            Doubt truth to be a liar,
                But never doubt I love.

O dear Ophelia, I am ill at these numbers. I have not
art to reckon my groans, but that I love thee best, O
most best, believe it. Adieu.   130

          Thine evermore, most dear lady, whilst
                   this machine is to him, Hamlet.

This, in obedience, hath my daughter shown me,
And more ⟨above,,⟩ hath his solicitings,
As they fell out by time, by means, and place,   135
All given to mine ear.

KING   But how hath she received his love?

POLONIUS   What do you think of me?

KING
As of a man faithful and honorable.

POLONIUS
I would fain prove so. But what might you think,   140
When I had seen this hot love on the wing
(As I perceived it, I must tell you that,
Before my daughter told me), what might you,
Or my dear Majesty your queen here, think,
If I had played the desk or table-book   145
Or given my heart a ⟨winking,⟩ mute and dumb,
Or looked upon this love with idle sight?
What might you think? No, I went round to work,
And my young mistress thus I did bespeak:
"Lord Hamlet is a prince, out of thy star.   150
This must not be." And then I prescripts gave her,
That she should lock herself from ⟨his⟩ resort,
Admit no messengers, receive no tokens;
Which done, she took the fruits of my advice,
And he, repelled (a short tale to make),   155
Fell into a sadness, then into a fast,
Thence to a watch, thence into a weakness,
Thence to ⟨a⟩ lightness, and, by this declension,
Into the madness wherein now he raves
And all we mourn for.   160

KING, ⌜*to Queen*⌝   Do you think ⟨'tis⟩ this?

QUEEN   It may be, very like.

POLONIUS
  Hath there been such a time (I would fain know
    that)
  That I have positively said " 'Tis so,"   165
  When it proved otherwise?

KING   Not that I know.

POLONIUS
  Take this from this, if this be otherwise.
  If circumstances lead me, I will find
  Where truth is hid, though it were hid, indeed,   170
  Within the center.

KING   How may we try it further?

POLONIUS
  You know sometimes he walks four hours together
  Here in the lobby.

QUEEN   So he does indeed.   175

POLONIUS
  At such a time I'll loose my daughter to him.
  ⌜*To the King.*⌝ Be you and I behind an arras then.
  Mark the encounter. If he love her not,
  And be not from his reason fall'n thereon,
  Let me be no assistant for a state,   180
  But keep a farm and carters.

KING   We will try it.

    Enter Hamlet ⟨reading on a book.⟩

QUEEN
  But look where sadly the poor wretch comes
    reading.

POLONIUS
  Away, I do beseech you both, away.   185
  I'll board him presently. O, give me leave.
              King and Queen exit ⌜with Attendants.⌝
  How does my good Lord Hamlet?

HAMLET   Well, God-a-mercy.

POLONIUS   Do you know me, my lord?

HAMLET   Excellent well. You are a fishmonger.   190

POLONIUS   Not I, my lord.

HAMLET   Then I would you were so honest a man.

POLONIUS   Honest, my lord?

HAMLET   Ay, sir. To be honest, as this world goes, is to
be one man picked out of ten thousand.   195

POLONIUS   That's very true, my lord.

HAMLET   For if the sun breed maggots in a dead
dog, being a good kissing carrion—Have you a
daughter?

POLONIUS   I have, my lord.   200

HAMLET   Let her not walk i' th' sun. Conception is a
blessing, but, as your daughter may conceive,
friend, look to 't.

POLONIUS, ⌐*aside*¬   How say you by that? Still harping on
my daughter. Yet he knew me not at first; he said I   205
was a fishmonger. He is far gone. And truly, in my
youth, I suffered much extremity for love, very near
this. I'll speak to him again.—What do you read, my
lord?

HAMLET   Words, words, words.   210

POLONIUS   What is the matter, my lord?

HAMLET   Between who?

POLONIUS   I mean the matter that you read, my lord.

HAMLET   Slanders, sir; for the satirical rogue says here
that old men have gray beards, that their faces are   215
wrinkled, their eyes purging thick amber and
plum-tree gum, and that they have a plentiful lack of
wit, together with most weak hams; all which, sir,
though I most powerfully and potently believe, yet I
hold it not honesty to have it thus set down; for   220
yourself, sir, shall grow old as I am, if, like a crab,
you could go backward.

POLONIUS, ⌐*aside*¬   Though this be madness, yet there is
method in 't.—Will you walk out of the air, my lord?

HAMLET Into my grave?   225

POLONIUS Indeed, that's out of the air. ⌜*Aside.*⌝ How
      pregnant sometimes his replies are! A happiness
      that often madness hits on, which reason and
      ⟨sanity⟩ could not so prosperously be delivered of. I
      will leave him ⟨and suddenly contrive the means of   230
      meeting between him⟩ and my daughter.—My lord,
      I will take my leave of you.

HAMLET You cannot, ⟨sir,⟩ take from me anything that I
      will more willingly part withal—except my life,
      except my life, except my life.   235

POLONIUS Fare you well, my lord.

HAMLET, ⌜*aside*⌝ These tedious old fools.

Enter Guildenstern and Rosencrantz.

POLONIUS You go to seek the Lord Hamlet. There he is.

ROSENCRANTZ, ⌜*to Polonius*⌝ God save you, sir.
                              ⌜*Polonius exits.*⌝

GUILDENSTERN My honored lord.   240

ROSENCRANTZ My most dear lord.

HAMLET My ⟨excellent⟩ good friends! How dost thou,
      Guildenstern? Ah, Rosencrantz! Good lads, how do
      you both?

ROSENCRANTZ
      As the indifferent children of the earth.   245

GUILDENSTERN
      Happy in that we are not ⟨overhappy.⟩
      On Fortune's ⟨cap,⟩ we are not the very button.

HAMLET Nor the soles of her shoe?

ROSENCRANTZ Neither, my lord.

HAMLET Then you live about her waist, or in the   250
      middle of her favors?

GUILDENSTERN Faith, her privates we.

HAMLET In the secret parts of Fortune? O, most true!
      She is a strumpet. What news?

ROSENCRANTZ None, my lord, but ⟨that⟩ the world's   255
      grown honest.

HAMLET   Then is doomsday near. But your news is not true. ⟨Let me question more in particular. What have you, my good friends, deserved at the hands of Fortune that she sends you to prison hither?   260

GUILDENSTERN   Prison, my lord?

HAMLET   Denmark's a prison.

ROSENCRANTZ   Then is the world one.

HAMLET   A goodly one, in which there are many confines, wards, and dungeons, Denmark being one o'   265 th' worst.

ROSENCRANTZ   We think not so, my lord.

HAMLET   Why, then, 'tis none to you, for there is nothing either good or bad but thinking makes it so. To me, it is a prison.   270

ROSENCRANTZ   Why, then, your ambition makes it one. 'Tis too narrow for your mind.

HAMLET   O God, I could be bounded in a nutshell and count myself a king of infinite space, were it not that I have bad dreams.   275

GUILDENSTERN   Which dreams, indeed, are ambition, for the very substance of the ambitious is merely the shadow of a dream.

HAMLET   A dream itself is but a shadow.

ROSENCRANTZ   Truly, and I hold ambition of so airy   280 and light a quality that it is but a shadow's shadow.

HAMLET   Then are our beggars bodies, and our monarchs and outstretched heroes the beggars' shadows. Shall we to th' court? For, by my fay, I cannot reason.   285

ROSENCRANTZ/GUILDENSTERN   We'll wait upon you.

HAMLET   No such matter. I will not sort you with the rest of my servants, for, to speak to you like an honest man, I am most dreadfully attended.⟩ But, in the beaten way of friendship, what make you at   290 Elsinore?

ROSENCRANTZ   To visit you, my lord, no other occasion.

HAMLET Beggar that I am, I am ⟨even⟩ poor in thanks;
but I thank you, and sure, dear friends, my thanks
are too dear a halfpenny. Were you not sent for? 295
Is it your own inclining? Is it a free visitation?
Come, come, deal justly with me. Come, come; nay,
speak.

GUILDENSTERN What should we say, my lord?

HAMLET Anything but to th' purpose. You were sent 300
for, and there is a kind of confession in your looks
which your modesties have not craft enough to
color. I know the good king and queen have sent for
you.

ROSENCRANTZ To what end, my lord? 305

HAMLET That you must teach me. But let me conjure
you by the rights of our fellowship, by the consonancy of our youth, by the obligation of our ever-
preserved love, and by what more dear a better
proposer can charge you withal: be even and direct 310
with me whether you were sent for or no.

ROSENCRANTZ, ⌜*to Guildenstern*⌝ What say you?

HAMLET, ⌜*aside*⌝ Nay, then, I have an eye of you.—If
you love me, hold not off.

GUILDENSTERN My lord, we were sent for. 315

HAMLET I will tell you why; so shall my anticipation
prevent your discovery, and your secrecy to the
King and Queen molt no feather. I have of late, but
wherefore I know not, lost all my mirth, forgone all
custom of exercises, and, indeed, it goes so heavily 320
with my disposition that this goodly frame, the
earth, seems to me a sterile promontory; this most
excellent canopy, the air, look you, this brave o'er-
hanging firmament, this majestical roof, fretted
with golden fire—why, it appeareth nothing to me 325
but a foul and pestilent congregation of vapors.
What ⟨a⟩ piece of work is a man, how noble in
reason, how infinite in faculties, in form and mov-

ing how express and admirable; in action how like
an angel, in apprehension how like a god: the 330
beauty of the world, the paragon of animals—and
yet, to me, what is this quintessence of dust? Man
delights not me, ⟨no,⟩ nor women neither, though by
your smiling you seem to say so.

ROSENCRANTZ My lord, there was no such stuff in my 335
thoughts.

HAMLET Why did you laugh, then, when I said "man
delights not me"?

ROSENCRANTZ To think, my lord, if you delight not in
man, what Lenten entertainment the players shall 340
receive from you. We coted them on the way, and
hither are they coming to offer you service.

HAMLET He that plays the king shall be welcome—his
Majesty shall have tribute on me. The adventurous
knight shall use his foil and target, the lover shall 345
not sigh gratis, the humorous man shall end his
part in peace, ⟨the clown shall make those laugh
whose lungs are ⌈tickle⌉ o' th' sear,⟩ and the lady
shall say her mind freely, or the ⟨blank⟩ verse shall
halt for 't. What players are they? 350

ROSENCRANTZ Even those you were wont to take such
delight in, the tragedians of the city.

HAMLET How chances it they travel? Their residence,
both in reputation and profit, was better both ways.

ROSENCRANTZ I think their inhibition comes by the 355
means of the late innovation.

HAMLET Do they hold the same estimation they did
when I was in the city? Are they so followed?

ROSENCRANTZ No, indeed are they not.

⟨HAMLET How comes it? Do they grow rusty? 360

ROSENCRANTZ Nay, their endeavor keeps in the wonted pace. But there is, sir, an aerie of children, little
eyases, that cry out on the top of question and are
most tyrannically clapped for 't. These are now the

fashion and so ⌈berattle⌉ the common stages (so 365
they call them) that many wearing rapiers are afraid
of goose quills and dare scarce come thither.

HAMLET What, are they children? Who maintains 'em?
How are they escoted? Will they pursue the quality
no longer than they can sing? Will they not say 370
afterwards, if they should grow themselves to common players (as it is ⌈most like,⌉ if their means are
no better), their writers do them wrong to make
them exclaim against their own succession?

ROSENCRANTZ Faith, there has been much ⌈to-do⌉ on 375
both sides, and the nation holds it no sin to tar
them to controversy. There was for a while no
money bid for argument unless the poet and the
player went to cuffs in the question.

HAMLET Is 't possible?   380

GUILDENSTERN O, there has been much throwing
about of brains.

HAMLET Do the boys carry it away?

ROSENCRANTZ Ay, that they do, my lord—Hercules
and his load too.⟩   385

HAMLET It is not very strange; for my uncle is King of
Denmark, and those that would make mouths at
him while my father lived give twenty, forty, fifty, a
hundred ducats apiece for his picture in little.
'Sblood, there is something in this more than nat- 390
ural, if philosophy could find it out.

                    A flourish ⟨for the Players.⟩

GUILDENSTERN There are the players.

HAMLET Gentlemen, you are welcome to Elsinore.
Your hands, come then. Th' appurtenance of welcome is fashion and ceremony. Let me comply 395
with you in this garb, ⟨lest my⟩ extent to the players,
which, I tell you, must show fairly outwards, should
more appear like entertainment than yours. You are
welcome. But my uncle-father and aunt-mother are
deceived.   400

GUILDENSTERN In what, my dear lord?

HAMLET I am but mad north-north-west. When the wind is southerly, I know a hawk from a handsaw.

Enter Polonius.

POLONIUS Well be with you, gentlemen.

HAMLET Hark you, Guildenstern, and you too—at each ear a hearer! That great baby you see there is not yet out of his swaddling clouts. 405

ROSENCRANTZ Haply he is the second time come to them, for they say an old man is twice a child.

HAMLET I will prophesy he comes to tell me of the players; mark it.—You say right, sir, a Monday morning, 'twas then indeed. 410

POLONIUS My lord, I have news to tell you.

HAMLET My lord, I have news to tell you: when Roscius was an actor in Rome— 415

POLONIUS The actors are come hither, my lord.

HAMLET Buzz, buzz.

POLONIUS Upon my honor—

HAMLET Then came each actor on his ass.

POLONIUS The best actors in the world, either for tragedy, comedy, history, pastoral, pastoral-comical, historical-pastoral, ⟨tragical-historical, tragical-comical-historical-pastoral,⟩ scene individable, or poem unlimited. Seneca cannot be too heavy, nor Plautus too light. For the law of writ and the liberty, these are the only men. 420 · 425

HAMLET O Jephthah, judge of Israel, what a treasure hadst thou!

POLONIUS What a treasure had he, my lord?

HAMLET Why, 430

> One fair daughter, and no more,
> The which he lovèd passing well.

POLONIUS, ⌜*aside*⌝ Still on my daughter.

HAMLET Am I not i' th' right, old Jephthah?

POLONIUS   If you call me "Jephthah," my lord: I have a   435
daughter that I love passing well.

HAMLET   Nay, that follows not.

POLONIUS   What follows then, my lord?

HAMLET   Why,

　　　　　　　As by lot, God wot   440

and then, you know,

　　　　　It came to pass, as most like it was—

the first row of the pious chanson will show you
more, for look where my abridgment comes.

Enter the Players.

You are welcome, masters; welcome all.—I am glad   445
to see thee well.—Welcome, good friends.—O ⟨my⟩
old friend! Why, thy face is valanced since I saw thee
last. Com'st thou to beard me in Denmark?—What,
my young lady and mistress! ⟨By'r⟩ Lady, your lady-
ship is nearer to heaven than when I saw you last, by   450
the altitude of a chopine. Pray God your voice, like a
piece of uncurrent gold, be not cracked within the
ring. Masters, you are all welcome. We'll e'en to 't
like ⟨French⟩ falconers, fly at anything we see. We'll
have a speech straight. Come, give us a taste of your   455
quality. Come, a passionate speech.

⟨FIRST⟩ PLAYER   What speech, my good lord?

HAMLET   I heard thee speak me a speech once, but it
was never acted, or, if it was, not above once; for
the play, I remember, pleased not the million: 460
'twas caviary to the general. But it was (as I
received it, and others whose judgments in such
matters cried in the top of mine) an excellent play,
well digested in the scenes, set down with as much
modesty as cunning. I remember one said there   465
were no sallets in the lines to make the matter
savory, nor no matter in the phrase that might indict
the author of ⟨affectation,⟩ but called it an honest

method, [as wholesome as sweet and, by very much,
more handsome than fine.] One speech in 't I   470
chiefly loved. 'Twas Aeneas' ⟨tale⟩ to Dido, and
thereabout of it especially when he speaks of
Priam's slaughter. If it live in your memory, begin at
this line—let me see, let me see:

The rugged Pyrrhus, like th' Hyrcanian beast—   475
'tis not so; it begins with Pyrrhus:
The rugged Pyrrhus, he whose sable arms,
Black as his purpose, did the night resemble
When he lay couchèd in th' ominous horse,
Hath now this dread and black complexion smeared   480
With heraldry more dismal. Head to foot,
Now is he total gules, horridly tricked
With blood of fathers, mothers, daughters, sons,
Baked and impasted with the parching streets,
That lend a tyrannous and a damnèd light   485
To their lord's murder. Roasted in wrath and fire,
And thus o'ersizèd with coagulate gore,
With eyes like carbuncles, the hellish Pyrrhus
Old grandsire Priam seeks.
So, proceed you.   490

POLONIUS 'Fore God, my lord, well spoken, with good
accent and good discretion.

⟨FIRST⟩ PLAYER   *Anon he finds him*
Striking too short at Greeks. His antique sword,
Rebellious to his arm, lies where it falls,   495
Repugnant to command. Unequal matched,
Pyrrhus at Priam drives, in rage strikes wide;
But with the whiff and wind of his fell sword
Th' unnervèd father falls. ⟨Then senseless Ilium,⟩
Seeming to feel this blow, with flaming top   500
Stoops to his base, and with a hideous crash
Takes prisoner Pyrrhus' ear. For lo, his sword,
Which was declining on the milky head
Of reverend Priam, seemed i' th' air to stick.

So as a painted tyrant Pyrrhus stood   505
⟨And,⟩ like a neutral to his will and matter,
Did nothing.
But as we often see against some storm
A silence in the heavens, the rack stand still,
The bold winds speechless, and the orb below   510
As hush as death, anon the dreadful thunder
Doth rend the region; so, after Pyrrhus' pause,
Aroused vengeance sets him new a-work,
And never did the Cyclops' hammers fall
On Mars's armor, forged for proof eterne,   515
With less remorse than Pyrrhus' bleeding sword
Now falls on Priam.
Out, out, thou strumpet Fortune! All you gods
In general synod take away her power,
Break all the spokes and ⌜fellies⌝ from her wheel,   520
And bowl the round nave down the hill of heaven
As low as to the fiends!
POLONIUS   This is too long.
HAMLET   It shall to the barber's with your beard.—
     Prithee say on. He's for a jig or a tale of bawdry, or   525
     he sleeps. Say on; come to Hecuba.
⟨FIRST⟩ PLAYER
But who, ah woe, had seen the mobled queen—
HAMLET   "The mobled queen"?
POLONIUS   That's good. ⟨⌜"Mobled⌝ queen" is good.⟩
⟨FIRST⟩ PLAYER
Run barefoot up and down, threat'ning the flames   530
With ⟨bisson rheum,⟩ a clout upon that head
Where late the diadem stood, and for a robe,
About her lank and all o'erteemed loins
A blanket, in the alarm of fear caught up—
Who this had seen, with tongue in venom steeped,   535
'Gainst Fortune's state would treason have
     pronounced.
But if the gods themselves did see her then

When she saw Pyrrhus make malicious sport
In mincing with his sword her ⟨husband's⟩ limbs,   540
The instant burst of clamor that she made
(Unless things mortal move them not at all)
Would have made milch the burning eyes of heaven
And passion in the gods.

POLONIUS Look whe'er he has not turned his color and   545
has tears in 's eyes. Prithee, no more.

HAMLET 'Tis well. I'll have thee speak out the rest of
this soon.—Good my lord, will you see the players
well bestowed? Do you hear, let them be well used,
for they are the abstract and brief chronicles of the   550
time. After your death you were better have a bad
epitaph than their ill report while you live.

POLONIUS My lord, I will use them according to their
desert.

HAMLET God's ⟨bodykins,⟩ man, much better! Use ev-   555
ery man after his desert and who shall 'scape
whipping? Use them after your own honor and
dignity. The less they deserve, the more merit is in
your bounty. Take them in.

POLONIUS Come, sirs.   560

HAMLET Follow him, friends. We'll hear a play tomorrow. ⌜*As Polonius and Players exit, Hamlet speaks to*
the First Player.⌝ Dost thou hear me, old friend? Can
you play "The Murder of Gonzago"?

⌜FIRST⌝ PLAYER Ay, my lord.   565

HAMLET We'll ha 't tomorrow night. You could, for ⟨a⟩
need, study a speech of some dozen or sixteen
lines, which I would set down and insert in 't,
could you not?

⌜FIRST⌝ PLAYER Ay, my lord.   570

HAMLET Very well. Follow that lord—and look you
mock him not. ⌜*First Player exits.*⌝ My good friends,
I'll leave you till night. You are welcome to Elsinore.

ROSENCRANTZ Good my lord.

HAMLET
  Ay, so, good-bye to you.   575
⌐*Rosencrantz and Guildenstern*⌐ *exit.*
Now I am alone.
O, what a rogue and peasant slave am I!
Is it not monstrous that this player here,
But in a fiction, in a dream of passion,
Could force his soul so to his own conceit   580
That from her working all ⟨his⟩ visage wanned,
Tears in his eyes, distraction in his aspect,
A broken voice, and his whole function suiting
With forms to his conceit—and all for nothing!
For Hecuba!   585
What's Hecuba to him, or he to ⟨Hecuba,⟩
That he should weep for her? What would he do
Had he the motive and ⟨the cue⟩ for passion
That I have? He would drown the stage with tears
And cleave the general ear with horrid speech,   590
Make mad the guilty and appall the free,
Confound the ignorant and amaze indeed
The very faculties of eyes and ears. Yet I,
A dull and muddy-mettled rascal, peak
Like John-a-dreams, unpregnant of my cause,   595
And can say nothing—no, not for a king
Upon whose property and most dear life
A damned defeat was made. Am I a coward?
Who calls me "villain"? breaks my pate across?
Plucks off my beard and blows it in my face?   600
Tweaks me by the nose? gives me the lie i' th' throat
As deep as to the lungs? Who does me this?
Ha! 'Swounds, I should take it! For it cannot be
But I am pigeon-livered and lack gall
To make oppression bitter, or ere this   605
I should ⟨have⟩ fatted all the region kites
With this slave's offal. Bloody, bawdy villain!
Remorseless, treacherous, lecherous, kindless
  villain!

⟨O vengeance!⟩　　　　　　　　　　　　　　　　610
Why, what an ass am I! This is most brave,
That I, the son of a dear ⌜father⌝ murdered,
Prompted to my revenge by heaven and hell,
Must, like a whore, unpack my heart with words
And fall a-cursing like a very drab,　　　　　　615
A ⟨scullion!⟩ Fie upon 't! Foh!
About, my brains!—Hum, I have heard
That guilty creatures sitting at a play
Have, by the very cunning of the scene,
Been struck so to the soul that presently　　　620
They have proclaimed their malefactions.
For murder, though it have no tongue, will speak
With most miraculous organ. I'll have these players
Play something like the murder of my father
Before mine uncle. I'll observe his looks;　　625
I'll tent him to the quick. If he do blench,
I know my course. The spirit that I have seen
May be a ⟨devil,⟩ and the ⟨devil⟩ hath power
T' assume a pleasing shape; yea, and perhaps,
Out of my weakness and my melancholy,　　　630
As he is very potent with such spirits,
Abuses me to damn me. I'll have grounds
More relative than this. The play's the thing
Wherein I'll catch the conscience of the King.
　　　　　　　　　　　　　　　　He exits.

⌜ACT 3⌝

⌜Scene 1⌝

Enter King, Queen, Polonius, Ophelia, Rosencrantz,
Guildenstern, ⟨and⟩ Lords.

KING
  And can you by no drift of conference
  Get from him why he puts on this confusion,
  Grating so harshly all his days of quiet
  With turbulent and dangerous lunacy?

ROSENCRANTZ
  He does confess he feels himself distracted,   5
  But from what cause he will by no means speak.

GUILDENSTERN
  Nor do we find him forward to be sounded,
  But with a crafty madness keeps aloof
  When we would bring him on to some confession
  Of his true state.   10

QUEEN   Did he receive you well?

ROSENCRANTZ   Most like a gentleman.

GUILDENSTERN
  But with much forcing of his disposition.

ROSENCRANTZ
  Niggard of question, but of our demands
  Most free in his reply.   15

QUEEN   Did you assay him to any pastime?

ROSENCRANTZ
  Madam, it so fell out that certain players

We o'erraught on the way. Of these we told him,
And there did seem in him a kind of joy
To hear of it. They are here about the court,   20
And, as I think, they have already order
This night to play before him.

POLONIUS   'Tis most true,
And he beseeched me to entreat your Majesties
To hear and see the matter.   25

KING
With all my heart, and it doth much content me
To hear him so inclined.
Good gentlemen, give him a further edge
And drive his purpose into these delights.

ROSENCRANTZ
We shall, my lord.   *Rosencrantz and Guildenstern*   30
                                ⌈*and Lords*⌉ *exit.*

KING   Sweet Gertrude, leave us ⟨too,⟩
For we have closely sent for Hamlet hither,
That he, as 'twere by accident, may here
Affront Ophelia.
Her father and myself ⟨⟨lawful espials⟩⟩   35
⟨Will⟩ so bestow ourselves that, seeing unseen,
We may of their encounter frankly judge
And gather by him, as he is behaved,
If 't be th' affliction of his love or no
That thus he suffers for.   40

QUEEN   I shall obey you.
And for your part, Ophelia, I do wish
That your good beauties be the happy cause
Of Hamlet's wildness. So shall I hope your virtues
Will bring him to his wonted way again,   45
To both your honors.

OPHELIA   Madam, I wish it may.
                                ⌈*Queen exits.*⌉

POLONIUS
Ophelia, walk you here.—Gracious, so please you,

We will bestow ourselves. ⌜*To Ophelia.*⌝
  book,
That show of such an exercise may colo
Your ⟨loneliness.⟩—We are oft to blame i
('Tis too much proved), that with devotion ⸺age
And pious action we do sugar o'er
The devil himself.   55

KING, ⌜*aside*⌝   O, 'tis too true!
  How smart a lash that speech doth give my
    conscience.
The harlot's cheek beautied with plast'ring art
Is not more ugly to the thing that helps it   60
Than is my deed to my most painted word.
O heavy burden!

POLONIUS
  I hear him coming. ⟨Let's⟩ withdraw, my lord.
                                    ⌜*They withdraw.*⌝

                    Enter Hamlet.

HAMLET
  To be or not to be—that is the question:
  Whether 'tis nobler in the mind to suffer   65
  The slings and arrows of outrageous fortune,
  Or to take arms against a sea of troubles
  And, by opposing, end them. To die, to sleep—
  No more—and by a sleep to say we end
  The heartache and the thousand natural shocks   70
  That flesh is heir to—'tis a consummation
  Devoutly to be wished. To die, to sleep—
  To sleep, perchance to dream. Ay, there's the rub,
  For in that sleep of death what dreams may come,
  When we have shuffled off this mortal coil,   75
  Must give us pause. There's the respect
  That makes calamity of so long life.
  For who would bear the whips and scorns of time,
  Th' oppressor's wrong, the proud man's contumely,

The pangs of despised love, the law's delay,   80
The insolence of office, and the spurns
That patient merit of th' unworthy takes,
When he himself might his quietus make
With a bare bodkin? Who would fardels bear,
To grunt and sweat under a weary life,   85
But that the dread of something after death,
The undiscovered country from whose bourn
No traveler returns, puzzles the will
And makes us rather bear those ills we have
Than fly to others that we know not of?   90
Thus conscience does make cowards ⟨of us all,⟩
And thus the native hue of resolution
Is ⟨sicklied⟩ o'er with the pale cast of thought,
And enterprises of great pitch and moment
With this regard their currents turn awry   95
And lose the name of action.—Soft you now,
The fair Ophelia.—Nymph, in thy orisons
Be all my sins remembered.

OPHELIA   Good my lord,
How does your Honor for this many a day?   100

HAMLET   I humbly thank you, well.

OPHELIA
My lord, I have remembrances of yours
That I have longèd long to redeliver.
I pray you now receive them.

HAMLET
No, not I. I never gave you aught.   105

OPHELIA
My honored lord, you know right well you did,
And with them words of so sweet breath composed
As made ⟨the⟩ things more rich. Their perfume
    lost,
Take these again, for to the noble mind   110
Rich gifts wax poor when givers prove unkind.
There, my lord.

HAMLET   Ha, ha, are you honest?

OPHELIA   My lord?

HAMLET   Are you fair?   115

OPHELIA   What means your lordship?

HAMLET   That if you be honest and fair, ⟨your honesty⟩ should admit no discourse to your beauty.

OPHELIA   Could beauty, my lord, have better commerce than with honesty?   120

HAMLET   Ay, truly, for the power of beauty will sooner transform honesty from what it is to a bawd than the force of honesty can translate beauty into his likeness. This was sometime a paradox, but now the time gives it proof. I did love you once.   125

OPHELIA   Indeed, my lord, you made me believe so.

HAMLET   You should not have believed me, for virtue cannot so ⟨inoculate⟩ our old stock but we shall relish of it. I loved you not.

OPHELIA   I was the more deceived.   130

HAMLET   Get thee ⟨to⟩ a nunnery. Why wouldst thou be a breeder of sinners? I am myself indifferent honest, but yet I could accuse me of such things that it were better my mother had not borne me: I am very proud, revengeful, ambitious, with more offenses at my beck than I have thoughts to put them in, imagination to give them shape, or time to act them in. What should such fellows as I do crawling between earth and heaven? We are arrant knaves ⟨all;⟩ believe none of us. Go thy ways to a nunnery.   140 Where's your father?

OPHELIA   At home, my lord.

HAMLET   Let the doors be shut upon him that he may play the fool nowhere but in 's own house. Farewell.

OPHELIA   O, help him, you sweet heavens!   145

HAMLET   If thou dost marry, I'll give thee this plague for thy dowry: be thou as chaste as ice, as pure as snow, thou shalt not escape calumny. Get thee to a

nunnery, farewell. Or if thou wilt needs marry,
marry a fool, for wise men know well enough what 150
monsters you make of them. To a nunnery, go, and
quickly too. Farewell.

OPHELIA Heavenly powers, restore him!

HAMLET I have heard of your paintings ⟨too,⟩ well
enough. God hath given you one face, and you 155
make yourselves another. You jig and amble, and
you ⟨lisp;⟩ you nickname God's creatures and make
your wantonness ⟨your⟩ ignorance. Go to, I'll no
more on 't. It hath made me mad. I say we will have
no more marriage. Those that are married already, 160
all but one, shall live. The rest shall keep as they are.
To a nunnery, go.   *He exits.*

OPHELIA
O, what a noble mind is here o'erthrown!
The courtier's, soldier's, scholar's, eye, tongue,
    sword,   165
⟨Th' expectancy⟩ and rose of the fair state,
The glass of fashion and the mold of form,
Th' observed of all observers, quite, quite down!
And I, of ladies most deject and wretched,
That sucked the honey of his musicked vows,   170
Now see ⟨that⟩ noble and most sovereign reason,
Like sweet bells jangled, out of time and harsh;
That unmatched form and stature of blown youth
Blasted with ecstasy. O, woe is me
T' have seen what I have seen, see what I see!   175

KING, ⌜*advancing with*⌝ *Polonius*
Love? His affections do not that way tend;
Nor what he spake, though it lacked form a little,
Was not like madness. There's something in his soul
O'er which his melancholy sits on brood,
And I do doubt the hatch and the disclose   180
Will be some danger; which for to prevent,
I have in quick determination

Thus set it down: he shall with speed to England
For the demand of our neglected tribute.
Haply the seas, and countries different,   185
With variable objects, shall expel
This something-settled matter in his heart,
Whereon his brains still beating puts him thus
From fashion of himself. What think you on 't?

POLONIUS
It shall do well. But yet do I believe   190
The origin and commencement of his grief
Sprung from neglected love.—How now, Ophelia?
You need not tell us what Lord Hamlet said;
We heard it all.—My lord, do as you please,
But, if you hold it fit, after the play   195
Let his queen-mother all alone entreat him
To show his grief. Let her be round with him;
And I'll be placed, so please you, in the ear
Of all their conference. If she find him not,
To England send him, or confine him where   200
Your wisdom best shall think.

KING　　　　　　　　　　　　It shall be so.
Madness in great ones must not ⟨unwatched⟩ go.
　　　　　　　　　　　　　　　　　　　　　　They exit.

⌜Scene 2⌝
Enter Hamlet and three of the Players.

HAMLET　Speak the speech, I pray you, as I pronounced
it to you, trippingly on the tongue; but if you mouth
it, as many of our players do, I had as lief the
town-crier spoke my lines. Nor do not saw the air
too much with your hand, thus, but use all gently;   5
for in the very torrent, tempest, and, as I may say,
whirlwind of your passion, you must acquire and
beget a temperance that may give it smoothness. O,

it offends me to the soul to hear a robustious,
periwig-pated fellow tear a passion to tatters, to very　10
rags, to split the ears of the groundlings, who for the
most part are capable of nothing but inexplicable
dumb shows and noise. I would have such a fellow
whipped for o'erdoing Termagant. It out-Herods
Herod. Pray you, avoid it.　15

PLAYER　I warrant your Honor.

HAMLET　Be not too tame neither, but let your own
discretion be your tutor. Suit the action to the
word, the word to the action, with this special
observance, that you o'erstep not the modesty of　20
nature.- For anything so o'erdone is from the purpose of playing, whose end, both at the first and
now, was and is to hold, as 'twere, the mirror up to
nature, to show virtue her ⟨own⟩ feature, scorn her
own image, and the very age and body of the time　25
his form and pressure. Now this overdone or come
tardy off, though it makes the unskillful laugh,
cannot but make the judicious grieve, the censure
of ⟨the⟩ which one must in your allowance o'erweigh
a whole theater of others. O, there be players that I　30
have seen play and heard others ⟨praise⟩ (and that
highly), not to speak it profanely, that, neither
having th' accent of Christians nor the gait of
Christian, pagan, nor man, have so strutted and
bellowed that I have thought some of nature's　35
journeymen had made men, and not made them
well, they imitated humanity so abominably.

PLAYER　I hope we have reformed that indifferently
with us, ⟨sir.⟩

HAMLET　O, reform it altogether. And let those that play　40
your clowns speak no more than is set down for
them, for there be of them that will themselves
laugh, to set on some quantity of barren spectators
to laugh too, though in the meantime some neces-

sary question of the play be then to be considered.   45
That's villainous and shows a most pitiful ambition
in the fool that uses it. Go make you ready.
⟨*Players exit.*⟩

Enter Polonius, Guildenstern, and Rosencrantz.

How now, my lord, will the King hear this piece of
work?

POLONIUS   And the Queen too, and that presently.   50

HAMLET   Bid the players make haste. ⟨*Polonius exits.*⟩
Will you two help to hasten them?

ROSENCRANTZ   Ay, my lord.   *They exit.*

HAMLET   What ho, Horatio!

Enter Horatio.

HORATIO   Here, sweet lord, at your service.   55

HAMLET
Horatio, thou art e'en as just a man
As e'er my conversation coped withal.

HORATIO
O, my dear lord—

⟨HAMLET⟩   Nay, do not think I flatter,
For what advancement may I hope from thee   60
That no revenue hast but thy good spirits
To feed and clothe thee? Why should the poor be
  flattered?
No, let the candied tongue lick absurd pomp
And crook the pregnant hinges of the knee   65
Where thrift may follow fawning. Dost thou hear?
Since my dear soul was mistress of her choice
And could of men distinguish, her election
Hath sealed thee for herself. For thou hast been
As one in suffering all that suffers nothing,   70
A man that Fortune's buffets and rewards
Hast ta'en with equal thanks; and blessed are those
Whose blood and judgment are so well
  commeddled

That they are not a pipe for Fortune's finger 75
To sound what stop she please. Give me that man
That is not passion's slave, and I will wear him
In my heart's core, ay, in my heart of heart,
As I do thee.—Something too much of this.—
There is a play tonight before the King. 80
One scene of it comes near the circumstance
Which I have told thee of my father's death.
I prithee, when thou seest that act afoot,
Even with the very comment of thy soul
Observe my uncle. If his occulted guilt 85
Do not itself unkennel in one speech,
It is a damnèd ghost that we have seen,
And my imaginations are as foul
As Vulcan's stithy. Give him heedful note,
For I mine eyes will rivet to his face, 90
And, after, we will both our judgments join
In censure of his seeming.

HORATIO   Well, my lord.
If he steal aught the whilst this play is playing
And 'scape ⟨detecting⟩, I will pay the theft. 95
                         ⟨*Sound a flourish.*⟩

HAMLET They are coming to the play. I must be idle.
    Get you a place.

*Enter Trumpets and Kettle Drums. ⟨Enter⟩ King, Queen,
Polonius, Ophelia, ⟨Rosencrantz, Guildenstern, and other
    Lords attendant with ⌐the King's¬ guard carrying
                    torches.⟩*

KING How fares our cousin Hamlet?
HAMLET Excellent, i' faith, of the chameleon's dish. I
    eat the air, promise-crammed. You cannot feed 100
    capons so.
KING I have nothing with this answer, Hamlet. These
    words are not mine.
HAMLET No, nor mine now. ⌐*To Polonius.*¬ My lord, you
    played once i' th' university, you say? 105

POLONIUS That did I, my lord, and was accounted a
  good actor.
HAMLET What did you enact?
POLONIUS I did enact Julius Caesar. I was killed i' th'
  Capitol. Brutus killed me.   110
HAMLET It was a brute part of him to kill so capital a
  calf there.—Be the players ready?
ROSENCRANTZ Ay, my lord. They stay upon your pa-
  tience.
QUEEN Come hither, my dear Hamlet, sit by me.   115
HAMLET No, good mother. Here's metal more
  attractive.   ⌜*Hamlet takes a place near Ophelia.*⌝
POLONIUS, ⌜*to the King*⌝ Oh, ho! Do you mark that?
HAMLET Lady, shall I lie in your lap?
OPHELIA No, my lord.   120
⟨HAMLET I mean, my head upon your lap?
OPHELIA Ay, my lord.⟩
HAMLET Do you think I meant country matters?
OPHELIA I think nothing, my lord.
HAMLET That's a fair thought to lie between maids'   125
  legs.
OPHELIA What is, my lord?
HAMLET Nothing.
OPHELIA You are merry, my lord.
HAMLET Who, I?   130
OPHELIA Ay, my lord.
HAMLET O God, your only jig-maker. What should a
  man do but be merry? For look you how cheerfully
  my mother looks, and my father died within 's two
  hours.   135
OPHELIA Nay, 'tis twice two months, my lord.
HAMLET So long? Nay, then, let the devil wear black,
  for I'll have a suit of sables. O heavens, die two
  months ago, and not forgotten yet? Then there's
  hope a great man's memory may outlive his life half   140
  a year. But, by'r Lady, he must build churches, then,

or else shall he suffer not thinking on, with the
hobby-horse, whose epitaph is "For oh, for oh, the
hobby-horse is forgot."

> *The trumpets sounds. Dumb show follows.*

Enter a King and a Queen, ⟨very lovingly,⟩ the Queen   145
embracing him and he her. ⟨She kneels and makes show of
protestation unto him.⟩ He takes her up and declines his
head upon her neck. He lies him down upon a bank of
flowers. She, seeing him asleep, leaves him. Anon
⟨comes⟩ in another man, takes off his crown, kisses it, pours   150
poison in the sleeper's ears, and leaves him. The Queen
returns, finds the King dead, makes passionate action. The
poisoner with some three or four come in again, seem to
condole with her. The dead body is carried away. The
poisoner woos the Queen with gifts. She seems harsh   155
awhile but in the end accepts ⟨his⟩ love.

> ⌜*Players exit.*⌝

OPHELIA   What means this, my lord?

HAMLET   Marry, this ⟨is miching⟩ mallecho. It means
mischief.

OPHELIA   Belike this show imports the argument of the   160
play.

> *Enter Prologue.*

HAMLET   We shall know by this fellow. The players
cannot keep ⟨counsel;⟩ they'll tell all.

OPHELIA   Will he tell us what this show meant?

HAMLET   Ay, or any show that you will show him. Be   165
not you ashamed to show, he'll not shame to tell you
what it means.

OPHELIA   You are naught, you are naught. I'll mark the
play.

PROLOGUE

> *For us and for our tragedy,*   17⟨
> *Here stooping to your clemency,*
> *We beg your hearing patiently.*   ⌜*He exits.*⌝

HAMLET Is this a prologue or the posy of a ring?
OPHELIA 'Tis brief, my lord.
HAMLET As woman's love.   175

    Enter ⌐the Player¬ King and Queen.

PLAYER KING
  Full thirty times hath Phoebus' cart gone round
  Neptune's salt wash and Tellus' ⟨orbèd⟩ ground,
  And thirty dozen moons with borrowed sheen
  About the world have times twelve thirties been
  Since love our hearts and Hymen did our hands   180
  Unite commutual in most sacred bands.

PLAYER QUEEN
  So many journeys may the sun and moon
  Make us again count o'er ere love be done!
  But woe is me! You are so sick of late,
  So far from cheer and from ⟨your⟩ former state,   185
  That I distrust you. Yet, though I distrust,
  Discomfort you, my lord, it nothing must.
  [For women fear too much, even as they love,]
  And women's fear and love hold quantity,
  In neither aught, or in extremity.   190
  Now what my ⟨love⟩ is, proof hath made you know,
  And, as my love is sized, my fear is so:
  [Where love is great, the littlest doubts are fear;
  Where little fears grow great, great love grows there.]

PLAYER KING
  Faith, I must leave thee, love, and shortly too. 195
  My operant powers their functions leave to do.
  And thou shalt live in this fair world behind,
  Honored, beloved; and haply one as kind
  For husband shalt thou—

PLAYER QUEEN   *O, confound the rest!* 200
  Such love must needs be treason in my breast.
  In second husband let me be accurst.
  None wed the second but who killed the first.

HAMLET That's wormwood!

PLAYER QUEEN
>*The instances that second marriage move*   205
>*Are base respects of thrift, but none of love.*
>*A second time I kill my husband dead*
>*When second husband kisses me in bed.*

PLAYER KING
>*I do believe you think what now you speak,*
>*But what we do determine oft we break.*   210
>*Purpose is but the slave to memory,*
>*Of violent birth, but poor validity,*
>*Which now, the fruit unripe, sticks on the tree*
>*But fall unshaken when they mellow be.*
>*Most necessary 'tis that we forget*   215
>*To pay ourselves what to ourselves is debt.*
>*What to ourselves in passion we propose,*
>*The passion ending, doth the purpose lose.*
>*The violence of either grief or joy*
>*Their own enactures with themselves destroy.*   220
>*Where joy most revels, grief doth most lament;*
>*Grief ⟨joys,⟩ joy grieves, on slender accident.*
>*This world is not for aye, nor 'tis not strange*
>*That even our loves should with our fortunes change;*
>*For 'tis a question left us yet to prove*   225
>*Whether love lead fortune or else fortune love.*
>*The great man down, you mark his favorite flies;*
>*The poor, advanced, makes friends of enemies.*
>*And hitherto doth love on fortune tend,*
>*For who not needs shall never lack a friend,*   230
>*And who in want a hollow friend doth try*
>*Directly seasons him his enemy.*
>*But, orderly to end where I begun:*
>*Our wills and fates do so contrary run*
>*That our devices still are overthrown;*   23
>*Our thoughts are ours, their ends none of our own.*
>*So think thou wilt no second husband wed,*
>*But die thy thoughts when thy first lord is dead.*

PLAYER QUEEN
Nor earth to me give food, nor heaven light,
Sport and repose lock from me day and night, 240
[*To desperation turn my trust and hope,*
⌜*An*⌝ *anchor's cheer in prison be my scope.*]
Each opposite that blanks the face of joy
Meet what I would have well and it destroy.
Both here and hence pursue me lasting strife, 245
If, once a widow, ever I be wife.

HAMLET If she should break it now!

PLAYER KING
'Tis deeply sworn. Sweet, leave me here awhile.
My spirits grow dull, and fain I would beguile
The tedious day with sleep. ⟨*Sleeps.*⟩ 250

PLAYER QUEEN   *Sleep rock thy brain,*
And never come mischance between us twain.
⌜*Player Queen exits.*⌝

HAMLET Madam, how like you this play?

QUEEN The lady doth protest too much, methinks.

HAMLET O, but she'll keep her word. 255

KING Have you heard the argument? Is there no offense in 't?

HAMLET No, no, they do but jest, poison in jest. No offense i' th' world.

KING What do you call the play? 260

HAMLET "The Mousetrap." Marry, how? Tropically. This play is the image of a murder done in Vienna. Gonzago is the duke's name, his wife Baptista. You shall see anon. 'Tis a knavish piece of work, but what of that? Your Majesty and we that have free 265 souls, it touches us not. Let the galled jade wince; our withers are unwrung.

Enter Lucianus.

This is one Lucianus, nephew to the king.

OPHELIA You are as good as a chorus, my lord.

HAMLET   I could interpret between you and your love, 270
    if I could see the puppets dallying.

OPHELIA   You are keen, my lord, you are keen.

HAMLET   It would cost you a groaning to take off mine
    edge.

OPHELIA   Still better and worse.   275

HAMLET   So you mis-take your husbands.—Begin,
    murderer. ⟨Pox,⟩ leave thy damnable faces and
    begin. Come, the croaking raven doth bellow for
    revenge.

LUCIANUS
    Thoughts black, hands apt, drugs fit, and time   280
      agreeing,
    ⟨Confederate⟩ season, else no creature seeing,
    Thou mixture rank, of midnight weeds collected,
    With Hecate's ban thrice blasted, thrice ⟨infected,⟩
    Thy natural magic and dire property   285
    On wholesome life ⟨usurp⟩ immediately.
               ⟨Pours the poison in his ears.⟩

HAMLET   He poisons him i' th' garden for his estate. His
    name's Gonzago. The story is extant and written in
    very choice Italian. You shall see anon how the
    murderer gets the love of Gonzago's wife.   290
                ⌈*Claudius rises.*⌉

OPHELIA   The King rises.

⟨HAMLET   What, frighted with false fire?⟩

QUEEN   How fares my lord?

POLONIUS   Give o'er the play.

KING   Give me some light. Away!   295

POLONIUS   Lights, lights, lights!
          All but Hamlet and Horatio exit.

HAMLET
    Why, let the strucken deer go weep,
      The hart ungallèd play.
    For some must watch, while some must sleep:
      Thus runs the world away.   30⟨

Would not this, sir, and a forest of feathers (if the
rest of my fortunes turn Turk with me) with ⟨two⟩
Provincial roses on my razed shoes, get me a
fellowship in a cry of players?

HORATIO   Half a share.   305

HAMLET   A whole one, I.
For thou dost know, O Damon dear,
    This realm dismantled was
Of Jove himself, and now reigns here
    A very very—pajock.   310

HORATIO   You might have rhymed.

HAMLET   O good Horatio, I'll take the ghost's word for
a thousand pound. Didst perceive?

HORATIO   Very well, my lord.

HAMLET   Upon the talk of the poisoning?   315

HORATIO   I did very well note him.

HAMLET   Ah ha! Come, some music! Come, the record-
ers!
For if the King like not the comedy,
    Why, then, belike he likes it not, perdy.   320
Come, some music!

Enter Rosencrantz and Guildenstern.

GUILDENSTERN   Good my lord, vouchsafe me a word
with you.

HAMLET   Sir, a whole history.

GUILDENSTERN   The King, sir—   325

HAMLET   Ay, sir, what of him?

GUILDENSTERN   Is in his retirement marvelous distempered.

HAMLET   With drink, sir?

GUILDENSTERN   No, my lord, with choler.   330

HAMLET   Your wisdom should show itself more richer
to signify this to the doctor, for for me to put him to
his purgation would perhaps plunge him into more
choler.

GUILDENSTERN Good my lord, put your discourse into 335
some frame and ⟨start⟩ not so wildly from my
affair.

HAMLET I am tame, sir. Pronounce.

GUILDENSTERN The Queen your mother, in most great
affliction of spirit, hath sent me to you. 340

HAMLET You are welcome.

GUILDENSTERN Nay, good my lord, this courtesy is not
of the right breed. If it shall please you to make me
a wholesome answer, I will do your mother's
commandment. If not, your pardon and my return 345
shall be the end of ⟨my⟩ business.

HAMLET Sir, I cannot.

ROSENCRANTZ What, my lord?

HAMLET Make you a wholesome answer. My wit's
diseased. But, sir, such answer as I can make, you 350
shall command—or, rather, as you say, my mother.
Therefore no more but to the matter. My mother,
you say—

ROSENCRANTZ Then thus she says: your behavior hath
struck her into amazement and admiration. 355

HAMLET O wonderful son that can so 'stonish a mother! But is there no sequel at the heels of this
mother's admiration? Impart.

ROSENCRANTZ She desires to speak with you in her
closet ere you go to bed. 360

HAMLET We shall obey, were she ten times our mother. Have you any further trade with us?

ROSENCRANTZ My lord, you once did love me.

HAMLET And do still, by these pickers and stealers.

ROSENCRANTZ Good my lord, what is your cause of 365
distemper? You do surely bar the door upon your
own liberty if you deny your griefs to your friend.

HAMLET Sir, I lack advancement.

ROSENCRANTZ How can that be, when you have the
voice of the King himself for your succession in 370
Denmark?

HAMLET Ay, sir, but "While the grass grows"—the proverb is something musty.

Enter the Players with recorders.

O, the recorders! Let me see one. ⌜*He takes a recorder and turns to Guildenstern.*⌝ To withdraw 375 with you: why do you go about to recover the wind of me, as if you would drive me into a toil?

GUILDENSTERN O, my lord, if my duty be too bold, my love is too unmannerly.

HAMLET I do not well understand that. Will you play 380 upon this pipe?

GUILDENSTERN My lord, I cannot.

HAMLET I pray you.

GUILDENSTERN Believe me, I cannot.

HAMLET I do beseech you. 385

GUILDENSTERN I know no touch of it, my lord.

HAMLET It is as easy as lying. Govern these ventages with your fingers and ⟨thumb,⟩ give it breath with your mouth, and it will discourse most eloquent music. Look you, these are the stops. 390

GUILDENSTERN But these cannot I command to any utt'rance of harmony. I have not the skill.

HAMLET Why, look you now, how unworthy a thing you make of me! You would play upon me, you would seem to know my stops, you would pluck 395 out the heart of my mystery, you would sound me from my lowest note to ⟨the top of⟩ my compass; and there is much music, excellent voice, in this little organ, yet cannot you make it speak. 'Sblood, do you think I am easier to be played on than a pipe? 400 Call me what instrument you will, though you ⟨can⟩ fret me, you cannot play upon me.

Enter Polonius.

God bless you, sir.

POLONIUS My lord, the Queen would speak with you,
  and presently.   405
HAMLET Do you see yonder cloud that's almost in
  shape of a camel?
POLONIUS By th' Mass, and 'tis like a camel indeed.
HAMLET Methinks it is like a weasel.
POLONIUS It is backed like a weasel.   410
HAMLET Or like a whale.
POLONIUS Very like a whale.
⟨HAMLET⟩ Then I will come to my mother by and by.
  ⌜*Aside.*⌝ They fool me to the top of my bent.—I will
  come by and by.   415
⟨POLONIUS⟩ I will say so.
⟨HAMLET⟩ "By and by" is easily said. Leave me,
  friends.

                  ⌜*All but Hamlet exit.*⌝

'Tis now the very witching time of night,
When churchyards yawn and hell itself ⟨breathes⟩   420
  out
Contagion to this world. Now could I drink hot
  blood
And do such ⟨bitter⟩ business as the day
Would quake to look on. Soft, now to my mother.   425
O heart, lose not thy nature; let not ever
The soul of Nero enter this firm bosom.
Let me be cruel, not unnatural.
I will speak ⟨daggers⟩ to her, but use none.
My tongue and soul in this be hypocrites: 430
How in my words somever she be shent,
To give them seals never, my soul, consent.

                        He exits.

⌜Scene 3⌝
Enter King, Rosencrantz, and Guildenstern.

KING
   I like him not, nor stands it safe with us
   To let his madness range. Therefore prepare you.
   I your commission will forthwith dispatch,
   And he to England shall along with you.
   The terms of our estate may not endure   5
   Hazard so near 's as doth hourly grow
   Out of his brows.
GUILDENSTERN   We will ourselves provide.
   Most holy and religious fear it is
   To keep those many many bodies safe   10
   That live and feed upon your Majesty.
ROSENCRANTZ
   The single and peculiar life is bound
   With all the strength and armor of the mind
   To keep itself from noyance, but much more
   That spirit upon whose weal depends and rests   15
   The lives of many. The cess of majesty
   Dies not alone, but like a gulf doth draw
   What's near it with it; or it is a massy wheel
   Fixed on the summit of the highest mount,
   To whose ⟨huge⟩ spokes ten thousand lesser things   20
   Are mortised and adjoined, which, when it falls,
   Each small annexment, petty consequence,
   Attends the boist'rous ⟨ruin.⟩ Never alone
   Did the king sigh, but ⟨with⟩ a general groan.
KING
   Arm you, I pray you, to this speedy voyage,   25
   For we will fetters put about this fear,
   Which now goes too free-footed.
ROSENCRANTZ   We will haste us.
          ⌜*Rosencrantz and Guildenstern*⌝ *exit.*

        Enter Polonius.

POLONIUS
   My lord, he's going to his mother's closet.
   Behind the arras I'll convey myself   30
   To hear the process. I'll warrant she'll tax him
     home;
   And, as you said (and wisely was it said),
   'Tis meet that some more audience than a mother,
   Since nature makes them partial, should o'erhear   35
   The speech of vantage. Fare you well, my liege.
   I'll call upon you ere you go to bed
   And tell you what I know.
KING   Thanks, dear my lord.
                       ⌜*Polonius*⌝ *exits.*

   O, my offense is rank, it smells to heaven;   40
   It hath the primal eldest curse upon 't,
   A brother's murder. Pray can I not,
   Though inclination be as sharp as will.
   My stronger guilt defeats my strong intent,
   And, like a man to double business bound,   45
   I stand in pause where I shall first begin
   And both neglect. What if this cursèd hand
   Were thicker than itself with brother's blood?
   Is there not rain enough in the sweet heavens
   To wash it white as snow? Whereto serves mercy   50
   But to confront the visage of offense?
   And what's in prayer but this twofold force,
   To be forestallèd ere we come to fall,
   Or ⟨pardoned⟩ being down? Then I'll look up.
   My fault is past. But, O, what form of prayer   55
   Can serve my turn? "Forgive me my foul murder"?
   That cannot be, since I am still possessed
   Of those effects for which I did the murder:
   My crown, mine own ambition, and my queen.
   May one be pardoned and retain th' offense?   60
   In the corrupted currents of this world,
   Offense's gilded hand may ⟨shove⟩ by justice,

And oft 'tis seen the wicked prize itself
Buys out the law. But 'tis not so above:
There is no shuffling; there the action lies   65
In his true nature, and we ourselves compelled,
Even to the teeth and forehead of our faults,
To give in evidence. What then? What rests?
Try what repentance can. What can it not?
Yet what can it, when one cannot repent?   70
O wretched state! O bosom black as death!
O limèd soul, that, struggling to be free,
Art more engaged! Help, angels! Make assay.
Bow, stubborn knees, and heart with strings of steel
Be soft as sinews of the newborn babe.   75
All may be well.   ⌜*He kneels.*⌝

Enter Hamlet.

HAMLET
Now might I do it ⟨pat,⟩ now he is a-praying,
And now I'll do 't.   ⌜*He draws his sword.*⌝
                    And so he goes to heaven,
And so am I ⟨revenged.⟩ That would be scanned: 80
A villain kills my father, and for that,
I, his sole son, do this same villain send
To heaven.
Why, this is ⟨hire⟩ and ⟨salary,⟩ not revenge.
He took my father grossly, full of bread,   85
With all his crimes broad blown, as flush as May;
And how his audit stands who knows save heaven.
But in our circumstance and course of thought
'Tis heavy with him. And am I then revenged
To take him in the purging of his soul,   90
When he is fit and seasoned for his passage?
No.
Up sword, and know thou a more horrid hent.
                    ⌜*He sheathes his sword.*⌝
When he is drunk asleep, or in his rage,

Or in th' incestuous pleasure of his bed,   95
At game a-swearing, or about some act
That has no relish of salvation in 't—
Then trip him, that his heels may kick at heaven,
And that his soul may be as damned and black
As hell, whereto it goes. My mother stays.   100
This physic but prolongs thy sickly days.

⌜*Hamlet*⌝ *exits.*

KING, ⌜*rising*⌝
My words fly up, my thoughts remain below;
→ Words without thoughts never to heaven go.

He exits.

artifice   art

read as unconscious   ⌜Scene 4⌝
fulfilling of O.C *Enter ⟨Queen⟩ and Polonius.*

POLONIUS
He will come straight. Look you lay home to him.
Tell him his pranks have been too broad to bear
   with
And that your Grace hath screened and stood
   between   5
Much heat and him. I'll silence me even here.
Pray you, be round ⟨with him.
HAMLET, *within* Mother, mother, mother!⟩
QUEEN I'll ⟨warrant⟩ you. Fear me not. Withdraw,
   I hear him coming.   10

⌜*Polonius hides behind the arras.*⌝

Enter Hamlet.

HAMLET Now, mother, what's the matter?
QUEEN
Hamlet, thou hast thy father much offended.
HAMLET
Mother, you have my father much offended.

QUEEN
  Come, come, you answer with an idle tongue.
HAMLET
  Go, go, you question with a wicked tongue.   15
QUEEN
  Why, how now, Hamlet?
HAMLET   What's the matter now?
QUEEN
  Have you forgot me?
HAMLET   No, by the rood, not so.
  You are the Queen, your husband's brother's wife,   20
  And (would it were not so) you are my mother.
QUEEN
  Nay, then I'll set those to you that can speak.
HAMLET
  Come, come, and sit you down; you shall not budge.
  You go not till I set you up a glass
  Where you may see the ⟨inmost⟩ part of you.   25

mirror / to see / nature

QUEEN
  What wilt thou do? Thou wilt not murder me?
  Help, ho!
POLONIUS, ⌜*behind the arras*⌝   What ho! Help!
HAMLET
  How now, a rat? Dead for a ducat, dead.
            ⌜*He ⟨kills Polonius⟩ by thrusting a rapier
                      through the arras.*⌝
POLONIUS, ⌜*behind the arras*⌝
  O, I am slain!   30
QUEEN   O me, what hast thou done?
HAMLET   Nay, I know not. Is it the King?
QUEEN
  O, what a rash and bloody deed is this!
HAMLET
  A bloody deed—almost as bad, good mother,
  As kill a king and marry with his brother.   35
QUEEN
  As kill a king?

HAMLET   Ay, lady, it was my word.
⌈*He pulls Polonius' body from behind the arras.*⌉
Thou wretched, rash, intruding fool, farewell.
I took thee for thy better. Take thy fortune.
Thou find'st to be too busy is some danger.   40
⌈*To Queen.*⌉ Leave wringing of your hands. Peace, sit
    you down,
And let me wring your heart; for so I shall
If it be made of penetrable stuff,
If damnèd custom have not brazed it so   45
That it be proof and bulwark against sense.

QUEEN
What have I done, that thou dar'st wag thy tongue
In noise so rude against me?

HAMLET   Such an act
That blurs the grace and blush of modesty,   50
Calls virtue hypocrite, takes off the rose
From the fair forehead of an innocent love
And sets a blister there, makes marriage vows
As false as dicers' oaths—O, such a deed
As from the body of contraction plucks   55
The very soul, and sweet religion makes
A rhapsody of words! Heaven's face does glow
O'er this solidity and compound mass
With heated visage, as against the doom,
Is thought-sick at the act.   60

QUEEN   Ay me, what act
That roars so loud and thunders in the index?

HAMLET
Look here upon this picture and on this,
The counterfeit presentment of two brothers.
See what a grace was seated on this brow,   65
Hyperion's curls, the front of Jove himself,
An eye like Mars' to threaten and command,
A station like the herald Mercury
New-lighted on a ⟨heaven⟩-kissing hill,

A combination and a form indeed   70
Where every god did seem to set his seal
To give the world assurance of a man.
This was your husband. Look you now what follows.
Here is your husband, like a mildewed ear
Blasting his wholesome brother. Have you eyes?   75
Could you on this fair mountain leave to feed
And batten on this moor? Ha! Have you eyes?
You cannot call it love, for at your age
The heyday in the blood is tame, it's humble
And waits upon the judgment; and what judgment   80
Would step from this to this? [Sense sure you have,
Else could you not have motion; but sure that sense
Is apoplexed; for madness would not err,
Nor sense to ecstasy was ne'er so thralled,
But it reserved some quantity of choice   85
To serve in such a difference.] What devil was 't
That thus hath cozened you at hoodman-blind?
[Eyes without feeling, feeling without sight,
Ears without hands or eyes, smelling sans all,
Or but a sickly part of one true sense   90
Could not so mope.] O shame, where is thy blush?
Rebellious hell,
If thou canst mutine in a matron's bones,
To flaming youth let virtue be as wax
And melt in her own fire. Proclaim no shame   95
When the compulsive ardor gives the charge,
Since frost itself as actively doth burn,
And reason ⟨panders⟩ will.
QUEEN   O Hamlet, speak no more!
       Thou turn'st my eyes into my ⟨very⟩ soul,   100
       And there I see such black and ⟨grainèd⟩ spots
       As will ⟨not⟩ leave their tint.
HAMLET   Nay, but to live
       In the rank sweat of an enseamèd bed,
       Stewed in corruption, honeying and making love   105
       Over the nasty sty!

QUEEN   O, speak to me no more!
  These words like daggers enter in my ears.
  No more, sweet Hamlet!
HAMLET   A murderer and a villain,   110
  A slave that is not twentieth part the ⟨tithe⟩
  Of your precedent lord; a vice of kings,
  A cutpurse of the empire and the rule,
  That from a shelf the precious diadem stole
  And put it in his pocket—   115
QUEEN   No more!
HAMLET   A king of shreds and patches—

Enter Ghost.

  Save me and hover o'er me with your wings,
  You heavenly guards!—What would your gracious
    figure?   120
QUEEN   Alas, he's mad.
HAMLET
  Do you not come your tardy son to chide,
  That, lapsed in time and passion, lets go by
  Th' important acting of your dread command?
  O, say!   125
GHOST   Do not forget. This visitation
  Is but to whet thy almost blunted purpose.
  But look, amazement on thy mother sits.
  O, step between her and her fighting soul.
  Conceit in weakest bodies strongest works.   130
  Speak to her, Hamlet.
HAMLET   How is it with you, lady?
QUEEN   Alas, how is 't with you,
  That you do bend your eye on vacancy
  And with th' incorporal air do hold discourse?   135
  Forth at your eyes your spirits wildly peep,
  And, as the sleeping soldiers in th' alarm,
  Your bedded hair, like life in excrements,
  Start up and stand an end. O gentle son,

Upon the heat and flame of thy distemper   140
Sprinkle cool patience! Whereon do you look?

HAMLET
On him, on him! Look you how pale he glares.
His form and cause conjoined, preaching to stones,
Would make them capable. ⌜*To the Ghost.*⌝ Do not
    look upon me,   145
Lest with this piteous action you convert
My stern effects. Then what I have to do
Will want true color—tears perchance for blood.

QUEEN   To whom do you speak this?

HAMLET   Do you see nothing there?   150

QUEEN
Nothing at all; yet all that is I see.

HAMLET   Nor did you nothing hear?

QUEEN   No, nothing but ourselves.

HAMLET
Why, look you there, look how it steals away!
My father, in his habit as he lived!   155
Look where he goes even now out at the portal!
                                        Ghost exits.

QUEEN
This is the very coinage of your brain.
This bodiless creation ecstasy ~~~~ madness
Is very cunning in.

HAMLET   ⟨Ecstasy?⟩   160
My pulse as yours doth temperately keep time
And makes as healthful music. It is not madness
That I have uttered. Bring me to the test,
And ⟨I⟩ the matter will reword, which madness
Would gambol from. Mother, for love of grace,   165
Lay not that flattering unction to your soul
That not your trespass but my madness speaks.
It will but skin and film the ulcerous place,
Whiles rank corruption, mining all within,
Infects unseen. Confess yourself to heaven,   170

Repent what's past, avoid what is to come,
And do not spread the compost on the weeds
To make them ranker. Forgive me this my virtue,
For, in the fatness of these pursy times,
Virtue itself of vice must pardon beg,   175
Yea, curb and woo for leave to do him good.

QUEEN
O Hamlet, thou hast cleft my heart in twain!

HAMLET
O, throw away the worser part of it,
And ⟨live⟩ the purer with the other half!
Good night. But go not to my uncle's bed.   180
Assume a virtue if you have it not.
[That monster, custom, who all sense doth eat,
Of habits devil, is angel yet in this,
That to the use of actions fair and good
He likewise gives a frock or livery   185
That aptly is put on.] Refrain ⟨tonight,⟩
And that shall lend a kind of easiness
To the next abstinence, [the next more easy;
For use almost can change the stamp of nature
And either ⌜ . . . ⌝ the devil or throw him out   190
With wondrous potency.] Once more, good night,
And, when you are desirous to be blest,
I'll blessing beg of you. For this same lord
                                ⌜*Pointing to Polonius.*⌝
I do repent; but heaven hath pleased it so
To punish me with this and this with me,   195
That I must be their scourge and minister.
I will bestow him and will answer well
The death I gave him. So, again, good night.
I must be cruel only to be kind.
This bad begins, and worse remains behind.   200
[One word more, good lady.]

QUEEN   What shall I do?

HAMLET
    Not this by no means that I bid you do:
    Let the bloat king tempt you again to bed,
    Pinch wanton on your cheek, call you his mouse,   205
    And let him, for a pair of reechy kisses
    Or paddling in your neck with his damned fingers,
    Make you to ravel all this matter out
    That I essentially am not in madness,
    But mad in craft. 'Twere good you let him know,   210
    For who that's but a queen, fair, sober, wise,
    Would from a paddock, from a bat, a gib,
    Such dear concernings hide? Who would do so?
    No, in despite of sense and secrecy,
    Unpeg the basket on the house's top,   215
    Let the birds fly, and like the famous ape,
    To try conclusions, in the basket creep
    And break your own neck down.
QUEEN
    Be thou assured, if words be made of breath
    And breath of life, I have no life to breathe   220
    What thou hast said to me.
HAMLET
    I must to England, you know that.
QUEEN   Alack,
    I had forgot! 'Tis so concluded on.
HAMLET
    [There's letters sealed; and my two schoolfellows,   225
    Whom I will trust as I will adders fanged,
    They bear the mandate; they must sweep my way
    And marshal me to knavery. Let it work,
    For 'tis the sport to have the enginer
    Hoist with his own petard; and 't shall go hard   230
    But I will delve one yard below their mines
    And blow them at the moon. O, 'tis most sweet
    When in one line two crafts directly meet.]
    This man shall set me packing.

I'll lug the guts into the neighbor room.   235
Mother, good night indeed. This counselor
Is now most still, most secret, and most grave,
Who was in life a foolish prating knave.—
Come, sir, to draw toward an end with you.
Good night, mother.   240
                ⌜*They*⌝ *exit,* ⟨*Hamlet tugging in Polonius.*⟩

⌜ACT 4⌝

⌜Scene 1⌝

*Enter King and Queen, with Rosencrantz and
Guildenstern.*

KING
There's matter in these sighs; these profound heaves
You must translate; 'tis fit we understand them.
Where is your son?

QUEEN
[Bestow this place on us a little while.]
⌜*Rosencrantz and Guildenstern exit.*⌝
Ah, mine own lord, what have I seen tonight!   5

KING   What, Gertrude? How does Hamlet?

QUEEN
Mad as the sea and wind when both contend
Which is the mightier. In his lawless fit,
Behind the arras hearing something stir,
Whips out his rapier, cries "A rat, a rat,"   10
And in this brainish apprehension kills
The unseen good old man.

KING   O heavy deed!
It had been so with us, had we been there.
His liberty is full of threats to all—   15
To you yourself, to us, to everyone.
Alas, how shall this bloody deed be answered?
It will be laid to us, whose providence

Should have kept short, restrained, and out of haunt
This mad young man. But so much was our love,   20
We would not understand what was most fit,
But, like the owner of a foul disease,
To keep it from divulging, let it feed
Even on the pith of life. Where is he gone?

QUEEN
To draw apart the body he hath killed,   25
O'er whom his very madness, like some ore
Among a mineral of metals base,
Shows itself pure: he weeps for what is done.

KING   O Gertrude, come away!
The sun no sooner shall the mountains touch   30
But we will ship him hence; and this vile deed
We must with all our majesty and skill
Both countenance and excuse.—Ho, Guildenstern!

Enter Rosencrantz and Guildenstern.

Friends both, go join you with some further aid.
Hamlet in madness hath Polonius slain,   35
And from his mother's closet hath he dragged him.
Go seek him out, speak fair, and bring the body
Into the chapel. I pray you, haste in this.
⟨*Rosencrantz and Guildenstern exit.*⟩
Come, Gertrude, we'll call up our wisest friends
And let them know both what we mean to do   40
And what's untimely done. ⌐ . . . ⌐
[Whose whisper o'er the world's diameter,
As level as the cannon to his blank
Transports his poisoned shot, may miss our name
And hit the woundless air.] O, come away!   45
My soul is full of discord and dismay.
                                              They exit.

⌜Scene 2⌝
⟨*Enter Hamlet.*⟩

HAMLET　Safely stowed.

⟨GENTLEMEN, *within*　Hamlet! Lord Hamlet!⟩

HAMLET　But soft, what noise? Who calls on Hamlet?
　　O, here they come.

　　Enter Rosencrantz, ⟨Guildenstern,⟩ and others.

ROSENCRANTZ
　　What have you done, my lord, with the dead body?　　5

HAMLET
　　⟨Compounded⟩ it with dust, whereto 'tis kin.

ROSENCRANTZ
　　Tell us where 'tis, that we may take it thence
　　And bear it to the chapel.

HAMLET　Do not believe it.

ROSENCRANTZ　Believe what?　　10

HAMLET　That I can keep your counsel and not mine
　　own. Besides, to be demanded of a sponge, what
　　replication should be made by the son of a king?

ROSENCRANTZ　Take you me for a sponge, my lord?

HAMLET　Ay, sir, that soaks up the King's countenance,　　15
　　his rewards, his authorities. But such officers do the
　　King best service in the end. He keeps them like ⟨an
　　ape⟩ an apple in the corner of his jaw, first mouthed,
　　to be last swallowed. When he needs what you have
　　gleaned, it is but squeezing you, and, sponge, you　　20
　　shall be dry again.

ROSENCRANTZ　I understand you not, my lord.

HAMLET　I am glad of it. A knavish speech sleeps in a
　　foolish ear.

ROSENCRANTZ　My lord, you must tell us where the　　25
　　body is and go with us to the King.

HAMLET　The body is with the King, but the King is not
　　with the body. The King is a thing—

GUILDENSTERN A "thing," my lord?

HAMLET Of nothing. Bring me to him. ⟨Hide fox, and   30
all after!⟩

They exit.

⌐Scene 3⌐
Enter King and two or three.

KING
I have sent to seek him and to find the body.
How dangerous is it that this man goes loose!
Yet must not we put the strong law on him.
He's loved of the distracted multitude,
Who like not in their judgment, but their eyes;   5
And, where 'tis so, th' offender's scourge is weighed,
But never the offense. To bear all smooth and even,
This sudden sending him away must seem
Deliberate pause. Diseases desperate grown
By desperate appliance are relieved   10
Or not at all.

Enter Rosencrantz.

How now, what hath befallen?

ROSENCRANTZ
Where the dead body is bestowed, my lord,
We cannot get from him.

KING   But where is he?   15

ROSENCRANTZ
Without, my lord; guarded, to know your pleasure.

KING
Bring him before us.

ROSENCRANTZ   Ho! Bring in the lord.

They enter ⌐with Hamlet.⌐

KING Now, Hamlet, where's Polonius?

HAMLET At supper.   2⟨

KING   At supper where?

HAMLET   Not where he eats, but where he is eaten. A
certain convocation of politic worms are e'en at
him. Your worm is your only emperor for diet. We
fat all creatures else to fat us, and we fat ourselves   25
for maggots. Your fat king and your lean beggar is
but variable service—two dishes but to one table.
That's the end.

[KING   Alas, alas!

HAMLET   A man may fish with the worm that hath eat   30
of a king and eat of the fish that hath fed of that
worm.]

KING   What dost thou mean by this?

HAMLET   Nothing but to show you how a king may go a
progress through the guts of a beggar.   35

KING   Where is Polonius?

HAMLET   In heaven. Send thither to see. If your messenger find him not there, seek him i' th' other
place yourself. But if, indeed, you find him not
within this month, you shall nose him as you go up   40
the stairs into the lobby.

KING, ⌜to Attendants.⌝   Go, seek him there.

HAMLET   He will stay till you come.   ⌜Attendants exit.⌝

KING
Hamlet, this deed, for thine especial safety
(Which we do tender, as we dearly grieve   45
For that which thou hast done) must send thee
hence
(With fiery quickness.) Therefore prepare thyself.
The bark is ready, and the wind at help,
Th' associates tend, and everything is bent   50
For England.

HAMLET   For England?

KING   Ay, Hamlet.

HAMLET   Good.

KING
So is it, if thou knew'st our purposes.   55

HAMLET
    I see a cherub that sees them. But come, for
      England.
    Farewell, dear mother.
KING   Thy loving father, Hamlet.
HAMLET
    My mother. Father and mother is man and wife,   60
    Man and wife is one flesh, ⟨and⟩ so, my mother.—
    Come, for England.   *He exits.*
KING
    Follow him at foot; tempt him with speed aboard.
    Delay it not. I'll have him hence tonight.
    Away, for everything is sealed and done   65
    That else leans on th' affair. Pray you, make haste.
                  ⌜*All but the King exit.*⌝
    And England, if my love thou hold'st at aught
    (As my great power thereof may give thee sense,
    Since yet thy cicatrice looks raw and red
    After the Danish sword, and thy free awe   70
    Pays homage to us), thou mayst not coldly set
    Our sovereign process, which imports at full,
    By letters congruing to that effect,
    The present death of Hamlet. Do it, England,
    For like the hectic in my blood he rages,   75
    And thou must cure me. Till I know 'tis done,
    Howe'er my haps, my joys ⟨were ne'er begun.⟩
                        He exits.

⌜Scene 4⌝
Enter Fortinbras with his army over the stage.

FORTINBRAS
    Go, Captain, from me greet the Danish king.
    Tell him that by his license Fortinbras
    Craves the conveyance of a promised march
    Over his kingdom. You know the rendezvous.

If that his Majesty would aught with us,   5
We shall express our duty in his eye;
And let him know so.
CAPTAIN   I will do 't, my lord.
FORTINBRAS   Go softly on.   ⌐*All but the Captain exit.*⌐

[*Enter Hamlet, Rosencrantz,* ⌐*Guildenstern,*⌐ *and others.*

HAMLET   Good sir, whose powers are these?   10
CAPTAIN   They are of Norway, sir.
HAMLET   How purposed, sir, I pray you?
CAPTAIN   Against some part of Poland.
HAMLET   Who commands them, sir?
CAPTAIN
The nephew to old Norway, Fortinbras.   15
HAMLET
Goes it against the main of Poland, sir,
Or for some frontier?
CAPTAIN
Truly to speak, and with no addition,
We go to gain a little patch of ground
That hath in it no profit but the name.   20
To pay five ducats, five, I would not farm it;
Nor will it yield to Norway or the Pole
A ranker rate, should it be sold in fee.
HAMLET
Why, then, the Polack never will defend it.
CAPTAIN
Yes, it is already garrisoned.   25
HAMLET
Two thousand souls and twenty thousand ducats
Will not debate the question of this straw.
This is th' impostume of much wealth and peace,
That inward breaks and shows no cause without
Why the man dies.—I humbly thank you, sir.   30
CAPTAIN   God be wi' you, sir.   ⌐*He exits.*⌐
ROSENCRANTZ   Will 't please you go, my lord?

HAMLET
   I'll be with you straight. Go a little before.
                     ⌈*All but Hamlet exit.*⌉

How all occasions do inform against me
And spur my dull revenge. What is a man   35
If his chief good and market of his time
Be but to sleep and feed? A beast, no more.
Sure He that made us with such large discourse,
Looking before and after, gave us not
That capability and godlike reason   40
To fust in us unused. Now whether it be
Bestial oblivion or some craven scruple
Of thinking too precisely on th' event
(A thought which, quartered, hath but one part
   wisdom   45
And ever three parts coward), I do not know
Why yet I live to say "This thing's to do,"
Sith I have cause, and will, and strength, and means
To do 't. Examples gross as earth exhort me:
Witness this army of such mass and charge,   50
Led by a delicate and tender prince,
Whose spirit with divine ambition puffed
Makes mouths at the invisible event,
Exposing what is mortal and unsure
To all that fortune, death, and danger dare,   55
Even for an eggshell. Rightly to be great
Is not to stir without great argument,
But greatly to find quarrel in a straw
When honor's at the stake. How stand I, then,
That have a father killed, a mother stained,   60
Excitements of my reason and my blood,
And let all sleep, while to my shame I see
The imminent death of twenty thousand men
That for a fantasy and trick of fame
Go to their graves like beds, fight for a plot   65
Whereon the numbers cannot try the cause,

Which is not tomb enough and continent
To hide the slain? O, from this time forth
My thoughts be bloody or be nothing worth!

            He exits.]

⌜Scene 5⌝
Enter Horatio, ⟨Queen,⟩ and a Gentleman.

QUEEN I will not speak with her.
GENTLEMAN She is importunate,
 Indeed distract; her mood will needs be pitied.
QUEEN What would she have?
GENTLEMAN
 She speaks much of her father, says she hears   5
 There's tricks i' th' world, and hems, and beats her
  heart,
 Spurns enviously at straws, speaks things in doubt
 That carry but half sense. Her speech is nothing,
 Yet the unshapèd use of it doth move   10
 The hearers to collection. They ⟨aim⟩ at it
 And botch the words up fit to their own thoughts;
 Which, as her winks and nods and gestures yield
  them,
 Indeed would make one think there might be   15
  thought,
 Though nothing sure, yet much unhappily.
HORATIO
 'Twere good she were spoken with, for she may
  strew
 Dangerous conjectures in ill-breeding minds.   20
⌜QUEEN⌝ Let her come in.   ⌜*Gentleman exits.*⌝
 ⌜*Aside.*⌝ To my sick soul (as sin's true nature is),
 Each toy seems prologue to some great amiss.
 So full of artless jealousy is guilt,
 It spills itself in fearing to be spilt.   25

⟨*Enter Ophelia distracted.*⟩

OPHELIA
Where is the beauteous Majesty of Denmark?

QUEEN   How now, Ophelia?

OPHELIA ⌜*sings*⌝
> *How should I your true love know*
> *From another one?*
> *By his cockle hat and staff*   30
> *And his sandal shoon.*

QUEEN
Alas, sweet lady, what imports this song?

OPHELIA   Say you? Nay, pray you, mark.
⌜*Sings.*⌝   *He is dead and gone, lady,*
> *He is dead and gone;*   35
> *At his head a grass-green turf,*
> *At his heels a stone.*

Oh, ho!

QUEEN   Nay, but Ophelia—

OPHELIA   Pray you, mark.   40
⌜*Sings.*⌝   *White his shroud as the mountain snow—*

Enter King.

QUEEN   Alas, look here, my lord.

OPHELIA ⌜*sings*⌝
> *Larded all with sweet flowers;*
> *Which bewept to the ground did not go*
> *With true-love showers.*   45

KING   How do you, pretty lady?

OPHELIA   Well, God dild you. They say the owl was a
baker's daughter. Lord, we know what we are but
know not what we may be. God be at your table.

KING   Conceit upon her father.   50

OPHELIA   Pray let's have no words of this, but when
they ask you what it means, say you this:

⌜*Sings.*⌝ *Tomorrow is Saint Valentine's day,*
    All in the morning betime,
    And I a maid at your window, 55
    To be your Valentine.
Then up he rose and donned his clothes
    And dupped the chamber door,
Let in the maid, that out a maid
    Never departed more. 60

KING   Pretty Ophelia—

OPHELIA
Indeed, without an oath, I'll make an end on 't:
⌜*Sings.*⌝ *By Gis and by Saint Charity,*
    Alack and fie for shame,
Young men will do 't, if they come to 't; 65
    By Cock, they are to blame.
Quoth she "Before you tumbled me,
    You promised me to wed."
He answers:
    "So would I 'a done, by yonder sun, 70
    An thou hadst not come to my bed."

KING   How long hath she been thus?

OPHELIA   I hope all will be well. We must be patient,
but I cannot choose but weep to think they would
lay him i' th' cold ground. My brother shall know of 75
it. And so I thank you for your good counsel. Come,
my coach! Good night, ladies, good night, sweet
ladies, good night, good night.   ⟨*She exits.*⟩

KING
Follow her close; give her good watch, I pray you.
                     ⌜*Horatio exits.*⌝
O, this is the poison of deep grief. It springs 80°
All from her father's death, and now behold!
O Gertrude, Gertrude,
When sorrows come, they come not single spies,
But in battalions: first, her father slain;
Next, your son gone, and he most violent author 85
Of his own just remove; the people muddied,

Thick, and unwholesome in ⟨their⟩ thoughts and
   whispers
For good Polonius' death, and we have done but
   greenly   90
In hugger-mugger to inter him; poor Ophelia
Divided from herself and her fair judgment,
Without the which we are pictures or mere beasts;
Last, and as much containing as all these,
Her brother is in secret come from France,   95
Feeds on ⟨his⟩ wonder, keeps himself in clouds,
And wants not buzzers to infect his ear
With pestilent speeches of his father's death,
Wherein necessity, of matter beggared,
Will nothing stick our person to arraign   100
In ear and ear. O, my dear Gertrude, this,
Like to a murd'ring piece, in many places
Gives me superfluous death.

                         A noise within.

⟨QUEEN   Alack, what noise is this?⟩
KING   Attend!   105
   Where is my Switzers? Let them guard the door.

              Enter a Messenger.

   What is the matter?
MESSENGER   Save yourself, my lord.
   The ocean, overpeering of his list,
Eats not the flats with more impiteous haste   110
Than young Laertes, in a riotous head,
O'erbears your officers. The rabble call him "lord,"
And, as the world were now but to begin,
Antiquity forgot, custom not known,
The ratifiers and props of every word,   115
⟨They⟩ cry "Choose we, Laertes shall be king!"
Caps, hands, and tongues applaud it to the clouds,
"Laertes shall be king! Laertes king!"
                        A noise within.

QUEEN
   How cheerfully on the false trail they cry.
   O, this is counter, you false Danish dogs!   120
KING   The doors are broke.

               Enter Laertes with others.

LAERTES
   Where is this king?—Sirs, stand you all without.
ALL   No, let's come in!
LAERTES   I pray you, give me leave.
ALL   We will, we will.   125
LAERTES
   I thank you. Keep the door. ⌜*Followers exit.*⌝ O, thou
      vile king,
   Give me my father!
QUEEN   Calmly, good Laertes.
LAERTES
   That drop of blood that's calm proclaims me   130
      bastard,
   Cries "cuckold" to my father, brands the harlot
   Even here between the chaste unsmirchèd brow
   Of my true mother.
KING   What is the cause, Laertes,   135
   That thy rebellion looks so giant-like?—
   Let him go, Gertrude. Do not fear our person.
   There's such divinity doth hedge a king
   That treason can but peep to what it would,
   Acts little of his will.—Tell me, Laertes,   140
   Why thou art thus incensed.—Let him go,
      Gertrude.—
   Speak, man.
LAERTES   Where is my father?
KING   Dead.   145
QUEEN
   But not by him.
KING   Let him demand his fill.

LAERTES
 How came he dead? I'll not be juggled with.
 To hell, allegiance! Vows, to the blackest devil!
 Conscience and grace, to the profoundest pit!   150
 I dare damnation. To this point I stand,
 That both the worlds I give to negligence,
 Let come what comes, only I'll be revenged
 Most throughly for my father.

KING Who shall stay you?   155

LAERTES My will, not all the ⟨world.⟩
 And for my means, I'll husband them so well
 They shall go far with little.

KING   Good Laertes,
 If you desire to know the certainty   160
 Of your dear father, is 't writ in your revenge
 That, swoopstake, you will draw both friend and
  foe,
 Winner and loser?

LAERTES None but his enemies.   165

KING Will you know them, then?

LAERTES
 To his good friends thus wide I'll ope my arms
 And, like the kind life-rend'ring pelican,
 Repast them with my blood.

KING   Why, now you speak   170
 Like a good child and a true gentleman.
 That I am guiltless of your father's death
 And am most sensibly in grief for it,
 It shall as level to your judgment 'pear
 As day does to your eye.   175

     A noise within: ⟨Let her come in.

LAERTES⟩ How now, what noise is that?

     Enter Ophelia.

 O heat, dry up my brains! Tears seven times salt
 Burn out the sense and virtue of mine eye!

By heaven, thy madness shall be paid with weight 180
Till our scale turn the beam! O rose of May,
Dear maid, kind sister, sweet Ophelia!
O heavens, is 't possible a young maid's wits
Should be as mortal as ⟨an old⟩ man's life?
⟨Nature is fine in love, and, where 'tis fine, 185
It sends some precious instance of itself
After the thing it loves.⟩

OPHELIA ⌜*sings*⌝
    They bore him barefaced on the bier,
    ⟨*Hey non nonny, nonny, hey nonny,*⟩
    And in his grave rained many a tear. 190
Fare you well, my dove.

LAERTES
Hadst thou thy wits and didst persuade revenge,
It could not move thus.

OPHELIA You must sing "A-down a-down"—and you
"Call him a-down-a."—O, how the wheel becomes 195
it! It is the false steward that stole his master's
daughter.

LAERTES This nothing's more than matter.

OPHELIA There's rosemary, that's for remembrance.
Pray you, love, remember. And there is pansies, 200
that's for thoughts.

LAERTES A document in madness: thoughts and remembrance fitted.

OPHELIA There's fennel for you, and columbines.
There's rue for you, and here's some for me; we 205
may call it herb of grace o' Sundays. You ⟨must⟩ wear
your rue with a difference. There's a daisy. I would
give you some violets, but they withered all when
my father died. They say he made a good end.
⌜*Sings.*⌝   *For bonny sweet Robin is all my joy.* 210

LAERTES
Thought and afflictions, passion, hell itself
She turns to favor and to prettiness.

OPHELIA ⌜*sings*⌝

> *And will he not come again?*
> *And will he not come again?*
>> *No, no, he is dead.*
>> *Go to thy deathbed.*
> *He never will come again.*

> *His beard was as white as snow,*
> ⟨*All*⟩ *flaxen was his poll.*
>> *He is gone, he is gone,*
>> *And we cast away moan.*
> *God 'a mercy on his soul.*

And of all Christians' souls, ⟨I pray God.⟩ God be wi'
you.   ⟨*She exits.*⟩

LAERTES Do you ⟨see⟩ this, O God?   225

KING
Laertes, I must commune with your grief,
Or you deny me right. Go but apart,
Make choice of whom your wisest friends you will,
And they shall hear and judge 'twixt you and me.
If by direct or by collateral hand   230
They find us touched, we will our kingdom give,
Our crown, our life, and all that we call ours,
To you in satisfaction; but if not,
Be you content to lend your patience to us,
And we shall jointly labor with your soul   235
To give it due content.

LAERTES   Let this be so.
His means of death, his obscure funeral
(No trophy, sword, nor hatchment o'er his bones,
No noble rite nor formal ostentation)   240
Cry to be heard, as 'twere from heaven to earth,
That I must call 't in question.

KING   So you shall,
And where th' offense is, let the great ax fall.
I pray you, go with me.   245

They exit.

⌜Scene 6⌝
Enter Horatio and others.

HORATIO What are they that would speak with me?

GENTLEMAN Seafaring men, sir. They say they have
letters for you.

HORATIO Let them come in. ⌜*Gentleman exits.*⌝ I do not
know from what part of the world I should be   5
greeted, if not from Lord Hamlet.

Enter Sailors.

SAILOR God bless you, sir.

HORATIO Let Him bless thee too.

SAILOR He shall, sir, ⟨an 't⟩ please Him. There's a letter
for you, sir. It came from th' ambassador that was   10
bound for England—if your name be Horatio, as I
am let to know it is.   ⌜*He hands Horatio a letter.*⌝

HORATIO ⟨*reads the letter*⟩ *Horatio, when thou shalt have*
overlooked this, give these fellows some means to the
King. They have letters for him. Ere we were two days   15
old at sea, a pirate of very warlike appointment gave
us chase. Finding ourselves too slow of sail, we put on
a compelled valor, and in the grapple I boarded them.
On the instant, they got clear of our ship; so I alone
became their prisoner. They have dealt with me like   20
thieves of mercy, but they knew what they did: I am to
do a ⟨good⟩ turn for them. Let the King have the letters
I have sent, and repair thou to me with as much speed
as thou wouldst fly death. I have words to speak in
thine ear will make thee dumb; yet are they much too   25
light for the ⟨bore⟩ of the matter. These good fellows
will bring thee where I am. Rosencrantz and Guilden-
stern hold their course for England; of them I have
much to tell thee. Farewell.

                    ⟨*He*⟩ *that thou knowest thine,*   30
                                      Hamlet.

Come, I will ⟨give⟩ you way for these your letters
And do 't the speedier that you may direct me
To him from whom you brought them.

They exit.

⌜Scene 7⌝
Enter King and Laertes.

KING
Now must your conscience my acquittance seal,
And you must put me in your heart for friend,
Sith you have heard, and with a knowing ear,
That he which hath your noble father slain
Pursued my life.   5
LAERTES   It well appears. But tell me
Why you ⟨proceeded⟩ not against these feats,
So criminal and so capital in nature,
As by your safety, greatness, wisdom, all things else,
You mainly were stirred up.   10
KING O, for two special reasons,
Which may to you perhaps seem much unsinewed,
But yet to me they're strong. The Queen his mother
Lives almost by his looks, and for myself
(My virtue or my plague, be it either which),   15
She is so ⟨conjunctive⟩ to my life and soul
That, as the star moves not but in his sphere,
I could not but by her. The other motive
Why to a public count I might not go
Is the great love the general gender bear him,   20
Who, dipping all his faults in their affection,
Work like the spring that turneth wood to stone,
Convert his gyves to graces, so that my arrows,
Too slightly timbered for so ⟨loud a wind,⟩
Would have reverted to my bow again,   25
But not where I have aimed them.
LAERTES
And so have I a noble father lost,

A sister driven into desp'rate terms,
Whose worth, if praises may go back again,
Stood challenger on mount of all the age   30
For her perfections. But my revenge will come.

KING

Break not your sleeps for that. You must not think
That we are made of stuff so flat and dull
That we can let our beard be shook with danger
And think it pastime. You shortly shall hear more.   35
I loved your father, and we love ourself,
And that, I hope, will teach you to imagine—

Enter a Messenger with letters.

⟨How now? What news?

MESSENGER   Letters, my lord, from
    Hamlet.⟩   40
These to your Majesty, this to the Queen.

KING   From Hamlet? Who brought them?

MESSENGER

Sailors, my lord, they say. I saw them not.
They were given me by Claudio. He received them
[Of him that brought them.]   45

KING   Laertes, you shall hear
    them.—
Leave us.   ⟨*Messenger exits.*⟩
    ⌜*Reads.*⌝ *High and mighty, you shall know I am set*
    naked on your kingdom. Tomorrow shall I beg leave to   50
    see your kingly eyes, when I shall (first asking ⟨your⟩
    pardon) thereunto recount the occasion of my sudden
    ⟨and more strange⟩ return. ⟨*Hamlet.*⟩
What should this mean? Are all the rest come back?
Or is it some abuse and no such thing?   55

LAERTES   Know you the hand?

KING   'Tis Hamlet's character. "Naked"—
And in a postscript here, he says "alone."
Can you ⟨advise⟩ me?

LAERTES
   I am lost in it, my lord. But let him come.   60
   It warms the very sickness in my heart
   That I ⟨shall⟩ live and tell him to his teeth
   "Thus didst thou."
KING   If it be so, Laertes
   (As how should it be so? how otherwise?),   65
   Will you be ruled by me?
LAERTES   Ay, my lord,
   So you will not o'errule me to a peace.
KING
   To thine own peace. If he be now returned,
   As ⟨checking⟩ at his voyage, and that he means   70
   No more to undertake it, I will work him
   To an exploit, now ripe in my device,
   Under the which he shall not choose but fall;
   And for his death no wind of blame shall breathe,
   But even his mother shall uncharge the practice   75
   And call it accident.
[LAERTES   My lord, I will be ruled,
   The rather if you could devise it so
   That I might be the organ.
KING   It falls right.   80
   You have been talked of since your travel much,
   And that in Hamlet's hearing, for a quality
   Wherein they say you shine. Your sum of parts
   Did not together pluck such envy from him
   As did that one, and that, in my regard,   85
   Of the unworthiest siege.
LAERTES   What part is that, my lord?
KING
   A very ribbon in the cap of youth—
   Yet needful too, for youth no less becomes
   The light and careless livery that it wears   90
   Than settled age his sables and his weeds,
   Importing health and graveness.] Two months since

Here was a gentleman of Normandy.
I have seen myself, and served against, the French,
And they can well on horseback, but this gallant   95
Had witchcraft in 't. He grew unto his seat,
And to such wondrous doing brought his horse
As had he been encorpsed and demi-natured
With the brave beast. So far he topped ⟨my⟩ thought
That I in forgery of shapes and tricks   100
Come short of what he did.
LAERTES   A Norman was 't?
KING   A Norman.
LAERTES
Upon my life, Lamord.
KING   The very same.   105
LAERTES
I know him well. He is the brooch indeed
And gem of all the nation.
KING   He made confession of you
And gave you such a masterly report
For art and exercise in your defense,   110
And for your rapier most especial,
That he cried out 'twould be a sight indeed
If one could match you. [The 'scrimers of their
        nation
He swore had neither motion, guard, nor eye,   115
If you opposed them.] Sir, this report of his
Did Hamlet so envenom with his envy
That he could nothing do but wish and beg
Your sudden coming-o'er, to play with you.
Now out of this—   120
LAERTES   What out of this, my lord?
KING
Laertes, was your father dear to you?
Or are you like the painting of a sorrow,
A face without a heart?
LAERTES   Why ask you this?   125

KING
　Not that I think you did not love your father,
　But that I know love is begun by time
　And that I see, in passages of proof,
　Time qualifies the spark and fire of it.
　[There lives within the very flame of love　　　　　130
　A kind of wick or snuff that will abate it,
　And nothing is at a like goodness still;
　For goodness, growing to a pleurisy,
　Dies in his own too-much. That we would do
　We should do when we would; for this "would"　　135
　　changes
　And hath abatements and delays as many
　As there are tongues, are hands, are accidents;
　And then this "should" is like a ⌈spendthrift⌉ sigh,
　That hurts by easing. But to the quick of th' ulcer:]　140
　Hamlet comes back; what would you undertake
　To show yourself indeed your father's son
　More than in words?
LAERTES　　　　　　　To cut his throat i' th' church.
KING
　No place indeed should murder sanctuarize;　　　145
　Revenge should have no bounds. But, good Laertes,
　Will you do this? Keep close within your chamber.
　Hamlet, returned, shall know you are come home.
　We'll put on those shall praise your excellence
　And set a double varnish on the fame　　　　　150
　The Frenchman gave you; bring you, in fine,
　　together
　And wager ⟨on⟩ your heads. He, being remiss,
　Most generous, and free from all contriving,
　Will not peruse the foils, so that with ease,　　155
　Or with a little shuffling, you may choose
　A sword unbated, and in a ⟨pass⟩ of practice
　Requite him for your father.

LAERTES   I will do 't,
  And for ⟨that⟩ purpose I'll anoint my sword.   160
  I bought an unction of a mountebank
  So mortal that, but dip a knife in it,
  Where it draws blood no cataplasm so rare,
  Collected from all simples that have virtue
  Under the moon, can save the thing from death   165
  That is but scratched withal. I'll touch my point
  With this contagion, that, if I gall him slightly,
  It may be death.
KING   Let's further think of this,
  Weigh what convenience both of time and means   170
  May fit us to our shape. If this should fail,
  And that our drift look through our bad
    performance,
  'Twere better not assayed. Therefore this project
  Should have a back or second that might hold   175
  If this did blast in proof. Soft, let me see.
  We'll make a solemn wager on your cunnings—
  I ha 't!
  When in your motion you are hot and dry
  (As make your bouts more violent to that end)   180
  And that he calls for drink, I'll have prepared
    him
  A chalice for the nonce, whereon but sipping,
  If he by chance escape your venomed stuck,
  Our purpose may hold there.—But stay, what   185
    noise?

Enter Queen.

QUEEN
  One woe doth tread upon another's heel,
  So fast they follow. Your sister's drowned, Laertcs.
LAERTES   Drowned? O, where?
QUEEN
  There is a willow grows askant the brook   190

That shows his ⟨hoar⟩ leaves in the glassy stream.
Therewith fantastic garlands did she make
Of crowflowers, nettles, daisies, and long purples,
That liberal shepherds give a grosser name,
But our cold maids do "dead men's fingers" call   195
  them.
There on the pendant boughs her coronet weeds
Clamb'ring to hang, an envious sliver broke,
When down her weedy trophies and herself
Fell in the weeping brook. Her clothes spread wide,   200
And mermaid-like awhile they bore her up,
Which time she chanted snatches of old lauds,
As one incapable of her own distress
Or like a creature native and endued
Unto that element. But long it could not be   205
Till that her garments, heavy with their drink,
Pulled the poor wretch from her melodious lay
To muddy death.
LAERTES   Alas, then she is drowned.
QUEEN Drowned, drowned.   210
LAERTES
Too much of water hast thou, poor Ophelia,
And therefore I forbid my tears. But yet
It is our trick; nature her custom holds,
Let shame say what it will. When these are gone,
The woman will be out.—Adieu, my lord.   215
I have a speech o' fire that fain would blaze,
But that this folly drowns it.   *He exits.*
KING   Let's follow, Gertrude.
How much I had to do to calm his rage!
Now fear I this will give it start again.   220
Therefore, let's follow.
                        They exit.

⌐ACT 5⌐

⌐Scene 1⌐
Enter ⌐*Gravedigger and Another.*⌐

⌐GRAVEDIGGER⌐ Is she to be buried in Christian burial,
when she willfully seeks her own salvation?

OTHER I tell thee she is. Therefore make her grave
straight. The crowner hath sat on her and finds it
Christian burial.   5

⌐GRAVEDIGGER⌐ How can that be, unless she drowned
herself in her own defense?

OTHER Why, 'tis found so.

⌐GRAVEDIGGER⌐ It must be ⟨*se offendendo*;⟩ it cannot be
else. For here lies the point: if I drown myself   10
wittingly, it argues an act, and an act hath three
branches—it is to act, to do, to perform. ⟨Argal,⟩ she
drowned herself wittingly.

OTHER Nay, but hear you, goodman delver—

⌐GRAVEDIGGER⌐ Give me leave. Here lies the water;   15
good. Here stands the man; good. If the man go to
this water and drown himself, it is (will he, nill he)
he goes; mark you that. But if the water come to him
and drown him, he drowns not himself. Argal, he
that is not guilty of his own death shortens not his   20
own life.

OTHER But is this law?

⌐GRAVEDIGGER⌐ Ay, marry, is 't—crowner's 'quest law.

OTHER   Will you ha' the truth on 't? If this had not been
a gentlewoman, she should have been buried out o'   25
Christian burial.

⌜GRAVEDIGGER⌝   Why, there thou sayst. And the more
pity that great folk should have count'nance in this
world to drown or hang themselves more than
their even-Christian. Come, my spade. There is no   30
ancient gentlemen but gard'ners, ditchers, and
grave-makers. They hold up Adam's profession.

OTHER   Was he a gentleman?

⌜GRAVEDIGGER⌝   He was the first that ever bore arms.

⟨OTHER   Why, he had none.   35

⌜GRAVEDIGGER⌝   What, art a heathen? How dost thou
understand the scripture? The scripture says Adam
digged. Could he dig without arms?⟩ I'll put another question to thee. If thou answerest me not to the
purpose, confess thyself—   40

OTHER   Go to!

⌜GRAVEDIGGER⌝   What is he that builds stronger than
either the mason, the shipwright, or the carpenter?

OTHER   The gallows-maker; for that ⟨frame⟩ outlives a
thousand tenants.   45

⌜GRAVEDIGGER⌝   I like thy wit well, in good faith. The
gallows does well. But how does it well? It does
well to those that do ill. Now, thou dost ill to say the
gallows is built stronger than the church. Argal, the
gallows may do well to thee. To 't again, come.   5⟨0⟩

OTHER   "Who builds stronger than a mason, a shipwright, or a carpenter?"

⌜GRAVEDIGGER⌝   Ay, tell me that, and unyoke.

OTHER   Marry, now I can tell.

⌜GRAVEDIGGER⌝   To 't.   5⟨⟩

OTHER   Mass, I cannot tell.

⟨_Enter Hamlet and Horatio afar off._⟩

⌜GRAVEDIGGER⌝   Cudgel thy brains no more about it,

for your dull ass will not mend his pace with
beating. And, when you are asked this question
next, say "a grave-maker." The houses he makes 60
lasts till doomsday. Go, get thee in, and fetch me a
stoup of liquor.

⌜*The Other Man exits
and the Gravedigger digs and sings.*⌝

In youth when I did love, did love,
Methought it was very sweet
To contract—O—the time for—a—my behove, 65
O, methought there—a—was nothing—a—meet.

HAMLET Has this fellow no feeling of his business? He
sings in grave-making.

HORATIO Custom hath made it in him a property of
easiness. 70

HAMLET 'Tis e'en so. The hand of little employment
hath the daintier sense.

⌜GRAVEDIGGER⌝ ⟨*sings*⟩

But age with his stealing steps
Hath clawed me in his clutch,
And hath shipped me into the land, 75
As if I had never been such.

⌜*He digs up a skull.*⌝

HAMLET That skull had a tongue in it and could sing
once. How the knave jowls it to the ground as if
'twere Cain's jawbone, that did the first murder!
This might be the pate of a politician which this ass 80
now o'erreaches, one that would circumvent God,
might it not?

HORATIO It might, my lord.

HAMLET Or of a courtier, which could say "Good
morrow, sweet lord! How dost thou, sweet lord?" 85
This might be my Lord Such-a-one that praised my
Lord Such-a-one's horse when he went to beg it,
might it not?

HORATIO Ay, my lord.

HAMLET Why, e'en so. And now my Lady Worm's,   90
    chapless and knocked about the ⟨mazard⟩ with a
    sexton's spade. Here's fine revolution, an we had
    the trick to see 't. Did these bones cost no more the
    breeding but to play at loggets with them? Mine
    ache to think on 't.   95
⌜GRAVEDIGGER⌝ ⟨*sings*⟩

> *A pickax and a spade, a spade,*
> *For and a shrouding sheet,*
> *O, a pit of clay for to be made*
> *For such a guest is meet.*
>
>   ⌜*He digs up more skulls.*⌝

HAMLET There's another. Why may not that be the   100
    skull of a lawyer? Where be his quiddities now, his
    quillities, his cases, his tenures, and his tricks? Why
    does he suffer this mad knave now to knock him
    about the sconce with a dirty shovel and will not tell
    him of his action of battery? Hum, this fellow might   105
    be in 's time a great buyer of land, with his statutes,
    his recognizances, his fines, his double vouchers,
    his recoveries. ⟨Is this the fine of his fines and the
    recovery of his recoveries,⟩ to have his fine pate full
    of fine dirt? Will ⟨his⟩ vouchers vouch him no more   110
    of his purchases, and ⟨double ones too,⟩ than the
    length and breadth of a pair of indentures? The very
    conveyances of his lands will scarcely lie in this box,
    and must th' inheritor himself have no more, ha?
HORATIO Not a jot more, my lord.   115
HAMLET Is not parchment made of sheepskins?
HORATIO Ay, my lord, and of calves' skins too.
HAMLET They are sheep and calves which seek out
    assurance in that. I will speak to this fellow.—
    Whose grave's this, sirrah?   120
⌜GRAVEDIGGER⌝ Mine, sir.
  ⌜*Sings.*⌝   ⟨*O,*⟩ *a pit of clay for to be made*
>   ⟨*For such a guest is meet.*⟩

HAMLET   I think it be thine indeed, for thou liest in 't.

⌜GRAVEDIGGER⌝   You lie out on 't, sir, and therefore 'tis 125
   not yours. For my part, I do not lie in 't, yet it is
   mine.

HAMLET   Thou dost lie in 't, to be in 't and say it is thine.
   'Tis for the dead, not for the quick; therefore thou
   liest.   130

⌜GRAVEDIGGER⌝   'Tis a quick lie, sir; 'twill away again
   from me to you.

HAMLET   What man dost thou dig it for?

⌜GRAVEDIGGER⌝   For no man, sir.

HAMLET   What woman then?   135

⌜GRAVEDIGGER⌝   For none, neither.

HAMLET   Who is to be buried in 't?

⌜GRAVEDIGGER⌝   One that was a woman, sir, but, rest
   her soul, she's dead.

HAMLET   How absolute the knave is! We must speak by 140
   the card, or equivocation will undo us. By the
   Lord, Horatio, this three years I have took note of
   it: the age is grown so picked that the toe of the
   peasant comes so near the heel of the courtier, he
   galls his kibe.—How long hast thou been grave- 145
   maker?

⌜GRAVEDIGGER⌝   Of ⟨all⟩ the days i' th' year, I came to 't
   that day that our last King Hamlet overcame
   Fortinbras.

HAMLET   How long is that since?   150

⌜GRAVEDIGGER⌝   Cannot you tell that? Every fool can
   tell that. It was that very day that young Hamlet
   was born—he that is mad, and sent into England.

HAMLET   Ay, marry, why was he sent into England?

⌜GRAVEDIGGER⌝   Why, because he was mad. He shall 155
   recover his wits there. Or if he do not, 'tis no great
   matter there.

HAMLET   Why?

⌜GRAVEDIGGER⌝   'Twill not be seen in him there. There
   the men are as mad as he.   160

HAMLET　How came he mad?

⌜GRAVEDIGGER⌝　Very strangely, they say.

HAMLET　How "strangely"?

⌜GRAVEDIGGER⌝　Faith, e'en with losing his wits.

HAMLET　Upon what ground? 165

⌜GRAVEDIGGER⌝　Why, here in Denmark. I have been sexton here, man and boy, thirty years.

HAMLET　How long will a man lie i' th' earth ere he rot?

⌜GRAVEDIGGER⌝　Faith, if he be not rotten before he die (as we have many pocky corses ⟨nowadays⟩ that will 170 scarce hold the laying in), he will last you some eight year or nine year. A tanner will last you nine year.

HAMLET　Why he more than another?

⌜GRAVEDIGGER⌝　Why, sir, his hide is so tanned with his 175 trade that he will keep out water a great while; and your water is a sore decayer of your whoreson dead body. Here's a skull now hath lien you i' th' earth three-and-twenty years.

HAMLET　Whose was it? 180

⌜GRAVEDIGGER⌝　A whoreson mad fellow's it was. Whose do you think it was?

HAMLET　Nay, I know not.

⌜GRAVEDIGGER⌝　A pestilence on him for a mad rogue! He poured a flagon of Rhenish on my head once. 185 This same skull, sir, was, sir, Yorick's skull, the King's jester.

HAMLET　This?

⌜GRAVEDIGGER⌝　E'en that.

HAMLET, ⌜*taking the skull*⌝ ⟨Let me see.⟩ Alas, poor 190 Yorick! I knew him, Horatio—a fellow of infinite jest, of most excellent fancy. He hath bore me on his back a thousand times, and now how abhorred in my imagination it is! My gorge rises at it. Here hung those lips that I have kissed I know not how oft. 195 Where be your gibes now? your gambols? your

songs? your flashes of merriment that were wont to
set the table on a roar? Not one now to mock your
own grinning? Quite chapfallen? Now get you to my
lady's ⟨chamber,⟩ and tell her, let her paint an inch　200
thick, to this favor she must come. Make her laugh
at that.—Prithee, Horatio, tell me one thing.

HORATIO　What's that, my lord?

HAMLET　Dost thou think Alexander looked o' this
fashion i' th' earth?　　　　　　　　　　　　　　205

HORATIO　E'en so.

HAMLET　And smelt so? Pah!　⌜*He puts the skull down.*⌝

HORATIO　E'en so, my lord.

HAMLET　To what base uses we may return, Horatio!
Why may not imagination trace the noble dust of　210
Alexander till he find it stopping a bunghole?

HORATIO　'Twere to consider too curiously to consider
so.

HAMLET　No, faith, not a jot; but to follow him thither,
with modesty enough and likelihood to lead it, ⟨as　215
thus:⟩ Alexander died, Alexander was buried, Alexander returneth to dust; the dust is earth; of earth
we make loam; and why of that loam whereto he
was converted might they not stop a beer barrel?

Imperious Caesar, dead and turned to clay,　　　220
Might stop a hole to keep the wind away.
O, that that earth which kept the world in awe
Should patch a wall t' expel the ⟨winter's⟩ flaw!

*Enter King, Queen, Laertes, ⟨Lords attendant,⟩ and the
　corpse ⌜of Ophelia, with a Doctor of Divinity.⌝*

But soft, but soft awhile! Here comes the King,
The Queen, the courtiers. Who is this they follow?　225
And with such maimèd rites? This doth betoken
The corse they follow did with desp'rate hand
Fordo its own life. 'Twas of some estate.
Couch we awhile and mark.　　　⌜*They step aside.*⌝

LAERTES What ceremony else?   230
HAMLET That is Laertes, a very noble youth. Mark.
LAERTES What ceremony else?
DOCTOR
  Her obsequies have been as far enlarged
  As we have warranty. Her death was doubtful,
  And, but that great command o'ersways the order,   235
  She should in ground unsanctified been lodged
  Till the last trumpet. For charitable prayers
  ⟨Shards,⟩ flints, and pebbles should be thrown on
      her.
  Yet here she is allowed her virgin crants,   240
  Her maiden strewments, and the bringing home
  Of bell and burial.
LAERTES
  Must there no more be done?
DOCTOR   No more be done.
  We should profane the service of the dead   245
  To sing a requiem and such rest to her
  As to peace-parted souls.
LAERTES   Lay her i' th' earth,
  And from her fair and unpolluted flesh
  May violets spring! I tell thee, churlish priest,   250
  A minist'ring angel shall my sister be
  When thou liest howling.
HAMLET, ⌜to Horatio⌝   What, the fair Ophelia?
QUEEN Sweets to the sweet, farewell!
                              ⌜*She scatters flowers.*⌝
  I hoped thou shouldst have been my Hamlet's wife;   255
  I thought thy bride-bed to have decked, sweet maid,
  And not have strewed thy grave.
LAERTES   O, treble woe
  Fall ten times ⟨treble⟩ on that cursèd head
  Whose wicked deed thy most ingenious sense   260
  Deprived thee of!—Hold off the earth awhile,
  Till I have caught her once more in mine arms.
                              ⟨*Leaps in the grave.*⟩

Now pile your dust upon the quick and dead,
Till of this flat a mountain you have made
T' o'ertop old Pelion or the skyish head   265
Of blue Olympus.

HAMLET, ⌐*advancing*¬
                    What is he whose grief
Bears such an emphasis, whose phrase of sorrow
Conjures the wand'ring stars and makes them stand
Like wonder-wounded hearers? This is I,   270
Hamlet the Dane.

LAERTES, ⌐*coming out of the grave*¬
                    The devil take thy soul!

HAMLET   Thou pray'st not well.   ⌐*They grapple.*¬
I prithee take thy fingers from my throat,
For though I am not splenitive ⟨and⟩ rash,   275
Yet have I in me something dangerous,
Which let thy wisdom fear. Hold off thy hand.

KING   Pluck them asunder.

QUEEN   Hamlet! Hamlet!

ALL   Gentlemen!   280

HORATIO   Good my lord, be quiet.
                    ⌐*Hamlet and Laertes are separated.*¬

HAMLET
Why, I will fight with him upon this theme
Until my eyelids will no longer wag!

QUEEN   O my son, what theme?

HAMLET
I loved Ophelia. Forty thousand brothers   285
Could not with all their quantity of love
Make up my sum. What wilt thou do for her?

KING   O, he is mad, Laertes!

QUEEN   For love of God, forbear him.

HAMLET   'Swounds, show me what thou't do.   290
Woo't weep, woo't fight, woo't fast, woo't tear
    thyself,
Woo't drink up eisel, eat a crocodile?

I'll do 't. Dost ⟨thou⟩ come here to whine?
To outface me with leaping in her grave?   295
Be buried quick with her, and so will I.
And if thou prate of mountains, let them throw
Millions of acres on us, till our ground,
Singeing his pate against the burning zone,
Make Ossa like a wart. Nay, an thou'lt mouth,   300
I'll rant as well as thou.

QUEEN   This is mere madness;
And ⟨thus⟩ awhile the fit will work on him.
Anon, as patient as the female dove
When that her golden couplets are disclosed,   305
His silence will sit drooping.

HAMLET   Hear you, sir,
What is the reason that you use me thus?
I loved you ever. But it is no matter.
Let Hercules himself do what he may,   310
The cat will mew, and dog will have his day.
                                        Hamlet exits.

KING
I pray thee, good Horatio, wait upon him.
                                        Horatio exits.
⌜*To Laertes.*⌝ Strengthen your patience in our last
    night's speech.
We'll put the matter to the present push.—   315
Good Gertrude, set some watch over your son.—
This grave shall have a living monument.
An hour of quiet ⟨shortly⟩ shall we see;
Till then in patience our proceeding be.
                                        They exit.

⌜Scene 2⌝
Enter Hamlet and Horatio.

HAMLET
  So much for this, sir. Now shall you see the other.
  You do remember all the circumstance?
HORATIO   Remember it, my lord!
HAMLET
  Sir, in my heart there was a kind of fighting
  That would not let me sleep. ⟨Methought⟩ I lay   5
  Worse than the mutines in the ⟨bilboes.⟩ Rashly—
  And praised be rashness for it: let us know,
  Our indiscretion sometime serves us well
  When our deep plots do pall; and that should learn
    us   10
  There's a divinity that shapes our ends,
  Rough-hew them how we will—
HORATIO   That is most
    certain.
HAMLET   Up from my cabin,   15
  My sea-gown scarfed about me, in the dark
  Groped I to find out them; had my desire,
  Fingered their packet, and in fine withdrew
  To mine own room again, making so bold
  (My fears forgetting manners) to unfold   20
  Their grand commission; where I found, Horatio,
  A royal knavery—an exact command,
  Larded with many several sorts of reasons
  Importing Denmark's health and England's too,
  With—ho!—such bugs and goblins in my life,   25
  That on the supervise, no leisure bated,
  No, not to stay the grinding of the ax,
  My head should be struck off.
HORATIO   Is 't possible?
HAMLET
  Here's the commission. Read it at more leisure.   30
                    ⌜*Handing him a paper.*⌝

But wilt thou hear now how I did proceed?
HORATIO   I beseech you.
HAMLET
Being thus benetted round with ⌐villainies,¬
Or I could make a prologue to my brains,
They had begun the play. I sat me down,   35
Devised a new commission, wrote it fair—
I once did hold it, as our statists do,
A baseness to write fair, and labored much
How to forget that learning; but, sir, now
It did me yeoman's service. Wilt thou know   40
Th' effect of what I wrote?
HORATIO   Ay, good my lord.
HAMLET
An earnest conjuration from the King,
As England was his faithful tributary,
As love between them like the palm might flourish,   45
As peace should still her wheaten garland wear
And stand a comma 'tween their amities,
And many suchlike ⌐ases¬ of great charge,
That, on the view and knowing of these contents,
Without debatement further, more or less,   50
He should those bearers put to sudden death,
Not shriving time allowed.
HORATIO   How was this sealed?
HAMLET
Why, even in that was heaven ordinant.
I had my father's signet in my purse,   55
Which was the model of that Danish seal;
Folded the writ up in the form of th' other,
⟨Subscribed⟩ it, gave 't th' impression, placed it
    safely,
The changeling never known. Now, the next day   60
Was our sea-fight; and what to this was sequent
Thou knowest already.
HORATIO
So Guildenstern and Rosencrantz go to 't.

HAMLET
⟨Why, man, they did make love to this employment.⟩
They are not near my conscience. Their defeat 65
Does by their own insinuation grow.
'Tis dangerous when the baser nature comes
Between the pass and fell incensèd points
Of mighty opposites.

HORATIO   Why, what a king is this! 70

HAMLET
Does it not, think thee, stand me now upon—
He that hath killed my king and whored my mother,
Popped in between th' election and my hopes,
Thrown out his angle for my proper life,
And with such cozenage—is 't not perfect 75
   conscience
⟨To quit him with this arm? And is 't not to be
   damned
To let this canker of our nature come
In further evil? 80

HORATIO
It must be shortly known to him from England
What is the issue of the business there.

HAMLET
It will be short. The interim's mine,
And a man's life's no more than to say "one."
But I am very sorry, good Horatio, 85
That to Laertes I forgot myself,
For by the image of my cause I see
The portraiture of his. I'll ⌈court⌉ his favors.
But, sure, the bravery of his grief did put me
Into a tow'ring passion. 90

HORATIO   Peace, who comes here?⟩

Enter ⟨Osric,⟩ a courtier.

OSRIC   Your lordship is right welcome back to Denmark.

HAMLET I ⟨humbly⟩ thank you, sir. ⌐*Aside to Horatio.*⌐
Dost know this waterfly?   95
HORATIO, ⌐*aside to Hamlet*⌐ No, my good lord.
HAMLET, ⌐*aside to Horatio*⌐ Thy state is the more gracious, for 'tis a vice to know him. He hath much
land, and fertile. Let a beast be lord of beasts and his
crib shall stand at the king's mess. 'Tis a chough,   100
but, as I say, spacious in the possession of dirt.
OSRIC Sweet lord, if your lordship were at leisure, I
should impart a thing to you from his Majesty.
HAMLET I will receive it, sir, with all diligence of
spirit. ⟨Put⟩ your bonnet to his right use: 'tis for the   105
head.
OSRIC I thank your lordship; it is very hot.
HAMLET No, believe me, 'tis very cold; the wind is
northerly.
OSRIC It is indifferent cold, my lord, indeed.   110
HAMLET But yet methinks it is very ⟨sultry⟩ and hot ⟨for⟩
my complexion.
OSRIC Exceedingly, my lord; it is very sultry, as
'twere—I cannot tell how. My lord, his Majesty
bade me signify to you that he has laid a great wager   115
on your head. Sir, this is the matter—
HAMLET I beseech you, remember. ⌐*He motions to
Osric to put on his hat.*⌐
OSRIC Nay, good my lord, for my ease, in good faith.
[Sir, here is newly come to court Laertes—believe
me, an absolute ⌐gentleman,⌐ full of most excellent   120
differences, of very soft society and great showing.
Indeed, to speak ⌐feelingly⌐ of him, he is the card or
calendar of gentry, for you shall find in him the
continent of what part a gentleman would see.
HAMLET Sir, his definement suffers no perdition in   125
you, though I know to divide him inventorially
would dozy th' arithmetic of memory, and yet but
yaw neither, in respect of his quick sail. But, in the

verity of extolment, I take him to be a soul of great
article, and his infusion of such dearth and rareness 130
as, to make true diction of him, his semblable is his
mirror, and who else would trace him, his umbrage,
nothing more.

OSRIC Your lordship speaks most infallibly of him.

HAMLET The concernancy, sir? Why do we wrap the 135
gentleman in our more rawer breath?

OSRIC Sir?

HORATIO, ⌈*aside to Hamlet*⌉ Is 't not possible to understand in another tongue? You will to 't, sir, really.

HAMLET, ⌈*to Osric*⌉ What imports the nomination of 140
this gentleman?

OSRIC Of Laertes?

HORATIO, ⌈*aside*⌉ His purse is empty already; all 's
golden words are spent.

HAMLET Of him, sir. 145

OSRIC I know you are not ignorant—

HAMLET I would you did, sir. Yet, in faith, if you did, it
would not much approve me. Well, sir?]

OSRIC You are not ignorant of what excellence Laertes
is— 150

[HAMLET I dare not confess that, lest I should compare
with him in excellence. But to know a man well
were to know himself.

OSRIC I mean, sir, for ⌈his⌉ weapon. But in the imputation laid on him by them, in his meed he's unfel- 155
lowed.]

HAMLET What's his weapon?

OSRIC Rapier and dagger.

HAMLET That's two of his weapons. But, well—

OSRIC The King, sir, hath wagered with him six Barba- 160
ry horses, against the which he has impawned, as I
take it, six French rapiers and poniards, with their
assigns, as girdle, ⟨hangers,⟩ and so. Three of the
carriages, in faith, are very dear to fancy, very

responsive to the hilts, most delicate carriages, and 165
of very liberal conceit.

HAMLET   What call you the "carriages"?

[HORATIO, ⌜*aside to Hamlet*⌝   I knew you must be edified
by the margent ere you had done.]

OSRIC   The ⟨carriages,⟩ sir, are the hangers. 170

HAMLET   The phrase would be more germane to the
matter if we could carry a cannon by our sides. I
would it ⟨might⟩ be "hangers" till then. But on. Six
Barbary horses against six French swords, their
assigns, and three liberal-conceited carriages— 175
that's the French bet against the Danish. Why is this
all ⌜"impawned,"⌝ ⟨as⟩ you call it?

OSRIC   The King, sir, hath laid, sir, that in a dozen
passes between yourself and him, he shall not
exceed you thrée hits. He hath laid on twelve for 180
nine, and it would come to immediate trial if your
lordship would vouchsafe the answer.

HAMLET   How if I answer no?

OSRIC   I mean, my lord, the opposition of your person
in trial. 185

HAMLET   Sir, I will walk here in the hall. If it please his
Majesty, it is the breathing time of day with me. Let
the foils be brought, the gentleman willing, and the
King hold his purpose, I will win for him, an I can.
If not, I will gain nothing but my shame and the odd 190
hits.

OSRIC   Shall I deliver you ⟨e'en⟩ so?

HAMLET   To this effect, sir, after what flourish your
nature will.

OSRIC   I commend my duty to your lordship. 195

HAMLET   Yours. ⌜*Osric exits.*⌝ ⟨He⟩ does well to commend it himself. There are no tongues else for 's
turn.

HORATIO   This lapwing runs away with the shell on his
head. 200

HAMLET He did ⟨comply,⟩ sir, with his dug before he
　　sucked it. Thus has he (and many more of the same
　　breed that I know the drossy age dotes on) only got
　　the tune of the time, and, out of an habit of
　　encounter, a kind of ⟨yeasty⟩ collection, which car- 205
　　ries them through and through the most ⌜fanned⌝
　　and ⟨winnowed⟩ opinions; and do but blow them to
　　their trial, the bubbles are out.

[*Enter a Lord.*

LORD My lord, his Majesty commended him to you by
　　young Osric, who brings back to him that you 210
　　attend him in the hall. He sends to know if your
　　pleasure hold to play with Laertes, or that you will
　　take longer time.
HAMLET I am constant to my purposes. They follow
　　the King's pleasure. If his fitness speaks, mine is 215
　　ready now or whensoever, provided I be so able as
　　now.
LORD The King and Queen and all are coming down.
HAMLET In happy time.
LORD The Queen desires you to use some gentle 220
　　entertainment to Laertes before you fall to play.
HAMLET She well instructs me. 　　　⌜*Lord exits.*⌝]
HORATIO You will lose, my lord.
HAMLET I do not think so. Since he went into France, I
　　have been in continual practice. I shall win at the 225
　　odds; ⟨but⟩ thou wouldst not think how ill all's here
　　about my heart. But it is no matter.
HORATIO Nay, good my lord—
HAMLET It is but foolery, but it is such a kind of
　　⟨gaingiving⟩ as would perhaps trouble a woman. 230
HORATIO If your mind dislike anything, obey it. I will
　　forestall their repair hither and say you are not fit.
HAMLET Not a whit. We defy augury. There is ⟨a⟩
　　special providence in the fall of a sparrow. If it be
　　⟨now,⟩ 'tis not to come; if it be not to come, it will be 235

now; if it be not now, yet it ⟨will⟩ come. The
readiness is all. Since no man of aught he leaves
knows, what is 't to leave betimes? Let be.

*A table prepared. ⟨Enter⟩ Trumpets, Drums, and Officers
with cushions, King, Queen, ⌈Osric,⌉ and all the state,
foils, daggers, ⟨flagons of wine,⟩ and Laertes.*

KING
Come, Hamlet, come and take this hand from me.
                    ⌈*He puts Laertes' hand into Hamlet's.*⌉
HAMLET, ⌈*to Laertes*⌉
Give me your pardon, sir. I have done you wrong;   240
But pardon 't as you are a gentleman. This presence
    knows,
And you must needs have heard, how I am punished
With a sore distraction. What I have done
That might your nature, honor, and exception   245
Roughly awake, I here proclaim was madness.
Was 't Hamlet wronged Laertes? Never Hamlet.
If Hamlet from himself be ta'en away,
And when he's not himself does wrong Laertes,
Then Hamlet does it not; Hamlet denies it.   250
Who does it, then? His madness. If 't be so,
Hamlet is of the faction that is wronged;
His madness is poor Hamlet's enemy.
⟨Sir, in this audience⟩
Let my disclaiming from a purposed evil   255
Free me so far in your most generous thoughts
That I have shot my arrow o'er the house
And hurt my brother.
LAERTES   I am satisfied in nature,
Whose motive in this case should stir me most   260
To my revenge; but in my terms of honor
I stand aloof and will no reconcilement
Till by some elder masters of known honor
I have a voice and precedent of peace
To ⟨keep⟩ my name ungored. But ⟨till⟩ that time   265

I do receive your offered love like love
And will not wrong it.

HAMLET   I embrace it freely
And will this brothers' wager frankly play.—
Give us the foils. ⟨Come on.⟩   270

LAERTES   .   Come, one for me.

HAMLET
I'll be your foil, Laertes; in mine ignorance
Your skill shall, like a star i' th' darkest night,
Stick fiery off indeed.

LAERTES   You mock me, sir.   275

HAMLET   No, by this hand.

KING
Give them the foils, young Osric. Cousin Hamlet,
You know the wager?

HAMLET   Very well, my lord.
Your Grace has laid the odds o' th' weaker side.   280

KING
I do not fear it; I have seen you both.
But, since he is better, we have therefore odds.

LAERTES
This is too heavy. Let me see another.

HAMLET
This likes me well. These foils have all a length?

OSRIC   Ay, my good lord.   285

⟨*Prepare to play.*⟩

KING
Set me the stoups of wine upon that table.—
If Hamlet give the first or second hit
Or quit in answer of the third exchange,
Let all the battlements their ordnance fire.
The King shall drink to Hamlet's better breath,   290
And in the cup an ⟨union⟩ shall he throw,
Richer than that which four successive kings
In Denmark's crown have worn. Give me the cups,

And let the kettle to the trumpet speak,
The trumpet to the cannoneer without,   295
The cannons to the heavens, the heaven to earth,
"Now the King drinks to Hamlet." Come, begin.
And you, the judges, bear a wary eye.
                                        Trumpets the while.

HAMLET   Come on, sir.
LAERTES   Come, my lord.   ⟨*They play.*⟩ 300
HAMLET   One.
LAERTES   No.
HAMLET   Judgment!
OSRIC   A hit, a very palpable hit.
LAERTES   Well, again.   305
KING
   Stay, give me drink.—Hamlet, this pearl is thine.
   Here's to thy health.
           ⌜*He drinks and then drops the pearl in the cup.*⌝
                         Drum, trumpets, and shot.
                   Give him the cup.

HAMLET
   I'll play this bout first. Set it by awhile.
   Come. ⌜*They play.*⌝ Another hit. What say you?   310
LAERTES
   ⟨A touch, a touch.⟩ I do confess 't.
KING
   Our son shall win.
QUEEN   He's fat and scant of breath.
   Here, Hamlet, take my napkin; rub thy brows.
   The Queen carouses to thy fortune, Hamlet.   315
                            ⌜*She lifts the cup.*⌝

HAMLET   Good madam.
KING   Gertrude, do not drink.
QUEEN
   I will, my lord; I pray you pardon me.   ⌜*She drinks.*⌝
KING, ⌜*aside*⌝
   It is the poisoned cup. It is too late.

HAMLET
  I dare not drink yet, madam—by and by.   320
QUEEN   Come, let me wipe thy face.
LAERTES, ⌐*to Claudius*¬
  My lord, I'll hit him now.
KING   I do not think 't.
LAERTES, ⌐*aside*¬
  And yet it is almost against my conscience.
HAMLET
  Come, for the third, Laertes. You do but dally.   325
  I pray you pass with your best violence.
  I am ⟨afeard⟩ you make a wanton of me.
LAERTES   Say you so? Come on.   ⟨*Play.*⟩
OSRIC   Nothing neither way.
LAERTES   Have at you now!   330
⌐*Laertes wounds Hamlet. Then ⟨in scuffling they change
          rapiers,⟩ and Hamlet wounds Laertes.*¬
KING   Part them. They are incensed.
HAMLET   Nay, come again.
                              ⌐*The Queen falls.*¬
OSRIC   Look to the Queen there, ho!
HORATIO
  They bleed on both sides.—How is it, my lord?
OSRIC   How is 't, Laertes?   335
LAERTES
  Why as a woodcock to mine own springe, Osric.
                              ⌐*He falls.*¬
  I am justly killed with mine own treachery.
HAMLET
  How does the Queen?
KING   She swoons to see them bleed.
QUEEN
  No, no, the drink, the drink! O, my dear Hamlet!   340
  The drink, the drink! I am poisoned.   ⌐*She dies.*¬
HAMLET
  O villainy! Ho! Let the door be locked.   ⌐*Osric exits.*¬
  Treachery! Seek it out.

LAERTES

   It is here, Hamlet. ⟨Hamlet,⟩ thou art slain.

   No med'cine in the world can do thee good. 345

   In thee there is not half an hour's life.

   The treacherous instrument is in ⟨thy⟩ hand,

   Unbated and envenomed. The foul practice

   Hath turned itself on me. Lo, here I lie,

   Never to rise again. Thy mother's poisoned. 350

   I can no more. The King, the King's to blame.

HAMLET

   The point envenomed too! Then, venom, to thy

     work. ⟨*Hurts the King.*⟩

ALL   Treason, treason!

KING

   O, yet defend me, friends! I am but hurt. 355

HAMLET

   Here, thou incestuous, ⟨murd'rous,⟩ damnèd Dane,

   Drink off this potion. Is ⟨thy union⟩ here?

            ⌈*Forcing him to drink the poison.*⌉

   Follow my mother. ⟨*King dies.*⟩

LAERTES   He is justly served.

   It is a poison tempered by himself. 360

   Exchange forgiveness with me, noble Hamlet.

   Mine and my father's death come not upon thee,

   Nor thine on me. ⟨*Dies.*⟩

HAMLET

   Heaven make thee free of it. I follow thee.—

   I am dead, Horatio.—Wretched queen, adieu.— 365

   You that look pale and tremble at this chance,

   That are but mutes or audience to this act,

   Had I but time (as this fell sergeant, Death,

   Is strict in his arrest), O, I could tell you—

   But let it be.—Horatio, I am dead. 370

   Thou livest; report me and my cause aright

   To the unsatisfied.

HORATIO   Never believe it.

I am more an antique Roman than a Dane.
Here's yet some liquor left.   ⌜*He picks up the cup.*⌝ 375
HAMLET   As thou'rt a man,
  Give me the cup. Let go! By heaven, I'll ha 't.
  O God, Horatio, what a wounded name,
  Things standing thus unknown, shall I leave behind
      me!   380
  If thou didst ever hold me in thy heart,
  Absent thee from felicity awhile
  And in this harsh world draw thy breath in pain
  To tell my story.
              A march afar off ⟨and ⌜shot⌝ within.⟩
                  What warlike noise is this?   385

                    Enter Osric.

OSRIC
  Young Fortinbras, with conquest come from Poland,
  To th' ambassadors of England gives
  This warlike volley.
HAMLET   O, I die, Horatio!
  The potent poison quite o'ercrows my spirit.   390
  I cannot live to hear the news from England.
  But I do prophesy th' election lights
  On Fortinbras; he has my dying voice.
  So tell him, with th' occurrents, more and less,
  Which have solicited—the rest is silence.   395
  ⟨O, O, O, O!⟩   ⟨*Dies.*⟩
HORATIO
  Now cracks a noble heart. Good night, sweet prince,
  And flights of angels sing thee to thy rest.
                              ⌜*March within.*⌝
  Why does the drum come hither?

*Enter Fortinbras with the ⌜English⌝ Ambassadors ⟨with
      Drum, Colors, and Attendants.⟩*

FORTINBRAS   Where is this sight?   400

HORATIO   What is it you would see?
  If aught of woe or wonder, cease your search.
FORTINBRAS
  This quarry cries on havoc. O proud Death,
  What feast is toward in thine eternal cell
  That thou so many princes at a shot   405
  So bloodily hast struck?
AMBASSADOR   The sight is dismal,
  And our affairs from England come too late.
  The ears are senseless that should give us hearing
  To tell him his commandment is fulfilled,   410
  That Rosencrantz and Guildenstern are dead.
  Where should we have our thanks?
HORATIO   Not from his
      mouth,
  Had it th' ability of life to thank you.   415
  He never gave commandment for their death.
  But since, so jump upon this bloody question,
  You from the Polack wars, and you from England,
  Are here arrived, give order that these bodies
  High on a stage be placed to the view,   420
  And let me speak to ⟨th'⟩ yet unknowing world
  How these things came about. So shall you hear
  Of carnal, bloody, and unnatural acts,
  Of accidental judgments, casual slaughters,
  Of deaths put on by cunning and ⟨forced⟩ cause,   425
  And, in this upshot, purposes mistook
  Fall'n on th' inventors' heads. All this can I
  Truly deliver.
FORTINBRAS   Let us haste to hear it
  And call the noblest to the audience.   430
  For me, with sorrow I embrace my fortune.
  I have some rights of memory in this kingdom,
  Which now to claim my vantage doth invite me.
HORATIO
  Of that I shall have also cause to speak,

And from his mouth whose voice will draw ⟨on⟩   435
   more.
But let this same be presently performed
Even while men's minds are wild, lest more
   mischance
On plots and errors happen.   440
FORTINBRAS   Let four captains
Bear Hamlet like a soldier to the stage,
For he was likely, had he been put on,
To have proved most royal; and for his passage,
The soldier's music and the rite of war   445
Speak loudly for him.
Take up the bodies. Such a sight as this
Becomes the field but here shows much amiss.
Go, bid the soldiers shoot.
       They exit, ⟨marching, after the which, a peal of
                    ordnance are shot off.⟩

Explanatory Notes

1.1 On the guards' platform at Elsinore, Horatio waits with Barnardo and Marcellus to question a ghost that has twice before appeared. The Ghost, in the form of the late King Hamlet of Denmark, appears but will not speak. Horatio decides to tell his fellow student, Prince Hamlet, about the Ghost's appearance.

2. **unfold yourself:** disclose your identity
14. **The rivals of my watch:** my fellow sentries
17. **the Dane:** the Danish king
30. **of us:** by us
34. **approve our eyes:** confirm our observation
43. **pole:** Polaris, the North Star
44. **his:** its
51. **harrows:** torments (A *harrow* is a farm implement used to break up the ground.)
57. **sometimes:** formerly
67. **sensible:** attested by the senses; **avouch:** guarantee, testimony
72. **Norway:** i.e., the king of Norway (the elder Fortinbras)
73. **parle:** parley, meeting
74. **smote:** attacked; or, perhaps, defeated; **sledded Polacks:** Polish military riding in sleds
76. **jump:** exactly

78–79. **In what . . . opinion:** i.e., I cannot be precise, but in my general **opinion**

81. **tell . . . knows:** i.e., let him who **knows tell me**

83. **toils:** causes to labor; wearies; **subject of the land:** i.e., subjects of the realm

85. **foreign mart:** international trade

86. **impress:** enforced service

88. **toward:** approaching, about to happen

95. **Thereto . . . pride:** stirred to do this (i.e., to dare King Hamlet to combat) by a proud desire to rival the Danish king

99. **heraldry:** the law of arms, regulating tournaments and battles

101. **stood seized of:** legally possessed

102. **a moiety competent:** an appropriate portion

103. **gagèd:** engaged, i.e., pledged

105. **comart:** bargain

106. **carriage of the article designed:** i.e., meaning carried by the agreement drawn up

108. **unimprovèd:** uncontrolled

110. **Sharked up:** i.e., gathered indiscriminately

112. **stomach:** spirit of adventure

118. **head:** fountainhead, source

119. **rummage:** bustle, commotion

121. **Well may it sort:** i.e., it would thus be fitting

125. **palmy:** triumphant, worthy to "bear the palm"

127. **sheeted:** wrapped in their shrouds

129–30. **As stars . . . sun:** These lines are awkward; probably some text has been lost.

130. **Disasters:** threatening signs; **moist star:** the moon, which governs the tides

131. **Upon . . . stands:** i.e., by whose influence the sea is controlled **Neptune:** Roman god of the sea

133. **precurse:** foreshadowing

134. **harbingers:** those that announce someone's or something's approach; **still:** always

135. **omen:** i.e., ominous event
137. **climatures:** geographic regions
138. **soft:** "wait a minute"
146. **happily:** perhaps; or, fortunately
169. **extravagant:** out of bounds; **erring:** wandering
171. **made probation:** demonstrated
173. **'gainst:** just before
177. **strike:** destroy through malign influence
178. **takes:** puts under a magic spell

1.2 In an audience chamber in Elsinore, Claudius, the new king of Denmark, holds court. After thanking his subjects for their recent support, he dispatches ambassadors to Norway to halt a threatened attack from Fortinbras. He gives Laertes permission to return to France but denies Hamlet's request to return to the university in Wittenberg. Hamlet, mourning for his father's death, is left alone to vent his despair at what he regards as his mother's all too hasty marriage to his uncle, Claudius. The audience learns that the marriage took place "within a month" of the former king's death.

Horatio, Barnardo, and Marcellus arrive and tell Hamlet about the Ghost. Hamlet, aroused by the news, agrees to join them that night.

8. **our sometime sister:** my former sister-in-law (Claudius uses the royal "we" throughout, when he is speaking as king.)

9. **jointress:** a woman who owns property jointly with her husband

11. **With . . . eye:** as if smiling with one **eye** and crying with the other

18. **a weak . . . worth:** i.e., a low opinion of my ability

21. **Colleaguèd:** i.e., in league with; **advantage:** i.e., superior position

29. **impotent:** helpless

31. **gait:** course

31–33. **in that . . . subject:** i.e., since the troops and supplies are drawn from Norway's own subjects

37. **To business:** to negotiate

38. **these . . . articles:** this detailed written account

39. **let . . . duty:** i.e., let your speedy departure take the place of ceremonious leave-taking

45. **lose your voice:** i.e., waste your words

48. **native:** naturally connected

60–61. **wrung . . . petition:** i.e., finally persuaded me to allow him

62. **Upon . . . consent:** i.e., I reluctantly agreed to his wishes

64–65. **Take . . . will:** a courteous formula giving Laertes permission to return to France

66. **cousin:** kinsman

67. **more than kin:** i.e., twice related: uncle/nephew and "father"/"son"; **less than kind:** i.e., in a less-than-natural relationship

69. **in the sun:** a pun on sun/son

70. **nighted color:** i.e., black (mourning) clothing

72. **vailèd lids:** i.e., lowered eyes

74. **common:** belonging to all human beings

78. **particular:** special, personal

80–86. **'Tis . . . truly:** i.e., it is not only my black clothes, my sighs and tears, my downcast face, and other outward signs of grief that indicate my real feelings

96. **obsequious:** dutiful (Claudius seems to be playing on the related word *obsequy,* funeral service.)

97. **obstinate condolement:** sorrow that refuses comfort

99. **incorrect to heaven:** uncorrected by the divine will

103. **most . . . sense:** most familiar object of perception

108. **still:** always, habitually

109. **corse:** corpse

111. **unprevailing:** futile, useless

113. **most immediate:** next in line of succession

116. **impart toward:** give to

118. **retrograde:** opposite, contrary

129. **jocund health:** merry toast

130. **tell:** count out

131. **rouse:** deep drink; **bruit:** report

133. **sullied:** stained, defiled (The Second Quarto [Q2] reads "sallied," an alternate spelling for "sullied"; the Folio [F] reads "solid.")

136. **canon:** law

143. **that was to this:** i.e., **that was**, in comparison **to this** king (Claudius)

144. **Hyperion to a satyr:** i.e., like the sun god as compared to a goatlike **satyr**

145. **might not beteem:** would not allow

151. **or ere:** before

153. **Niobe:** In Greek mythology, Niobe, so grief-stricken at the loss of her children that she could not cease crying, was transformed into a stone from which water continually flowed.

154. **wants . . . reason:** lacks the ability to reason

158. **Hercules:** in Greek mythology, a hero of extraordinary strength and courage

160. **Had . . . eyes:** i.e., had stopped turning her **eyes** red

161. **post:** rush (as in riding a post-horse)

162. **incestuous:** Hamlet calls the marriage of his mother and his uncle "incestuous"—i.e., a violation of the laws against intercourse between close kin. The Ghost will also make this charge (1.5.49). Other members of the Danish court seem to see the marriage of Gertrude and Claudius as legal and legitimate. Debates about the incestuousness of a marriage between a widow and her dead husband's brother were heated in the sixteenth century (especially during the divorce trial of Henry VIII and Catherine of Aragon). The Bible gives conflicting commands about such marriages. How one is to view the mar-

riage of Gertrude and Claudius is an ongoing focus of interest for students of *Hamlet*.

169. **I'll . . . you:** i.e., instead of your calling yourself
my "servant," we'll call each other "friend"

170. **what . . . from:** what are you doing away from

186. **hard upon:** soon after

188. **coldly:** served cold (as leftovers)

189. **dearest:** most grievous; bitterest

194. **goodly:** admirable, excellent

201. **Season your admiration:** i.e., control your as-
tonishment

202. **attent:** attentive

210. **at point exactly, cap-à-pie:** at every point, from
head to foot

213. **oppressed and fear-surprisèd:** terrified

214. **truncheon:** short staff (here carried as a symbol
of authority)

215. **the act of fear:** the action of **fear** upon them

245. **beaver:** front piece of a helmet

259. **grizzled:** gray

269. **tenable:** withheld, kept secret

278. **doubt . . . play:** suspect some treacherous action

1.3 In Polonius's chambers, Laertes says good-bye to his
sister, Ophelia, and tells her not to trust Hamlet's promises of love. Polonius joins them, sends Laertes off, then
echoes Laertes's warnings to Ophelia, finally ordering her
not to see Hamlet again.

3. **convey is assistant:** ships are available

7. **fashion:** a temporary enthusiasm; **toy in blood:**
amorous flirtation

8. **in . . . nature:** in the early days of its prime

9. **Forward:** ardent, eager

10. **perfume . . . minute:** that which makes the moment sweet and fills it with pleasure

14–15. nature . . . bulk: i.e., a growing human does not increase only in strength and size

15. this temple: the body; **waxes:** grows larger

17. withal: at the same time

18. cautel: deceit

20. greatness: high rank

23. Carve: i.e., choose

26. that body: i.e., the Danish state

31. give his saying deed: put his words into action

34. credent: gullible; **list:** listen to

35–36. your chaste . . . importunity: i.e., surrender your chastity to his uncontrolled pleading

38. keep . . . affection: i.e., hold yourself back from actions your feelings would lead you into (The metaphor is from warfare, and is continued in the next line.)

40. chariest: most careful

43. The canker . . . spring: the cankerworm destroys the early spring blossoms

44. buttons: buds

46. blastments: withering blights

48. Youth . . . else near: i.e., youth loses self-control even without a tempter

51. ungracious: ungodly

52–54. Show me . . . treads: i.e., show me how to live a strict and virtuous life while you yourself follow a life of self-indulgence (See Matthew 7.13–14.)

55. recks not his own rede: does not heed his own advice

58. A double . . . grace: i.e., to receive one's father's **blessing** twice is a **double** favor from heaven

59. Occasion smiles upon: i.e., opportunity (personified as "Occasion") kindly grants me

65. Look thou character: see that you inscribe

67. familiar: friendly; **vulgar:** i.e., indiscriminate

71. unfledged courage: spirited youngster

75. censure: synonymous with **judgment**

76. **habit:** clothing

80. **Are . . . in that:** This puzzling line reads, in Q2, "Or of a most select and generous, chiefe in that"; in F it reads, "Are of a most . . . cheff in that." The line seems to mean, generally: the French show their refinement chiefly in the way they choose their apparel.

83. **husbandry:** management of one's money

89. **invests:** i.e., presses upon (Many editors prefer the Folio's "invites.")

98. **Marry:** indeed (formerly, a mild oath derived from "By the Virgin Mary")

103. **so 'tis put on me:** so I have been told

108-9. **tenders . . . to me:** offers **to me** of **his affection**

111. **Unsifted in:** i.e., naive about

115. **tenders:** coins that should be "legal tender" but are not because they **are not sterling**

116. **Tender yourself more dearly:** regard yourself at a higher rate

117-18. **not to . . . thus:** not to run the phrase, as if it were a horse, so hard that it becomes winded

118. **tender me a fool:** (1) show yourself to me as a **fool**; (2) make me look like a **fool**; (3) present me with a grandchild (The word *fool* was used as a term of endearment for a child.)

124. **springes:** snares; **woodcocks:** birds thought to be stupid and easily captured

127-28. **extinct . . . a-making:** i.e., both the **light** and the **heat** of such **blazes** die out almost as soon as they appear

131-32. **Set . . . parle:** Polonius here uses images from finance (**Set . . . at a higher rate**), diplomacy (**entreatments:** negotiations), and the military (**a command to parle:** an order to meet in conference) in order to tell Ophelia to spend less time talking to Hamlet.

136-40. **brokers . . . beguile:** i.e., they are panders

(**brokers, bawds:** go-betweens in sexual intrigues) who are not as holy as their dress (**investments**) would indicate; instead, they are merely urgers (**implorators**) of sinful actions (**unholy suits**) speaking (**breathing**) as if they were holy, in order to entice (**beguile**) (**Bawds** was suggested by Lewis Theobald; Q2 and F read "bonds.")

142. **slander:** disgrace by misusing

1.4 While Claudius drinks away the night, Hamlet, Horatio, and Marcellus are visited by the Ghost. It signals to Hamlet. Hamlet's friends try to stop him from following the Ghost, but Hamlet will not be held back.

1. **shrewdly:** keenly, intensely
2. **eager:** sharp (from the French *aigre*)
7. **held his wont:** has been accustomed
9. **doth . . . rouse:** stays awake tonight drinking
10. **Keeps wassail:** carouses; **upspring:** a German dance, particularly associated with heavy drinking
11. **Rhenish:** Rhine wine
13. **triumph of his pledge:** his feat of emptying the cup in one draft
17. **to the manner born:** destined through birth to accept this custom
20. **taxed of:** censured by
21. **clepe:** call
22. **addition:** titles of honor
25. **pith and marrow:** essence; **attribute:** reputation
26. **So:** in the same way; **oft it chances in:** it often happens with
27. **mole of nature:** natural fault
30. **o'ergrowth . . . complexion:** i.e., the increase of one of the four "humors," which were thought to control man's physical and emotional being
31. **pales and forts:** palings and ramparts
32. **o'erleavens:** radically changes

33. **plausive:** pleasing

35. **nature's livery:** i.e., something by which one is marked by nature (**as in their birth**, or **the o'ergrowth of some complexion**); **fortune's star:** something determined by luck (as in the accidental forming of **some habit**)

36. **His virtues else:** the other **virtues** of these men

39–41. **The dram . . . scandal:** These difficult lines have never been satisfactorily repaired, but the general sense may be that a small amount of evil makes even something admirable seem disreputable.

48. **questionable:** problematic

52. **canonized:** i.e., buried in accord with the canons of the church (accent on second syllable)

59–61. **and we . . . our souls:** and causing us weak humans to agitate our minds with thoughts that go **beyond** what even **our souls** can reach to

64. **some . . . desire: did desire** to impart something

73. **a pin's fee:** the cost of a pin

81. **deprive your sovereignty of reason:** depose **reason** as ruler of your mind

83. **toys of desperation:** desperate impulses

92. **arture:** artery (Arteries were believed to be the veins that carried the body's invisible "vital spirits.")

93. **the Nemean lion's nerve:** the sinews of the lion killed by Hercules as one of his twelve "labors"

95. **lets me:** holds me back

1.5 The Ghost tells Hamlet a tale of horror. Saying that he is the spirit of Hamlet's father, he demands that Hamlet avenge King Hamlet's murder at the hands of Claudius. Hamlet, horrified, vows to "remember" and swears his friends to secrecy about what they have seen.

3. **Mark me:** pay attention to me
9. **lend thy serious hearing:** listen intently

11. **bound:** ready (The word also means "in duty bound" and "obligated," which is the sense to which the Ghost responds in the following line.)

16. **for:** during

21. **harrow up:** tear up (agricultural image)

22–23. **stars . . . spheres:** In Ptolemaic astronomy, each planet (star) was carried around the earth in a crystalline sphere.

25. **an end:** on end

26. **fearful porpentine:** uneasy (threatened) porcupine

27. **eternal blazon:** description of that which is **eternal**

39. **duller . . . be:** you would **be duller**; **fat:** thick

40. **Lethe wharf:** the bank of the river Lethe (the river of forgetfulness)

41. **Wouldst thou not:** if you did not

42. **orchard:** palace garden

44. **forgèd process:** false story

45. **Rankly abused:** completely misled

57–58. **decline / Upon:** turn to (with the sense of "declining" as falling, bending downward)

65. **soft:** "enough," or "wait a minute"

69. **hebona:** a poison (The word may be linked to "henbane," a poisonous weed, or to "ebony," the sap of which was thought to be poisonous. Marlowe, in *The Jew of Malta*, mentions "the juice of hebon" as deadly.)

71. **leprous distilment:** distillation causing a condition like leprosy

75. **posset:** clot

76. **eager:** acid

78–80. **a most instant tetter . . . body:** i.e., sores and scabs, as on a leper, covered my body with a vile crust like the bark of a tree **tetter:** a skin disease marked by sores and scabs **lazar-like:** like a leper

82. **dispatched:** dispossessed

84. **Unhouseled . . . unaneled:** without having received final rites

90. **luxury:** lust

96. **matin:** morning

104. **globe:** Hamlet perhaps gestures to his head.

105. **table:** table-book or slate, used here metaphorically (Hamlet wants to wipe his memory clean, as one would erase a slate or table-book. Later [lines 114–16], he takes out actual "tables.")

106. **fond records:** foolish jottings (**records** accented on the second syllable)

108. **youth and observation:** youthful **observation**

114. **meet it is:** it is appropriate that

125. **Hillo, ho . . . bird, come:** Hamlet mocks Marcellus's call, as if it were the call of a falconer.

138. **arrant:** complete

142. **circumstance:** ceremony

154. **honest:** genuine

165. **Upon my sword:** an appropriate object on which to swear an oath, in that the hilts form a cross

170. **truepenny:** honest fellow

177. **Hic et ubique:** here and everywhere (Latin)

184. **pioner:** a foot soldier who marches in advance of the army to dig trenches and clear the way; a digger or miner; **remove:** move to another spot

186. **as a stranger give it welcome:** welcome it as one should welcome **a stranger**

188. **your philosophy:** i.e., **philosophy** in general

189–202. **never . . . help you:** i.e., swear never to note, even through gestures and hints, that you know anything about me, no matter how strangely I act

190. **How . . . some'er:** howsoever

191–92. **As I . . . on:** since I may in the future think it appropriate to act bizarrely

194. **With arms . . . headshake:** with your **arms** folded or shaking your head in a knowing way

195. **doubtful:** ambiguous
196. **an if:** if
198. **list:** should choose
200. **giving-out:** expression; **note:** indicate
204. **Rest, rest, perturbèd spirit:** These words suggest that Horatio and Marcellus have sworn the oath demanded by Hamlet and the Ghost; Q2 and F give no stage direction to indicate when they do so.

2.1 Polonius sends his servant Reynaldo to Paris to question Laertes's acquaintances. Ophelia enters, deeply disturbed about a visit she has just had from an apparently mad Hamlet. Polonius decides that Hamlet has become insane because Ophelia is refusing to see him. Polonius rushes off to tell the king.

4–5. **make inquire / Of:** ask questions about
8. **Inquire me:** i.e., **inquire** on my behalf; **Danskers:** Danes
9. **what means:** what is their supply of money
10. **keep:** live
12. **encompassment and drift of question:** roundabout conversation (Polonius's language itself tends to be roundabout.)
13–14. **come you ... touch it:** i.e., you will come closer (to getting answers) than you would by specific questions
15. **Take you, as 'twere:** assume, as it were
21. **put on him:** accuse him of
22. **forgeries:** invented faults; **rank:** great; offensive
24. **wanton:** rebellious
25–26. **are companions ... liberty:** are known to accompany youthful activity
27. **gaming:** gambling
29. **drabbing:** dealing with prostitutes
31. **season ... charge:** make **the charge** seem less serious by your way of stating it   **season:** temper

33. **open to incontinency:** is habitually inclined to sexual indulgence

35. **quaintly:** cunningly

36. **taints of liberty:** slight faults that accompany independence

38–39. **A savageness . . . assault:** i.e., a wildness in untamed **blood,** which all young people can be accused of

44. **fetch of wit:** clever trick

46. **soiled i' th' working:** i.e., as cloth may be soiled as it is being worked with

48. **sound: sound** out or question

49. **prenominate crimes:** before-named wrongdoings

51. **closes . . . consequence:** agrees with you as follows

53. **addition:** form of address

66. **o'ertook in 's rouse:** overcome by drink

69. **Videlicet:** namely, that is to say (Latin)

69–70. **See . . . truth:** i.e., **you** can **see** this deceptive **bait** capture a real fish

71. **reach:** mental ability

72. **windlasses . . . bias:** indirect approaches, a **windlass** being an indirect course in hunting, the **bias** being the curve that brings the ball to the desired point in the game of bowls

75. **Shall you my son: you shall** (find out) **my son**

79. **in yourself:** yourself (instead of in reports)

87. **closet:** private room

88. **doublet:** close-fitting jacket; **unbraced:** unfastened

89. **fouled:** dirty

90. **down-gyvèd to his ankle:** fallen down around his ankles like gyves or chains

114. **ecstasy:** madness

115. **violent property:** characteristic violence; **fordoes:** destroys

125. **coted:** observed

126. **wrack:** destroy; **beshrew my jealousy:** curse my suspicious thoughts

127. **proper to our age:** characteristic of the old

128. **cast beyond ourselves:** go too far (The image may come from casting a net, or the word **cast** may have the meaning "plan, devise.")

130. **discretion:** good judgment

131. **close:** hidden

131-33. **might . . . love:** i.e., this love **might** cause **more grief** if hidden than hatred if told about

2.2 Claudius and Gertrude set Rosencrantz and Guildenstern, two boyhood friends of Hamlet, to spy on him to discover the cause of his apparent madness. After the returned ambassadors announce their success in stopping Fortinbras's planned invasion of Denmark, Polonius reports his "discovery" that Hamlet is mad for love. Claudius is unpersuaded but agrees to join Polonius in spying on Hamlet.

When Hamlet himself enters, he is confronted first by Polonius and then by Rosencrantz and Guildenstern, whom he quickly identifies as Claudius's spies. As they talk, a company of touring actors enters. Hamlet persuades one of them to deliver a speech, and recognizes, to his shame, that he has shown less intensity in avenging his father's murder than the actor has done in performance. Hamlet hopes that when the players stage *The Murder of Gonzago* for the court, he can determine whether Claudius is guilty of King Hamlet's death.

6. **Sith:** since; **nor . . . nor:** neither . . . nor

12. **havior:** manners

13. **vouchsafe your rest:** agree to stay

18. **opened:** laid bare, revealed

22. **gentry:** generosity (or, perhaps, courtesy)

32. **in the full bent:** fully, totally (The term suggests a bow, in archery, bent to its limit.)

40. **practices:** actions (with perhaps a suggestion of intrigues, maneuvers, and plots)

50. **Hunts . . . sure:** i.e., does not follow so successfully **the trail of** political cunning

55. **fruit:** dessert

59. **the main:** the central point

61. **sift:** examine closely (as if through a sieve)

65. **Upon our first:** at **our first** approach

71. **borne in hand:** systematically deceived; **arrests:** orders to desist

75. **give . . . against:** attack, assault

84. **On such . . . allowance:** according to **such** terms **of safety** for Denmark and of permission for Fortinbras

86. **likes:** pleases

93. **expostulate:** make a speech about

97. **brevity . . . wit:** i.e., in a wise speech, a few words carry the central meaning

98. **flourishes:** ornaments

103. **More . . . art:** i.e., get to the point more quickly by cutting out the rhetorical ornamentations

104. **I use no art:** i.e., my language is natural

106. **figure:** figure of speech

113. **Perpend:** consider carefully

121. **etc.:** Polonius, in reading the letter, says "et cetera" in order to indicate that he is skipping over the letter's formal compliments.

123. **stay:** wait; **will be faithful:** will read accurately

124–27. **Doubt . . . I love:** Hamlet's poem plays on different meanings of **doubt:** (1) to be skeptical about (as about the ancient truths about **the stars** and **the sun**); (2) to suspect (that, e.g., **truth** might be **a liar**); (3) to disbelieve (e.g., Hamlet's love).

128. **ill . . . numbers:** unskilled at writing verse

129. **reckon my groans:** count (and rhythmically count out) my lover's sighs

131–32. **whilst . . . to him:** i.e., while I still occupy this body

134. **above:** besides

145. **played . . . table-book:** remained silent, keeping this knowledge hidden as if I had put it in a **desk** or a diary

146. **given . . . winking:** made **my heart** close its eyes to what was going on

149. **my young mistress:** this young lady (i.e., Ophelia); **bespeak:** speak to

155–59. **he . . . Fell into . . . madness:** Polonius lists what were supposed to be the classic stages of the **declension** (decline) into love-madness: from **sadness,** to **a fast** (failure to eat), to **a watch** (insomnia), to **weakness,** to light-headedness, to insanity.

168. **Take this from this:** Polonius gestures to his head and his shoulder (or to his chain of office and his neck, or to his staff of office and his hand), indicating that he would yield up his life (or his office) if proved wrong.

171. **center:** the earth's center, which, in the Ptolemaic system, is also the center of the universe

176. **loose:** turn her loose (The figure is that of releasing an animal from its chains, either for the hunt or for purposes of mating.)

177. **arras:** a hanging screen of rich tapestry fabric

186. **board:** i.e., speak to; **presently:** immediately

198. **a good kissing carrion:** This puzzling phrase is often changed to read "a god kissing carrion."

218. **wit:** understanding; **hams:** buttocks and thighs

220. **honesty:** good manners

227. **pregnant:** full of meaning; **happiness:** aptness of phrasing

245. **As . . . earth:** like the general run of mortals

252. **privates:** intimates, with a pun on living within Fortune's "private parts" (This sexual punning begins with Hamlet's reference to Fortune's "favors" and continues in

Hamlet's "in the secret parts of Fortune" and his calling Fortune "a strumpet.")

264. **goodly:** large

264–65. **confines:** places of confinement

282–84. **beggars bodies ... beggars' shadows:** i.e., if ambition is but a "shadow's shadow," then **beggars** (who are without ambition) are the only humans with substantial **bodies** and kings and heroes (ruled by ambition) are only **the beggars' shadows**

284. **fay:** faith

286. **wait upon:** accompany; serve

287. **sort you with:** put you in the same class with

295. **too dear a halfpenny:** not worth **a halfpenny**

307–8. **the consonancy of our youth:** the harmony we enjoyed when we were younger

309. **by ... dear:** by whatever is more valuable

310. **proposer:** speaker; **charge you withal:** urge you with

313. **of:** on

316–17. **my anticipation ... discovery:** my saying it first will keep you from having to reveal it

317–18. **your secrecy ... molt no feather: your** promise of **secrecy** not be diminished

324. **fretted:** adorned

329. **express:** well framed

330. **apprehension:** understanding

332. **quintessence:** the very essence (The word is usually used to describe that which transcends the four earthly essences, but here is used ironically to describe mankind as, in essence, **dust**—made from dust to return to dust. See Genesis 2.7, 3.19.)

340. **Lenten:** i.e., meager

341. **coted:** passed

345. **foil and target:** blunted smallsword and shield

346. **the humorous man:** the actor playing the eccentric character

347. **the clown:** the actor who plays the comic roles

348. **tickle o' th' sear:** i.e., easily made to laugh **sear:** the catch in a gunlock that keeps the hammer cocked (When the sear is tickle or loose, the gun goes off easily.); **the lady:** the actor playing the female role

350. **halt:** limp; go awkwardly or irregularly

353. **Their residence:** their remaining in the city

355–56. **their . . . innovation:** The **inhibition** that forces the tragedians from the city and the **innovation** that caused it may reflect London theatrical or political happenings.

361–62. **keeps . . . pace:** continues as usual

362–63. **an aerie of . . . little eyases:** a nest of young hawks (i.e., the child actors)

363. **cry out . . . question:** speak their lines in loud, shrill voices

365. **berattle the common stages:** noisily attack the public theaters

366–67. **are afraid of goose quills:** fear the satirical pens of the poets writing for boy actors

369. **escoted:** financially supported

369–70. **pursue . . . sing:** follow the acting profession only until their voices change in adolescence

376. **tar:** provoke, incite

377–79. **There was . . . in the question:** i.e, no plays were salable that did not take up the quarrel between the children's poets and the adult players

383. **carry it away:** carry off the victory

384–85. **Hercules and his load too:** i.e., the boy actors win over the whole world of playgoers (Hercules' **load** was the globe, which he bore on his shoulders for Atlas.)

387. **mouths:** contorted faces

389. **picture in little:** miniature portrait

390. **'Sblood:** an oath (by Christ's or God's blood)

394. **Th' appurtenance of:** that which belongs to

395–96. comply ... garb: use courteous action with you in this way

396. my extent: i.e., what I show

402. mad north-north-west: only at certain times (when "the wind sits" in certain directions)

403. I know ... a handsaw: a proverb that means "I can distinguish between things that do not resemble each other"

414. Roscius: an actor in the first century B.C.E.

417. Buzz, buzz: a rude response, suggesting that Polonius's news is old news

423–24. scene ... unlimited: i.e., plays that observe the classical unities of time and place, as well as those that pay no attention to such limits

424. Seneca: a Roman philosopher and writer of tragedies

425. Plautus: a Roman writer of comedies; **For the law ... liberty:** i.e., for plays that follow the rules of composition and those that do not

427. Jephthah: According to the biblical story (Judges 11.29–40), Jephthah unintentionally sacrificed his daughter through a rash vow. Hamlet goes on to sing lines from a popular ballad based on Jephthah's story.

432. passing: surpassingly, exceedingly

440. lot: chance; **wot:** knows

443. row: stanza; **pious chanson:** scriptural ballad

444. abridgment: that which cuts short my recitation

447. valanced: fringed (i.e., with a beard)

449. my young lady and mistress: addressed to the boy actor who plays the women's parts

451. the altitude of a chopine: the height of the thick sole of a shoe called a **chopine**—i.e., the boy has grown several inches in height

451–53. a piece ... ring: Hamlet thus expresses his hope that the boy's voice is not **cracked** but is still suitable for female parts. (A coin is not lawful money if it has

a crack that extends inward from the edge into the ring
that surrounds the image of the sovereign's head.)

453. **e'en to 't:** go at it

454. **fly at anything we see:** i.e., undertake anything,
no matter how difficult

455. **straight:** at once

456. **quality:** professional ability

461. **caviary to the general:** i.e., like caviar, too exotic
for average tastes

463. **cried . . . of:** spoke with more authority than

464. **digested:** ordered, arranged

465. **modesty:** restraint

466. **sallets:** i.e., spicy (indelicate or vulgar) words

470. **fine:** gaudy

471–73. **Aeneas' tale . . . of Priam's slaughter:** Aeneas, hero of Virgil's *Aeneid*, tells Dido, queen of Carthage,
stories of the Trojan War. Among them is that of Priam,
king of Troy, who was killed by Pyrrhus seeking revenge
for his father Achilles' death.

475. **Hyrcanian beast:** a tiger (Hyrcania, in Roman
times, was the name of a region now in Iran at the southern end of the Caspian Sea. In the *Aeneid*, it is associated
with tigers.)

479. **horse:** the wooden horse in which the Greeks hid
themselves to gain entry into Troy

482. **gules:** red (a heraldic term); **tricked:** decorated

487. **o'ersizèd:** covered as with "size," a glaze or filler

488. **carbuncles:** deep red glowing jewels

492. **discretion:** judgment, discernment

496. **Repugnant to:** opposing, resisting

498. **fell:** cruel

499. **senseless:** without human senses; **Ilium:** the
fortress within Troy

509. **rack:** clouds high above, driven by the wind

514. **Cyclops:** Titans who forged thunderbolts for
Jove, king of the Greco-Roman gods

515. **Mars:** the Roman god of war; **for proof eterne:** to stand the test of eternity

520. **fellies:** sections of the wheel's rim; **wheel:** Fortune was often pictured as controlling human life by turning a great **wheel** on which she stood or sat.

521. **nave:** hub of the wheel

525. **jig:** a lively, mocking song

526. **Hecuba:** the wife of Priam and queen of Troy

527. **moblèd:** i.e., her head and face were muffled

531. **bisson rheum:** blinding tears; **clout:** piece of cloth

533. **lank and all o'erteemèd:** shrunken and worn out with childbearing

536–37. **'Gainst . . . pronounced:** would have uttered treasonous statements against Fortune's rule

543. **milch:** wet with tears, milky

544. **passion:** deep emotion

545. **whe'er:** whether

549. **bestowed:** lodged, housed

550. **abstract:** summary

555. **God's bodykins:** a mild oath (by God's "little body")

580–81. **Could . . . wanned:** i.e., could work **his soul** into such accord with his thought that, from his soul's **working** on his body, his face grew pale

583–84. **his whole function . . . conceit:** i.e., all the bodily powers that express emotion responding with outward appearances to match his thoughts

591. **Make mad . . . free:** i.e., madden guilty spectators and terrify those who are innocent

592. **amaze:** astound

594. **muddy-mettled:** dull-spirited; **peak:** mope

595. **John-a-dreams:** a proverbial name for an absent-minded dreamer; **unpregnant of:** unfilled by, and therefore never to give birth (to action)

598. **defeat:** overthrow

601–2. **gives me . . . lungs:** i.e., calls me an absolute liar

603. **'Swounds:** an oath, by Christ's wounds

606. **kites:** birds of prey

608. **kindless:** unnatural

611. **brave:** admirable

615. **drab:** prostitute

616. **scullion:** kitchen servant

617. **About, . . . !:** i.e., turn around

619. **cunning:** art, skill; **scene:** performance

620. **presently:** instantly

626. **tent:** probe (as into a wound)

631. **spirits:** i.e., emotional states (such as **melancholy**)

632. **Abuses:** deceives, deludes

633. **relative:** pertinent

3.1 After Rosencrantz and Guildenstern report their failure to find the cause of Hamlet's madness, Polonius places Ophelia where he and Claudius may secretly observe a meeting between her and Hamlet. Hamlet is at first courteous to Ophelia, but suddenly he turns on her: he denies having loved her, asks where her father is, attacks womankind, and tells her she should enter a nunnery. After Hamlet exits, Claudius decides that Hamlet's erratic behavior is not caused by love and announces a plan to send Hamlet on an embassy to England. Polonius persuades Claudius to take no action until Gertrude talks with Hamlet after the play, which is scheduled for that evening.

2. **puts . . . confusion:** acts in this distracted way

5. **distracted:** perturbed, unsettled

7. **forward . . . sounded:** i.e., eager to be questioned

14–15. **Niggard . . . reply:** not inclined to talk, but willing to answer fully our questions

16. **assay:** tempt
18. **o'erraught:** overtook
28. **give ... edge:** i.e., sharpen his desire
32. **closely:** privately
34. **Affront:** meet face to face
35. **espials:** spies
38. **as he is behaved:** according to how he acts
51–52. **show ... loneliness:** i.e., Ophelia's apparent reading of a Bible or prayer book would give a pretext for her being alone
52. **to blame:** i.e., guilty, blameworthy
59–61. **The harlot's ... word:** i.e., the pockmarked cheek of the whore is not uglier, when compared to the illusion of beauty she creates with cosmetics, than is what I have done in comparison to my story of what happened
73. **rub:** obstacle (a technical term from the game of bowls, where a "rub" is any obstruction that hinders or deflects the course of the bowl)
75. **shuffled off this mortal coil:** i.e., untangled ourselves from the flesh; also, detached ourselves from the turmoil of human affairs.
77. **makes calamity of so long life:** i.e., makes us put up with unhappiness for such a long time
80. **despised:** unrequited (accent on first syllable)
81. **office:** i.e., those in **office**
83. **his quietus make:** settle his own account (from *quietus est,* a legal term meaning "he is quit")
84. **bare bodkin:** a mere dagger (or, an unsheathed dagger); **fardels:** burdens, loads
87. **undiscovered:** unexplored; **bourn:** frontier
88. **puzzles:** i.e., paralyzes
91. **conscience:** i.e., knowledge, consciousness
92. **native hue:** natural color
93. **cast:** shade
94. **pitch:** height (The *pitch* is the highest point in a falcon's flight.) **moment:** importance

95. **With this regard:** on this account; **their currents turn awry:** i.e., the great enterprises are like rivers that, turned aside from their main channels, lose momentum and become stagnant

96. **Soft you now:** an exclamation to interrupt speech ("wait a moment," "hold," "enough")

113. **honest:** chaste (with perhaps also the meaning of "truthful")

118. **discourse to:** conversation with

123. **his:** its

124. **sometime:** formerly; **paradox:** a statement contrary to what is generally thought

125. **the time:** the present age

127–29. **virtue . . . relish of it:** The metaphor here is of grafting a bud or branch to produce better fruit. Virtue, Hamlet says, may be grafted onto (may **inoculate**) sinful human nature (**our old stock**), but the sinfulness will still leave its taste (**relish**) in the fruit that is produced.

131. **nunnery:** convent (The word was sometimes used mockingly to refer to a brothel.)

132–33. **indifferent honest:** reasonably virtuous

151. **monsters:** cuckolds (In the standard joke, a cuckold had horns growing out of the forehead.)

157. **nickname:** call by the wrong name

157–58. **make . . . ignorance:** call your immorality **ignorance** (The word **wantonness** may here have the less frequent meaning of "affectation.")

159. **on 't:** of it

164–65. **courtier's . . . sword:** i.e., the **courtier's eye**, the **scholar's tongue**, the **soldier's sword**

167. **glass of fashion:** mirror of proper behavior; **mold of form:** model of attractiveness

172. **out of time:** out of correct rhythm

173. **blown:** vigorous, fresh (The word, applied to flowers in bloom, picks up the earlier **rose of the . . . state** [line 166].)

174. **Blasted with ecstasy:** blighted by madness
176. **affections:** emotions, mental state
180. **doubt:** fear; **the hatch and the disclose:** Both **hatch** and **disclose** mean to break out of the egg—here, the "egg" on which Hamlet's **melancholy sits on brood** (line 179).
187. **something-settled:** somehow fixed
197. **round:** plainspoken
199. **find him not:** i.e., does not discover his secret

3.2 Hamlet gives direction to the actors and asks Horatio to help him observe Claudius's reaction to the play. When the court arrive, Hamlet makes bawdy and bitter comments to Ophelia. The traveling actors perform, in dumb show and then with dialogue, a story that includes many elements of Claudius's alleged seduction of Gertrude and murder of King Hamlet. At the moment that the Player King is murdered by his nephew, Claudius stops the play and rushes out. Hamlet is exuberant in his belief that the Ghost's word has been proved true. Rosencrantz and Guildenstern return to tell Hamlet that Claudius is furious and that Gertrude wishes to see Hamlet at once in her sitting room. Hamlet promises himself that he will not harm her, though he will "speak daggers."

3. **I had as lief:** I'd just as soon
9. **robustious:** noisy, boisterous
11. **groundlings:** spectators who stood rather than sat, and thus paid less to go to the theater
12. **capable of:** able to appreciate
14. **Termagant:** imaginary Muslim god, shown in early drama as noisy and unrestrained
15. **Herod:** Herod of Judea, who appears in medieval drama as a raging tyrant
20. **modesty:** moderation, absence of excess

21. **from:** opposite to
22. **playing:** acting
25. **the . . . time:** i.e., the present exactly as it is
26. **his:** its; **pressure:** shape
26–27. **come tardy off:** done inadequately
27. **unskillful:** those lacking judgment
28–29. **the censure . . . one:** the judgment of even one of which
29. **allowance:** estimation
32. **not to speak it profanely:** not intending to be profane in what I'm about to say
33. **Christians:** an informal usage, meaning humans as opposed to animals
36. **journeymen:** hirelings who work for daily wages
38. **indifferently:** pretty well
42. **of them:** i.e., some **of them**
43. **barren:** dull, not intelligent
57. **my conversation coped withal:** my experience has brought me into contact with
61. **revenue:** accent on second syllable
65. **pregnant:** ready (to bend)
66. **thrift:** profit
67. **dear:** highly prized
68. **election:** choice
74. **commeddled:** mixed together
75. **pipe:** small wind instrument, like a flute
84. **comment:** observation
85. **occulted:** deliberately hidden
86. **unkennel:** reveal, as when a fox is driven from its lair
89. **Vulcan's stithy:** forge of the Roman god of fire and metalworking
99. **chameleon's dish:** Chameleons were thought to live off air.
132. **your only jig-maker:** the best comic of them all
138. **a suit of sables:** clothing trimmed with sable furs

142. **suffer not thinking on:** endure oblivion

142–43. **the hobby-horse:** a character in morris dances (The song that Hamlet quotes expresses sorrow that such figures are gone and forgotten.)

144 SD. **Dumb show:** a scene without words

158. **miching mallecho:** skulking misdeed (**Miching** is dialect for "sneaking," **mallecho** is the Spanish *malhecho*, "misdeed.")

160. **Belike:** perhaps; **argument:** plot

168. **naught:** naughty, indecent

173. **posy of a ring:** a poem inscribed in a ring

176. **Phoebus' cart:** the chariot of the sun god, which appears to make its cycle around the earth annually (The language of this play-within-the-play is set apart from that surrounding it by complicated word order and noticeably poetic language.)

177. **Neptune's salt wash:** the ocean **Neptune:** Roman god of the sea; **Tellus:** Roman goddess of the earth

180. **Hymen:** god of marriage

186. **distrust you:** fear for you

188. **For women . . . love:** This line is part of an incomplete couplet; perhaps the completing line was dropped in the printing house, or perhaps the couplet was incompletely crossed out by Shakespeare.

189–90. **women's . . . extremity:** i.e., women's **love** and **fear** are parallel: where they love, they also fear

196. **My operant powers . . . leave to do:** i.e., my vital powers cease to function

204. **wormwood:** i.e., bitter, harsh

205. **instances:** causes

206. **thrift:** worldly profit

211. **Purpose is but the slave to memory:** i.e., a **purpose** must be remembered if it is to be carried out

212. **validity:** vigor

215–16. **Most . . . debt:** i.e., **we** conveniently **forget** the promises we make to **ourselves**

220. **enactures:** enactments

223. **aye:** ever

231. **try:** test (his friendship)

235. **devices still:** plans always

242. **An anchor's cheer:** an anchorite's (hermit's) food and drink

243. **opposite . . . joy:** obstacle that makes joy's **face** turn pale (or, perhaps, that deprives joy's **face** of all expression)

251. **rock:** soothe

256. **argument:** plot

261. **Tropically:** i.e., as a trope, a figure of speech

265. **free:** innocent

266–67. **Let . . . unwrung:** a proverb that says, in effect: let guilty persons flinch; we have clear consciences **galled jade:** a horse with raw skin **withers:** ridge between the horse's shoulders **unwrung:** not chafed

269. **a chorus:** a character who (as in Shakespeare's *Henry V*) tells the audience what they are about to see

270–71. **I could . . . dallying:** i.e., I could play the role of narrator at a puppet show in which you and your lover are shown making love

273–74. **take off mine edge:** make me less sharp; satisfy my desire (Hamlet gives a sexual meaning to Ophelia's "You are keen" [i.e., sharp, penetrating] and responds with this double entendre.)

275. **better and worse:** more witty and more offensive

276. **so you mis-take:** i.e., in the same way, you take falsely (Wives promise to "take" their husbands "for better, for worse.")

278–79. **the croaking . . . revenge:** Hamlet here amusingly condenses two lines from the anonymous *The True Tragedy of Richard III* (c. 1591): "The screeking **raven** sits **croaking** for **revenge.** / Whole herds of beasts comes bellowing **for revenge.**"

282. **Confederate season:** i.e., time being my ally; **else:** otherwise

284. **With Hecate's ban:** by the curse of Hecate, the goddess of sorcery and witchcraft

292. **false fire:** discharge of a gun loaded only with powder

301. **feathers:** worn on actors' hats

302. **turn Turk with me:** turn against me

303. **Provincial:** possibly, of Provence (in France); **razed:** slashed decoratively

303–4. **a fellowship in a cry of players:** a partnership in a theater company

307. **Damon:** renowned, in Roman mythology, for the depth of his friendship for his friend Pythias

308. **dismantled:** stripped

310. **pajock:** possibly "peacock" (In the natural history of Shakespeare's day, the peacock had a reputation for lust and cruelty.)

311. **rhymed:** The obvious rhyme word is *ass.*

317–18. **recorders:** wooden flutes with mouthpieces

320. **perdy:** from the French *par dieu,* "by God"

327–28. **distempered:** upset (with a second meaning of "ill," which is how Hamlet chooses to interpret it)

330. **choler:** biliousness (The word has a second meaning of "anger," which Hamlet plays on at line 334.)

333. **purgation:** medical cleansing; spiritual purification

336. **start:** shy away (like a nervous or wild horse)

344. **wholesome:** sane

345. **pardon:** permission to depart

355. **admiration:** wonder

360. **closet:** private chamber

364. **by these . . . stealers:** i.e., by these hands (The phrase borrows from the catechism, where one is told "to keep [one's] hands from picking and stealing.")

372. **"While the grass grows":** The rest of the proverb reads "the horse starves."

373. **something musty:** somewhat stale, i.e., so famil-

iar it need not be quoted in full (The proverb, in Latin, was in use 350 years before *Hamlet* was written.)

376–77. **go . . . toil:** try to get to the windward side of me, as if to force me into a trap (Hamlet speaks as if they were hunters and he their quarry.)

381. **this pipe:** the recorder

387. **ventages:** finger holes, or **stops** (line 390), of the recorder

396. **sound me:** (1) play me like a musical instrument; (2) measure my depths, as with a fathom line; (3) test me for my secrets (a triple pun)

397. **compass:** (1) full range of an instrument's sound; (2) limits, scope

399. **organ:** musical instrument; **'Sblood:** an oath (by God's, or Christ's, blood)

402. **fret:** (1) annoy; (2) provide an instrument with frets (On stringed instruments, frets are the raised parts that guide the fingers.)

413. **by and by:** soon, before long; or, perhaps, right away

427. **Nero:** murderer of his mother, Agrippina

431. **How . . . somever:** however; **shent:** punished

432. **give them seals:** i.e., validate my words (by putting them into action)

3.3 Claudius orders Rosencrantz and Guildenstern to take Hamlet to England immediately. Polonius arrives to tell Claudius of his plans to spy on Hamlet's conversation with Gertrude. Left alone, Claudius reveals to the audience his remorse for killing his brother, and he tries to pray. Hamlet comes upon him kneeling and draws his sword, but then stops to think that if he kills Claudius at prayer, Claudius will go to heaven. Hamlet decides to kill Claudius when the king is committing a sin so that Claudius will instead go to hell. After Hamlet leaves, Claudius rises, saying that he has been unable to pray.

1. **I . . . not:** i.e., I do not like the way he is acting

3. **dispatch:** prepare at once

5. **The terms of our estate:** my position as a king

12. **single and peculiar:** individual and private

14. **noyance:** injury

16. **cess:** cessation, decease

17. **gulf:** whirlpool

21. **mortised:** securely fastened

25. **Arm you . . . to:** i.e., prepare yourself for

31–32. **tax him home:** reprimand him strongly

36. **of vantage:** from the vantage point of concealment

41. **primal eldest curse:** The first curse, which condemned Cain to a life of "a fugitive and a vagabond," was laid on him for his murder of his brother, Abel (Genesis 4.10–12).

50–51. **Whereto . . . offense?:** i.e., what purpose does **mercy** serve except **to confront** the face of condemnation? (The promise of the New Testament is that mercy, in the person of Christ, will, at the Last Judgment, oppose itself to the face of the offended Deity, and thus secure forgiveness of our sins.)

53–54. **forestallèd . . . down:** i.e., the **twofold force** of prayer is that we not be "led into temptation" and that we be "forgiven our trespasses"

60. **th' offense:** that which has been gained through the crime

61. **currents:** course of events

62. **Offense's gilded hand:** the golden hand of the offender, **gilded** through money illegally obtained; **shove by:** thrust aside

64. **'tis not so above:** this is not the case in heaven

65. **There is no shuffling:** in heaven, one cannot escape through evasion

65–68. **the action . . . in evidence:** i.e., in God's court, **the** legal **action** must be brought in accord with the facts; we are forced even to testify against **ourselves**

68. **rests:** remains

72. **limèd:** trapped, like a bird caught in birdlime

73. **engaged:** entangled; **Make assay:** put forth all your efforts

80. **would be scanned:** i.e., needs to be examined

84. **hire and salary:** i.e., something Claudius should pay me for

85. **grossly, full of bread:** in the full enjoyment of the world (See Ezekiel 16.49: "Pride, fullness of bread, and abundance of idleness.")

87. **audit:** final account

89. **heavy with him:** i.e., his spirit is in a serious condition

90. **him:** i.e., Claudius

93. **know thou a more horrid hent:** i.e., wait for a more horrible occasion

100. **stays:** waits

101. **This physic:** this medicine (i.e., this postponement of the killing; or, Claudius's purging of himself through prayer)

3.4 In Gertrude's room, Polonius hides behind a tapestry. Hamlet's entrance so alarms Gertrude that she cries out for help. Polonius echoes her cry, and Hamlet, thinking Polonius to be Claudius, stabs him to death. Hamlet then verbally attacks his mother for marrying Claudius. In the middle of Hamlet's attack, the Ghost returns to remind Hamlet that his real purpose is to avenge his father's death. Gertrude cannot see the Ghost and pities Hamlet's apparent madness. After the Ghost exits, Hamlet urges Gertrude to abandon Claudius's bed. He then tells her about Claudius's plan to send him to England and reveals his suspicions that the journey is a plot against him, which he resolves to counter violently. He exits dragging out Polonius's body.

1. **straight:** immediately; **lay home to him:** reprove him thoroughly

7. **round:** blunt

9. **Fear me not:** don't doubt me

14. **idle:** foolish

18. **forgot me:** forgotten who I am

24. **glass:** mirror

29. **Dead for a ducat:** i.e., **dead**, I'll wager **a ducat**

45. **damnèd custom:** habitual wickedness

46. **proof:** invulnerable (like armor); **sense:** feeling

55. **contraction:** i.e., the marriage contract

57. **rhapsody:** jumble

58. **this . . . mass:** i.e., the earth

59. **against the doom:** when Judgment Day comes

60. **Is thought-sick:** i.e., Heaven **is thought-sick**

62. **That roars . . . index:** i.e., that receives such a violent introduction (**The index** was the table of contents introducing a book.)

64. **counterfeit presentment:** representation in portraits (These are perhaps miniatures—Claudius's on a chain around Gertrude's neck, King Hamlet's around Prince Hamlet's neck—or are perhaps paintings hung upon the wall.)

66. **Hyperion:** the sun god, the most beautiful of the pagan deities; **front:** brow

68. **A station . . . Mercury:** a way of standing that is like that of the winged messenger of the gods

74. **ear:** i.e., of a cereal plant like wheat

75. **Blasting:** blighting; **his:** its

76. **leave to feed:** stop feeding

77. **batten:** glut yourself; **moor:** barren land

79. **heyday:** state of excitement; **blood:** passion

81. **Sense:** perception through the senses

83. **apoplexed:** suffering from apoplexy, hence without sensation or consciousness

84. **sense . . . thralled:** i.e., the five senses are never so

subjected by lunacy (Hamlet's argument is that even in madness, Gertrude's senses would have **reserved some quantity of choice** [line 85]—i.e., retained a trace of the power to choose.)

87. **cozened:** tricked; **hoodman-blind:** the game of blindman's buff

89. **sans all:** without the other senses

91. **so mope:** be so stupefied

93. **mutine:** incite rebellion

94–95. **be . . . fire:** i.e., **melt** like the **wax** in a burning candle

95–98. **Proclaim . . . will:** i.e., do not call it shameful when youthful passion acts impetuously, since the **frost** of age is itself aflame and **reason** is acting as a pander for desire instead of controlling it

101. **grainèd:** indelible (*Grain* was a "fast" or permanent dye.)

102. **leave their tinct:** give up their color

104. **enseamèd:** greasy

112. **a vice of kings:** a buffoon of a king (a reference to the comic Vice of the morality plays)

113. **cutpurse:** thief

123. **lapsed in time and passion:** i.e., having let **time** slip by and **passion** cool

124. **important:** importunate, urgent

128. **amazement on thy mother sits:** i.e., your **mother** is in a state of extreme shock

130. **Conceit:** imagination

135. **incorporal:** immaterial

137. **in th' alarm:** waked by the call to arms

138. **hair, like life in excrements:** as if **hair**, a lifeless outgrowth ("excrement"), had come to **life**

139. **an end:** on **end**

144. **capable:** responsive

147. **effects:** purposes

148. **want:** lack

155. **in ... lived:** dressed as he did when **he lived**

158. **ecstasy:** madness

165. **gambol from:** skip away from

166. **flattering unction:** soothing salve

174. **fatness:** grossness; **pursy:** fat, flabby

176. **curb:** bow

182–83. **That monster ... devil:** This passage may contain mistakes in the printing (editors often change "devil" to "evil"). The general meaning may be "**Custom, a monster** that consumes **all sense**, is therefore like a **devil** in suggesting evil habits."

184. **use:** habit

186. **aptly:** easily

190. **either ⌈ ... ⌉ the devil:** A word seems to have been lost; Q2 reads "either the devil"; many editors (to complete the line and the thought) insert the verb "master," found in the quarto of *Hamlet* printed in 1611 (Q3).

196. **their scourge and minister:** heaven's **scourge** (of punishment—and therefore subject to punishment himself) and heaven's **minister** (agent of divine retribution) **their:** heaven's

200. **remains behind:** is yet to come

203. **Not ... means ... :** After this general statement of negation, Hamlet lists the things he would have Gertrude *not* do (e.g., go to bed with Claudius).

206. **reechy:** filthy

210. **'Twere good you let him know:** said very sarcastically, as are lines 211–18

212. **paddock:** toad; **gib:** tomcat

213. **Such dear concernings:** such important matters

215–18. **Unpeg the basket ... and break your own neck down:** The story that Hamlet alludes to here is lost. **Unpeg:** unfasten **To try conclusions:** to experiment

229–30. **to have the enginer ... petard:** to have the maker of military devices blown up by his own explosives

230–31. **and 't ... I will:** i.e., with any luck, **I will**

234. packing: leaving the country; carrying off a burden

239. to draw toward an end with you: to come to the end of my business with you (with a pun on **draw,** as Hamlet drags him away)

4.1 Gertrude reports Polonius's death to Claudius, who sends Rosencrantz and Guildenstern to find Hamlet and recover the body.

   1. **matter:** significance
  11. **brainish apprehension:** brain-sick belief
  12. **unseen:** hidden
  13. **heavy:** dreadful
  18. **laid to us, whose providence:** charged against me, whose foresight
  19. **short:** i.e., on a short leash; **out of haunt:** away from others
  23. **divulging:** coming to light
  26–27. **like . . . base:** perhaps, like a vein of gold in a mine of **base metals**; or, perhaps, like gold that separates out as liquid from **base metals** when the metal is heated
  32–33. **with all our majesty . . . excuse:** i.e., with all my royal authority I **must countenance**, and with all my **skill** I must **excuse**
  34. **join you . . . aid:** find others to help you
  41. **and what's untimely done:** Both Q2 and F print this short line; the four lines following in Q2 require that some words be inserted to provide a reference for "Whose whisper" in line 42. Many editions accept the eighteenth-century editorial insertion of "So haply slander" to complete line 41.
  43. **As level . . . blank:** with as sure an aim as **the cannon** hitting its mark

4.2 Hamlet refuses to tell Rosencrantz and Guildenstern where he has put Polonius's body.

6. **dust . . . kin:** "for dust thou art, and unto dust shalt thou return" (Genesis 3.19)

12–13. **to be demanded . . . what replication:** being questioned by . . . what reply

15. **countenance:** favorable looks

17–18. **like an ape an apple:** as **an ape** keeps **an apple**

23. **sleeps in:** is not understood by

30–31. **Hide fox . . . :** perhaps a line from a child's game like hide-and-seek

4.3 Hamlet is brought to Claudius, who tells him that he is to leave immediately for England. Alone, at the end of this scene, Claudius discloses to the audience that he is sending Hamlet to his death.

4. **loved of:** loved by; **distracted:** unsettled

6–7. **where 'tis so . . . offense:** i.e., where the people love with **their eyes** instead of their reason, they judge the punishment (the **scourge**) rather than the crime (the **offense**)

7. **To bear . . . even:** to manage everything smoothly and evenly

9. **Deliberate pause:** the result of careful thought

9–10. **Diseases . . . relieved:** Proverbial: **desperate diseases** require **desperate** remedies.

23. **convocation of politic worms:** perhaps an allusion to the Diet of Worms, a **convocation** (council) summoned at the city of Worms by the Holy Roman emperor in 1521

35. **progress:** royal journey

45. **Which . . . grieve: which we tender** as dearly (value as highly) **as we dearly** (deeply) **grieve**

49. **at help:** favorable

50. **tend:** attend you, wait for you; **bent:** ready

56. **I see a cherub . . . :** Heaven's angels (cherubim), Hamlet suggests, can see Claudius's purposes.

63. **at foot:** at his heels, close behind

67. **England:** the king of England

68. **As . . . sense: as my power** may give you a **sense thereof** (i.e., of the value of retaining my love)

69. **cicatrice:** scar

70–71. **thy free awe . . . us:** i.e., **awe** of Denmark's power makes England pay **homage** (acknowledge allegiance; or, perhaps, pay tribute) to Denmark

71–72. **thou . . . process:** i.e., England may not lightly regard my royal command

74. **present:** immediate

75. **the hectic:** continual fever

77. **Howe'er my haps:** whatever my fortunes

4.4 Fortinbras and his army march across Hamlet's path on their way to Poland. Hamlet finds in Fortinbras's vigorous activity a model for himself in avenging his father's murder; Hamlet resolves upon bloody action.

2–4. **by his license . . . Over his kingdom:** In formal language, Fortinbras, having been given **license** from Claudius to **march** across Denmark, now asks for an escort (see 2.2.81–85). **conveyance of:** escort during

5. **would aught with us:** wishes anything of me (Note his use of the royal "we.")

6. **in his eye:** in his presence

9. **softly:** slowly

16. **the main: the main** part

18. **with no addition:** without added details

20. **the name: the** mere **name** of conquest

21. **To pay . . . farm it:** I would not **pay** five ducats to rent it.

23. **ranker:** higher; **in fee:** outright

27. **Will not debate . . . this straw:** are not enough to pay for settling this trifling quarrel

28. **impostume:** abscess

29. **without:** on the outside

34. **inform against:** denounce

38–39. **discourse, . . . before and after:** power of thought that looks into the past and the future

41. **fust:** become moldy

42. **Bestial oblivion:** mindlessness like the beasts'

42–43. **craven scruple / Of thinking:** cowardly hesitation that results from **thinking**

49. **gross as earth:** as evident as the **earth** itself

53. **Makes mouths at: makes** faces at (i.e., holds in contempt)

56–59. **Rightly . . . at the stake:** i.e., to be truly **great,** one should not fight except when the **argument** is itself **great,** unless honor is at risk **at the stake:** at risk (as in gambling)

64. **trick of fame:** illusion of honor

66. **Whereon . . . cause:** on which **the numbers** of fighting men do not have room to fight the battle

67–68. **Which is not . . . hide the slain: which is not** large enough to be a **tomb** or receptacle for those who will be killed **continent:** container

4.5 Reports reach Gertrude that Ophelia is mad. Ophelia enters singing about death and betrayal. After Ophelia has gone, Claudius agonizes over her madness and over the stir created by the return of an angry Laertes. When Laertes breaks in on Claudius and Gertrude, Claudius asserts his innocence with regard to Polonius's death. The reappearance of the mad Ophelia is devastating to Laertes.

3. **distract:** distraught; **will needs be:** must be

6. **tricks:** plots, deception

8. **Spurns enviously at straws:** takes offense angrily at trifles; **in doubt:** obscurely (?)

9–11. **Her speech . . . to collection:** i.e., **her speech** makes no sense, but its very formlessness makes her **hearers** draw conclusions

12. **botch . . . up:** patch together

13–15. **Which . . . make one think: the words** (line 12), together with her **gestures,** would **make one think**

22. **as sin's true nature is:** i.e., sin, in its **true nature**, is a sickness of the **soul**

23. **toy:** trifle; **amiss:** disaster

24. **artless:** awkward, stupid; **jealousy:** unreasonable suspicions

25. **spills:** destroys; **spilt:** divulged

28–31. **How should I . . . shoon:** Ophelia sings a version of a ballad preserved in many editions of music of the time. The song continues in lines 34–37 and 41, 43–45.

30. **cockle hat:** A hat with a cockle shell denoted a pilgrim returning from the shrine of St. James of Compostela.

31. **shoon:** shoes

44. **did not go:** The word "not" has been inserted into the ballad, perhaps as Ophelia's addition, or perhaps by mistake by the printer.

47. **God dild you:** God yield (reward) you

47–48. **the owl . . . daughter:** According to an old story, an ungenerous **baker's daughter** was transformed into an **owl** as punishment for her stinginess.

50. **Conceit upon:** i.e., (she is) thinking about

53–60. **Tomorrow . . . more:** The song alludes to the ancient custom that the first girl a man sees on Valentine's day is to be his true love. The song continues in lines 63–68, 70–71. **betime:** early **dupped:** opened

63. **Gis:** Jesus

66. **Cock:** a substitution for "God" in oaths

74. **cannot . . . weep:** cannot help weeping

83. **spies:** individual soldiers sent by the army to scout out the territory

85–86. most violent . . . remove: the cause, through his violence, of his justly earned removal   **author:** cause

86. muddied: stirred up, confused

89–90. we have . . . greenly: I have acted foolishly

91. In hugger-mugger: without proper ceremony

96. in clouds: i.e., in a cloud of suspicion

97. wants not buzzers: does not lack gossipers

99. of matter beggared: lacking facts

100. Will nothing stick . . . arraign: not hesitate to accuse me of the crime

101–3. this . . . superfluous death: i.e., this (battalion of troubles) kills me over and over, as if I were shot at by a **murd'ring piece**, a cannon that scatters its shots

105. Attend: listen

106. Switzers: Swiss bodyguards

109–12. The ocean . . . your officers: i.e., Laertes and his followers are overbearing the king's **officers** as quickly and pitilessly as an **ocean** flooding its flatlands   **overpeering of his list:** overflowing its shore   **head:** armed force

113–16. as the world . . . They cry: as if **the world were to begin** right now, with tradition and custom completely forgotten   **ratifiers and props of every word:** probably refers to **Antiquity** and **custom**, the supports of words and promises

117. Caps: Their **caps**, that is, are thrown into the air.

120. counter: In hunting, a dog goes "counter" when it follows the trail in the wrong direction.

122. without: outside

132. cuckold: betrayed husband

134. true: faithful, chaste

137. fear our: fear for my

139. would: i.e., **would** like to do

140. his: its

148. juggled with: manipulated and thus deceived

152. both . . . negligence: I don't care what happens to me in this world or the next

154. **throughly:** thoroughly

162. **swoopstake:** a term from gambling, as is **draw**; literally, take all the stakes on the gambling table (Here the meaning is "are you determined to take revenge on friends and enemies both?")

168. **life-rend'ring pelican:** The mother pelican was thought to feed her young with her own blood.

173. **sensibly:** intensely

174. **level:** intelligible, plain

179. **virtue:** power

180–81. **paid . . . beam:** avenged (The image is of putting an excess of weight in one scale until it overbalances the other scale, or turns **the beam.**)

185. **fine in:** refined by

186. **instance of itself:** sample or proof of its refined nature (In this case, the sample is Ophelia's wits, which, Laertes says, have been sent after the dead Polonius.)

193. **could not move thus:** could not be this moving

194–95. **You must sing ". . . a-down-a":** Ophelia perhaps instructs others on the stage to sing refrains to her song.

195. **the wheel:** perhaps, the refrain of the song; or, perhaps the turning of the spinning wheel, to which motion ballads were sung

196. **false steward:** perhaps a reference to a story or ballad no longer known

198. **This nothing's . . . matter:** i.e., this nonsense speaks more eloquently than does serious speech

199. **There's rosemary:** Ophelia begins here to distribute real or imaginary flowers.

202. **document:** lesson, instruction

202–3. **thoughts . . . fitted:** i.e., Ophelia has wisely linked **thoughts** and **remembrance**

204. **fennel:** In flower symbolism, fennel symbolized flattery and deceit.

205. **rue:** symbol of sorrow or repentance

207. **with a difference:** a heraldic term for a variation in a coat of arms, but here meaning, perhaps, "for a different reason"; **daisy:** symbol of dissembling

208. **violets:** symbol of faithfulness

211. **Thought:** melancholy; **passion:** suffering

219. **poll:** head

230. **collateral:** i.e., as an accessory

231. **find us touched:** find me implicated

239. **hatchment:** tablet displaying his coat of arms

240. **ostentation:** ceremony

242. **That:** so that

4.6 Horatio is given a letter from Hamlet telling of the prince's boarding of a pirate ship and his subsequent return to Denmark.

10. **th' ambassador:** i.e., Hamlet

14. **overlooked:** read; **means:** means of access

16. **pirate . . . appointment:** pirate ship well equipped for battle

17–18. **put on a compelled valor:** became, under compulsion, courageous

21. **thieves of mercy:** merciful **thieves**

23. **repair thou:** come

25–26. **too light for the bore of the matter: too light for the** caliber of the gun; i.e., inadequate

32. **way:** means of access

4.7 Claudius, in conversation with Laertes, also gets a letter from Hamlet announcing the prince's return. Claudius enlists Laertes's willing help in devising another plot against Hamlet's life. Laertes agrees to kill Hamlet with a poisoned rapier in a fencing match. If he fails, Claudius will give Hamlet a poisoned cup of wine. Gertrude interrupts their plotting to announce that Ophelia has drowned.

1. **my acquittance seal:** ratify my acquittal, i.e., acknowledge my innocence

8. **capital:** deadly

10. **mainly:** greatly

12. **unsinewed:** weak

16. **conjunctive:** closely joined

17. **star . . . sphere:** In Ptolemaic astronomy each planet (**star**) was carried around earth in a crystalline **sphere** from which it was inseparable.

19. **count:** accounting, judgment

20. **the general gender:** the common people

22. **Work . . . stone:** function like springs of water that petrify **wood**

23. **Convert his gyves:** transform his shackles

28. **terms:** condition

29. **if praises . . . again:** if I may praise what she used to be

30–31. **Stood challenger . . . perfections:** i.e., her worth challenged all the age to equal her excellence

50. **naked:** defenseless

52. **pardon:** permission

57. **character:** handwriting

68. **So:** provided that

70. **checking at:** refusing to continue (The image is of a falcon in flight turning away from the prey she is supposed to be pursuing.); **that:** if that (i.e., if)

72. **device:** devising, planning

75. **uncharge the practice:** not blame his death on our plot **uncharge:** lift a burden from **practice:** stratagem, treachery

79. **organ:** agent, instrument

83. **Your . . . parts:** all of your qualities combined

86. **unworthiest siege:** least important rank

88. **A very . . . youth:** a mere decoration in youth's **cap**

89–92. **youth no less becomes . . . graveness:** i.e., clothes worn by **youth** are as becoming to the young as the garments of **age** are to their comfortably prosperous wearers   **sables:** rich robes with sable trim   **weeds:** garments   **Importing:** signifying

95. **can well:** are skillful

98. **As had he been:** as if he had been; **encorpsed and demi-natured:** made into a single body (with the horse) to form a double-natured creature like the centaur (half man, half horse)

99. **brave:** noble; **topped:** surpassed

100–101. **in forgery . . . he did:** i.e., in imagining his feats, I fall short of his actual performance

108. **made confession of you:** acknowledged you

110. **art and exercise . . . defense:** theory and practice of fencing

113. **'scrimers:** fencers (French *escrimeurs*)

119. **play:** fence

128. **passages of proof:** proven instances

129. **qualifies:** diminishes, lessens

131. **snuff:** the burned part of the wick of a candle

132. **is at a like goodness still:** remains always at the same level of perfection

133. **pleurisy:** excess (not to be confused with the disease of the same name)

134. **his own too-much:** its own excess

139–40. **spendthrift . . . by easing:** According to old notions of medicine, a sigh eases distress but draws blood away from the heart.

140. **to . . . th' ulcer:** i.e., to the main point

142. **indeed:** in fact; also, in action

145. **should murder sanctuarize:** i.e., should protect a murderer (like Hamlet) from punishment

149. **put on those shall:** incite those who shall

151. **in fine:** in conclusion

153. **remiss:** carelessly indifferent

154. **generous:** noble-minded

157. **unbated:** not blunted (as rapiers for such

matches should be); **a pass of practice:** a treacherous thrust

161. **of a mountebank:** from a quack doctor

162. **mortal:** deadly

163. **cataplasm:** poultice

164. **Collected from:** composed of; **simples:** medicinal plants; **virtue:** medicinal power

167. **contagion:** poison that infects the blood

167–68. **if . . . death:** if I scratch him he will die

171. **May fit us to our shape:** may suit our plan

172–73. **drift . . . performance:** intention reveal itself through our bungling

175. **back or second:** backup position

176. **blast in proof:** blow up in the testing

177. **your cunnings:** yours and Hamlet's skills

184. **stuck:** thrust (a fencing term)

190. **askant:** aslant

191. **hoar:** gray

192. **Therewith:** i.e., with willow garlands

193. **long purples:** orchids

194. **liberal:** plainspoken

195. **cold:** chaste

198. **envious sliver:** malicious branch

202. **lauds:** hymns

203. **incapable of:** without ability to understand

204. **endued:** naturally adapted

213. **It . . . trick:** i.e., weeping is natural

214–15. **When these . . . out:** i.e., when these tears are shed, my female-like weakness will be spent

5.1 Hamlet, returned from his journey, enters a graveyard with Horatio where a gravedigger is singing as he digs. Hamlet tries to find out who the grave is for and meditates on the skulls that are being dug up. A funeral procession approaches. Hamlet soon realizes that the corpse is Ophelia's. When Laertes in his grief leaps into her grave and curses Hamlet as the cause of Ophelia's death, Hamlet comes forward. He and Laertes struggle, with Hamlet protesting his own love and grief for Ophelia.

0 SD. Enter Gravedigger and Another: In Q2 and Folio *Hamlet*, this stage direction reads "Enter two clowns," thus indicating that the Gravedigger and his companion were played by actors who did comic roles.

4. straight: straightway, immediately; **crowner:** coroner; **sat on her:** conducted a formal inquest into her death; **finds it:** decided that her death warrants

9. se offendendo: in self-offense (the gravedigger's mistake for the common legal phrase *se defendendo*, "in self-defense")

11. wittingly: deliberately

12. Argal: a mistake for Latin *ergo*, "therefore"

15. Give me leave: let me go on

17. will he, nill he: willy-nilly, whether wished or not

23. 'quest: inquest

27. there thou sayst: you said it correctly

28. count'nance: legal approval

30. even-Christian: their fellow Christians

32. hold up: maintain

34. bore arms: was given heraldic insignia (with a pun on "arms" as part of the body)

41. Go to: an exclamation of impatience

53. unyoke: i.e., quit, as a farmer does when he unyokes his team of oxen

56. Mass: by the Mass

58–59. your . . . beating: i.e., a stupid donkey does not move more quickly because it is beaten

63–66, 73–76, 96–99, 122–23. In youth . . . : The words of the Gravedigger's song are found, with variations, printed in Richard Tottel's *Miscellany* (1557), entitled "The aged lover renounceth love." The "O" and "a's" (lines 65–66)

may mark the breathing or grunts of the Gravedigger, or may be part of his song, much of which makes little sense.

69–70. Custom . . . easiness: i.e., habit makes it easy for him

71. of little employment: not frequently used

72. hath the daintier sense: is more sensitive

78. jowls: dashes

81. o'erreaches: gets the better of

91. chapless: without a lower jaw; **mazard:** head (a slang term)

94. loggets: a game played by throwing pieces of wood at a stake

101. quiddities: hair-splitting definitions

102. quillities: subtle distinctions, quibbles; **tenures:** holdings

104. sconce: head (a slang term)

106–7. his statutes, his recognizances . . . : Hamlet begins here a list of legal terms referring to buying and holding property.

112. indentures: contracts

113. conveyances: deeds; **this box:** i.e., this skull

114. inheritor: owner

125. out on 't: outside of it

129. quick: living

131. quick: quickly moving

140. absolute: precise

140–41. by the card: i.e., with precision

143–45. the age . . . kibe: i.e., **the** present **age** has become so affected that peasants walk on the very heels of courtiers **picked:** affected **his kibe:** the courtier's sore heel

170. pocky: rotten, as if infected with syphilis

171. scarce hold the laying in: barely hold together long enough to be buried

177. your water: i.e., **water**

177–78. your . . . body: i.e., bodies **whoreson:** vile

178. lien you: lain

199. **chapfallen:** without the lower jaw; also, perhaps, dejected

199–200. **my lady's chamber:** i.e., the room of the gentlewoman you would entertain

201. **favor:** appearance

204. **Alexander:** Alexander the Great, who died in 323 B.C.E. as ruler of the known world

212. **curiously:** elaborately

215. **modesty:** moderation, reserve

220. **Imperious:** imperial; majestic

223. **flaw:** gust of wind

226. **maimèd:** impaired, diminished

228. **Fordo:** destroy; **some estate:** high rank

229. **Couch we:** let us hide

234. **doubtful:** suspicious

235. **but that . . . order:** except for the fact that the king's **command** overrides the rule of the church

236–37. **in ground . . . trumpet: in** unhallowed **ground** been buried until the Judgment Day (See 1 Corinthians 15.51–52: ". . . for **the trumpet** shall sound, and the dead shall be raised incorruptible. . . .")

237. **For:** instead of

238. **Shards:** bits of pottery

240. **crants:** garlands

241. **strewments:** flowers strewn on a grave

241–42. **bringing . . . burial:** being brought to the grave, her last **home,** to the sound of the **bell**

246. **such rest:** i.e., to pray for **such rest**

247. **peace-parted:** i.e., that depart in peace

252. **howling:** i.e., in hell

254. **Sweets to the sweet:** sweet flowers to the sweet maiden

260–61. **thy most . . . Deprived thee of:** i.e., **deprived** you **of** your mind

265. **Pelion:** a high mountain on which, in Greek mythology, the giants placed Mount Ossa in their attempt to scale Mount Olympus

269. **wand'ring stars:** planets

275. **splenitive:** quick-tempered

289. **forbear him:** be patient with him

290. **thou't:** thou wilt

291. **Woo't:** wilt thou

293. **eisel:** vinegar

296. **quick:** alive

299. **the burning zone:** that **zone** in the celestial sphere, paralleling the earth's equator, in which the sun seems to circle the earth

300. **Ossa:** See note to line 265.

304. **Anon:** soon

305. **golden couplets:** twin birds covered with yellow down; **disclosed:** hatched

312. **wait upon him:** accompany him

313. **in:** by thinking of

315. **to the present push:** into immediate action

5.2   In the hall of the castle, Hamlet tells Horatio how he discovered the king's plot against him and how he turned the tables on Rosencrantz and Guildenstern. Osric enters to ask, on Claudius's behalf, that Hamlet fence with Laertes. Hamlet agrees to the contest, despite his misgivings.

Hamlet is winning the match when Gertrude drinks from the poisoned cup that Claudius has prepared for Hamlet. Laertes then wounds Hamlet with the poisoned rapier. In the scuffle that follows, Hamlet forces an exchange of rapiers, and Hamlet wounds Laertes. As Gertrude dies, Laertes, himself dying, discloses his and Claudius's plot against Hamlet. Hamlet kills Claudius. Before Hamlet dies, he asks Horatio to tell the full story that has led to these deaths and names Fortinbras heir to the Danish throne. After Hamlet's death, Fortinbras arrives, claims the crown, and orders a military funeral for Hamlet.

6. **mutines:** mutineers; **bilboes:** shackles

8. **indiscretion:** acting impulsively

9. **pall:** lose strength; **learn:** teach

11. **our ends:** outcome of our actions

12. **Rough-hew them how we will:** no matter how roughly we ourselves shape them

23. **Larded:** ornamented

25. **bugs and goblins in my life:** causes of alarm if I were allowed to live   **bugs:** bugbears

26. **on . . . bated:** As soon as the document has been read, Hamlet is to be executed, the immediacy of the execution not being reduced (**bated**) by any delay (**leisure**).

34. **Or:** before

36. **fair:** in the clear hand of a clerk

37–38. **hold it . . . A baseness:** consider it, as our statesmen do, a lower-class skill

40. **yeoman's:** substantial, loyal

41. **effect:** substance

44–52. **As England . . . allowed:** In this passage, Hamlet parodies the formal language he used in writing the **new commission** (line 36). **tributary:** a nation that pays tribute (a form of tax) to its conqueror

47. **stand . . . amities:** serve to link their friendships

48. **suchlike ases of great charge:** similar "whereas" legal phrases of **great** significance

52. **shriving time:** time for confession

54. **ordinant:** working to control events

55. **signet:** small seal

56. **model:** replica

58. **Subscribed it, gave 't th' impression:** signed it, sealed it with the signet on wax

60. **changeling:** exchange (As the fairies substituted elves or imps for human babies, so Hamlet has replaced the king's document with his own forged one.)

61. **what to this was sequent:** what followed this

65. **defeat:** destruction

66. **insinuation:** winding themselves into the affair

67. **baser:** inferior

68. **pass:** thrust; **fell:** fierce

71. **Does . . . upon—:** is it not now my duty—

73. **election:** The play suggests, here and elsewhere, that the Danish king is somehow elected.

74. **angle:** fishhook; **proper:** very

77. **quit:** requite, pay back

80. **In:** into

87–88. **by . . . his:** i.e., I see the portrait of Laertes's situation in that of my own

89. **bravery:** boastful showiness

95. **waterfly:** an iridescent insect

99–100. **Let a beast . . . king's mess:** i.e., if a man, no matter how bestial, has enough money he will be welcome at **the king's** table **crib:** stall of an ox **mess:** place where groups (usually military) were fed

105. **Put your bonnet . . . use:** i.e., put on your hat (Hats were commonly worn by men, even indoors, but removed in the presence of superiors. Osric continues to hold his hat in his hand despite Hamlet's insistence; see 5.2.117.)

110. **indifferent:** somewhat

112. **complexion:** temperament

118–95. Throughout these passages, Osric's language is florid, affected, and imprecise; Hamlet answers him in a style even more exaggerated. Often we can only guess at what they may be saying.

122–23. **the card or calendar of gentry:** the model of courtly manners (?)

124. **continent:** that which contains

125. **definement:** definition; **perdition:** loss

126–28. **to divide him . . . quick sail:** i.e., to inventory his qualities would stagger one's **memory,** but the inventory would fall short of his excellence (?)

129–33. **a soul . . . nothing more:** Hamlet's mockingly

affected language says, in essence, that Laertes is a fine man, so special that he can be matched only by his image in a mirror; everyone else in comparison to him is only his shadow.

135–36. **wrap . . . breath?** i.e., why are we talking about him?

138. **possible:** i.e., **possible** for Osric

140. **nomination:** naming

143. **all 's:** all his

148. **approve:** commend

154–55. **imputation:** reputation

155. **meed:** merit

155–56. **unfellowed:** unmatched

158. **Rapier and dagger:** In rapier fencing, the **rapier**, carried in the right hand, led the attack; the **dagger**, in the left hand, parried the opponent's attack.

·162–63. **poniards:** daggers; **assigns:** accessories; **girdle, hangers, and so:** sword belt, attaching straps, and so forth

164. **carriages:** literally, wheeled supports on which cannons are mounted; **dear to fancy:** fancifully designed

165. **responsive:** well matched

166. **liberal conceit:** imaginative design (?)

167. **What call you the "carriages"?:** i.e., what are you calling "carriages"?

168–69. **edified by the margent:** aided through a note in the margin

178. **laid:** bet

178–79. **a dozen passes between yourself and him:** a dozen exchanges between Hamlet and Laertes

180–81. **twelve for nine:** No one has satisfactorily explained this phrase so that it fits in with the terms of the wager.

182. **vouchsafe the answer:** consent to meet Laertes in this match (Hamlet chooses to understand the statement differently.)

187. **breathing time of day:** the time I take my exercise

188. **foils:** weapons blunted for fencing

195. **commend:** offer my services (The word also means "praise," as Hamlet takes it at lines 196–97.)

197–98. **for 's turn:** for his purpose (i.e., to praise him)

201. **comply . . . with his dug:** say polite things to the breast he was about to nurse from

203. **drossy:** worthless

204. **tune:** manner of speaking

204–7. **out . . . opinions:** perhaps, out of repeated social encounters, they have got a collection of frothy language that wins acceptance from refined persons

207–8. **blow . . . out:** In this image, Osric and his kind are themselves composed of froth; when one blows on them to see if there is anything to them, they collapse like **bubbles**.

215–16. **If . . . ready:** i.e., if the king is ready, so am I

219. **In happy time:** opportunely (a courteous phrase)

220–21. **use some gentle entertainment:** receive him in a friendly way

225–26. **at the odds:** with **the odds** (advantage) allowed me

230. **gaingiving:** misgiving

232. **repair:** coming

233–34. **a special providence . . . a sparrow:** See Matthew 10.29–31: "Are not two sparrows sold for a farthing, and one of them shall not fall on the ground without your Father? . . . Fear ye not, therefore, ye are of more value than many sparrows."

237–38. **of aught he leaves knows: knows** anything about what **he leaves** behind

238. **betimes:** early

241. **This presence:** this royal audience

243. **needs:** necessarily

244. **sore:** severe, grave

246. **Roughly awake:** harshly awaken

255. **disclaiming from:** proclaiming my innocence (disavowing all part in); **purposed:** intended

257. **That I have:** as if I had

259. **in nature:** in terms of my natural affection for my father and for my sister

261. **terms of honor:** offense to my honor

262–65. **will no reconcilement . . . ungored:** will accept no reconciliation until experts in those questions give a decision that may serve as a precedent for making peace, thus freeing my reputation from a charge of dishonor **voice:** authority **name ungored:** reputation unwounded

269. **frankly:** freely, willingly

272. **your foil:** the background against which you will shine (a courteous pun on the word **foils**, used at line 270 to request the blunted weapons)

274. **Stick fiery off:** stand out in brilliant contrast

280. **laid the odds . . . side:** i.e., the king's stake, much greater than Laertes's, is bet on Hamlet, who here again claims to be weaker than Laertes

282. **we have therefore odds:** i.e., we have been given "odds" (in that Laertes must make three more hits than Hamlet in order to win)

283. **Let me see another:** Here Laertes selects the sharpened, poisoned rapier.

284. **This likes me:** I like this; **have all a length:** are all the same **length**

285 SD. **play:** fence

288. **quit in answer of the third exchange:** requite (Laertes) for earlier hits by scoring the third hit

291. **union:** large pearl

294. **kettle:** kettledrum

314. **napkin:** handkerchief

315. **carouses:** drinks a toast

326. **pass:** thrust

327. **make a wanton of me:** play with me as if I were a child

330 SD. **in scuffling they change rapiers:** This stage direction, in Q1, reads "they catch one anothers' rapiers," which suggests that Hamlet forces the exchange through a contemporary method of disarm called the "left-hand seizure."

336. **woodcock:** a proverbially stupid bird; **to mine own springe:** caught in my own trap

348. **Unbated and envenomed:** sharp and poisoned

357. **union:** probable pun on "union" as "pearl" and "union" in marriage and death

360. **tempered:** mixed, compounded

366. **this chance:** these events

367. **mutes:** actors without speaking parts

368. **fell sergeant:** cruel **sergeant** at arms (arresting officer)

382. **Absent thee from felicity awhile:** i.e., keep yourself from the happiness of death

386–88. **Young Fortinbras . . . volley:** i.e., Fortinbras, returning victoriously from Poland, has shot off a volley of gunfire to salute the ambassadors approaching from England

390. **o'ercrows:** triumphs over

393. **voice:** vote

394–95. **occurrents . . . solicited:** occurrences that have brought on

396. **O, O, O, O!:** This series of *O*s, usually omitted by editors, may simply be an indication for the actor to make the sounds appropriate to Hamlet's dying.

403. **This quarry . . . havoc:** i.e., this heap of dead bodies proclaims that **havoc** has been at work

404. **toward:** in preparation

409. **senseless:** incapable of sensing

410. **him:** i.e., Claudius

417. **jump upon this bloody question:** so immediately after **this bloody** quarrel

420. **stage:** platform

424. **casual:** occurring by chance

425. **put on:** instigated

428. **deliver:** tell

432. **rights of memory:** rights remembered

433. **Which . . . me:** which my presence here at this advantageous time invites me to claim

435–36. **And from his mouth . . . on more:** i.e., with words **from** Hamlet's **mouth,** whose "voice" will be seconded by others

437. **presently:** immediately

440. **On . . . happen:** i.e., **happen** as a result of **plots and errors**

443. **put on:** put to the test

444. **passage:** passing, death

448. **field: field** of battle

Textual Notes

The reading of the present text appears to the left of the square bracket. The earliest sources of readings not in Q2, the Second Quarto text, are indicated as follows: **Q1** is the First Quarto of 1603; **Q3** is the Third Quarto of 1611; **Q4** is the Fourth Quarto of ?1622; **Q5** is the Fifth Quarto of 1637; **F** is the First Folio of 1623; **F2** is the Second Folio of 1632; **F3** is the Third Folio of 1663–64; **F4** is the Fourth Folio of 1685; **Ed.** is an earlier editor of Shakespeare, beginning with Rowe in 1709. **SD** means stage direction; **SP** means speech prefix; **uncorr.** means first or uncorrected state; **corr.** means second or corrected state.

1.1. 19. soldier] F; souldiers Q2   51. harrows] F; horrowes Q2   74. Polacks] Ed.; pollax Q2; Pollax F   84. why . . . cast] F; with . . . cost Q2   100. those] F; these Q2   103. returned] F; returne Q2   106. designed] F2; desseigne Q2; designe F   120–37. Q2 *only*   133. feared] Ed.; feare Q2   150. you] F; your Q2   156. SD *1 line later in* F; *omit* Q2

1.2. 1. SP KING] F; *Claud.* Q2   41. SD F; *omit* Q2   60–62. wrung . . . consent] Q2 *only*   69. so, my] F; so much my Q2   80. good] F; coold Q2   85. shapes] Q3; chapes Q2; shewes F   86. denote] F; deuote Q2   100. a] F; or Q2   136. self-slaughter] F; seale slaughter Q2   137. weary] F; wary Q2   141. to this] F; thus Q2   147. would] F; should Q2   153. even she] *omit* Q2   182. you to drink deep ere] F; you for to drinke ere Q2   185. see] F; *omit* Q2   219. Where, as] Q1 (Where as); Whereas Q2, F   257. SP BARNARDO/MARCELLUS] Ed.; *Both.* Q2; *All.* F   262. tonight] Q4; to nigh Q2; to Night F   276. SD *All . . . exit.*] Ed.; *Exeunt.* Q2, F   279. Foul] F; fonde Q2

1.3.   3. is] F; in Q2   15. bulk] F; bulkes Q2   21. *omit*
Q2   24. the health] Ed.; health Q2, F   53. like] F; *omit*
Q2   80. Are] F; Or Q2   81. be] F; boy Q2   82. loan] F;
loue Q2   83. dulls the] F; dulleth Q2   118. Running]
Ed.; Wrong Q2; Roaming F   124. springes] F; springs
Q2   134. tether] F; tider Q2   138. implorators] F; im-
ploratotors Q2   139. bawds] Ed.; bonds Q2, F   140. be-
guile] F; beguide Q2

1.4.   2. a] F; *omit* Q2   19–41. Q2 *only*   19. revel] Q5;
reueale Q2   30. the] Ed.; their Q2   39. evil] Ed.; eale Q2
62. SD *Ghost beckons.*] Ed.; *Beckins.* Q2; *Ghost beckens
Hamlet.* F   83–86. Q2 *only*   97. imagination] F; imagion
Q2

1.5.   50. wit] Ed; wits Q2, F   54. a] F; *omit* Q2   62.
lust] F; but Q2   63. sate] F; sort Q2   75. posset] F; pos-
sesse Q2   84. unaneled] F; vnanueld Q2   86. With all] F;
Withall Q2   98. SD F; *omit* Q2   102. stiffly] F; swiftly Q2
125. bird] F; and Q2   136. SP HORATIO/MARCELLUS] Ed.;
Booth. Q2; *Both.* F   136. my lord] F; *omit* Q2   161. SP
HORATIO/MARCELLUS] Ed.; *Booth.* Q2; *Both.* F   205. With
all] F; Withall Q2

2.1.   0. SD *old . . . Reynaldo*] Ed.; *old Polonius, with his
man or two* Q2; *Polonius, and Reynoldo* F   31. no] F; *omit*
Q2   46. i' th'] F; with Q2   59–60. at "friend . . . gentleman."] F; *omit* Q2   66. o'ertook] F; or tooke Q2

2.2.   0. SD *and Attendants*] *omit* Q2; *Cum aliis* F   17.
Q2 *only*   60. o'erhasty] F; hastie Q2   61. SD *Enter . . .
Polonius.*] *Enter Polonius, Voltumand, and Cornelius.* F
91. SD *Voltemand and Cornelius exit.*] Ed.; *Exeunt
Embassadors.* Q2; *Exit Ambass.* F   97. since] F; *omit*
Q2   116. SD *He reads.*] Ed.; *The Letter.* F; *omit* Q2   123.
SD *He reads the letter.*] *Letter.* Q2; *omit* F   134. above]
F; about Q2   146. winking] F; working Q2   152. his]
F; her Q2   158. a] F; *omit* Q2   161. 'tis] F; *omit* Q2
229. sanity] F; sanctity Q2   230–31. and . . . him] F; *omit*
Q2   233. sir] F; *omit* Q2   234. will more] F; will not more

Q2 242. excellent] F; extent Q2 246. overhappy] F; euer
happy Q2 247. cap] F; lap Q2 255. that] F; *omit* Q2
258–89. Let ... attended] F; *omit* Q2 286. SP ROSEN-
CRANTZ/GUILDENSTERN] Ed.; *Both* F 293. even] F; euer Q2
327. a] F; *omit* Q2 333. no] F; *omit* Q2 347–48. the
clown ... sear] F; *omit* Q2 348. tickle] Ed.; tickled F
349. blank] F; black Q2 360–85. F; *omit* Q2 365. berat-
tle] F2; be-ratled F 372. most like] Ed.; like most F 396.
lest my] F; let me Q2 422–23. tragical- ... -pastoral] F;
omit Q2 446. my] F; *omit* Q2 449. By'r] F; by Q2 454.
French falconers] F; friendly Fankners Q2 457, 493, 527,
530. SP FIRST] F; *omit* Q2 468. affectation] F; affection Q2
469–70. as wholesome ... fine] Q2; *omit* F 471. tale] F;
talke Q2 499. *Then ... Ilium*] F; *omit* Q2 506. *And*] F;
omit Q2 520. *fellies*] Ed.; follies Q2; Fallies F 529.
"Moblèd queen" is good] Ed.; *omit* Q2; Inobled Queene is
good F 531. *bisson rheum*] F; *Bison* rehume Q2 540.
husband's] F; husband Q2 555. bodykins] F; bodkin Q2
562. SD *As ... Player.*] this ed.; *Exeunt Pol. and Players.* Q2
after line 573; *Exit Polon.* F *after line 560* 566. a] F; *omit*
Q2 567. dozen or] F; dosen lines, or Q2 575. SD *Rosencrantz ... exit.*] *Exeunt.* Q2; *Exeunt. Manet Hamlet.* F, *both
after line 574* 581. his] F; the Q2 586. to Hecuba] F; to
her Q2 588. the cue] F; that Q2 606. have] F; a Q2 610.
F; *omit* Q2 612. father] Q3; *omit* Q2, F 616. scullion] F;
stallyon Q2 628. devil ... devil] F; deale ... deale Q2

3.1. 0. SD *and*] F; *omit* Q2 31. too] F; two Q2 35.
lawful espials] F; *omit* Q2 36. Will] F; Wee'le Q2 52.
loneliness] F; lowlines Q2 63. Let's] F; *omit* Q2 91. of
us all] F; *omit* Q2 93. sicklied] F; sickled Q2 108. the]
F; these Q2 117. your honesty] F; you Q2 128. inocu-
late] F; euocutat Q2 131. to] F; *omit* Q2 140. all] F;
omit Q2 154. too] F; *omit* Q2 157. lisp] F; list Q2 158.
wantonness your] F; wantonness Q2 166. expectancy] F;
expectation Q2 171. that] F; what Q2 176. SP KING, *ad-*

vancing with Polonius] Ed.; *Enter King and Polonius.* Q2,
F   203. unwatched] F; vnmatcht Q2

3.2.   24. own] F; *omit* Q2   29. the] F; *omit* Q2   31.
praise] F; praysd Q2   39. sir] F; *omit* Q2   47. SD *Players*
exit.] F; *omit* Q2   51. SD *Polonius exits.*] F; *omit* Q2   53.
SD *They exit.*] F; *Exeunt they two.* Q2   59. SP HAMLET] F;
omit Q2   69. Hath] F; S'hath Q2   95. detecting] F; de-
tected Q2   95. SD *omit* Q2; *following 97* SD *in* F   97. SD
the King's] Ed.; *his* F   97. SD *torches*] *Torches. Danish*
March F   115. SP QUEEN] F; *Ger.* Q2   121–22. F; *omit* Q2
145. *very lovingly*] F; *omit* Q2   146–47. *She . . . him*] F;
omit Q2   150. *comes*] F; *come* Q2   156. *his*] F; *omit* Q2
156. SD *Players exit.*] Ed.; *Exeunt* F; *omit* Q2   158. is
miching] F; munching Q2   163. counsel] F; *omit* Q2
176 *and hereafter to line 248.* SP PLAYER KING] Ed.; *King*
Q2, F   177. *orbèd*] F; orb'd the Q2   182 *and hereafter*
until line 251. SP PLAYER QUEEN] *Quee.* Q2; *Bap.* F   185.
your] F; our Q2   188. Q2 *only*   190. *In*] F; Eyther none,
in Q2   191. *love*] F; Lord Q2   193–94. Q2 *only*   205. SP
omit Q2; *Bapt.* F   222. *joys*] F; ioy Q2   241–42. Q2 *only*
242. *An*] Ed.; *And* Q2   246. *once a . . . be wife*] F; once I be
a . . . be a wife Q2   247. *printed after line 245 in* Q2   252.
SD Ed.; *Exeunt.* Q2; *Exit* F   277. Pox] F; *omit* Q2   282.
Confederate] F; Considerat Q2   284. *infected*] F; inuected
Q2   286. *usurp*] F; vsurps Q2   286. SD F; *omit* Q2   292.
F; *omit* Q2   302. two] F; *omit* Q2   336. start] F; stare Q2
346. my] F; *omit* Q2   388. thumb] F; the vmber Q2   397.
the top of] F; *omit* Q2   401–2. you can fret] F; you fret Q2
402. me, you] F; me not, you Q2   413. SP HAMLET] F; *omit*
Q2   416. SP POLONIUS] F; *omit* Q2   417. SP HAMLET] F;
omit Q2   417–18. Leave me, friends] *placed here in* F;
after line 415 in Q2   418. SD *omit* Q2; *Exit.* F *after line 416*
420. breathes] F; breakes Q2   424. bitter business as the
day] F; busines as the bitter day Q2   429. daggers] F; dagger Q2

3.3.   20. huge] F; hough Q2   23. ruin] F; raine Q2   24.

with] F; *omit* Q2   28. SD *Rosencrantz . . . exit.*] Ed.; *Exeunt Gent.* Q2, F   39. SD *Polonius exits.*] Ed.; *Exit.* Q2 *after line 38; omit* F   54. pardoned] F; pardon Q2   62. shove] F; showe Q2   77. pat] F; *omit* Q2   80. revenged] F; reuendge Q2   84. hire and salary] F; base and silly Q2   86. With all] F; Withal Q2

3.4.   0. SD *Queen*] F; *Gertrard* Q2   7. with him] F; *omit* Q2   8. F; *omit* Q2   9. SP *and hereafter in 3.4 and 4.1* QUEEN] F; *Ger.* Q2, *except line 61: "Quee."*   9. warrant] F; wait Q2   25. inmost] F; most Q2   29. SD *kills Polonius.*] F *1 line later; omit* Q2   62. That] F; *Ham.* That Q2   63. SP HAMLET] F; *omit* Q2   69. heaven] F; heaue, a Q2   81–86. Sense . . . difference] Q2 *only*   88–91. Eyes . . . mope] Q2 *only*   98. panders] F; pardons Q2   100. eyes into my very soul] F; very eyes into my soule Q2   101. grainèd] F; greeued Q2   102. not leave their] F; leaue there their Q2   111. tithe] F; kyth Q2   160. F; *omit* Q2   164. I] F; *omit* Q2   179. live] F; leaue Q2   182–86. That . . . on] Q2 *only*   186. Refrain tonight] F; to refraine night Q2   188–91. the . . . potency] Q2 *only*   201. Q2 *only*   225–33. Q2 *only*   238. a foolish] F; a most foolish Q2   240. SD *They . . . Polonius.*] Ed.; *Exit.* Q2; *Exit Hamlet . . . Polonius.* F

4.1.   4. Q2 *only*   38. SD *Rosencrantz . . . exit.*] F (*Exit Gent.*); *omit* Q2   42–45. Whose . . . air] Q2 *only*

4.2.   0. SD *Enter Hamlet.*] F; *Enter Hamlet, Rosencraus, and others.* Q2   2. F; *omit* Q2   3. SP HAMLET] F; *omit* Q2   4. SD *Enter . . . others.*] F (*Enter Ros. and Guildensterne.*)   6. Compounded] F; Compound Q2   17–18. an ape] F; *omit* Q2   30–31. Hide . . . after] F; *omit* Q2

4.3.   11. SD *Enter Rosencrantz.*] F; *Enter Rosencraus and all the rest.* Q2   18. SD *They . . . Hamlet.*] Ed.; *They enter.* Q2; *Enter Hamlet and Guildensterne.* F   29–32. Q2 *only*   33. SP KING] F; *King. King.* Q2   48. With fiery quickness] F; *omit* Q2   61. and so] F; so Q2   77. were ne'er begun] F; will nere begin Q2

4.4. 9. SD *All . . . others.*] Ed.; *Enter Hamlet, Rosencraus, &c.* Q2; *Exit.* F   10–69. Q2 *only*

4.5. 0. SD *Queen*] F; *Gertrard* Q2; *Enter Queene and Horatio.* F   11. aim] F; yawne Q2   21. SP QUEEN] Ed.; *omit* Q2, F   22. SP To] F; *Quee.* Q2   25. SD *Enter . . . distracted.*] F; *Enter Ophelia.* Q2 *after line 21*   28. SD *sings*] Ed.; *shee sings.* Q2 *after line 27; omit* F   34. SD *Sings*] Ed.; *Song.* Q2 *after line 35; omit* F   43. SD *sings*] Ed.; *Song.* Q2 *after line 44; omit* F   53. SD *Sings*] Ed.; *Song.* Q2 *after line 53; omit* F   78. SD F; *omit* Q2   87. their] F; *omit* Q2   96. his] F; this Q2   104. F; *omit* Q2   116. They] F; The Q2   156. world] F; worlds Q2   176. F; *Laer.* Let her come in. Q2, *printed after "Enter Ophelia."*   177. SP LAERTES] F; *omit* Q2   184. an old] F; a poore Q2   185–87. F; *omit* Q2   188. SD *sings*] Ed.; *Song.* Q2 *after line 188; omit* F   189. F; *omit* Q2   206. must] F; may Q2   213. SD *sings*] Ed.; *Song.* Q2 *after line 213; omit* F   219. *All*] F; *omit* Q2   223. I pray God] F; *omit* Q2   224. SD *She exits.*] *omit* Q2; *Exeunt Ophelia* F   225. see] F; *omit* Q2

4.6. 9. an 't] F; and Q2   22. *good*] F; *omit* Q2   26. *bore*] F; bord Q2   30. *He*] F; *So* Q2   32. SP Come] F; *Hor.* Come Q2   32. give] F; *omit* Q2

4.7. 7. proceeded] F; proceede Q2   16. conjunctive] F; concliue Q2   24. loud a wind] F; loued Arm'd Q2   38–40. F; *omit* Q2   41. SP These] Ed.; *Messen.* These Q2; This F   45. Q2 *only*   51. *your*] F; you Q2   53. *and more strange*] F; *omit* Q2   53. *Hamlet*] F; *omit* Q2   54. SP What] F; *King.* What Q2   59. advise] F; deuise Q2   62. shall] F; *omit* Q2   70. checking] F; the King Q2   77–92. LAERTES . . . graveness] Q2 *only*   99. my] F; me Q2   113–16. The . . . them] Q2 *only*   130–40. Q2 *only*   139. spendthrift] Q5; spend thirfts Q2   153. on] F; ore Q2   157. pass] F; pace Q2   160. that] F; *omit* Q2   181. prepared] F; prefard Q2   191. hoar] F; horry Q2   195. our cold] F; our cull-cold Q2

5.1. 0. SD *Enter . . . Another.*] Ed.; *Enter two Clownes.* Q2, F 1 and throughout scene SP GRAVEDIGGER] Ed.; *Clowne* Q2, F 9. *se offendendo*] F; so offended Q2 12. Argal] F; or all Q2 35–38. OTHER . . . arms] F; *omit* Q2 44. frame] F; *omit* Q2 56. SD F; *omit* Q2 62. stoup] F; soope Q2 62. SD this ed.; *Sings.* F; *Song.* Q2 *after line 63* 67. SP HAMLET] F; *Enter Hamlet and Horatio. Ham.* Q2 73. SD *sings*] F; *Song.* Q2 *after line 73* 91. mazard] F; massene Q2 96. SD sings] F; *Song.* Q2 108–9. Is . . . recoveries] F; *omit* Q2 110. his] F; *omit* Q2 111. double ones too] F; doubles Q2 122. *O*] F; or Q2 123. F; *omit* Q2 147. all] F; *omit* Q2 170. nowadays] F; *omit* Q2 190. Let me see] F; *omit* Q2 200. chamber] F; table Q2 215–16. as thus] F; *omit* Q2 223. winter's] F; waters Q2 223. SD *Enter . . . attendant.*] Ed.; *Enter K. Q. Laertes and the corse.* Q2 *after line 224; Enter King, Queene, Laertes, and a Coffin, with Lords attendant.* F *after line 224* 238. Shards] F; *omit* Q2 259. treble] F; double Q2 262. SD F; *omit* Q2 275. and] F; *omit* Q2 294. thou] F; *omit* Q2 303. thus] F; this Q2 318. shortly] F; thirtie Q2

5.2. 5. Methought] F; my thought Q2 6. bilboes] F; bilbo Q2 33. villainies] Ed.; villaines Q2, F 48. *as*es] Ed.; as sir Q2; Assis F 58. Subscribed] F; Subscribe Q2 64. F; *omit* Q2 77–91. F; *omit* Q2 88. court] Ed.; count F 91. SD *Enter . . . courtier.*] *Enter a Courtier.* Q2; *Enter young Osricke.* F 94. humbly] F; humble Q2 105. Put] F; *omit* Q2 111. sultry . . . for] F; sully . . . or Q2 119–48. Q2 *only* 120. gentleman] Q3; gentlemen Q2 122. feelingly] Q3; sellingly Q2 *uncorr.;* fellingly Q2 *corr.* 151–56. Q2 *only* 154. his] Q5; this Q2 163. hangers] F; hanger Q2 168–69. Q2 *only* 170. carriages] F; carriage Q2 173. might be] F; be Q2 *uncorr.;* be might Q2 *corr.* 176–77. this all "impawned," as you] Ed.; this all you Q2; this impon'd as F 192. e'en] F; *omit* Q2 196. Yours . . . He does] Ed.; Yours doo's Q2; Yours, yours; hee does F 201. did comply, sir] did sir Q2 *uncorr.;* did so sir Q2 *corr.;*

did Complie F 205. yeasty] F; histy Q2 206–7. fanned and winnowed] Ed.; prophane and trennowed Q2; fond and winnowed F 208 SD–222. Q2 *only* 226. but] F; *omit* Q2 230. gaingiving] F; gamgiuing Q2 233. a] F; *omit* Q2 235. now] F; *omit* Q2 236. will] F; well Q2 238. SD Q2; *Enter King, Queene, Laertes and Lords, with other Attendants with Foyles, and Gauntlets, a Table and Flagons of Wine on it.* F 254. F; *omit* Q2 265. keep] F; *omit* Q2 265. till] F; all Q2 270. Come on] F; *omit* Q2 285. SD F *1 line earlier; omit* Q2 291. union] F; Vnice Q2 300. SD F; *omit* Q2 307. SD Q2 *(after line 304 and adding "Florish, a peece goes off.");* Trumpets sound, and shot goes off.* F *after line 308* 311. A touch, a touch] F; *omit* Q2 327. afeard] F; sure Q2 328. SD F; *omit* Q2 330. SD F; *omit* Q2 344. Hamlet. Hamlet] F; Hamlet Q2 347. thy] F; my Q2 353. SD F; *omit* Q2 356. murd'rous] F; *omit* Q2 357. thy union] F; the Onixe Q2 358. SD F; *omit* Q2 363. SD F; *omit* Q2 384. SD *A march a farre off.* Q2; *March afarre off, and shout within.* F 396. F; *omit* Q2 396. SD F; *omit* Q2 399. SD Q2; *Enter Fortinbras and English Ambassador, with Drumme, Colours, and Attendants.* F 403. proud] F; prou'd Q2 421. th'] F; *omit* Q2 425. forced] F; for no Q2 435. on] F; no Q2 449. SD *Exeunt.* Q2; *Exeunt . . . off.* F

The Tragedy of

MACBETH

Shakespeare's *Macbeth*

In 1603, at about the middle of Shakespeare's career as a playwright, a new monarch ascended the throne of England. He was James VI of Scotland, who then also became James I of England. Immediately, Shakespeare's London was alive with an interest in things Scottish. Many Scots followed their king to London and attended the theaters there. Shakespeare's company, which became the King's Men under James's patronage, now sometimes staged their plays for the new monarch's entertainment, just as they had for Queen Elizabeth before him. It was probably within this context that Shakespeare turned to Raphael Holinshed's history of Scotland for material for a tragedy.

In Scottish history of the eleventh century, Shakespeare found a spectacle of violence—the slaughter of whole armies and of innocent families, the assassination of kings, the ambush of nobles by murderers, the brutal execution of rebels. He also came upon stories of witches and wizards providing advice to traitors. Such accounts could feed the new Scottish King James's belief in a connection between treason and witchcraft. James had already himself executed women as witches. Shakespeare's *Macbeth* supplied its audience with a sensational view of witches and supernatural apparitions and equally sensational accounts of bloody battles in which, for example, a rebel was "unseamed . . . from the nave [navel] to th' chops [jaws]."

It is possible, then, that in writing *Macbeth* Shakespeare was mainly intent upon appealing to the new interests in London brought about by James's kingship. What he created, though, is a play that has fascinated generations of readers and audiences that care little about Scottish history. In its depiction of a man who murders his king and kinsman in order to gain the crown, only to lose all that humans seem to need in order to be happy—sleep, nourishment, friends, love—*Macbeth* teases us with huge questions. Why do people do evil knowing that it is evil? Does Macbeth represent someone who murders because fate tempts him? Because his wife pushes him into it? Because he is overly ambitious? Having killed Duncan, why does Macbeth fall apart, unable to sleep, seeing ghosts, putting spies in everyone's home, killing his friends and innocent women and children? Why does the success of Macbeth and Lady Macbeth—prophesied by the witches, promising the couple power and riches and "peace to all their nights and days to come"—turn so quickly to ashes, destroying the Macbeths' relationship, their world, and, finally, both of them?

In earlier centuries, Macbeth's story was seen as a powerful study of a heroic individual who commits an evil act and pays an enormous price as his conscience—and the natural forces for good in the universe—destroy him. More recently his story was applied to nations that overreach themselves, his speeches of despair quoted to show that Shakespeare shared late-twentieth-century feelings of alienation. Today, the line between Macbeth's evil and the supposed good of those who oppose him is being blurred, new attitudes about witches and witchcraft are being expressed, new questions raised about the ways that maleness and femaleness are portrayed in the play. As with so many of Shakespeare's plays, *Macbeth* speaks to each generation with a new voice.

Characters in the Play

Three Witches, the Weïrd Sisters

DUNCAN, king of Scotland
MALCOLM, his elder son
DONALBAIN, Duncan's younger son

MACBETH, thane of Glamis
LADY MACBETH
SEYTON, attendant to Macbeth
Three Murderers in Macbeth's service
A Doctor
A Gentlewoman } *both attending upon Lady Macbeth*
A Porter

BANQUO, commander, with Macbeth, of Duncan's army
FLEANCE, his son

MACDUFF, a Scottish noble
LADY MACDUFF
Their son

LENNOX
ROSS
ANGUS } *Scottish nobles*
MENTEITH
CAITHNESS

SIWARD, commander of the English forces
YOUNG SIWARD, Siward's son

A Captain in Duncan's army
An Old Man
A Doctor at the English court

389

HECATE

Apparitions: an Armed Head, a Bloody Child, a Crowned
    Child, and eight nonspeaking kings

Three Messengers, Three Servants, a Lord, a Soldier

Attendants, a Sewer, Servants, Lords, Thanes, Soldiers
    (all nonspeaking)

Lady Macbeth is identified
as such, only in relation
to Macbeth.

Is this a way of saying
that Macbeth has something
akin to MPD (bipolar personality)
conflicting personalities?

ACT 1

Scene 1
Thunder and lightning. Enter three Witches.

FIRST WITCH
   When shall we three meet again?
   In thunder, lightning, or in rain?
SECOND WITCH
   When the hurly-burly's done,
   When the battle's lost and won.
THIRD WITCH
   That will be ere the set of sun.   5
FIRST WITCH
   Where the place?
SECOND WITCH   Upon the heath.
THIRD WITCH
   There to meet with Macbeth.
FIRST WITCH   I come, Graymalkin.
⌜SECOND WITCH⌝ Paddock calls.   10
⌜THIRD WITCH⌝ Anon.
ALL
   Fair is foul, and foul is fair,
   Hover through the fog and filthy air.

                             They exit.

Scene 2

Alarum within. Enter King ⌐Duncan,¬ Malcolm,
Donalbain, Lennox, with Attendants, meeting a bleeding
Captain.

DUNCAN
What bloody man is that? He can report,
As seemeth by his plight, of the revolt
The newest state.
MALCOLM   This is the sergeant
Who, like a good and hardy soldier, fought   5
'Gainst my captivity.—Hail, brave friend!
Say to the King the knowledge of the broil
As thou didst leave it.
CAPTAIN   Doubtful it stood,
As two spent swimmers that do cling together   10
And choke their art. The merciless Macdonwald
(Worthy to be a rebel, for to that
The multiplying villainies of nature
Do swarm upon him) from the Western Isles
Of kerns and ⌐gallowglasses¬ is supplied;   15
And Fortune, on his damnèd ⌐quarrel¬ smiling,
Showed like a rebel's whore. But all's too weak;
For brave Macbeth (well he deserves that name),
Disdaining Fortune, with his brandished steel,
Which smoked with bloody execution,   20
Like valor's minion, carved out his passage
Till he faced the slave;
Which ne'er shook hands, nor bade farewell to him,
Till he unseamed him from the nave to th' chops,
And fixed his head upon our battlements.   25
DUNCAN
O valiant cousin, worthy gentleman!
CAPTAIN
As whence the sun 'gins his reflection
Shipwracking storms and direful thunders ⌐break,¬

So from that spring whence comfort seemed to
   come   30
Discomfort swells. Mark, King of Scotland, mark:
No sooner justice had, with valor armed,
Compelled these skipping kerns to trust their heels,
But the Norweyan lord, surveying vantage,
With furbished arms and new supplies of men,   35
Began a fresh assault.

DUNCAN
Dismayed not this our captains, Macbeth and
   Banquo?

CAPTAIN
Yes, as sparrows eagles, or the hare the lion.
If I say sooth, I must report they were   40
As cannons overcharged with double cracks,
So they doubly redoubled strokes upon the foe.
Except they meant to bathe in reeking wounds
Or memorize another Golgotha,
I cannot tell—   45
But I am faint. My gashes cry for help.

DUNCAN
So well thy words become thee as thy wounds:
They smack of honor both.—Go, get him surgeons.
      ⌜*The Captain is led off by Attendants.*⌝

      Enter Ross and Angus.

Who comes here?

MALCOLM   The worthy Thane of Ross.   50

LENNOX
What a haste looks through his eyes!
So should he look that seems to speak things
   strange.

ROSS   God save the King.

DUNCAN   Whence cam'st thou, worthy thane?   55

ROSS   From Fife, great king,
Where the Norweyan banners flout the sky

And fan our people cold.
Norway himself, with terrible numbers,
Assisted by that most disloyal traitor, 60
The Thane of Cawdor, began a dismal conflict,
Till that Bellona's bridegroom, lapped in proof,
Confronted him with self-comparisons,
Point against point, rebellious arm 'gainst arm,
Curbing his lavish spirit. And to conclude, 65
The victory fell on us.

DUNCAN   Great happiness!

ROSS   That now Sweno,
The Norways' king, craves composition.
Nor would we deign him burial of his men 70
Till he disbursèd at Saint Colme's Inch
Ten thousand dollars to our general use.

DUNCAN
No more that Thane of Cawdor shall deceive
Our bosom interest. Go, pronounce his present
  death, 75
And with his former title greet Macbeth.

ROSS   I'll see it done.

DUNCAN
What he hath lost, noble Macbeth hath won.
                                        They exit.

Scene 3
Thunder. Enter the three Witches.

FIRST WITCH   Where hast thou been, sister?
SECOND WITCH   Killing swine.
THIRD WITCH   Sister, where thou?
FIRST WITCH
A sailor's wife had chestnuts in her lap
And munched and munched and munched. "Give 5
  me," quoth I.
"Aroint thee, witch," the rump-fed runnion cries.

Her husband's to Aleppo gone, master o' th' *Tiger;*
But in a sieve I'll thither sail,
And, like a rat without a tail,
I'll do, I'll do, and I'll do.   10

SECOND WITCH
  I'll give thee a wind.

FIRST WITCH
  Th' art kind.

THIRD WITCH
  And I another.

FIRST WITCH
  I myself have all the other,   15
  And the very ports they blow,
  All the quarters that they know
  I' th' shipman's card.
  I'll drain him dry as hay.
  Sleep shall neither night nor day   20
  Hang upon his penthouse lid.
  He shall live a man forbid.
  Weary sev'nnights, nine times nine,
  Shall he dwindle, peak, and pine.
  Though his bark cannot be lost,   25
  Yet it shall be tempest-tossed.
  Look what I have.

SECOND WITCH   Show me, show me.

FIRST WITCH
  Here I have a pilot's thumb,
  Wracked as homeward he did come.   *Drum within.*   30

THIRD WITCH
  A drum, a drum!
  Macbeth doth come.

ALL, ⌜*dancing in a circle*⌝
  The Weïrd Sisters, hand in hand,
  Posters of the sea and land,
  Thus do go about, about,   35
  Thrice to thine and thrice to mine

And thrice again, to make up nine.
Peace, the charm's wound up.

Enter Macbeth and Banquo.

MACBETH
So foul and fair a day I have not seen.
BANQUO
How far is 't called to ⌈Forres?⌉—What are these,   40
So withered, and so wild in their attire,
That look not like th' inhabitants o' th' earth
And yet are on 't?—Live you? Or are you aught
That man may question? You seem to understand
    me   45
By each at once her choppy finger laying
Upon her skinny lips. You should be women,
And yet your beards forbid me to interpret
That you are so.
MACBETH   Speak if you can. What are you?   50
FIRST WITCH
All hail, Macbeth! Hail to thee, Thane of Glamis!
SECOND WITCH
All hail, Macbeth! Hail to thee, Thane of Cawdor!
THIRD WITCH
All hail, Macbeth, that shalt be king hereafter!
BANQUO
Good sir, why do you start and seem to fear
Things that do sound so fair?—I' th' name of truth,   55
Are you fantastical, or that indeed
Which outwardly you show? My noble partner
You greet with present grace and great prediction
Of noble having and of royal hope,
That he seems rapt withal. To me you speak not.   60
If you can look into the seeds of time
And say which grain will grow and which will not,
Speak, then, to me, who neither beg nor fear
Your favors nor your hate.

FIRST WITCH Hail! 65
SECOND WITCH Hail!
THIRD WITCH Hail!
FIRST WITCH
  Lesser than Macbeth and greater.
SECOND WITCH
  Not so happy, yet much happier.
THIRD WITCH
  Thou shalt get kings, though thou be none. 70
  So all hail, Macbeth and Banquo!
FIRST WITCH
  Banquo and Macbeth, all hail!
MACBETH
  Stay, you imperfect speakers. Tell me more.
  By Sinel's death I know I am Thane of Glamis.
  But how of Cawdor? The Thane of Cawdor lives 75
  A prosperous gentleman, and to be king
  Stands not within the prospect of belief,
  No more than to be Cawdor. Say from whence
  You owe this strange intelligence or why
  Upon this blasted heath you stop our way 80
  With such prophetic greeting. Speak, I charge you.
                              Witches vanish.
BANQUO
  The earth hath bubbles, as the water has,
  And these are of them. Whither are they vanished?
MACBETH
  Into the air, and what seemed corporal melted,
  As breath into the wind. Would they had stayed! 85
BANQUO
  Were such things here as we do speak about?
  Or have we eaten on the insane root
  That takes the reason prisoner?
MACBETH
  Your children shall be kings.
BANQUO   You shall be king. 90

MACBETH
  And Thane of Cawdor too. Went it not so?
BANQUO
  To th' selfsame tune and words.—Who's here?

            Enter Ross and Angus.

ROSS
  The King hath happily received, Macbeth,
  The news of thy success, and, when he reads
  Thy personal venture in the rebels' fight,   95
  His wonders and his praises do contend
  Which should be thine or his. Silenced with that,
  In viewing o'er the rest o' th' selfsame day
  He finds thee in the stout Norweyan ranks,
  Nothing afeard of what thyself didst make,   100
  Strange images of death. As thick as tale
  ⌜Came⌝ post with post, and every one did bear
  Thy praises in his kingdom's great defense,
  And poured them down before him.
ANGUS   We are sent   105
  To give thee from our royal master thanks,
  Only to herald thee into his sight,
  Not pay thee.
ROSS
  And for an earnest of a greater honor,
  He bade me, from him, call thee Thane of Cawdor,   110
  In which addition, hail, most worthy thane,
  For it is thine.
BANQUO   What, can the devil speak true?
MACBETH
  The Thane of Cawdor lives. Why do you dress me
  In borrowed robes?   115
ANGUS   Who was the Thane lives yet,
  But under heavy judgment bears that life
  Which he deserves to lose. Whether he was
    combined

With those of Norway, or did line the rebel   120
With hidden help and vantage, or that with both
He labored in his country's wrack, I know not;
But treasons capital, confessed and proved,
Have overthrown him.
MACBETH, ⌜*aside*⌝   Glamis and Thane of Cawdor!   125
  The greatest is behind. ⌜*To Ross and Angus.*⌝ Thanks
    for your pains.
  ⌜*Aside to Banquo.*⌝ Do you not hope your children
    shall be kings
  When those that gave the Thane of Cawdor to me   130
  Promised no less to them?
BANQUO   That, trusted home,
  Might yet enkindle you unto the crown,
  Besides the Thane of Cawdor. But 'tis strange.
  And oftentimes, to win us to our harm,   135
  The instruments of darkness tell us truths,
  Win us with honest trifles, to betray 's
  In deepest consequence.—
  Cousins, a word, I pray you.   ⌜*They step aside.*⌝
MACBETH, ⌜*aside*⌝   Two truths are told   140
  As happy prologues to the swelling act
  Of the imperial theme.—I thank you, gentlemen.
  ⌜*Aside.*⌝ This supernatural soliciting
  Cannot be ill, cannot be good. If ill,
  Why hath it given me earnest of success   145
  Commencing in a truth? I am Thane of Cawdor.
  If good, why do I yield to that suggestion
  Whose horrid image doth unfix my hair
  And make my seated heart knock at my ribs
  Against the use of nature? Present fears   150
  Are less than horrible imaginings.
  My thought, whose murder yet is but fantastical,
  Shakes so my single state of man
  That function is smothered in surmise,
  And nothing is but what is not.   155

BANQUO Look how our partner's rapt.

MACBETH, ⌈*aside*⌉
  If chance will have me king, why, chance may
    crown me
  Without my stir.

BANQUO   New honors come upon him,   160
  Like our strange garments, cleave not to their mold
  But with the aid of use.

MACBETH, ⌈*aside*⌉   Come what come may,
  Time and the hour runs through the roughest day.

BANQUO
  Worthy Macbeth, we stay upon your leisure.   165

MACBETH
  Give me your favor. My dull brain was wrought
  With things forgotten. Kind gentlemen, your pains
  Are registered where every day I turn
  The leaf to read them. Let us toward the King.
  ⌈*Aside to Banquo.*⌉ Think upon what hath chanced,   170
    and at more time,
  The interim having weighed it, let us speak
  Our free hearts each to other.

BANQUO Very gladly.

MACBETH Till then enough.—Come, friends.   175

                                    They exit.

Scene 4
Flourish. Enter King ⌈Duncan,⌉ Lennox, Malcolm,
Donalbain, and Attendants.

DUNCAN
  Is execution done on Cawdor? ⌈Are⌉ not
  Those in commission yet returned?

MALCOLM   My liege,
  They are not yet come back. But I have spoke
  With one that saw him die, who did report   5

That very frankly he confessed his treasons,
Implored your Highness' pardon, and set forth
A deep repentance. Nothing in his life
Became him like the leaving it. He died
As one that had been studied in his death   10
To throw away the dearest thing he owed
As 'twere a careless trifle.

DUNCAN   There's no art
To find the mind's construction in the face.
He was a gentleman on whom I built   15
An absolute trust.

Enter Macbeth, Banquo, Ross, and Angus.

                          O worthiest cousin,
The sin of my ingratitude even now
Was heavy on me. Thou art so far before
That swiftest wing of recompense is slow   20
To overtake thee. Would thou hadst less deserved,
That the proportion both of thanks and payment
Might have been mine! Only I have left to say,
More is thy due than more than all can pay.

MACBETH
The service and the loyalty I owe   25
In doing it pays itself. Your Highness' part
Is to receive our duties, and our duties
Are to your throne and state children and servants,
Which do but what they should by doing everything
Safe toward your love and honor.   30

DUNCAN   Welcome hither.
I have begun to plant thee and will labor
To make thee full of growing.—Noble Banquo,
That hast no less deserved nor must be known
No less to have done so, let me enfold thee   35
And hold thee to my heart.

BANQUO   There, if I grow,
The harvest is your own.

DUNCAN   My plenteous joys,
Wanton in fullness, seek to hide themselves   40
In drops of sorrow.—Sons, kinsmen, thanes,
And you whose places are the nearest, know
We will establish our estate upon
Our eldest, Malcolm, whom we name hereafter
The Prince of Cumberland; which honor must   45
Not unaccompanied invest him only,
But signs of nobleness, like stars, shall shine
On all deservers.—From hence to Inverness
And bind us further to you.

MACBETH
The rest is labor which is not used for you.   50
I'll be myself the harbinger and make joyful
The hearing of my wife with your approach.
So humbly take my leave.

DUNCAN   My worthy Cawdor.

MACBETH, ⌈*aside*⌉
The Prince of Cumberland! That is a step   55
On which I must fall down or else o'erleap,
For in my way it lies. Stars, hide your fires;
Let not light see my black and deep desires.
The eye wink at the hand, yet let that be
Which the eye fears, when it is done, to see.   60

                                        He exits.

DUNCAN
True, worthy Banquo. He is full so valiant,
And in his commendations I am fed:
It is a banquet to me.—Let's after him,
Whose care is gone before to bid us welcome.
It is a peerless kinsman.   65

                              Flourish. They exit.

Scene 5
Enter Macbeth's Wife, alone, with a letter.

LADY MACBETH, ⌐*reading the letter*¬ *They met me in the*
day of success, and I have learned by the perfect'st
report they have more in them than mortal knowledge.
When I burned in desire to question them further, they
made themselves air, into which they vanished.   5
Whiles I stood rapt in the wonder of it came missives
from the King, who all-hailed me "Thane of Cawdor,"
by which title, before, these Weïrd Sisters saluted me
and referred me to the coming on of time with "Hail,
king that shalt be." This have I thought good to deliver 10
thee, my dearest partner of greatness, that thou
might'st not lose the dues of rejoicing by being igno-
rant of what greatness is promised thee. Lay it to thy
heart, and farewell.

Glamis thou art, and Cawdor, and shalt be   15
What thou art promised. Yet do I fear thy nature;
It is too full o' th' milk of human kindness
To catch the nearest way. Thou wouldst be great,
Art not without ambition, but without
The illness should attend it. What thou wouldst   20
   highly,
That wouldst thou holily; wouldst not play false
And yet wouldst wrongly win. Thou'd'st have, great
   Glamis,
That which cries "Thus thou must do," if thou have   25
   it,
And that which rather thou dost fear to do,
Than wishest should be undone. Hie thee hither,
That I may pour my spirits in thine ear
And chastise with the valor of my tongue   30
All that impedes thee from the golden round,
Which fate and metaphysical aid doth seem
To have thee crowned withal.

Enter Messenger.

What is your tidings?

MESSENGER
The King comes here tonight.   35

LADY MACBETH   Thou 'rt mad to say it.
Is not thy master with him, who, were 't so,
Would have informed for preparation?

MESSENGER
So please you, it is true. Our thane is coming.
One of my fellows had the speed of him,   40
Who, almost dead for breath, had scarcely more
Than would make up his message.

LADY MACBETH   Give him tending.
He brings great news.   *Messenger exits.*

The raven himself is hoarse   45
That croaks the fatal entrance of Duncan
Under my battlements. Come, you spirits
That tend on mortal thoughts, unsex me here,
And fill me from the crown to the toe top-full
Of direst cruelty. Make thick my blood.   50
Stop up th' access and passage to remorse,
That no compunctious visitings of nature
Shake my fell purpose, nor keep peace between
Th' effect and it. Come to my woman's breasts
And take my milk for gall, you murd'ring ministers,   55
Wherever in your sightless substances
You wait on nature's mischief. Come, thick night,
And pall thee in the dunnest smoke of hell,
That my keen knife see not the wound it makes,
Nor heaven peep through the blanket of the dark   60
To cry "Hold, hold!"

Enter Macbeth.

Great Glamis, worthy Cawdor,
Greater than both by the all-hail hereafter!

Thy letters have transported me beyond
This ignorant present, and I feel now   65
The future in the instant.

MACBETH   My dearest love,
Duncan comes here tonight.

LADY MACBETH   And when goes hence?

MACBETH
Tomorrow, as he purposes.   70

LADY MACBETH   O, never
Shall sun that morrow see!
Your face, my thane, is as a book where men
May read strange matters. To beguile the time,
Look like the time. Bear welcome in your eye,   75
Your hand, your tongue. Look like th' innocent
    flower,
But be the serpent under 't. He that's coming
Must be provided for; and you shall put
This night's great business into my dispatch,   80
Which shall to all our nights and days to come
Give solely sovereign sway and masterdom.

MACBETH
We will speak further.

LADY MACBETH   Only look up clear.
To alter favor ever is to fear.   85
Leave all the rest to me.

                                        They exit.

Scene 6

Hautboys and Torches. Enter King ⌜*Duncan,*⌝ *Malcolm,*
Donalbain, Banquo, Lennox, Macduff, Ross, Angus, and
Attendants.

DUNCAN
This castle hath a pleasant seat. The air
Nimbly and sweetly recommends itself
Unto our gentle senses.

BANQUO   This guest of summer,
  The temple-haunting ⌈martlet,⌉ does approve,   5
  By his loved ⌈mansionry,⌉ that the heaven's breath
  Smells wooingly here. No jutty, frieze,
  Buttress, nor coign of vantage, but this bird
  Hath made his pendant bed and procreant cradle.
  Where they ⌈most⌉ breed and haunt, I have   10
    observed,
  The air is delicate.

                Enter Lady ⌈Macbeth.⌉

DUNCAN   See, see our honored hostess!—
  The love that follows us sometime is our trouble,
  Which still we thank as love. Herein I teach you   15
  How you shall bid God 'ild us for your pains
  And thank us for your trouble.
LADY MACBETH   All our service,
  In every point twice done and then done double,
  Were poor and single business to contend   20
  Against those honors deep and broad wherewith
  Your Majesty loads our house. For those of old,
  And the late dignities heaped up to them,
  We rest your hermits.
DUNCAN   Where's the Thane of Cawdor?   25
  We coursed him at the heels and had a purpose
  To be his purveyor; but he rides well,
  And his great love (sharp as his spur) hath helped
    him
  To his home before us. Fair and noble hostess,   30
  We are your guest tonight.
LADY MACBETH   Your servants ever
  Have theirs, themselves, and what is theirs in compt
  To make their audit at your Highness' pleasure,
  Still to return your own.   35
DUNCAN   Give me your hand.

⌜*Taking her hand.*⌝

Conduct me to mine host. We love him highly
And shall continue our graces towards him.
By your leave, hostess.

They exit.

Scene 7

Hautboys. Torches. Enter a Sewer and divers Servants
with dishes and service over the stage. Then enter
Macbeth.

MACBETH

If it were done when 'tis done, then 'twere well
It were done quickly. If th' assassination
Could trammel up the consequence and catch
With his surcease success, that but this blow
Might be the be-all and the end-all here,   5
But here, upon this bank and ⌜shoal⌝ of time,
We'd jump the life to come. But in these cases
We still have judgment here, that we but teach
Bloody instructions, which, being taught, return
To plague th' inventor. This even-handed justice   10
Commends th' ingredience of our poisoned chalice
To our own lips. He's here in double trust:
First, as I am his kinsman and his subject,
Strong both against the deed; then, as his host,
Who should against his murderer shut the door,   15
Not bear the knife myself. Besides, this Duncan
Hath borne his faculties so meek, hath been
So clear in his great office, that his virtues
Will plead like angels, trumpet-tongued, against
The deep damnation of his taking-off;   20
And pity, like a naked newborn babe
Striding the blast, or heaven's cherubin horsed

Upon the sightless couriers of the air,
Shall blow the horrid deed in every eye,
That tears shall drown the wind. I have no spur   25
To prick the sides of my intent, but only
Vaulting ambition, which o'erleaps itself
And falls on th' other—

Enter Lady ⌜Macbeth.⌝

How now, what news?

LADY MACBETH
He has almost supped. Why have you left the   30
     chamber?

MACBETH
Hath he asked for me?

LADY MACBETH   Know you not he has?

MACBETH
We will proceed no further in this business.
He hath honored me of late, and I have bought   35
Golden opinions from all sorts of people,
Which would be worn now in their newest gloss,
Not cast aside so soon.

LADY MACBETH   Was the hope drunk
Wherein you dressed yourself? Hath it slept since?   4⟨0⟩
And wakes it now, to look so green and pale
At what it did so freely? From this time
Such I account thy love. Art thou afeard
To be the same in thine own act and valor
As thou art in desire? Wouldst thou have that   4⟨5⟩
Which thou esteem'st the ornament of life
And live a coward in thine own esteem,
Letting "I dare not" wait upon "I would,"
Like the poor cat i' th' adage?

MACBETH   Prithee, peace.   ⟨50⟩
I dare do all that may become a man.
Who dares ⌜do⌝ more is none.

LADY MACBETH   What beast was 't,
   then,
  That made you break this enterprise to me?   55
  When you durst do it, then you were a man;
  And to be more than what you were, you would
  Be so much more the man. Nor time nor place
  Did then adhere, and yet you would make both.
  They have made themselves, and that their fitness   60
   now
  Does unmake you. I have given suck, and know
  How tender 'tis to love the babe that milks me.
  I would, while it was smiling in my face,
  Have plucked my nipple from his boneless gums   65
  And dashed the brains out, had I so sworn as you
  Have done to this.
MACBETH   If we should fail—
LADY MACBETH   We fail?
  But screw your courage to the sticking place   70
  And we'll not fail. When Duncan is asleep
  (Whereto the rather shall his day's hard journey
  Soundly invite him), his two chamberlains
  Will I with wine and wassail so convince
  That memory, the warder of the brain,   75
  Shall be a fume, and the receipt of reason
  A limbeck only. When in swinish sleep
  Their drenchèd natures lies as in a death,
  What cannot you and I perform upon
  Th' unguarded Duncan? What not put upon   80
  His spongy officers, who shall bear the guilt
  Of our great quell?
MACBETH   Bring forth men-children only,
  For thy undaunted mettle should compose
  Nothing but males. Will it not be received,   85
  When we have marked with blood those sleepy two
  Of his own chamber and used their very daggers,
  That they have done 't?

LADY MACBETH   Who dares receive it other,
As we shall make our griefs and clamor roar   90
Upon his death?

MACBETH   I am settled and bend up
Each corporal agent to this terrible feat.
Away, and mock the time with fairest show.
False face must hide what the false heart doth   95
   know.

                                     They exit.

ACT 2

Scene 1
Enter Banquo, and Fleance with a torch before him.

BANQUO How goes the night, boy?

FLEANCE
The moon is down. I have not heard the clock.

BANQUO And she goes down at twelve.

FLEANCE I take 't 'tis later, sir.

BANQUO
Hold, take my sword. ⌜*Giving his sword to Fleance.*⌝ 5
                There's husbandry in heaven;
Their candles are all out. Take thee that too.
A heavy summons lies like lead upon me,
And yet I would not sleep. Merciful powers,
Restrain in me the cursèd thoughts that nature 10
Gives way to in repose.

     Enter Macbeth, and a Servant with a torch.

                Give me my sword.—Who's
  there?

MACBETH A friend.

BANQUO
What, sir, not yet at rest? The King's abed. 15
He hath been in unusual pleasure, and
Sent forth great largess to your offices.
This diamond he greets your wife withal,

411

By the name of most kind hostess, and shut up
In measureless content.   20
⌐*He gives Macbeth a diamond.*⌐
MACBETH   Being unprepared,
Our will became the servant to defect,
Which else should free have wrought.
BANQUO All's well.
I dreamt last night of the three Weïrd Sisters.   25
To you they have showed some truth.
MACBETH   I think not of
   them.
Yet, when we can entreat an hour to serve,
We would spend it in some words upon that   30
   business,
If you would grant the time.
BANQUO   At your kind'st leisure.
MACBETH
If you shall cleave to my consent, when 'tis,
It shall make honor for you.   35
BANQUO   So I lose none
In seeking to augment it, but still keep
My bosom franchised and allegiance clear,
I shall be counseled.
MACBETH   Good repose the while.   40
BANQUO Thanks, sir. The like to you.
                        Banquo ⌐*and Fleance*⌐ *exit.*
MACBETH
Go bid thy mistress, when my drink is ready,
She strike upon the bell. Get thee to bed.
                              ⌐*Servant*⌐ *exits.*
Is this a dagger which I see before me,
The handle toward my hand? Come, let me clutch   45
   thee.
I have thee not, and yet I see thee still.
Art thou not, fatal vision, sensible
To feeling as to sight? Or art thou but

A dagger of the mind, a false creation   50
Proceeding from the heat-oppressèd brain?
I see thee yet, in form as palpable
As this which now I draw.   ⌐*He draws his dagger.*⌐
Thou marshal'st me the way that I was going,
And such an instrument I was to use.   55
Mine eyes are made the fools o' th' other senses
Or else worth all the rest. I see thee still,
And, on thy blade and dudgeon, gouts of blood,
Which was not so before. There's no such thing.
It is the bloody business which informs   60
Thus to mine eyes. Now o'er the one-half world
Nature seems dead, and wicked dreams abuse
The curtained sleep. Witchcraft celebrates
Pale Hecate's off'rings, and withered murder,
Alarumed by his sentinel, the wolf,   65
Whose howl's his watch, thus with his stealthy pace,
With Tarquin's ravishing ⌐strides,⌐ towards his
   design
Moves like a ghost. Thou ⌐sure⌐ and firm-set earth,
Hear not my steps, which ⌐way they⌐ walk, for fear   70
Thy very stones prate of my whereabouts
And take the present horror from the time,
Which now suits with it. Whiles I threat, he lives.
Words to the heat of deeds too cold breath gives.
                                        A bell rings.
I go, and it is done. The bell invites me.   75
Hear it not, Duncan, for it is a knell
That summons thee to heaven or to hell.
                                        He exits.

Scene 2
Enter Lady ⌜Macbeth.⌝

LADY MACBETH
That which hath made them drunk hath made me
   bold.
What hath quenched them hath given me fire.
   Hark!—Peace.
It was the owl that shrieked, the fatal bellman,   5
Which gives the stern'st good-night. He is about it.
The doors are open, and the surfeited grooms
Do mock their charge with snores. I have drugged
   their possets,
That death and nature do contend about them   10
Whether they live or die.
MACBETH, ⌜*within*⌝   Who's there? what, ho!
LADY MACBETH
Alack, I am afraid they have awaked,
And 'tis not done. Th' attempt and not the deed
Confounds us. Hark!—I laid their daggers ready;   15
He could not miss 'em. Had he not resembled
My father as he slept, I had done 't.

Enter Macbeth ⌜with bloody daggers.⌝

My husband?
MACBETH
I have done the deed. Didst thou not hear a noise?
LADY MACBETH
I heard the owl scream and the crickets cry.   20
Did not you speak?
MACBETH   When?
LADY MACBETH   Now.
MACBETH   As I descended?
LADY MACBETH Ay.   25
MACBETH Hark!—Who lies i' th' second chamber?
LADY MACBETH Donalbain.

MACBETH This is a sorry sight.
LADY MACBETH
  A foolish thought, to say a sorry sight.
MACBETH
  There's one did laugh in 's sleep, and one cried   30
    "Murder!"
  That they did wake each other. I stood and heard
    them.
  But they did say their prayers and addressed them
  Again to sleep.   35
LADY MACBETH   There are two lodged together.
MACBETH
  One cried "God bless us" and "Amen" the other,
  As they had seen me with these hangman's hands,
  List'ning their fear. I could not say "Amen"
  When they did say "God bless us."   40
LADY MACBETH Consider it not so deeply.
MACBETH
  But wherefore could not I pronounce "Amen"?
  I had most need of blessing, and "Amen"
  Stuck in my throat.
LADY MACBETH   These deeds must not be thought   45
  After these ways; so, it will make us mad.
MACBETH
  Methought I heard a voice cry "Sleep no more!
  Macbeth does murder sleep"—the innocent sleep,
  Sleep that knits up the raveled sleave of care,
  The death of each day's life, sore labor's bath,   50
  Balm of hurt minds, great nature's second course,
  Chief nourisher in life's feast.
LADY MACBETH   What do you mean?
MACBETH
  Still it cried "Sleep no more!" to all the house.
  "Glamis hath murdered sleep, and therefore   55
    Cawdor
  Shall sleep no more. Macbeth shall sleep no more."

LADY MACBETH
 Who was it that thus cried? Why, worthy thane,
 You do unbend your noble strength to think
 So brainsickly of things. Go get some water   60
 And wash this filthy witness from your hand.—
 Why did you bring these daggers from the place?
 They must lie there. Go, carry them and smear
 The sleepy grooms with blood.

MACBETH   I'll go no more.   65
 I am afraid to think what I have done.
 Look on 't again I dare not.

LADY MACBETH   Infirm of purpose!
 Give me the daggers. The sleeping and the dead
 Are but as pictures. 'Tis the eye of childhood   70
 That fears a painted devil. If he do bleed,
 I'll gild the faces of the grooms withal,
 For it must seem their guilt.
     She exits ⌜with the daggers.⌝ Knock within.

MACBETH   Whence is that
 knocking?   75
 How is 't with me when every noise appalls me?
 What hands are here! Ha, they pluck out mine eyes.
 Will all great Neptune's ocean wash this blood
 Clean from my hand? No, this my hand will rather
 The multitudinous seas incarnadine,   80
 Making the green one red.

     Enter Lady ⌜Macbeth.⌝

LADY MACBETH
 My hands are of your color, but I shame
 To wear a heart so white.   *Knock.*
      I hear a knocking
 At the south entry. Retire we to our chamber.   85
 A little water clears us of this deed.
 How easy is it, then! Your constancy
 Hath left you unattended.   *Knock.*

                    Hark, more knocking.
Get on your nightgown, lest occasion call us   90
And show us to be watchers. Be not lost
So poorly in your thoughts.

MACBETH
To know my deed 'twere best not know myself.
                                        Knock.
Wake Duncan with thy knocking. I would thou
    couldst.   95
                                     They exit.

                         Scene 3
              Knocking within. Enter a Porter.

PORTER Here's a knocking indeed! If a man were
    porter of hell gate, he should have old turning the
    key. *(Knock.)* Knock, knock, knock! Who's there, i'
    th' name of Beelzebub? Here's a farmer that hanged
    himself on th' expectation of plenty. Come in time!   5
    Have napkins enough about you; here you'll sweat
    for 't. *(Knock.)* Knock, knock! Who's there, in th'
    other devil's name? Faith, here's an equivocator
    that could swear in both the scales against either
    scale, who committed treason enough for God's   10
    sake yet could not equivocate to heaven. O, come in,
    equivocator. *(Knock.)* Knock, knock, knock! Who's
    there? Faith, here's an English tailor come hither for
    stealing out of a French hose. Come in, tailor. Here
    you may roast your goose. *(Knock.)* Knock, knock!   15
    Never at quiet.—What are you?—But this place is
    too cold for hell. I'll devil-porter it no further. I had
    thought to have let in some of all professions that go
    the primrose way to th' everlasting bonfire. *(Knock.)*
    Anon, anon!   20

⌜*The Porter opens the door to*⌝ *Macduff and Lennox.*

I pray you, remember the porter.

MACDUFF
Was it so late, friend, ere you went to bed
That you do lie so late?

PORTER Faith, sir, we were carousing till the second
cock, and drink, sir, is a great provoker of three 25
things.

MACDUFF What three things does drink especially provoke?

PORTER Marry, sir, nose-painting, sleep, and urine.
Lechery, sir, it provokes and unprovokes. It pro- 30
vokes the desire, but it takes away the performance. Therefore much drink may be said to be an
equivocator with lechery. It makes him, and it
mars him; it sets him on, and it takes him off; it
persuades him and disheartens him; makes him 35
stand to and not stand to; in conclusion, equivo-
cates him in a sleep and, giving him the lie, leaves
him.

MACDUFF I believe drink gave thee the lie last night.

PORTER That it did, sir, i' th' very throat on me; but I 40
requited him for his lie, and, I think, being too
strong for him, though he took up my legs sometime, yet I made a shift to cast him.

MACDUFF Is thy master stirring?

Enter Macbeth.

Our knocking has awaked him. Here he comes. 45
⌜*Porter exits.*⌝

LENNOX
Good morrow, noble sir.

MACBETH   Good morrow, both.

MACDUFF
Is the King stirring, worthy thane?

MACBETH   Not yet.

MACDUFF
He did command me to call timely on him. 50
I have almost slipped the hour.

MACBETH   I'll bring you to him.

MACDUFF
  I know this is a joyful trouble to you,
  But yet 'tis one.

MACBETH
  The labor we delight in physics pain.   55
  This is the door.

MACDUFF   I'll make so bold to call,
  For 'tis my limited service.   *Macduff exits.*

LENNOX   Goes the King hence today?

MACBETH   He does. He did appoint so.   60

LENNOX
  The night has been unruly. Where we lay,
  Our chimneys were blown down and, as they say,
  Lamentings heard i' th' air, strange screams of
      death,
  And prophesying, with accents terrible,   65
  Of dire combustion and confused events
  New hatched to th' woeful time. The obscure bird
  Clamored the livelong night. Some say the earth
  Was feverous and did shake.

MACBETH   'Twas a rough night.   70

LENNOX
  My young remembrance cannot parallel
  A fellow to it.

                  Enter Macduff.

MACDUFF   O horror, horror, horror!
  Tongue nor heart cannot conceive nor name thee!

MACBETH and LENNOX   What's the matter?   75

MACDUFF
  Confusion now hath made his masterpiece.
  Most sacrilegious murder hath broke ope
  The Lord's anointed temple and stole thence
  The life o' th' building.

MACBETH   What is 't you say? The life?   80
LENNOX   Mean you his Majesty?
MACDUFF
   Approach the chamber and destroy your sight
   With a new Gorgon. Do not bid me speak.
   See and then speak yourselves.

                      Macbeth and Lennox exit.
                      Awake, awake!   85
   Ring the alarum bell.—Murder and treason!
   Banquo and Donalbain, Malcolm, awake!
   Shake off this downy sleep, death's counterfeit,
   And look on death itself. Up, up, and see
   The great doom's image. Malcolm, Banquo,   90
   As from your graves rise up and walk like sprites
   To countenance this horror.—Ring the bell.

                          Bell rings.

        Enter Lady ⌈Macbeth.⌉

LADY MACBETH   What's the business,
   That such a hideous trumpet calls to parley
   The sleepers of the house? Speak, speak!   95
MACDUFF   O gentle lady,
   'Tis not for you to hear what I can speak.
   The repetition in a woman's ear
   Would murder as it fell.

                Enter Banquo.

                O Banquo, Banquo,   100
   Our royal master's murdered.
LADY MACBETH   Woe, alas!
   What, in our house?
BANQUO   Too cruel anywhere.—
   Dear Duff, I prithee, contradict thyself   105
   And say it is not so.

Enter Macbeth, Lennox, and Ross.

MACBETH
Had I but died an hour before this chance,
I had lived a blessèd time; for from this instant
There's nothing serious in mortality.
All is but toys. Renown and grace is dead.   110
The wine of life is drawn, and the mere lees
Is left this vault to brag of.

Enter Malcolm and Donalbain.

DONALBAIN   What is amiss?
MACBETH   You are, and do not know 't.
The spring, the head, the fountain of your blood   115
Is stopped; the very source of it is stopped.
MACDUFF
Your royal father's murdered.
MALCOLM   O, by whom?
LENNOX
Those of his chamber, as it seemed, had done 't.
Their hands and faces were all badged with blood.   120
So were their daggers, which unwiped we found
Upon their pillows. They stared and were distracted.
No man's life was to be trusted with them.
MACBETH
O, yet I do repent me of my fury,
That I did kill them.   125
MACDUFF   Wherefore did you so?
MACBETH
Who can be wise, amazed, temp'rate, and furious,
Loyal, and neutral, in a moment? No man.
Th' expedition of my violent love
Outrun the pauser, reason. Here lay Duncan,   130
His silver skin laced with his golden blood,
And his gashed stabs looked like a breach in nature
For ruin's wasteful entrance; there the murderers,

Steeped in the colors of their trade, their daggers
Unmannerly breeched with gore. Who could refrain　135
That had a heart to love, and in that heart
Courage to make 's love known?

LADY MACBETH　　　　　　　　　　Help me hence, ho!

MACDUFF
　Look to the lady.

MALCOLM, ⌜*aside to Donalbain*⌝ Why do we hold our　140
　　tongues,
　That most may claim this argument for ours?

DONALBAIN, ⌜*aside to Malcolm*⌝
　What should be spoken here, where our fate,
　Hid in an auger hole, may rush and seize us?
　Let's away. Our tears are not yet brewed.　145

MALCOLM, ⌜*aside to Donalbain*⌝
　Nor our strong sorrow upon the foot of motion.

BANQUO　Look to the lady.
　　　　　　　⌜*Lady Macbeth is assisted to leave.*⌝
　And when we have our naked frailties hid,
　That suffer in exposure, let us meet
　And question this most bloody piece of work　150
　To know it further. Fears and scruples shake us.
　In the great hand of God I stand, and thence
　Against the undivulged pretense I fight
　Of treasonous malice.

MACDUFF　　　　　　　And so do I.　155

ALL　　　　　　　　　　So all.

MACBETH
　Let's briefly put on manly readiness
　And meet i' th' hall together.

ALL　　　　　　　　Well contented.
　　　　　　⌜*All but Malcolm and Donalbain*⌝ *exit.*

MALCOLM
　What will you do? Let's not consort with them.　160
　To show an unfelt sorrow is an office
　Which the false man does easy. I'll to England.

DONALBAIN
To Ireland I. Our separated fortune
Shall keep us both the safer. Where we are,
There's daggers in men's smiles. The near in blood,   165
The nearer bloody.
MALCOLM   This murderous shaft that's shot
Hath not yet lighted, and our safest way
Is to avoid the aim. Therefore to horse,
And let us not be dainty of leave-taking   170
But shift away. There's warrant in that theft
Which steals itself when there's no mercy left.
                                        They exit.

Scene 4
Enter Ross with an Old Man.

OLD MAN
Threescore and ten I can remember well,
Within the volume of which time I have seen
Hours dreadful and things strange, but this sore
    night
Hath trifled former knowings.   5
ROSS   Ha, good father,
Thou seest the heavens, as troubled with man's act,
Threatens his bloody stage. By th' clock 'tis day,
And yet dark night strangles the traveling lamp.
Is 't night's predominance or the day's shame   10
That darkness does the face of earth entomb
When living light should kiss it?
OLD MAN   'Tis unnatural,
Even like the deed that's done. On Tuesday last
A falcon, tow'ring in her pride of place,   15
Was by a mousing owl hawked at and killed.
ROSS
And Duncan's horses (a thing most strange and
    certain),

Beauteous and swift, the minions of their race,
Turned wild in nature, broke their stalls, flung out,   20
Contending 'gainst obedience, as they would
Make war with mankind.

OLD MAN   'Tis said they eat each
   other.

ROSS
   They did so, to th' amazement of mine eyes   25
   That looked upon 't.

                     Enter Macduff.

                     Here comes the good
      Macduff.—
   How goes the world, sir, now?

MACDUFF   Why, see you not?   30

ROSS
   Is 't known who did this more than bloody deed?

MACDUFF
   Those that Macbeth hath slain.

ROSS   Alas the day,
   What good could they pretend?

MACDUFF   They were suborned.   35
   Malcolm and Donalbain, the King's two sons,
   Are stol'n away and fled, which puts upon them
   Suspicion of the deed.

ROSS   'Gainst nature still!
   Thriftless ambition, that will ravin up   40
   Thine own lives' means. Then 'tis most like
   The sovereignty will fall upon Macbeth.

MACDUFF
   He is already named and gone to Scone
   To be invested.

ROSS   Where is Duncan's body?   4

MACDUFF   Carried to Colmekill,
   The sacred storehouse of his predecessors
   And guardian of their bones.

ROSS   Will you to Scone?

MACDUFF
  No, cousin, I'll to Fife.   50

ROSS   Well, I will thither.

MACDUFF
  Well, may you see things well done there. Adieu,
  Lest our old robes sit easier than our new.

ROSS   Farewell, father.

OLD MAN
  God's benison go with you and with those   55
  That would make good of bad and friends of foes.

                                        All exit.

ACT 3

Scene 1
Enter Banquo.

BANQUO
Thou hast it now—King, Cawdor, Glamis, all
As the Weïrd Women promised, and I fear
Thou played'st most foully for 't. Yet it was said
It should not stand in thy posterity,
But that myself should be the root and father   5
Of many kings. If there come truth from them
(As upon thee, Macbeth, their speeches shine)
Why, by the verities on thee made good,
May they not be my oracles as well,
And set me up in hope? But hush, no more.   10

Sennet sounded. Enter Macbeth as King, Lady
⌈*Macbeth,*⌉ *Lennox, Ross, Lords, and Attendants.*

MACBETH
Here's our chief guest.
LADY MACBETH   If he had been forgotten,
It had been as a gap in our great feast
And all-thing unbecoming.
MACBETH
Tonight we hold a solemn supper, sir,   1
And I'll request your presence.
BANQUO   Let your Highness

426

Command upon me, to the which my duties
Are with a most indissoluble tie
Forever knit.   20

MACBETH Ride you this afternoon?

BANQUO Ay, my good lord.

MACBETH
We should have else desired your good advice
(Which still hath been both grave and prosperous)
In this day's council, but we'll take tomorrow.   25
Is 't far you ride?

BANQUO
As far, my lord, as will fill up the time
'Twixt this and supper. Go not my horse the better,
I must become a borrower of the night
For a dark hour or twain.   30

MACBETH   Fail not our feast.

BANQUO My lord, I will not.

MACBETH
We hear our bloody cousins are bestowed
In England and in Ireland, not confessing
Their cruel parricide, filling their hearers   35
With strange invention. But of that tomorrow,
When therewithal we shall have cause of state
Craving us jointly. Hie you to horse. Adieu,
Till you return at night. Goes Fleance with you?

BANQUO
Ay, my good lord. Our time does call upon 's.   40

MACBETH
I wish your horses swift and sure of foot,
And so I do commend you to their backs.
Farewell.   *Banquo exits.*
Let every man be master of his time
Till seven at night. To make society   45
The sweeter welcome, we will keep ourself
Till suppertime alone. While then, God be with you.
          Lords ⌈and all but Macbeth and a Servant⌉ exit.

Sirrah, a word with you. Attend those men
Our pleasure?

SERVANT
They are, my lord, without the palace gate.   50

MACBETH
Bring them before us.   *Servant exits.*
     To be thus is nothing,
But to be safely thus. Our fears in Banquo
Stick deep, and in his royalty of nature
Reigns that which would be feared. 'Tis much he   55
 dares,
And to that dauntless temper of his mind
He hath a wisdom that doth guide his valor
To act in safety. There is none but he
Whose being I do fear; and under him   60
My genius is rebuked, as it is said
Mark Antony's was by Caesar. He chid the sisters
When first they put the name of king upon me
And bade them speak to him. Then, prophet-like,
They hailed him father to a line of kings.   65
Upon my head they placed a fruitless crown
And put a barren scepter in my grip,
Thence to be wrenched with an unlineal hand,
No son of mine succeeding. If 't be so,
For Banquo's issue have I filed my mind;   70
For them the gracious Duncan have I murdered,
Put rancors in the vessel of my peace
Only for them, and mine eternal jewel
Given to the common enemy of man
To make them kings, the seeds of Banquo kings.   75
Rather than so, come fate into the list,
And champion me to th' utterance.—Who's there?

Enter Servant and two Murderers.

⌈*To the Servant.*⌉ Now go to the door, and stay there
 till we call.   *Servant exits.*

Was it not yesterday we spoke together? 80
⌈MURDERERS⌉
  It was, so please your Highness.
MACBETH   Well then, now
  Have you considered of my speeches? Know
  That it was he, in the times past, which held you
  So under fortune, which you thought had been 85
  Our innocent self. This I made good to you
  In our last conference, passed in probation with you
  How you were borne in hand, how crossed, the
    instruments,
  Who wrought with them, and all things else that 90
    might
  To half a soul and to a notion crazed
  Say "Thus did Banquo."
FIRST MURDERER   You made it known to us.
MACBETH
  I did so, and went further, which is now 95
  Our point of second meeting. Do you find
  Your patience so predominant in your nature
  That you can let this go? Are you so gospeled
  To pray for this good man and for his issue,
  Whose heavy hand hath bowed you to the grave 100
  And beggared yours forever?
FIRST MURDERER   We are men, my liege.
MACBETH
  Ay, in the catalogue you go for men,
  As hounds and greyhounds, mongrels, spaniels,
    curs, 105
  Shoughs, water-rugs, and demi-wolves are clept
  All by the name of dogs. The valued file
  Distinguishes the swift, the slow, the subtle,
  The housekeeper, the hunter, every one
  According to the gift which bounteous nature 110
  Hath in him closed; whereby he does receive

Particular addition, from the bill
That writes them all alike. And so of men.
Now, if you have a station in the file,
Not i' th' worst rank of manhood, say 't,   115
And I will put that business in your bosoms
Whose execution takes your enemy off,
Grapples you to the heart and love of us,
Who wear our health but sickly in his life,
Which in his death were perfect.   120

SECOND MURDERER   I am one, my liege,
Whom the vile blows and buffets of the world
Hath so incensed that I am reckless what
I do to spite the world.

FIRST MURDERER   And I another   125
So weary with disasters, tugged with fortune,
That I would set my life on any chance,
To mend it or be rid on 't.

MACBETH   Both of you
Know Banquo was your enemy.   130

⌜MURDERERS⌝   True, my lord.

MACBETH
So is he mine, and in such bloody distance
That every minute of his being thrusts
Against my near'st of life. And though I could
With barefaced power sweep him from my sight   135
And bid my will avouch it, yet I must not,
For certain friends that are both his and mine,
Whose loves I may not drop, but wail his fall
Who I myself struck down. And thence it is
That I to your assistance do make love,   140
Masking the business from the common eye
For sundry weighty reasons.

SECOND MURDERER   We shall, my lord,
Perform what you command us.

FIRST MURDERER   Though our lives—   145

MACBETH
    Your spirits shine through you. Within this hour at
      most
    I will advise you where to plant yourselves,
    Acquaint you with the perfect spy o' th' time,
    The moment on 't, for 't must be done tonight   150
    And something from the palace; always thought
    That I require a clearness. And with him
    (To leave no rubs nor botches in the work)
    Fleance, his son, that keeps him company,
    Whose absence is no less material to me   155
    Than is his father's, must embrace the fate
    Of that dark hour. Resolve yourselves apart.
    I'll come to you anon.
⌜MURDERERS⌝ We are resolved, my lord.
MACBETH
    I'll call upon you straight. Abide within.   160
                        ⌜*Murderers exit.*⌝
    It is concluded. Banquo, thy soul's flight,
    If it find heaven, must find it out tonight.
                          ⌜*He exits.*⌝

Scene 2
Enter Macbeth's Lady and a Servant.

LADY MACBETH Is Banquo gone from court?
SERVANT
    Ay, madam, but returns again tonight.
LADY MACBETH
    Say to the King I would attend his leisure
    For a few words.
SERVANT Madam, I will.   *He exits.*   5
LADY MACBETH Naught's had, all's spent,
    Where our desire is got without content.
    'Tis safer to be that which we destroy
    Than by destruction dwell in doubtful joy.

Enter Macbeth.

How now, my lord, why do you keep alone,   10
Of sorriest fancies your companions making,
Using those thoughts which should indeed have died
With them they think on? Things without all remedy
Should be without regard. What's done is done.

MACBETH
We have scorched the snake, not killed it.   15
She'll close and be herself whilst our poor malice
Remains in danger of her former tooth.
But let the frame of things disjoint, both the worlds
    suffer,
Ere we will eat our meal in fear, and sleep   20
In the affliction of these terrible dreams
That shake us nightly. Better be with the dead,
Whom we, to gain our peace, have sent to peace,
Than on the torture of the mind to lie
In restless ecstasy. Duncan is in his grave.   25
After life's fitful fever he sleeps well.
Treason has done his worst; nor steel nor poison,
Malice domestic, foreign levy, nothing
Can touch him further.

LADY MACBETH   Come on, gentle my lord,   30
Sleek o'er your rugged looks. Be bright and jovial
Among your guests tonight.

MACBETH   So shall I, love,
And so I pray be you. Let your remembrance
Apply to Banquo; present him eminence   35
Both with eye and tongue: unsafe the while that we
Must lave our honors in these flattering streams
And make our faces vizards to our hearts,
Disguising what they are.

LADY MACBETH   You must leave this.   40

MACBETH
O, full of scorpions is my mind, dear wife!
Thou know'st that Banquo and his Fleance lives.

LADY MACBETH
  But in them nature's copy's not eterne.

MACBETH
  There's comfort yet; they are assailable.
  Then be thou jocund. Ere the bat hath flown   45
  His cloistered flight, ere to black Hecate's summons
  The shard-borne beetle with his drowsy hums
  Hath rung night's yawning peal, there shall be done
  A deed of dreadful note.

LADY MACBETH   What's to be done?   50

MACBETH
  Be innocent of the knowledge, dearest chuck,
  Till thou applaud the deed.—Come, seeling night,
  Scarf up the tender eye of pitiful day
  And with thy bloody and invisible hand
  Cancel and tear to pieces that great bond
  Which keeps me pale. Light thickens, and the crow
  Makes wing to th' rooky wood.
  Good things of day begin to droop and drowse,
  Whiles night's black agents to their preys do
    rouse.—   60
  Thou marvel'st at my words, but hold thee still.
  Things bad begun make strong themselves by ill.
  So prithee go with me.

                                  They exit.

                      Scene 3
                Enter three Murderers.

FIRST MURDERER
  But who did bid thee join with us?

THIRD MURDERER   Macbeth.

SECOND MURDERER, ⌈*to the First Murderer*⌉
  He needs not our mistrust, since he delivers
  Our offices and what we have to do
  To the direction just.   5

FIRST MURDERER   Then stand with us.—
  The west yet glimmers with some streaks of day.
  Now spurs the lated traveler apace
  To gain the timely inn, ⌜and⌝ near approaches
  The subject of our watch.   10
THIRD MURDERER   Hark, I hear horses.
BANQUO, *within*   Give us a light there, ho!
SECOND MURDERER   Then 'tis he. The rest
  That are within the note of expectation
  Already are i' th' court.   15
FIRST MURDERER   His horses go about.
THIRD MURDERER
  Almost a mile; but he does usually
  (So all men do) from hence to th' palace gate
  Make it their walk.

      Enter Banquo and Fleance, with a torch.

SECOND MURDERER   A light, a light!   20
THIRD MURDERER   'Tis he.
FIRST MURDERER   Stand to 't.
BANQUO   It will be rain tonight.
FIRST MURDERER   Let it come down!
                      ⌜*The three Murderers attack.*⌝
BANQUO
  O treachery! Fly, good Fleance, fly, fly, fly!   25
  Thou mayst revenge—O slave!
                      ⌜*He dies. Fleance exits.*⌝
THIRD MURDERER
  Who did strike out the light?
FIRST MURDERER   Was 't not the way?
THIRD MURDERER   There's but one down. The son is
  fled.   30
SECOND MURDERER   We have lost best half of our
  affair.
FIRST MURDERER
  Well, let's away and say how much is done.
                                          They exit.

Scene 4

Banquet prepared. Enter Macbeth, Lady ⌐Macbeth,⌐
Ross, Lennox, Lords, and Attendants.

MACBETH
   You know your own degrees; sit down. At first
   And last, the hearty welcome.   ⌐*They sit.*⌐
LORDS   Thanks to your Majesty.
MACBETH
   Ourself will mingle with society
   And play the humble host.   5
   Our hostess keeps her state, but in best time
   We will require her welcome.
LADY MACBETH
   Pronounce it for me, sir, to all our friends,
   For my heart speaks they are welcome.

      Enter First Murderer ⌐to the door.⌐

MACBETH
   See, they encounter thee with their hearts' thanks.   10
   Both sides are even. Here I'll sit i' th' midst.
   Be large in mirth. Anon we'll drink a measure
   The table round. ⌐*Approaching the Murderer.*⌐ There's
      blood upon thy face.
MURDERER   'Tis Banquo's then.   15
MACBETH
   'Tis better thee without than he within.
   Is he dispatched?
MURDERER
   My lord, his throat is cut. That I did for him.
MACBETH
   Thou art the best o' th' cutthroats,
   Yet he's good that did the like for Fleance.   20
   If thou didst it, thou art the nonpareil.
MURDERER
   Most royal sir, Fleance is 'scaped.
MACBETH, ⌐*aside*⌐
   Then comes my fit again. I had else been perfect,

Whole as the marble, founded as the rock,
As broad and general as the casing air.   25
But now I am cabined, cribbed, confined, bound in
To saucy doubts and fears.—But Banquo's safe?

MURDERER
Ay, my good lord. Safe in a ditch he bides,
With twenty trenchèd gashes on his head,
The least a death to nature.   30

MACBETH   Thanks for that.
There the grown serpent lies. The worm that's fled
Hath nature that in time will venom breed,
No teeth for th' present. Get thee gone. Tomorrow
We'll hear ourselves again.   *Murderer exits.*   35

LADY MACBETH   My royal lord,
You do not give the cheer. The feast is sold
That is not often vouched, while 'tis a-making,
'Tis given with welcome. To feed were best at home;
From thence, the sauce to meat is ceremony;   40
Meeting were bare without it.

Enter the Ghost of Banquo, and sits in Macbeth's place.

MACBETH, ⌜*to Lady Macbeth*⌝ Sweet remembrancer!—
Now, good digestion wait on appetite
And health on both!

LENNOX   May 't please your Highness sit.   45

MACBETH
Here had we now our country's honor roofed,
Were the graced person of our Banquo present,
Who may I rather challenge for unkindness
Than pity for mischance.

ROSS   His absence, sir,   50
Lays blame upon his promise. Please 't your
    Highness
To grace us with your royal company?

MACBETH
The table's full.

LENNOX   Here is a place reserved, sir.   55
MACBETH   Where?
LENNOX
  Here, my good lord. What is 't that moves your
    Highness?
MACBETH
  Which of you have done this?
LORDS   What, my good lord?   60
MACBETH, ⌜*to the Ghost*⌝
  Thou canst not say I did it. Never shake
  Thy gory locks at me.
ROSS
  Gentlemen, rise. His Highness is not well.
LADY MACBETH
  Sit, worthy friends. My lord is often thus
  And hath been from his youth. Pray you, keep seat.   65
  The fit is momentary; upon a thought
  He will again be well. If much you note him
  You shall offend him and extend his passion.
  Feed and regard him not. ⌜*Drawing Macbeth aside.*⌝
                          Are you a man?   70
MACBETH
  Ay, and a bold one, that dare look on that
  Which might appall the devil.
LADY MACBETH   O, proper stuff!
  This is the very painting of your fear.
  This is the air-drawn dagger which you said   75
  Led you to Duncan. O, these flaws and starts,
  Impostors to true fear, would well become
  A woman's story at a winter's fire,
  Authorized by her grandam. Shame itself!
  Why do you make such faces? When all's done,   80
  You look but on a stool.
MACBETH
  Prithee, see there. Behold, look! ⌜*To the Ghost.*⌝ Lo,
    how say you?

Why, what care I? If thou canst nod, speak too.—
If charnel houses and our graves must send   85
Those that we bury back, our monuments
Shall be the maws of kites.   ⌜*Ghost exits.*⌝
LADY MACBETH   What, quite unmanned in folly?
MACBETH
  If I stand here, I saw him.
LADY MACBETH   Fie, for shame!   90
MACBETH
  Blood hath been shed ere now, i' th' olden time,
  Ere humane statute purged the gentle weal;
  Ay, and since too, murders have been performed
  Too terrible for the ear. The ⌜time⌝ has been
  That, when the brains were out, the man would die,   95
  And there an end. But now they rise again
  With twenty mortal murders on their crowns
  And push us from our stools. This is more strange
  Than such a murder is.
LADY MACBETH   My worthy lord,   100
  Your noble friends do lack you.
MACBETH   I do forget.—
  Do not muse at me, my most worthy friends.
  I have a strange infirmity, which is nothing
  To those that know me. Come, love and health to   105
    all.
  Then I'll sit down.—Give me some wine. Fill full.

                     Enter Ghost.

  I drink to th' general joy o' th' whole table
  And to our dear friend Banquo, whom we miss.
  Would he were here! To all and him we thirst,   110
  And all to all.
LORDS   Our duties, and the pledge.
                    ⌜*They raise their drinking cups.*⌝
MACBETH, ⌜*to the Ghost*⌝
  Avaunt, and quit my sight! Let the earth hide thee.
  Thy bones are marrowless; thy blood is cold;

Thou hast no speculation in those eyes   115
Which thou dost glare with.

LADY MACBETH   Think of this, good
    peers,
But as a thing of custom. 'Tis no other;
Only it spoils the pleasure of the time.   120

MACBETH, ⌜*to the Ghost*⌝   What man dare, I dare.
Approach thou like the rugged Russian bear,
The armed rhinoceros, or th' Hyrcan tiger;
Take any shape but that, and my firm nerves
Shall never tremble. Or be alive again   125
And dare me to the desert with thy sword.
If trembling I inhabit then, protest me
The baby of a girl. Hence, horrible shadow!
Unreal mock'ry, hence!   ⌜*Ghost exits*
                    Why so, being gone,   130
I am a man again.—Pray you sit still.

LADY MACBETH
You have displaced the mirth, broke the good
    meeting
With most admired disorder.

MACBETH   Can such things be   135
And overcome us like a summer's cloud,
Without our special wonder? You make me strange
Even to the disposition that I owe,
When now I think you can behold such sights
And keep the natural ruby of your cheeks   140
When mine is blanched with fear.

ROSS   What sights, my
    lord?

LADY MACBETH
I pray you, speak not. He grows worse and worse.
Question enrages him. At once, good night.   145
Stand not upon the order of your going,
But go at once.

LENNOX   Good night, and better health
Attend his Majesty.

LADY MACBETH   A kind good night to all.   150
  Lords ⌐and all but Macbeth and Lady Macbeth⌐ exit.
MACBETH
  It will have blood, they say; blood will have blood.
  Stones have been known to move, and trees to
    speak;
  Augurs and understood relations have
  By maggot pies and choughs and rooks brought   155
    forth
  The secret'st man of blood.—What is the night?
LADY MACBETH
  Almost at odds with morning, which is which.
MACBETH
  How say'st thou that Macduff denies his person
  At our great bidding?   160
LADY MACBETH   Did you send to him, sir?
MACBETH
  I hear it by the way; but I will send.
  There's not a one of them but in his house
  I keep a servant fee'd. I will tomorrow
  (And betimes I will) to the Weïrd Sisters.   165
  More shall they speak, for now I am bent to know
  By the worst means the worst. For mine own good,
  All causes shall give way. I am in blood
  Stepped in so far that, should I wade no more,
  Returning were as tedious as go o'er.   170
  Strange things I have in head, that will to hand,
  Which must be acted ere they may be scanned.
LADY MACBETH
  You lack the season of all natures, sleep.
MACBETH
  Come, we'll to sleep. My strange and self-abuse
  Is the initiate fear that wants hard use.   17
  We are yet but young in deed.
                                    They exit.

Scene 5
Thunder. Enter the three Witches, meeting Hecate.

FIRST WITCH
Why, how now, Hecate? You look angerly.
HECATE
Have I not reason, beldams as you are?
Saucy and overbold, how did you dare
To trade and traffic with Macbeth
In riddles and affairs of death,   5
And I, the mistress of your charms,
The close contriver of all harms,
Was never called to bear my part
Or show the glory of our art?
And which is worse, all you have done   10
Hath been but for a wayward son,
Spiteful and wrathful, who, as others do,
Loves for his own ends, not for you.
But make amends now. Get you gone,
And at the pit of Acheron   15
Meet me i' th' morning. Thither he
Will come to know his destiny.
Your vessels and your spells provide,
Your charms and everything beside.
I am for th' air. This night I'll spend   20
Unto a dismal and a fatal end.
Great business must be wrought ere noon.
Upon the corner of the moon
There hangs a vap'rous drop profound.
I'll catch it ere it come to ground,   25
And that, distilled by magic sleights,
Shall raise such artificial sprites
As by the strength of their illusion
Shall draw him on to his confusion.
He shall spurn fate, scorn death, and bear   30
His hopes 'bove wisdom, grace, and fear.

And you all know, security
Is mortals' chiefest enemy.

                              Music and a song.
Hark! I am called. My little spirit, see,
Sits in a foggy cloud and stays for me. ⌜*Hecate exits.*⌝   35
            Sing within "Come away, come away," etc.

FIRST WITCH
Come, let's make haste. She'll soon be back again.
                                          They exit.

                        Scene 6
            Enter Lennox and another Lord.

LENNOX
My former speeches have but hit your thoughts,
Which can interpret farther. Only I say
Things have been strangely borne. The gracious
    Duncan
Was pitied of Macbeth; marry, he was dead.   5
And the right valiant Banquo walked too late,
Whom you may say, if 't please you, Fleance killed,
For Fleance fled. Men must not walk too late.
Who cannot want the thought how monstrous
It was for Malcolm and for Donalbain   10
To kill their gracious father? Damnèd fact,
How it did grieve Macbeth! Did he not straight
In pious rage the two delinquents tear
That were the slaves of drink and thralls of sleep?
Was not that nobly done? Ay, and wisely, too,   15
For 'twould have angered any heart alive
To hear the men deny 't. So that I say
He has borne all things well. And I do think
That had he Duncan's sons under his key
(As, an 't pleasc heaven, he shall not) they should   20
    find
What 'twere to kill a father. So should Fleance.

But peace. For from broad words, and 'cause he
    failed
His presence at the tyrant's feast, I hear   25
Macduff lives in disgrace. Sir, can you tell
Where he bestows himself?

LORD   The ⌜son⌝ of Duncan
  (From whom this tyrant holds the due of birth)
Lives in the English court and is received   30
Of the most pious Edward with such grace
That the malevolence of fortune nothing
Takes from his high respect. Thither Macduff
Is gone to pray the holy king upon his aid
To wake Northumberland and warlike Siward   35
That, by the help of these (with Him above
To ratify the work), we may again
Give to our tables meat, sleep to our nights,
Free from our feasts and banquets bloody knives,
Do faithful homage, and receive free honors,   40
All which we pine for now. And this report
Hath so exasperate ⌜the⌝ King that he
Prepares for some attempt of war.

LENNOX   Sent he to Macduff?

LORD
  He did, and with an absolute "Sir, not I,"   45
The cloudy messenger turns me his back
And hums, as who should say "You'll rue the time
That clogs me with this answer."

LENNOX   And that well might
  Advise him to a caution ⌜t' hold⌝ what distance   50
His wisdom can provide. Some holy angel
Fly to the court of England and unfold
His message ere he come, that a swift blessing
May soon return to this our suffering country
Under a hand accursed.   55

LORD   I'll send my prayers with him.

                        They exit.

ACT 4

Scene 1
Thunder. Enter the three Witches.

FIRST WITCH
  Thrice the brinded cat hath mewed.

SECOND WITCH
  Thrice, and once the hedge-pig whined.

THIRD WITCH
  Harpier cries " 'Tis time, 'tis time!"

FIRST WITCH
  Round about the cauldron go;
  In the poisoned entrails throw.   5
  Toad, that under cold stone
  Days and nights has thirty-one
  Sweltered venom sleeping got,
  Boil thou first i' th' charmèd pot.
                    ⌜*The Witches circle the cauldron.*⌝

ALL
  Double, double toil and trouble;   10
  Fire burn, and cauldron bubble.

SECOND WITCH
  Fillet of a fenny snake
  In the cauldron boil and bake.
  Eye of newt and toe of frog,
  Wool of bat and tongue of dog,   15
  Adder's fork and blindworm's sting,

Lizard's leg and howlet's wing,
For a charm of powerful trouble,
Like a hell-broth boil and bubble.

ALL
Double, double toil and trouble;   20
Fire burn, and cauldron bubble.

THIRD WITCH
Scale of dragon, tooth of wolf,
Witch's mummy, maw and gulf
Of the ravined salt-sea shark,
Root of hemlock digged i' th' dark,   25
Liver of blaspheming Jew,
Gall of goat and slips of yew
Slivered in the moon's eclipse,
Nose of Turk and Tartar's lips,
Finger of birth-strangled babe   30
Ditch-delivered by a drab,
Make the gruel thick and slab.
Add thereto a tiger's chaudron
For th' ingredient of our cauldron.

ALL
Double, double toil and trouble;   35
Fire burn, and cauldron bubble.

SECOND WITCH
Cool it with a baboon's blood.
Then the charm is firm and good.

Enter Hecate ⌜*to*⌝ *the other three Witches.*

HECATE
O, well done! I commend your pains,
And everyone shall share i' th' gains.   40
And now about the cauldron sing
Like elves and fairies in a ring,
Enchanting all that you put in.
  Music and a song: "Black Spirits," etc. ⌜*Hecate exits.*⌝

SECOND WITCH
By the pricking of my thumbs,
Something wicked this way comes.   45
Open, locks,
Whoever knocks.

Enter Macbeth.

MACBETH
How now, you secret, black, and midnight hags?
What is 't you do?
ALL   A deed without a name.   50
MACBETH
I conjure you by that which you profess
(Howe'er you come to know it), answer me.
Though you untie the winds and let them fight
Against the churches, though the yeasty waves
Confound and swallow navigation up,   55
Though bladed corn be lodged and trees blown
     down,
Though castles topple on their warders' heads,
Though palaces and pyramids do slope
Their heads to their foundations, though the   60
     treasure
Of nature's ⌜germens⌝ tumble ⌜all together⌝
Even till destruction sicken, answer me
To what I ask you.
FIRST WITCH   Speak.   65
SECOND WITCH   Demand.
THIRD WITCH   We'll answer.
FIRST WITCH
Say if th' hadst rather hear it from our mouths
Or from our masters'.
MACBETH   Call 'em. Let me see 'em.   70
FIRST WITCH
Pour in sow's blood that hath eaten
Her nine farrow; grease that's sweaten

From the murderers' gibbet throw
Into the flame.

ALL   Come high or low;   75
Thyself and office deftly show.

Thunder. First Apparition, an Armed Head.

MACBETH
Tell me, thou unknown power—

FIRST WITCH   He knows thy
thought.
Hear his speech but say thou naught.   80

FIRST APPARITION
Macbeth! Macbeth! Macbeth! Beware Macduff!
Beware the Thane of Fife! Dismiss me. Enough.
                              He descends.

MACBETH
Whate'er thou art, for thy good caution, thanks.
Thou hast harped my fear aright. But one word
   more—   85

FIRST WITCH
He will not be commanded. Here's another
More potent than the first.

Thunder. Second Apparition, a Bloody Child.

SECOND APPARITION   Macbeth! Macbeth! Macbeth!—
MACBETH   Had I three ears, I'd hear thee.

SECOND APPARITION
Be bloody, bold, and resolute. Laugh to scorn   90
The power of man, for none of woman born
Shall harm Macbeth.   ⌈*He*⌉ *descends.*

MACBETH
Then live, Macduff; what need I fear of thee?
But yet I'll make assurance double sure
And take a bond of fate. Thou shalt not live,   95
That I may tell pale-hearted fear it lies,
And sleep in spite of thunder.

*Thunder. Third Apparition, a Child Crowned, with a tree
in his hand.*

　　　　　　　　　　　　What is this
That rises like the issue of a king
And wears upon his baby brow the round　　　　　　100
And top of sovereignty?
ALL　　Listen but speak not to 't.
THIRD APPARITION
Be lion-mettled, proud, and take no care
Who chafes, who frets, or where conspirers are.
Macbeth shall never vanquished be until　　　　　　105
Great Birnam Wood to high Dunsinane Hill
Shall come against him.　　　　　　⌜*He*⌝ *descends.*
MACBETH　　　　　　　That will never be.
Who can impress the forest, bid the tree
Unfix his earthbound root? Sweet bodements, good!　　110
Rebellious dead, rise never till the wood
Of Birnam rise, and our high-placed Macbeth
Shall live the lease of nature, pay his breath
To time and mortal custom. Yet my heart
Throbs to know one thing. Tell me, if your art　　　　115
Can tell so much: shall Banquo's issue ever
Reign in this kingdom?
ALL　　　　　　　　Seek to know no more.
MACBETH
I will be satisfied. Deny me this,
And an eternal curse fall on you! Let me know!　　　120
　　　　　　　⌜*Cauldron sinks.*⌝ *Hautboys.*
Why sinks that cauldron? And what noise is this?
FIRST WITCH　Show.
SECOND WITCH　Show.
THIRD WITCH　Show.
ALL
Show his eyes and grieve his heart.　　　　　　　125
Come like shadows; so depart.

A show of eight kings, ⌐the eighth king⌐ with a glass in
his hand, and Banquo last.

MACBETH
Thou art too like the spirit of Banquo. Down!
Thy crown does sear mine eyeballs. And thy hair,
Thou other gold-bound brow, is like the first.
A third is like the former.—Filthy hags,   130
Why do you show me this?—A fourth? Start, eyes!
What, will the line stretch out to th' crack of doom?
Another yet? A seventh? I'll see no more.
And yet the eighth appears who bears a glass
Which shows me many more, and some I see   135
That twofold balls and treble scepters carry.
Horrible sight! Now I see 'tis true,
For the blood-boltered Banquo smiles upon me
And points at them for his.
                  ⌐*The Apparitions disappear.*⌐
                  What, is this so?   140

FIRST WITCH
Ay, sir, all this is so. But why
Stands Macbeth thus amazedly?
Come, sisters, cheer we up his sprites
And show the best of our delights.
I'll charm the air to give a sound   145
While you perform your antic round,
That this great king may kindly say
Our duties did his welcome pay.
        Music. The Witches dance and vanish.

MACBETH
Where are they? Gone? Let this pernicious hour
Stand aye accursèd in the calendar!—   150
Come in, without there.

        Enter Lennox.

LENNOX   What's your Grace's will?

MACBETH
　Saw you the Weïrd Sisters?
LENNOX　　　　　　　　　No, my lord.
MACBETH
　Came they not by you?　　　　　　　　　　　　155
LENNOX　　　　　　　　No, indeed, my lord.
MACBETH
　Infected be the air whereon they ride,
　And damned all those that trust them! I did hear
　The galloping of horse. Who was 't came by?
LENNOX
　'Tis two or three, my lord, that bring you word　160
　Macduff is fled to England.
MACBETH　　　　　　　　Fled to England?
LENNOX　Ay, my good lord.
MACBETH, ⌜*aside*⌝
　Time, thou anticipat'st my dread exploits.
　The flighty purpose never is o'ertook　　　　　165
　Unless the deed go with it. From this moment
　The very firstlings of my heart shall be
　The firstlings of my hand. And even now,
　To crown my thoughts with acts, be it thought and
　　done:　　　　　　　　　　　　　　　　170
　The castle of Macduff I will surprise,
　Seize upon Fife, give to th' edge o' th' sword
　His wife, his babes, and all unfortunate souls
　That trace him in his line. No boasting like a fool;
　This deed I'll do before this purpose cool.　　175
　But no more sights!—Where are these gentlemen?
　Come bring me where they are.
　　　　　　　　　　　　　　　　They exit.

Scene 2
Enter Macduff's Wife, her Son, and Ross.

LADY MACDUFF
  What had he done to make him fly the land?
ROSS
  You must have patience, madam.
LADY MACDUFF   He had none.
  His flight was madness. When our actions do not,
  Our fears do make us traitors.   5
ROSS   You know not
  Whether it was his wisdom or his fear.
LADY MACDUFF
  Wisdom? To leave his wife, to leave his babes,
  His mansion and his titles in a place
  From whence himself does fly? He loves us not;   10
  He wants the natural touch; for the poor wren
  (The most diminutive of birds) will fight,
  Her young ones in her nest, against the owl.
  All is the fear, and nothing is the love,
  As little is the wisdom, where the flight   15
  So runs against all reason.
ROSS   My dearest coz,
  I pray you school yourself. But for your husband,
  He is noble, wise, judicious, and best knows
  The fits o' th' season. I dare not speak much   20
    further;
  But cruel are the times when we are traitors
  And do not know ourselves; when we hold rumor
  From what we fear, yet know not what we fear,
  But float upon a wild and violent sea   25
  Each way and move—I take my leave of you.
  Shall not be long but I'll be here again.
  Things at the worst will cease or else climb upward
  To what they were before.—My pretty cousin,
  Blessing upon you.   30

LADY MACDUFF
  Fathered he is, and yet he's fatherless.
ROSS
  I am so much a fool, should I stay longer
  It would be my disgrace and your discomfort.
  I take my leave at once.   *Ross exits.*
LADY MACDUFF   Sirrah, your father's dead.   35
  And what will you do now? How will you live?
SON
  As birds do, mother.
LADY MACDUFF   What, with worms and flies?
SON
  With what I get, I mean; and so do they.
LADY MACDUFF
  Poor bird, thou'dst never fear the net nor lime,   40
  The pitfall nor the gin.
SON
  Why should I, mother? Poor birds they are not set
    for.
  My father is not dead, for all your saying.
LADY MACDUFF
  Yes, he is dead. How wilt thou do for a father?   45
SON   Nay, how will you do for a husband?
LADY MACDUFF
  Why, I can buy me twenty at any market.
SON   Then you'll buy 'em to sell again.
LADY MACDUFF   Thou speak'st with all thy wit,
  And yet, i' faith, with wit enough for thee.   50
SON   Was my father a traitor, mother?
LADY MACDUFF   Ay, that he was.
SON   What is a traitor?
LADY MACDUFF   Why, one that swears and lies.
SON   And be all traitors that do so?   55
LADY MACDUFF   Every one that does so is a traitor
    and must be hanged.
SON   And must they all be hanged that swear and lie?

LADY MACDUFF Every one.

SON Who must hang them?   60

LADY MACDUFF Why, the honest men.

SON Then the liars and swearers are fools, for there
are liars and swearers enough to beat the honest
men and hang up them.

LADY MACDUFF Now God help thee, poor monkey! But   65
how wilt thou do for a father?

SON If he were dead, you'd weep for him. If you would
not, it were a good sign that I should quickly have a
new father.

LADY MACDUFF Poor prattler, how thou talk'st!   70

Enter a Messenger.

MESSENGER
Bless you, fair dame. I am not to you known,
Though in your state of honor I am perfect.
I doubt some danger does approach you nearly.
If you will take a homely man's advice,
Be not found here. Hence with your little ones!   75
To fright you thus methinks I am too savage;
To do worse to you were fell cruelty,
Which is too nigh your person. Heaven preserve
    you!
I dare abide no longer.   *Messenger exits.*   80

LADY MACDUFF   Whither should I fly?
I have done no harm. But I remember now
I am in this earthly world, where to do harm
Is often laudable, to do good sometime
Accounted dangerous folly. Why then, alas,   85
Do I put up that womanly defense
To say I have done no harm?

Enter Murderers.

                          What are these faces?

MURDERER Where is your husband?

LADY MACDUFF
    I hope in no place so unsanctified   90
    Where such as thou mayst find him.
MURDERER   He's a traitor.
SON
    Thou liest, thou shag-eared villain!
MURDERER   What, you egg?
    ⌜*Stabbing him.*⌝ Young fry of treachery!   95
SON   He has killed
        me, mother.
    Run away, I pray you.
    ⌜*Lady Macduff*⌝ *exits, crying "Murder!"* ⌜*followed by the*
                    Murderers bearing the Son's body.⌝

                    Scene 3
            Enter Malcolm and Macduff.

MALCOLM
    Let us seek out some desolate shade and there
    Weep our sad bosoms empty.
MACDUFF   Let us rather
    Hold fast the mortal sword and, like good men,
    Bestride our ⌜downfall'n⌝ birthdom. Each new morn   5
    New widows howl, new orphans cry, new sorrows
    Strike heaven on the face, that it resounds
    As if it felt with Scotland, and yelled out
    Like syllable of dolor.
MALCOLM   What I believe, I'll wail;   10
    What know, believe; and what I can redress,
    As I shall find the time to friend, I will.
    What you have spoke, it may be so, perchance.
    This tyrant, whose sole name blisters our tongues,
    Was once thought honest. You have loved him well.   15
    He hath not touched you yet. I am young, but
        something

You may ⌜deserve⌝ of him through me, and wisdom
To offer up a weak, poor, innocent lamb
T' appease an angry god.   20

MACDUFF
  I am not treacherous.

MALCOLM   But Macbeth is.
  A good and virtuous nature may recoil
  In an imperial charge. But I shall crave your
    pardon.   25
  That which you are, my thoughts cannot transpose.
  Angels are bright still, though the brightest fell.
  Though all things foul would wear the brows of
    grace,
  Yet grace must still look so.   30

MACDUFF   I have lost my hopes.

MALCOLM
  Perchance even there where I did find my doubts.
  Why in that rawness left you wife and child,
  Those precious motives, those strong knots of love,
  Without leave-taking? I pray you,   35
  Let not my jealousies be your dishonors,
  But mine own safeties. You may be rightly just,
  Whatever I shall think.

MACDUFF   Bleed, bleed, poor country!
  Great tyranny, lay thou thy basis sure,   40
  For goodness dare not check thee. Wear thou thy
    wrongs;
  The title is affeered.—Fare thee well, lord.
  I would not be the villain that thou think'st
  For the whole space that's in the tyrant's grasp, 45
  And the rich East to boot.

MALCOLM   Be not offended.
  I speak not as in absolute fear of you.
  I think our country sinks beneath the yoke.
  It weeps, it bleeds, and each new day a gash   50
  Is added to her wounds. I think withal

There would be hands uplifted in my right;
And here from gracious England have I offer
Of goodly thousands. But, for all this,
When I shall tread upon the tyrant's head   55
Or wear it on my sword, yet my poor country
Shall have more vices than it had before,
More suffer, and more sundry ways than ever,
By him that shall succeed.

MACDUFF   What should he be?   60

MALCOLM
It is myself I mean, in whom I know
All the particulars of vice so grafted
That, when they shall be opened, black Macbeth
Will seem as pure as snow, and the poor state
Esteem him as a lamb, being compared   65
With my confineless harms.

MACDUFF   Not in the legions
Of horrid hell can come a devil more damned
In evils to top Macbeth.

MALCOLM   I grant him bloody,   70
Luxurious, avaricious, false, deceitful,
Sudden, malicious, smacking of every sin
That has a name. But there's no bottom, none,
In my voluptuousness. Your wives, your daughters,
Your matrons, and your maids could not fill up   75
The cistern of my lust, and my desire
All continent impediments would o'erbear
That did oppose my will. Better Macbeth
Than such an one to reign.

MACDUFF   Boundless intemperance   80
In nature is a tyranny. It hath been
Th' untimely emptying of the happy throne
And fall of many kings. But fear not yet
To take upon you what is yours. You may
Convey your pleasures in a spacious plenty   85
And yet seem cold—the time you may so hoodwink.

We have willing dames enough. There cannot be
That vulture in you to devour so many
As will to greatness dedicate themselves,
Finding it so inclined.   90

MALCOLM   With this there grows
In my most ill-composed affection such
A stanchless avarice that, were I king,
I should cut off the nobles for their lands,
Desire his jewels, and this other's house;   95
And my more-having would be as a sauce
To make me hunger more, that I should forge
Quarrels unjust against the good and loyal,
Destroying them for wealth.

MACDUFF   This avarice   100
Sticks deeper, grows with more pernicious root
Than summer-seeming lust, and it hath been
The sword of our slain kings. Yet do not fear.
Scotland hath foisons to fill up your will
Of your mere own. All these are portable,   105
With other graces weighed.

MALCOLM
But I have none. The king-becoming graces,
As justice, verity, temp'rance, stableness,
Bounty, perseverance, mercy, lowliness,
Devotion, patience, courage, fortitude,   110
I have no relish of them but abound
In the division of each several crime,
Acting it many ways. Nay, had I power, I should
Pour the sweet milk of concord into hell,
Uproar the universal peace, confound   115
All unity on earth.

MACDUFF   O Scotland, Scotland!

MALCOLM
If such a one be fit to govern, speak.
I am as I have spoken.

MACDUFF   Fit to govern?   120

No, not to live.—O nation miserable,
With an untitled tyrant bloody-sceptered, .
When shalt thou see thy wholesome days again,
Since that the truest issue of thy throne
By his own interdiction stands ⌜accursed⌝   125
And does blaspheme his breed?—Thy royal father
Was a most sainted king. The queen that bore thee,
Oft'ner upon her knees than on her feet,
Died every day she lived. Fare thee well.
These evils thou repeat'st upon thyself   130
Hath banished me from Scotland.—O my breast,
Thy hope ends here!
MALCOLM   Macduff, this noble passion,
Child of integrity, hath from my soul
Wiped the black scruples, reconciled my thoughts   135
To thy good truth and honor. Devilish Macbeth
By many of these trains hath sought to win me
Into his power, and modest wisdom plucks me
From overcredulous haste. But God above
Deal between thee and me, for even now   140
I put myself to thy direction and
Unspeak mine own detraction, here abjure
The taints and blames I laid upon myself
For strangers to my nature. I am yet
Unknown to woman, never was forsworn,   145
Scarcely have coveted what was mine own,
At no time broke my faith, would not betray
The devil to his fellow, and delight
No less in truth than life. My first false speaking
Was this upon myself. What I am truly   150
Is thine and my poor country's to command—
Whither indeed, before ⌜thy⌝ here-approach,
Old Siward with ten thousand warlike men,
Already at a point, was setting forth.
Now we'll together, and the chance of goodness   15
Be like our warranted quarrel. Why are you silent?

MACDUFF

Such welcome and unwelcome things at once
'Tis hard to reconcile.

Enter a Doctor.

MALCOLM

Well, more anon.—Comes the King forth,
I pray you?   160

DOCTOR

Ay, sir. There are a crew of wretched souls
That stay his cure. Their malady convinces
The great assay of art, but at his touch
(Such sanctity hath heaven given his hand)
They presently amend.   165

MALCOLM   I thank you, doctor.

⌜*Doctor*⌝ *exits.*

MACDUFF

What's the disease he means?

MALCOLM   'Tis called the evil:
A most miraculous work in this good king,
Which often since my here-remain in England   170
I have seen him do. How he solicits heaven
Himself best knows, but strangely visited people
All swoll'n and ulcerous, pitiful to the eye,
The mere despair of surgery, he cures,
Hanging a golden stamp about their necks,   175
Put on with holy prayers; and, 'tis spoken,
To the succeeding royalty he leaves
The healing benediction. With this strange virtue,
He hath a heavenly gift of prophecy,
And sundry blessings hang about his throne   180
That speak him full of grace.

Enter Ross.

MACDUFF   See who comes here.

MALCOLM

My countryman, but yet I know him ⌜not.⌝

MACDUFF
  My ever-gentle cousin, welcome hither.
MALCOLM
  I know him now.—Good God betimes remove   185
  The means that makes us strangers!
ROSS   Sir, amen.
MACDUFF
  Stands Scotland where it did?
ROSS   Alas, poor country,
  Almost afraid to know itself. It cannot   190
  Be called our mother, but our grave, where nothing
  But who knows nothing is once seen to smile;
  Where sighs and groans and shrieks that rent the air
  Are made, not marked; where violent sorrow seems
  A modern ecstasy. The dead man's knell   195
  Is there scarce asked for who, and good men's lives
  Expire before the flowers in their caps,
  Dying or ere they sicken.
MACDUFF
  O relation too nice and yet too true!
MALCOLM What's the newest grief?   200
ROSS
  That of an hour's age doth hiss the speaker.
  Each minute teems a new one.
MACDUFF   How does my wife?
ROSS Why, well.
MACDUFF And all my children?   205
ROSS Well too.
MACDUFF
  The tyrant has not battered at their peace?
ROSS
  No, they were well at peace when I did leave 'em.
MACDUFF
  Be not a niggard of your speech. How goes 't?
ROSS
  When I came hither to transport the tidings   21

Which I have heavily borne, there ran a rumor
Of many worthy fellows that were out;
Which was to my belief witnessed the rather
For that I saw the tyrant's power afoot.
Now is the time of help. Your eye in Scotland   215
Would create soldiers, make our women fight
To doff their dire distresses.

MALCOLM   Be 't their comfort
We are coming thither. Gracious England hath
Lent us good Siward and ten thousand men;   220
An older and a better soldier none
That Christendom gives out.

ROSS   Would I could answer
This comfort with the like. But I have words
That would be howled out in the desert air,   225
Where hearing should not latch them.

MACDUFF   What concern
     they—
The general cause, or is it a fee-grief
Due to some single breast?   230

ROSS   No mind that's honest
But in it shares some woe, though the main part
Pertains to you alone.

MACDUFF   If it be mine,
Keep it not from me. Quickly let me have it.   235

ROSS
Let not your ears despise my tongue forever,
Which shall possess them with the heaviest sound
That ever yet they heard.

MACDUFF   Hum! I guess at it.

ROSS
Your castle is surprised, your wife and babes   240
Savagely slaughtered. To relate the manner
Were on the quarry of these murdered deer
To add the death of you.

MALCOLM   Merciful heaven!

What, man, ne'er pull your hat upon your brows.   245
Give sorrow words. The grief that does not speak
Whispers the o'erfraught heart and bids it break.

MACDUFF My children too?

ROSS
Wife, children, servants, all that could be found.

MACDUFF
And I must be from thence? My wife killed too?   250

ROSS I have said.

MALCOLM Be comforted.
Let's make us med'cines of our great revenge
To cure this deadly grief.

MACDUFF
He has no children. All my pretty ones?   255
Did you say "all"? O hell-kite! All?
What, all my pretty chickens and their dam
At one fell swoop?

MALCOLM Dispute it like a man.

MACDUFF I shall do so,   260
But I must also feel it as a man.
I cannot but remember such things were
That were most precious to me. Did heaven look on
And would not take their part? Sinful Macduff,
They were all struck for thee! Naught that I am,   265
Not for their own demerits, but for mine,
Fell slaughter on their souls. Heaven rest them now.

MALCOLM
Be this the whetstone of your sword. Let grief
Convert to anger. Blunt not the heart; enrage it.

MACDUFF
O, I could play the woman with mine eyes   270
And braggart with my tongue! But, gentle heavens,
Cut short all intermission! Front to front
Bring thou this fiend of Scotland and myself.
Within my sword's length set him. If he 'scape,
Heaven forgive him too.   27!

MALCOLM   This ⌜tune⌝ goes manly.
  Come, go we to the King. Our power is ready;
  Our lack is nothing but our leave. Macbeth
  Is ripe for shaking, and the powers above
  Put on their instruments. Receive what cheer you   280
    may.
  The night is long that never finds the day.

They exit.

ACT 5

Scene 1
Enter a Doctor of Physic and a Waiting-Gentlewoman.

DOCTOR I have two nights watched with you but can
perceive no truth in your report. When was it she
last walked?

GENTLEWOMAN Since his Majesty went into the field, I
have seen her rise from her bed, throw her night-   5
gown upon her, unlock her closet, take forth paper,
fold it, write upon 't, read it, afterwards seal it, and
again return to bed; yet all this while in a most fast
sleep.

DOCTOR A great perturbation in nature, to receive at   10
once the benefit of sleep and do the effects of
watching. In this slumb'ry agitation, besides her
walking and other actual performances, what at any
time have you heard her say?

GENTLEWOMAN That, sir, which I will not report after   15
her.

DOCTOR You may to me, and 'tis most meet you
should.

GENTLEWOMAN Neither to you nor anyone, having no
witness to confirm my speech.   20

Enter Lady ⌜Macbeth⌝ with a taper.

Lo you, here she comes. This is her very guise and,
upon my life, fast asleep. Observe her; stand close.

DOCTOR How came she by that light?

GENTLEWOMAN Why, it stood by her. She has light by her continually. 'Tis her command. 25

DOCTOR You see her eyes are open.

GENTLEWOMAN Ay, but their sense are shut.

DOCTOR What is it she does now? Look how she rubs her hands.

GENTLEWOMAN It is an accustomed action with her to 30 seem thus washing her hands. I have known her continue in this a quarter of an hour.

LADY MACBETH Yet here's a spot.

DOCTOR Hark, she speaks. I will set down what comes from her, to satisfy my remembrance the more 35 strongly.

LADY MACBETH Out, damned spot, out, I say! One. Two. Why then, 'tis time to do 't. Hell is murky. Fie, my lord, fie, a soldier and afeard? What need we fear who knows it, when none can call our power to 40 account? Yet who would have thought the old man to have had so much blood in him?

DOCTOR Do you mark that?

LADY MACBETH The Thane of Fife had a wife. Where is she now? What, will these hands ne'er be clean? No 45 more o' that, my lord, no more o' that. You mar all with this starting.

DOCTOR Go to, go to. You have known what you should not.

GENTLEWOMAN She has spoke what she should not, 50 I am sure of that. Heaven knows what she has known.

LADY MACBETH Here's the smell of the blood still. All the perfumes of Arabia will not sweeten this little hand. O, O, O! 55

DOCTOR What a sigh is there! The heart is sorely charged.

GENTLEWOMAN I would not have such a heart in my bosom for the dignity of the whole body.

DOCTOR Well, well, well.   60

GENTLEWOMAN Pray God it be, sir.

DOCTOR This disease is beyond my practice. Yet I have
     known those which have walked in their sleep,
     who have died holily in their beds.

LADY MACBETH Wash your hands. Put on your night-   65
     gown. Look not so pale. I tell you yet again, Ban-
     quo's buried; he cannot come out on 's grave.

DOCTOR Even so?

LADY MACBETH To bed, to bed. There's knocking at the
     gate. Come, come, come, come. Give me your   70
     hand. What's done cannot be undone. To bed, to
     bed, to bed.   *Lady ⌜Macbeth⌝ exits.*

DOCTOR Will she go now to bed?

GENTLEWOMAN Directly.

DOCTOR
     Foul whisp'rings are abroad. Unnatural deeds   75
     Do breed unnatural troubles. Infected minds
     To their deaf pillows will discharge their secrets.
     More needs she the divine than the physician.
     God, God forgive us all. Look after her.
     Remove from her the means of all annoyance   80
     And still keep eyes upon her. So, good night.
     My mind she has mated, and amazed my sight.
     I think but dare not speak.

GENTLEWOMAN   Good night, good doctor.
                                   They exit.

Scene 2
Drum and Colors. Enter Menteith, Caithness, Angus,
Lennox, ⌜and⌝ Soldiers.

MENTEITH
     The English power is near, led on by Malcolm,
     His uncle Siward, and the good Macduff.

Revenges burn in them, for their dear causes
Would to the bleeding and the grim alarm
Excite the mortified man.

ANGUS   Near Birnam Wood   5
Shall we well meet them. That way are they coming.

CAITHNESS
Who knows if Donalbain be with his brother?

LENNOX
For certain, sir, he is not. I have a file
Of all the gentry. There is Siward's son   10
And many unrough youths that even now
Protest their first of manhood.

MENTEITH   What does the tyrant?

CAITHNESS
Great Dunsinane he strongly fortifies.
Some say he's mad; others that lesser hate him   15
Do call it valiant fury. But for certain
He cannot buckle his distempered cause
Within the belt of rule.

ANGUS   Now does he feel
His secret murders sticking on his hands.   20
Now minutely revolts upbraid his faith-breach.
Those he commands move only in command,
Nothing in love. Now does he feel his title
Hang loose about him, like a giant's robe
Upon a dwarfish thief.   25

MENTEITH   Who, then, shall blame
His pestered senses to recoil and start
When all that is within him does condemn
Itself for being there?

CAITHNESS   Well, march we on   30
To give obedience where 'tis truly owed.
Meet we the med'cine of the sickly weal,
And with him pour we in our country's purge
Each drop of us.

LENNOX   Or so much as it needs   35

To dew the sovereign flower and drown the weeds.
Make we our march towards Birnam.

They exit marching.

Scene 3
Enter Macbeth, ⌜the⌝ Doctor, and Attendants.

MACBETH
Bring me no more reports. Let them fly all.
Till Birnam Wood remove to Dunsinane
I cannot taint with fear. What's the boy Malcolm?
Was he not born of woman? The spirits that know
All mortal consequences have pronounced me thus: 5
"Fear not, Macbeth. No man that's born of woman
Shall e'er have power upon thee." Then fly, false
   thanes,
And mingle with the English epicures.
The mind I sway by and the heart I bear   10
Shall never sag with doubt nor shake with fear.

Enter Servant.

The devil damn thee black, thou cream-faced loon!
Where got'st thou that goose-look?
SERVANT   There is ten thousand—
MACBETH   Geese, villain?   15
SERVANT   Soldiers, sir.
MACBETH
Go prick thy face and over-red thy fear,
Thou lily-livered boy. What soldiers, patch?
Death of thy soul! Those linen cheeks of thine
Are counselors to fear. What soldiers, whey-face?   20
SERVANT   The English force, so please you.
MACBETH
Take thy face hence.   ⌜*Servant exits.*⌝
         Seyton!—I am sick at heart
When I behold—Seyton, I say!—This push

Will cheer me ever or ⌜disseat⌝ me now.   25
I have lived long enough. My way of life
Is fall'n into the sere, the yellow leaf,
And that which should accompany old age,
As honor, love, obedience, troops of friends,
I must not look to have, but in their stead   30
Curses, not loud but deep, mouth-honor, breath
Which the poor heart would fain deny and dare
        not.—
Seyton!

Enter Seyton.

SEYTON
  What's your gracious pleasure?   35
MACBETH   What news more?
SEYTON
  All is confirmed, my lord, which was reported.
MACBETH
  I'll fight till from my bones my flesh be hacked.
  Give me my armor.
SEYTON   'Tis not needed yet.   40
MACBETH   I'll put it on.
  Send out more horses. Skirr the country round.
  Hang those that talk of fear. Give me mine
        armor.—
  How does your patient, doctor?   45
DOCTOR   Not so sick, my lord,
  As she is troubled with thick-coming fancies
  That keep her from her rest.
MACBETH   Cure ⌜her⌝ of that.
  Canst thou not minister to a mind diseased,   50
  Pluck from the memory a rooted sorrow,
  Raze out the written troubles of the brain,
  And with some sweet oblivious antidote
  Cleanse the stuffed bosom of that perilous stuff
  Which weighs upon the heart?   55

DOCTOR   Therein the patient
  Must minister to himself.

MACBETH
  Throw physic to the dogs. I'll none of it.—
  Come, put mine armor on. Give me my staff.
                ⌜*Attendants begin to arm him.*⌝
  Seyton, send out.—Doctor, the thanes fly from   60
    me.—
  Come, sir, dispatch.—If thou couldst, doctor, cast
  The water of my land, find her disease,
  And purge it to a sound and pristine health,
  I would applaud thee to the very echo   65
  That should applaud again.—Pull 't off, I say.—
  What rhubarb, senna, or what purgative drug
  Would scour these English hence? Hear'st thou of
    them?

DOCTOR
  Ay, my good lord. Your royal preparation   70
  Makes us hear something.

MACBETH   Bring it after me.—
  I will not be afraid of death and bane
  Till Birnam Forest come to Dunsinane.

DOCTOR, ⌜*aside*⌝
  Were I from Dunsinane away and clear,   75
  Profit again should hardly draw me here.
                         They exit.

Scene 4
Drum and Colors. Enter Malcolm, Siward, Macduff,
Siward's son, Menteith, Caithness, Angus, and Soldiers,
marching.

MALCOLM
  Cousins, I hope the days are near at hand
  That chambers will be safe.

MENTEITH   We doubt it nothing.
SIWARD
  What wood is this before us?
MENTEITH   The wood of Birnam.   5
MALCOLM
  Let every soldier hew him down a bough
  And bear 't before him. Thereby shall we shadow
  The numbers of our host and make discovery
  Err in report of us.
SOLDIER   It shall be done.   10
SIWARD
  We learn no other but the confident tyrant
  Keeps still in Dunsinane and will endure
  Our setting down before 't.
MALCOLM   'Tis his main hope;
  For, where there is advantage to be given,   15
  Both more and less have given him the revolt,
  And none serve with him but constrainèd things
  Whose hearts are absent too.
MACDUFF   Let our just censures
  Attend the true event, and put we on   20
  Industrious soldiership.
SIWARD   The time approaches
  That will with due decision make us know
  What we shall say we have and what we owe.
  Thoughts speculative their unsure hopes relate,   25
  But certain issue strokes must arbitrate;
  Towards which, advance the war.

They exit marching.

Scene 5
Enter Macbeth, Seyton, and Soldiers, with Drum and Colors.

MACBETH
Hang out our banners on the outward walls.
The cry is still "They come!" Our castle's strength
Will laugh a siege to scorn. Here let them lie
Till famine and the ague eat them up.
Were they not forced with those that should be   5
    ours,
We might have met them dareful, beard to beard,
And beat them backward home.
                              A cry within of women.
                         What is that noise?

SEYTON
It is the cry of women, my good lord.   ⌜*He exits.*⌝   10
MACBETH
I have almost forgot the taste of fears.
The time has been my senses would have cooled
To hear a night-shriek, and my fell of hair
Would at a dismal treatise rouse and stir
As life were in 't. I have supped full with horrors.   15
Direness, familiar to my slaughterous thoughts,
Cannot once start me.

                    ⌜*Enter Seyton.*⌝

                    Wherefore was that cry?
SEYTON   The Queen, my lord, is dead.
MACBETH   She should have died hereafter.   20
There would have been a time for such a word.
Tomorrow and tomorrow and tomorrow
Creeps in this petty pace from day to day
To the last syllable of recorded time,
And all our yesterdays have lighted fools
The way to dusty death. Out, out, brief candle!

Life's but a walking shadow, a poor player
That struts and frets his hour upon the stage
And then is heard no more. It is a tale
Told by an idiot, full of sound and fury,   30
Signifying nothing.

Enter a Messenger.

Thou com'st to use thy tongue: thy story quickly.
MESSENGER   Gracious my lord,
I should report that which I say I saw,
But know not how to do 't.   35
MACBETH   Well, say, sir.
MESSENGER
As I did stand my watch upon the hill,
I looked toward Birnam, and anon methought
The wood began to move.
MACBETH   Liar and slave!   40
MESSENGER
Let me endure your wrath, if 't be not so.
Within this three mile may you see it coming.
I say, a moving grove.
MACBETH   If thou speak'st false,
Upon the next tree shall thou hang alive   45
Till famine cling thee. If thy speech be sooth,
I care not if thou dost for me as much.—
I pull in resolution and begin
To doubt th' equivocation of the fiend,
That lies like truth. "Fear not till Birnam Wood   50
Do come to Dunsinane," and now a wood
Comes toward Dunsinane.—Arm, arm, and out!—
If this which he avouches does appear,
There is nor flying hence nor tarrying here.
I 'gin to be aweary of the sun   55
And wish th' estate o' th' world were now
    undone.—

Ring the alarum bell!—Blow wind, come wrack,
At least we'll die with harness on our back.

They exit.

Scene 6

*Drum and Colors. Enter Malcolm, Siward, Macduff, and
their army, with boughs.*

MALCOLM
Now near enough. Your leafy screens throw down
And show like those you are.—You, worthy uncle,
Shall with my cousin, your right noble son,
Lead our first battle. Worthy Macduff and we
Shall take upon 's what else remains to do,   5
According to our order.

SIWARD   Fare you well.
Do we but find the tyrant's power tonight,
Let us be beaten if we cannot fight.

MACDUFF
Make all our trumpets speak; give them all breath,   10
Those clamorous harbingers of blood and death.

*They exit.
Alarums continued.*

Scene 7

Enter Macbeth.

MACBETH
They have tied me to a stake. I cannot fly,
But, bear-like, I must fight the course. What's he
That was not born of woman? Such a one
Am I to fear, or none.

Enter young Siward.

YOUNG SIWARD   What is thy name?

MACBETH   Thou'lt be afraid to hear it.

YOUNG SIWARD
  No, though thou call'st thyself a hotter name
  Than any is in hell.

MACBETH   My name's Macbeth.

YOUNG SIWARD
  The devil himself could not pronounce a title   10
  More hateful to mine ear.

MACBETH   No, nor more fearful.

YOUNG SIWARD
  Thou liest, abhorrèd tyrant. With my sword
  I'll prove the lie thou speak'st.
                    ⌈*They*⌉ *fight, and young Siward* ⌈*is*⌉ *slain.*

MACBETH   Thou wast born of   15
    woman.
  But swords I smile at, weapons laugh to scorn,
  Brandished by man that's of a woman born.
                                        He exits.

          Alarums. Enter Macduff.

MACDUFF
  That way the noise is. Tyrant, show thy face!
  If thou beest slain, and with no stroke of mine,   20
  My wife and children's ghosts will haunt me still.
  I cannot strike at wretched kerns, whose arms
  Are hired to bear their staves. Either thou, Macbeth,
  Or else my sword with an unbattered edge
  I sheathe again undeeded. There thou shouldst be;   25
  By this great clatter, one of greatest note
  Seems bruited. Let me find him, Fortune,
  And more I beg not.   *He exits. Alarums.*

          Enter Malcolm and Siward.

SIWARD
  This way, my lord. The castle's gently rendered.
  The tyrant's people on both sides do fight,   30

The noble thanes do bravely in the war,
The day almost itself professes yours,
And little is to do.

MALCOLM   We have met with foes
That strike beside us.   35

SIWARD   Enter, sir, the castle.
                              They exit. Alarum.

⌜Scene 8⌝
Enter Macbeth.

MACBETH
Why should I play the Roman fool and die
On mine own sword? Whiles I see lives, the gashes
Do better upon them.

Enter Macduff.

MACDUFF   Turn, hellhound, turn!
MACBETH
Of all men else I have avoided thee.   5
But get thee back. My soul is too much charged
With blood of thine already.

MACDUFF   I have no words;
My voice is in my sword, thou bloodier villain
Than terms can give thee out.   *Fight. Alarum.*   10

MACBETH   Thou losest labor.
As easy mayst thou the intrenchant air
With thy keen sword impress as make me bleed.
Let fall thy blade on vulnerable crests;
I bear a charmèd life, which must not yield   1�
To one of woman born.

MACDUFF   Despair thy charm,
And let the angel whom thou still hast served
Tell thee Macduff was from his mother's womb
Untimely ripped.   2�

MACBETH
  Accursèd be that tongue that tells me so,
  For it hath cowed my better part of man!
  And be these juggling fiends no more believed
  That palter with us in a double sense,
  That keep the word of promise to our ear   25
  And break it to our hope. I'll not fight with thee.
MACDUFF   Then yield thee, coward,
  And live to be the show and gaze o' th' time.
  We'll have thee, as our rarer monsters are,
  Painted upon a pole, and underwrit   30
  "Here may you see the tyrant."
MACBETH   I will not yield
  To kiss the ground before young Malcolm's feet
  And to be baited with the rabble's curse.
  Though Birnam Wood be come to Dunsinane   35
  And thou opposed, being of no woman born,
  Yet I will try the last. Before my body
  I throw my warlike shield. Lay on, Macduff,
  And damned be him that first cries "Hold! Enough!"
                      They exit fighting. Alarums.

⌜*They*⌝ *enter fighting, and Macbeth* ⌜*is*⌝ *slain.* ⌜*Macduff*
exits carrying off Macbeth's body.⌝ *Retreat and flourish.*
Enter, with Drum and Colors, Malcolm, Siward, Ross,
            Thanes, and Soldiers.

MALCOLM
  I would the friends we miss were safe arrived.   40
SIWARD
  Some must go off; and yet by these I see
  So great a day as this is cheaply bought.
MALCOLM
  Macduff is missing, and your noble son.
ROSS
  Your son, my lord, has paid a soldier's debt.
  He only lived but till he was a man,   45

The which no sooner had his prowess confirmed
In the unshrinking station where he fought,
But like a man he died.

SIWARD   Then he is dead?

ROSS
Ay, and brought off the field. Your cause of sorrow   50
Must not be measured by his worth, for then
It hath no end.

SIWARD   Had he his hurts before?

ROSS
Ay, on the front.

SIWARD   Why then, God's soldier be he!   55
Had I as many sons as I have hairs,
I would not wish them to a fairer death;
And so his knell is knolled.

MALCOLM
He's worth more sorrow, and that I'll spend for
     him.   60

SIWARD   He's worth no more.
They say he parted well and paid his score,
And so, God be with him. Here comes newer
     comfort.

Enter Macduff with Macbeth's head.

MACDUFF
Hail, King! for so thou art. Behold where stands   65
Th' usurper's cursèd head. The time is free.
I see thee compassed with thy kingdom's pearl,
That speak my salutation in their minds,
Whose voices I desire aloud with mine.
Hail, King of Scotland!   70

ALL   Hail, King of Scotland!   *Flourish.*

MALCOLM
We shall not spend a large expense of time
Before we reckon with your several loves
And make us even with you. My thanes and
     kinsmen,

Henceforth be earls, the first that ever Scotland
In such an honor named. What's more to do,
Which would be planted newly with the time,
As calling home our exiled friends abroad
That fled the snares of watchful tyranny,   80
Producing forth the cruel ministers
Of this dead butcher and his fiend-like queen
(Who, as 'tis thought, by self and violent hands,
Took off her life)—this, and what needful else
That calls upon us, by the grace of grace,   85
We will perform in measure, time, and place.
So thanks to all at once and to each one,
Whom we invite to see us crowned at Scone.

Flourish. All exit.

Explanatory Notes

1.1   Three witches plan to meet Macbeth.

3. **hurly-burly:** commotion
5. **ere:** before
9. **Graymalkin:** the name of the first witch's "familiar" (an attendant spirit serving her in the form of a cat)
10. **Paddock:** a toad, the "familiar" of the second witch
11. **Anon:** immediately (perhaps, the response of the third witch to her "familiar")

1.2   Duncan, king of Scotland, hears an account of the success in battle of his noblemen Macbeth and Banquo. Duncan orders the execution of the rebel thane of Cawdor and sends messengers to announce to Macbeth that he has been given Cawdor's title.

0 SD. **Alarum:** a trumpet "call to arms"
4. **sergeant:** soldier, officer (also called *Captain* in the Folio stage directions and speech prefixes)
7. **broil:** battle
10. **spent:** exhausted
11. **choke their art:** prevent each other from using their skill (in swimming)   **art:** skill
12. **to that:** to make him that (i.e., a rebel)
13. **villainies:** shameful evils
14. **Western Isles:** the Hebrides (islands off the west coast of Scotland)
15. **kerns and gallowglasses:** lightly armed undisciplined foot soldiers and soldiers heavily armed and well trained (The terms were usually applied to Irish soldiers.)

16. **damnèd quarrel:** the accursed cause (for which he fought)

17. **Showed . . . whore:** appeared to have granted the rebellious Macdonwald her favors; **all:** everything that Macdonwald and Fortune can do

21. **valor's minion:** the chosen darling of Valor

22. **slave:** villain (i.e., Macdonwald)

24. **unseamed . . . chops:** ripped him open from his navel to his jaw

27. **his reflection:** its apparent backward turning

34. **the Norweyan lord:** i.e., the king of Norway; **surveying vantage:** seeing his chance

40. **say sooth:** speak truthfully

41. **cracks:** i.e., explosive charges

43. **Except:** unless

44. **memorize another Golgotha:** make the event (or place) memorable by turning it into a second Golgotha **Golgotha:** "the place of dead men's skulls" (Mark 15.22) where Jesus was crucified

48. **smack:** have the flavor, taste

50. **Thane:** a title used in Scotland as the equivalent of "baron"

52. **should:** is likely to

58. **people:** i.e., troops

59. **Norway himself:** i.e., the king of Norway

61. **dismal:** ominous

62. **Bellona:** Roman goddess of war (Her **bridegroom** would be the fiercest of warriors.); **lapped in proof:** dressed in proven armor

63. **him:** the king of Norway; **self-comparisons:** (attacks) that matched his own

65. **lavish:** unrestrained

69. **Norways':** Norwegians'; **craves composition:** asks for terms

71. **Saint Colme's Inch:** i.e., Inchcolm, a small island in the Firth of Forth **Colme's:** pronounced "kollums"

73–74. deceive / Our bosom interest: betray my dearest concerns **Our:** i.e., my (the royal "we")

74. present: immediate

1.3 The three witches greet Macbeth as "Thane of Glamis" (as he is), "Thane of Cawdor," and "king hereafter." They then promise Banquo that he will father kings, and they disappear. Almost as soon as they are gone, Ross and Angus arrive with news that the king has named Macbeth "Thane of Cawdor." Macbeth contemplates killing Duncan in order to become "king hereafter" as the witches have called him.

7. Aroint thee: begone; **rump-fed:** fed on rump meat; fat-rumped; **runnion:** perhaps "scabby woman" or "fat woman"

8. Tiger: the name of the sailor's ship

10. like: in the form of

15. the other: i.e., **the other** winds

16. And . . . blow: and (I have) **the ports** from which the winds **blow**

17. quarters: i.e., directions

18. card: compass card

21. penthouse lid: eyelid

22. forbid: under a curse

25. bark: ship; **lost:** destroyed

29. pilot: helmsman

30. Wracked: wrecked; also, tormented

33. Weïrd: fateful, fate-determining (In the Folio, the spelling is "weyward" or "weyard.") **Weïrd** is the Scottish form of *wyrd*, the Old English word for fate or destiny.

34. Posters: those who post, i.e., travel rapidly

38. wound up: coiled (i.e., like a spring ready for action)

39. have not seen: have never **seen** before

40. is 't called: is it said to be

46. **choppy:** chapped; or, deeply wrinkled

47. **should be:** must **be** (i.e., most of your features indicate that you are)

56. **fantastical:** figments of the imagination

58. **present grace:** i.e., the title of "Thane of Glamis," already possessed by Macbeth

59. **noble having:** i.e., possession of **noble** titles; **royal hope: hope** of **royal** status

60. **That he seems rapt withal:** so **that he seems** transported by it all

63–64. **neither . . . hate:** neither **beg** your **favors** nor **fear** your **hate**

69. **happy:** fortunate

70. **get:** beget, father

74. **Sinel:** Macbeth's father

79. **owe:** own

87. **insane root:** plant that causes insanity

93. **happily:** with satisfaction

96–97. **His wonders . . . his:** i.e., the wonder he feels, which makes him speechless, vies with his desire to offer praise (Since he is **silenced** [line 97], his wonder wins the battle.)

101–2. **As thick . . . post:** couriers arrived as rapidly as they could be counted **tale:** count

109. **earnest:** a small payment to seal a bargain; thus, a promise of a greater reward to come

111. **addition:** title

116. **Who:** he who

119. **combined:** in conspiracy

120. **line the rebel:** i.e., reinforce Macdonwald

126. **The greatest is behind:** the greater part of the prophecy is already accomplished

132. **home:** i.e., fully

137. **betray 's: betray** us

141. **happy:** fortunate

143. **soliciting:** seduction, temptation

144. **ill:** evil
148. **unfix my hair:** make **my hair** stand on end
149. **seated:** i.e., fixed in its place
150. **Against . . . nature:** unnaturally **use:** custom; **Present fears:** causes of fear that are **present**
151. **horrible imaginings:** imaginary horrors
152. **fantastical:** imaginary
154. **function:** ability to act; **surmise:** speculation
155. **but:** except
159. **stir:** stirring; taking action
161. **our strange garments:** i.e., new clothes; **cleave . . . mold:** do not fit the body's form
162. **But:** except
172. **The interim having weighed it:** i.e., having thought about it in **the interim**

1.4 Duncan demands and receives assurances that the former thane of Cawdor has been executed. When Macbeth, Banquo, Ross, and Angus join Duncan, he offers thanks to Macbeth and Banquo. He then announces his intention to have his son Malcolm succeed him as king and his plan to visit Macbeth at Inverness. Macbeth sets out ahead of him to prepare for the royal visit. Now that Malcolm has been named Duncan's successor, Macbeth is convinced that he can become king only by killing Duncan.

0 SD. **Flourish:** fanfare of trumpets
2. **in commission:** i.e., commissioned (to carry out the execution)
11. **owed:** owned
12. **careless:** uncared for, worthless
22–23. **That the proportion . . . mine:** that both my **thanks** and my **payment** might have exceeded what you deserve
24. **all:** i.e., **all** I possess

26. **pays itself:** i.e., is its own reward

27–28. **our duties . . . servants:** i.e., we, as dutiful subjects, owe to you the obligations that **children** owe parents **and servants** owe masters

30. **Safe toward:** protective of

40. **Wanton:** unrestrained

43. **We . . . estate:** i.e., I name as my heir

44. **hereafter:** henceforth, from now on

45. **Prince of Cumberland:** heir to the throne

46. **Not . . . only:** i.e., not be bestowed on him without accompanying honors to others

48. **Inverness:** Macbeth's castle

50. **rest:** leisure, repose

51. **harbinger:** one who signals the approach of another

59. **The eye . . . hand:** i.e., let my **eye** not see what my **hand** does

61. **full so valiant:** perhaps, quite as **valiant** as you have said him to be (If this is the correct reading, Duncan is here responding to a comment made to him by Banquo during Macbeth's "aside.")

62. **his commendations:** the praises given him

64. **before:** ahead

1.5   Lady Macbeth reads her husband's letter about his meeting the witches. She fears that Macbeth lacks the ruthlessness he needs to kill Duncan and fulfill the witches' second prophecy. When she learns that Duncan is coming to visit, she calls upon supernatural agents to fill her with cruelty. Macbeth arrives, and Lady Macbeth tells him that she will take charge of the preparations for Duncan's visit and for his murder.

12. **dues of rejoicing:** i.e., the due measure of joy

16. **fear:** worry about

18. **catch:** take; **wouldst:** wish to

20. **illness:** i.e., ruthlessness

20–21. **wouldst highly:** would greatly like (to have); also, would like to do ambitiously—or idealistically

22. **wouldst thou holily:** would like (to do) in a saintly way

23–28. **Thou'd'st ... undone:** Lady Macbeth's avoidance of such terms as "murder" and "assassination" leads to imprecise use of **that** and **it.**

28. **should be undone:** i.e., should not be done

29. **spirits:** vital power, energy

30. **chastise:** rebuke; also, inflict punishment on

31. **round:** i.e., the crown

32. **metaphysical:** supernatural

33. **withal:** i.e., with

37. **were 't so:** i.e., if the king were coming

38. **informed for preparation:** sent word so that we could be prepared

40. **had the speed of him:** outrode him

43. **Give him tending:** tend to (take care of) him

46. **fatal:** directed by fate; **fatal** to Duncan

48. **mortal:** deadly

49. **crown:** top of the head

51. **remorse:** compassion

52. **compunctious:** remorseful; **visitings:** promptings; **nature:** natural feelings

53. **fell:** cruel; deadly

53–54. **keep ... it:** prevent my purpose from having its effect

55. **for gall:** in exchange for bile, the humor associated with envy and hatred; **ministers:** agents

56. **sightless:** invisible

57. **wait on:** attend; also, perhaps, lie in wait for, or accompany; **mischief:** evil

58. **pall thee:** cover yourself as with a pall, a dark cloth that is put over a coffin; **dunnest:** darkest

63. **all-hail hereafter:** i.e., future kingship

65. **ignorant:** i.e., unaware of the future
66. **instant:** present moment
74. **beguile the time:** deceive those around us
80. **dispatch:** management (with a secondary sense of "putting to death")
82. **solely sovereign:** absolute; **sway:** power
85. **favor:** expression; **fear:** frighten

1.6 Duncan and his attendants arrive at Inverness. Lady Macbeth welcomes them.

0 SD. **Hautboys:** powerful double-reed woodwind instruments, also called "shawms," designed for outdoor ceremonials (Oboes are later descendants of hautboys, with a much softer tone, designed for use in orchestras.)
5. **martlet:** house martin; **approve:** demonstrate
6. **By his loved mansionry:** i.e., by the fact that he loves to build nests here
7. **wooingly:** invitingly; **jutty:** projection
8. **coign of vantage:** i.e., protruding corner **of vantage:** affording a good observation point
9. **pendant:** hanging, suspended; **procreant cradle: cradle** where he breeds
14–15. **The love . . . as love:** i.e., the affection of others who attend on us is sometimes inconvenient, but we are still grateful for it
15–17. **Herein . . . trouble:** i.e., in saying this, **I teach you how** to say "thank you" for the **trouble** I'm causing you, since it is the result of my love **God 'ild:** God yield (i.e., thank you)
20. **single:** trivial
20–21. **contend / Against:** rival, try to match
22. **those:** i.e., those honors
23. **late:** recent
24. **We rest your hermits:** we remain your beadsmen (Beadsmen repaid gifts with prayers for the donor.)

26. **We:** i.e., I (royal plural); **coursed:** pursued

27. **purveyor:** a servant who makes advance preparations for a noble master

33. **theirs:** i.e., their dependents; **what is theirs:** what they own; **in compt:** in trust (from the king)

35. **Still:** always

1.7 Macbeth contemplates the reasons why it is a terrible thing to kill Duncan. Lady Macbeth mocks his fears and offers a plan for Duncan's murder, which Macbeth accepts.

0 SD. **Sewer:** butler

1–2. **If . . . quickly:** This sentence plays with several meanings of **done** (finished with, accomplished, performed) and for the moment leaves **it** unspecified.

3. **trammel up:** catch as in a net

4. **his surcease:** Duncan's death; or its (the assassination's) completion; **that but:** if only

7. **jump the life to come:** risk the fate of my soul

17. **Hath . . . meek:** has exercised his power so humbly (or so compassionately)

18. **clear:** blameless

19. **plead . . . against:** as in a court of law

20. **taking-off:** i.e., murder

22. **Striding the blast:** riding the wind; **cherubin:** In other plays, Shakespeare uses the word **cherubin** to refer to cherubs (winged angels, depicted as infants or youths with wings and rosy, smiling faces); here, the reference seems to be to the powerful supernatural winged creature described in Ezekiel 10 and referred to in Psalm 18.10, where God comes to the rescue of the psalmist, David, riding on a cherub (". . . he rode upon a Cherub and did fly, and he came flying upon the wings of the wind").

23. **sightless couriers:** invisible coursers or steeds

25. **That:** so that; **tears shall drown the wind:** i.e., **tears** as thick as rain will still **the wind**

27. **which o'erleaps itself:** i.e., the rider, in vaulting into the saddle, jumps too far and **falls** on the other side

35. **bought:** acquired

37. **would be:** ought to **be,** wish to **be**

41. **green and pale:** sickly, as if hungover from drinking

43. **Such:** i.e., fickle, like his hope and resolution

48. **wait upon:** always follow, accompany

49. **the poor cat i' th' adage:** i.e., the **cat** who would eat fish but would not get its feet wet (proverbial) **adage:** proverb

52. **none:** i.e., not a man

55. **break:** broach, disclose

56. **durst:** dared

58. **Nor . . . nor:** neither . . . nor

59. **adhere:** agree, conjoin

60. **that their fitness:** their very convenience (for the assassination)

62. **unmake:** i.e., unman, unnerve

70. **But:** only; **screw . . . place:** i.e., **screw** up **your courage** (Perhaps the image is that of a crossbow string that is mechanically tightened into its notch.)

72. **Whereto the rather:** to which all the sooner

73. **Soundly invite him:** i.e., **invite him** to sleep **soundly; chamberlains:** servants of the bedchamber

74. **wassail:** carousing; **convince:** overpower (Latin *vincere,* to conquer)

75. **warder:** guardian

76. **receipt of reason:** container that encloses **reason**

77. **limbeck:** alembic (the upper part of a still into which fumes rise)

78. **drenchèd natures:** drowned faculties

80. **put upon:** impute to, blame on

81. **spongy:** i.e., having soaked up wine

82. **quell:** murder

84. **mettle:** spirit; metal

85. **received:** accepted as true
89. **other:** otherwise
92. **settled:** determined
92–93. **bend . . . agent:** exert all the power in my body
93. **to:** i.e., to perform
94. **mock:** deceive

2.1 Banquo, who has accompanied Duncan to Inverness, is uneasy because he too is tempted by the witches' prophecies, although only in his dreams. Macbeth pretends to have forgotten them. Left alone by Banquo, Macbeth imagines that he sees a gory dagger leading him to Duncan's room. Hearing the bell rung by Lady Macbeth to signal completion of her preparations for Duncan's death, Macbeth exits to kill the king.

6. **husbandry:** careful use of resources, frugality
7. **Take thee that:** perhaps giving Fleance his dagger
8. **heavy summons: summons** to sleep
17. **largess:** gifts, tips; **offices:** i.e., servants
19. **shut up:** concluded (his remarks); or summed up (what he had to say)
22–23. **Our will . . . wrought:** our desire (to entertain the king properly) was limited (by our lack of time to prepare); otherwise our desire would have operated freely, liberally **will:** desire **became the servant to defect:** was subjected to deficiency **wrought:** operated
29. **entreat an hour to serve:** i.e., find a time that suits us
34. **cleave to my consent:** i.e., support me, join my party **cleave:** adhere
37. **still:** always, continue to
38. **My bosom franchised:** my inmost being free
39. **I shall be counseled:** I will be willing to listen; or, I will follow your counsel
48. **fatal vision:** an apparition (1) that is ominous or

fateful, (2) that represents a deadly weapon, or (3) that shows what is fated, sent by Fate

48–49. sensible / To feeling: perceptible to the sense of touch

50. false: unreal

51. heat-oppressèd: feverishly excited

54. marshal'st: lead

56. made the fools o' th' other senses: made fools of by the evidence given by my sense of touch

57. Or else worth all the rest: or else my eyes alone report the truth

58. dudgeon: handle; **gouts:** clots

59. There's no such thing: i.e., the dagger does not exist

62. abuse: deceive

64. Hecate: goddess of witchcraft (**pale** because of the connection with the moon); **off'rings:** sacrifices, rituals

65. Alarumed: summoned to action (_all' arme_, to arms!)

66. watch: i.e., cry, like that of a watchman; **thus:** Macbeth here begins to move with the stealthy pace of a murderer, toward his design.

67. Tarquin: a Roman infamous for his rape of Lucrece (Shakespeare had told the story of the rape and Lucrece's suicide in his _The Rape of Lucrece_ [1594].); **ravishing:** ravenous; leading to rape

72. take . . . time: take away (with the sound of his footsteps) **the horror** of the moment's absolute silence

73. suits: agrees, fits in

74. Words . . . gives: i.e., talking simply cools off **the heat** that drives action

2.2 Lady Macbeth waits anxiously for Macbeth to return from killing Duncan. When Macbeth enters, he is horrified by what he has done. He has brought with him the daggers that he used on Duncan, instead of leaving them

in the room with Duncan's servants as Lady Macbeth had
planned. When he finds himself incapable of returning
the daggers, Lady Macbeth does so. She returns to find
Macbeth still paralyzed with horror and urges him to put
on his gown and wash the blood from his hands.

5. **bellman:** town crier, who sounded the hours of the
night and tolled the bell on the evening before an execution (Here, the **owl** is a bellman because, according to
superstition, the hoot of the owl portends death. He is
fatal perhaps because sent by Fate, or perhaps because he
predicts death.)

6. **He:** Macbeth

8. **mock their charge:** make a mockery of their
responsibility

9. **possets:** hot drinks, containing milk and liquor

15. **Confounds:** ruins

16. **He:** Macbeth; **he:** Duncan

28. **sorry:** deplorable, wretched

34. **addressed them:** applied themselves

38. **As:** as if; **hangman's:** executioner's (The hangman
also had to cut the body to pieces, hence his bloody
hands.)

39. **List'ning:** i.e., listening to

46. **so:** if so

49. **raveled sleave:** tangled threads

51. **second course:** i.e., main **course**

59. **unbend:** loosen, slacken (contrasts with "bend up"
at 1.7.92)

60. **brainsickly:** madly; or, morbidly

61. **witness:** evidence

72. **gild:** i.e., smear; **withal:** with it (i.e., with Duncan's
blood)

80. **multitudinous:** vast; **incarnadine:** turn bloodred

81. **one red:** i.e., a uniform **red** color

82. **shame:** would be ashamed

87. **constancy:** firmness of mind

88. **left you unattended:** abandoned you

90. **nightgown:** dressing gown; **occasion:** circumstances

91. **show us to be watchers:** reveal that we are still up and awake

92. **poorly:** poor-spiritedly, dispiritedly

2.3 A drunken porter goes to answer a knocking at the gate, all the while playing the role of a devil-porter at the gates of hell. He admits Macduff and Lennox, who have come to wake Duncan. Macbeth appears and greets them. Macduff exits to wake Duncan, then returns to announce Duncan's murder. Macbeth and Lennox go to see for themselves. When they return, Lennox announces that Duncan's servants are the murderers. Macbeth reveals that he has slain the servants. When his motives are questioned, Lady Macbeth interrupts by calling for help for herself. Duncan's sons, Malcolm and Donalbain, plan to flee for their lives, Malcolm to England, Donalbain to Ireland.

0 SD. **Porter:** gatekeeper

2. **old:** i.e., plenty of

4. **Beelzebub:** Matthew 12.24: "Beelzebub, the prince of the devils"

4–5. **farmer . . . plenty:** perhaps, the **farmer** hoarded crops only to face an unexpected surplus and dropping prices

6. **napkins:** handkerchiefs (to mop up his sweat)

8. **equivocator:** one who intentionally speaks ambiguously, either by using words that can be taken more than one way or by mentally hedging or limiting his or her words (Jesuits were charged with equivocation, and many scholars see this passage as referring to the 1606 trial and execution for treason of a Jesuit, Father Garnett, whose

defense included the claim that by the doctrine of equivocation, a lie is not a lie if the speaker intends a second,
true meaning by his words.)

14. **stealing . . . hose: stealing** cloth in the process of
making breeches (with perhaps an obscene suggestion)

15. **roast your goose:** heat your tailor's iron ("Goose"
was also a slang term for prostitute.)

19. **primrose way . . . bonfire:** the broad and pleasur-
able path to hell (See Matthew 7.13.)

20. **Anon:** right away

21. **I pray you, remember the porter:** This is a
request for a tip.

24–25. **the second cock:** i.e., 3 A.M.

29. **nose-painting:** reddening the nose through drink

37. **giving him the lie:** lying to him; laying him out

40. **i' th' very throat on me:** in my **very throat** (To
"give a lie in the throat" was to accuse someone of deliberate lying.)   **on:** of

42. **took up my legs:** lifted my feet off the ground (an
image from wrestling), perhaps in a drunken stagger

43. **made a shift:** managed; **cast him:** give him a fall
(as in wrestling); throw it out (vomit, urinate)

50. **timely:** early

51. **slipped the hour:** allowed **the hour** to slip by

55. **physics:** relieves (To *physic* was to treat an illness
with physic, or medicine.)

58. **limited service:** appointed duty

60. **appoint:** plan to do

62. **as:** i.e., so

66. **combustion:** tumult, confusion

67. **obscure bird: bird** of darkness, the owl   **obscure:**
accent first syllable

76. **Confusion:** destruction

78. **The Lord's anointed temple:** the body of the king,
which was represented by Renaissance monarchies as
having been **anointed** by God

83. **Gorgon:** a mythological figure the sight of which brought instant death

90. **great doom's image:** a sight as terrible as doomsday

91. **As . . . sprites:** as if, at the Last Judgment, you **rise from your graves** like ghosts

92. **countenance:** be in keeping with

94. **calls to parley:** The image is of the battlefield, where a *parley* is a conference.

98. **repetition:** report, account

107. **but:** only; **chance:** occurrence

109. **nothing serious in mortality:** nothing important in life

110. **toys:** trifles; **grace:** honor

111–12. **The wine . . . brag of:** i.e., the **vault** has had **the wine** drawn off and nothing is left but the dregs (**lees**)

113–14. **What is amiss? / You are:** i.e., "What is wrong?" "You are damaged (**amiss**) in that your father is killed."

115. **head:** fountainhead

120. **badged:** marked, as with badges

122. **distracted:** distraught

127. **amazed:** utterly confused, bewildered

128. **in a moment:** simultaneously

129. **expedition:** haste

132. **breach:** gap (technically, a break in a fortification caused by battering)

133. **wasteful:** destructive

134. **Steeped:** soaked

135. **Unmannerly breeched with gore:** i.e., improperly clothed with blood (instead of being properly sheathed); **refrain:** hold himself back

137. **make 's: make** his

138. **Help me hence, ho!:** Lady Macbeth perhaps faints—or pretends to faint—at this point.

142. **That . . . ours:** i.e., that have the best right to speak on this subject

144. **Hid in an auger hole:** concealed in a tiny crack (i.e., hiding in ambush)
146. **upon the foot of motion:** ready to move, to take action
148. **naked frailties hid:** i.e., clothed our frail bodies
150. **question:** examine
151. **scruples:** suspicions
153. **undivulged pretense:** unrevealed purpose (of the traitor)
157. **briefly:** quickly; **put on manly readiness:** clothe ourselves properly (with perhaps also a sense of emotional readiness)
160. **consort:** join in league
161. **office:** function
165–66. **The near . . . bloody:** a common expression, reminiscent of Matthew 10.36: "a man's foes shall be they of his own household"   **near:** nearer
170. **dainty of:** polite about
171. **shift away:** go away stealthily

2.4 An old man and Ross exchange accounts of recent unnatural happenings. Macduff joins them to report that Malcolm and Donalbain are now accused of having bribed the servants who supposedly killed Duncan. Macduff also announces that Macbeth has been chosen king. Ross leaves for Scone and Macbeth's coronation, but Macduff resolves to stay at his own castle at Fife.

1. **Threescore and ten:** seventy years
3. **sore:** dreadful
5. **trifled former knowings:** made my earlier experiences seem trivial
8. **his bloody stage:** i.e., the earth, on which man performs his **bloody** acts
10–12. **Is 't night's . . . kiss it?:** i.e., is it dark because night has become more powerful than day, or because day is hiding its face in shame?

15. **tow'ring in her pride of place:** circling at the top of her ascent

16. **by a mousing owl hawked at:** attacked on the wing by an **owl**, whose normal prey is mice

19. **minions of their race:** choicest examples of their breed

21. **as:** as if

23. **eat:** ate

34. **good:** i.e., benefit (for themselves); **pretend:** intend

35. **suborned:** secretly bribed

40. **Thriftless:** unprofitable; **ravin up:** devour hungrily

43. **Scone:** the ancient royal city where Scottish kings were crowned

44. **invested:** dressed in his coronation robes; crowned

46. **Colmekill:** the small island (now called Iona), off the coast of Scotland, where Scottish kings were buried

47. **storehouse:** i.e., crypt, where the bodies were placed

50. **Fife:** Macduff's castle

51. **thither:** i.e., to Scone

55. **benison:** blessing

3.1 Banquo suspects that Macbeth killed Duncan in order to become king. Macbeth invites Banquo to a feast that night. Banquo promises to return in time. Macbeth, fearing that Banquo's children, not his own, will be the future kings of Scotland, seizes upon the opportunity provided by Banquo's scheduled return after dark to arrange for his murder. To carry out the crime, Macbeth employs two men whom he has persuaded to regard Banquo as an enemy.

4. **stand:** remain

8. **by:** judging by; **on thee made good: made good** with regard to you

10 SD. **Sennet:** flourish of trumpets to announce the entrance of a person of high degree

13. **It had:** it would have; **as:** like

14. **all-thing:** wholly

15. **solemn:** ceremonial

18. **Command upon me:** i.e., royally invite me (as opposed to **request,** line 16); **the which:** i.e., your commands; **duties:** obligations

29–30. **I . . . twain:** i.e., I must ride an **hour** or two after dark

33. **cousins:** Malcolm and Donalbain

36. **invention:** fictions

37. **therewithal:** in addition to that; **cause of state:** state affairs

38. **Craving us jointly:** requiring the attention of both of us; **Hie:** hurry

45. **society:** (your) companionship

46. **The sweeter welcome:** the more sweetly welcome (to me)

46–47. **we will . . . alone:** I will stay . . . alone

47. **While then, God be with you:** until then, goodbye

48. **Sirrah:** term of address to a social inferior

48–49. **Attend . . . pleasure:** i.e., are **those men** waiting to see me?

50. **without:** outside

55. **would be:** ought to **be**

57. **to:** in addition to

61. **genius:** attendant spirit; **rebuked:** checked

62. **Caesar:** i.e., Octavius Caesar (Shakespeare will write about this again in *Antony and Cleopatra.*)

66. **fruitless:** without offspring

70. **issue:** descendants; **filed:** made foul, defiled

72. **rancors:** bitter ill-feelings

73. **eternal jewel:** i.e., soul

74. **common enemy:** i.e., the devil   **common:** general

75. **seeds:** sons

76. **come fate:** let **fate come**; **list:** lists, arena for trial by combat

77. **champion me:** oppose me; **to th' utterance:** to the death (*à l'outrance*, to the uttermost, to extremity)

77 SD. **Murderers:** Although the two men are called "murderers" in the Folio stage directions and speech prefixes, Macbeth's speeches to them suggest that the men are not yet murderers, but are rather very poor men who are desperate and who can thus be persuaded to kill for the king. The thrust of Macbeth's speeches to them is, first, that Banquo is the one responsible for their extreme poverty and, second, that Macbeth will reward them handsomely for the killing. The secondary meanings of such terms as **crossed** and **instruments** (lines 88, 89) suggest that the men have been **beggared** (line 101) by being dispossessed of their property by a greedy landowner (a process described in many writings of the time); they are now **reckless what [they] do** (lines 123–24), willing to undertake anything that will **mend** their lives (line 128).

87. **in probation:** in proving it

88. **borne in hand:** deceived, deluded (from the French *maintenir*); **crossed:** thwarted; also barred, debarred, shut out

89. **instruments:** means; also legal **instruments** such as were often used to strip men of their property

92. **To half a soul:** i.e., even to a half-wit; **a notion:** an understanding, a mind

98. **gospeled:** ruled by the Gospel's "love your enemies"

101. **yours:** your descendants

103. **catalogue:** list (of human types); **go for:** i.e., are counted as

106. **Shoughs:** rough-haired lapdogs; **water-rugs:** perhaps, water spaniels; **demi-wolves:** crossbreeds of dog and wolf   **demi:** half; **clept:** called

107. **valued file:** a list that evaluates each breed

109. **housekeeper:** watchdog

111. **closed:** enclosed

112. **Particular addition:** a special name or title

112–13. **from the bill . . . alike:** in distinction from the catalogue that simply lists them all as **dogs** (line 107)

119. **in his life:** because Banquo is alive

120. **were perfect:** would be completely contented

126. **tugged with:** pulled about by

127. **set:** stake, venture; **chance:** eventuality

128. **on 't:** of it

132. **in such bloody distance:** in such mortal hostility; or, within such a **distance** (a technical term in fencing) that I am made **bloody** (the image continues with the term **thrusts** [line 133])

134. **my near'st of life:** i.e., the part most essential to **life**—the heart; my most vital spot

136. **bid my will avouch it:** offer my desire for Banquo's death as sufficient justification for killing him

137. **For:** because of

138. **but wail:** i.e., but I must, instead, bewail

140. **to . . . make love:** court your help

146. **spirits:** courage, vital powers

149. **perfect spy o' th' time:** perhaps, exact information about when the deed should be done

150. **on 't:** of it

151. **something from:** somewhat away from; **always thought:** it being always understood

152. **I require a clearness:** I must be kept clear

153. **rubs nor botches:** flaws or defects

155. **material:** important

157. **Resolve yourselves apart:** make up your minds in private

160. **straight:** straightway, immediately

161. **concluded:** decided

3.2 Both Lady Macbeth and Macbeth express their unhappiness. Macbeth speaks of his fear of Banquo especially. He refers to a dreadful deed that will happen that night but does not confide his plan for Banquo's murder to Lady Macbeth.

6. **spent:** used up, exhausted

11. **sorriest:** most wretched

13. **without:** beyond

15. **scorched:** slashed (from *score*, to slash as with a knife)

16. **close:** come back together, heal; **our poor malice:** your and my weak hostility

17. **her former tooth:** i.e., the snake's **tooth** (her poisoned fang) as it was before she was **scorched**

18. **frame:** structure; **disjoint:** come apart

18–19. **both the worlds suffer:** (let) heaven and earth perish

25. **In restless ecstasy:** in a frenzy of sleeplessness

27. **his:** its; **nor . . . nor:** neither . . . nor

28. **Malice domestic:** civil ill will; **foreign levy:** armies from abroad

30. **gentle my lord:** **my** noble **lord**

31. **Sleek o'er:** smooth over; **rugged looks:** i.e., furrowed brows

35–36. **present . . . tongue:** give him special honor by look and speech

36. **unsafe the while that:** (you and I) are **unsafe** during this time in which

37. **lave our honors:** wash our reputations

38. **vizards:** masks, visors

40. **leave this:** stop talking and thinking this way

43. **nature's copy's not eterne:** i.e., they have not been granted eternal life **copy:** perhaps, copyhold tenure (a lease held by the lord of the manor); or, the individual copied from **nature's** mold

46. **cloistered:** secluded (in the dark buildings and belfries where **the bat** flies); **Hecate:** a powerful goddess and the patron of witches

47. **shard-borne:** borne on wings that are like shards (pieces of pottery)

48. **rung night's yawning peal:** i.e., finished announcing, with its **hums**, the coming of sleepy night (The image is of the pealing of the curfew bell.)

52. **seeling night:** i.e., **night** which blinds the eyes (The image is of the sewing together of the eyelids of the falcon to keep it temporarily in darkness.)

53. **Scarf up:** blindfold; **pitiful:** compassionate

57. **rooky:** perhaps, filled with rooks

3.3 A third man joins the two whom Macbeth has already sent to kill Banquo and Fleance. The three assassins manage to kill Banquo. Fleance escapes.

3. **He:** i.e., the third murderer; **delivers:** reports

4. **offices:** duties

5. **To the direction just:** exactly according to (our) instructions (from Macbeth)

8. **lated:** belated, tardy

9. **timely:** opportune, welcome

10. **The subject of our watch:** the person we are waiting for

14. **within the note of expectation:** i.e., included in the list of expected guests

16. **His horses go about:** perhaps, the **horses** are being led or ridden on a more circuitous route

3.4 As Macbeth's banquet begins, one of Banquo's murderers appears at the door to tell Macbeth of Banquo's death and Fleance's escape. Returning to the table, Macbeth is confronted by Banquo's ghost, invisible to all but Macbeth. While Lady Macbeth is able to dismiss as a momentary fit Macbeth's expressions of horror at the ghost's first appearance, the reappearance of the ghost and Macbeth's outcries in response to it force Lady Macbeth to send all the guests away. Alone with Lady Macbeth, Macbeth resolves to meet the witches again. He foresees a future marked by further violence.

1. **degrees:** relative status (and hence where you are entitled to sit)

1–2. **At first / And last:** to all in whatever degree

6. **keeps her state:** remains on her throne; **in best time:** at the most proper moment

7. **require:** request

10. **encounter thee:** respond to your welcome (perhaps with low bows as they take their places)

11. **Both sides are even:** (1) the thanks of the guests balance the welcome of Lady Macbeth, so the hostess and guests **are even**; or, (2) there are equal numbers on **both sides** of the table

12. **large:** liberal, unrestrained; **Anon:** soon; **measure:** i.e., a toast

21. **the nonpareil:** without equal

23. **I . . . perfect:** I would otherwise have been fully secure, complete

24. **founded:** rooted, stable

25. **broad:** free; **casing:** surrounding, enclosing

26. **cabined, cribbed:** closed in, cramped (as in a cabin or hovel)

27. **saucy:** insolent; **safe:** i.e., safely disposed of

28. **bides:** remains; waits

30. **The least a death to nature:** the smallest one of which would have been fatal

32. **worm:** serpent larva (i.e., a creature that will grow up to be a serpent)

35. **hear ourselves:** talk

37. **give the cheer:** i.e., entertain your guests properly;

sold: i.e., as opposed to **given** (line 39), as if the host were an innkeeper (The sense, lines 37–39, is that a **feast** is no better than a meal in an inn if the host does not keep assuring his guests of their welcome.)

39. **To feed ... home:** i.e., mere eating is best done **at home**

40. **From thence:** i.e., (when one is) away from home; **meat:** food; **ceremony:** the practice of courtesy

41. SD. **Enter the Ghost:** The ghost is not observed by Macbeth until line 54. The ghost may, in fact, enter at line 41, unobserved by Macbeth and the other characters onstage. Or it is possible that the entrance is marked at line 41 because the Folio reproduces a stage manager's note to remind the actor playing Banquo to get ready to enter, at around line 47, when "summoned" by Macbeth.

43. **wait on:** serve, and therefore follow upon

46. **our country's honor roofed:** i.e., all the nobility of the country under one roof

48–49. **Who ... mischance:** whom I hope I should blame for unkindly staying away on purpose rather than pity for some accident that has happened to him

51. **Lays ... promise:** i.e., calls into question **his promise** (to be here)

57. **moves:** disturbs

66. **upon a thought:** in a moment

67. **note:** pay attention to

68. **passion:** disturbed state

75. **air-drawn:** made of air

76. **flaws and starts:** outbursts

77. **to:** in comparison to; **well become:** be very appropriate for

79. **Authorized by:** vouched for, with a sense also of "authored by" (accent on second syllable); **Shame itself!:** i.e., for **shame!**

85. **charnel houses:** vaults or small buildings for the bones of the dead

86–87. **our monuments . . . kites:** i.e., our only burial vaults (**monuments**) will be the stomachs (**maws**) of birds of prey (**kites**)

92. **humane:** human; also, **humane** or kindly; **purged the gentle weal:** cleansed the commonwealth of violence and made it gentle

101. **lack you:** miss your company

107 SD. **Enter Ghost:** The ghost is not observed by Macbeth until line 113. See note on 3.4.41 SD.

113. **Avaunt:** begone; **quit:** leave

115. **speculation:** ability to see

119. **a thing of custom:** something customary

123. **Hyrcan:** from Hyrcania, a part of the Roman Empire located at the southern end of the Caspian Sea (In the *Aeneid,* Hyrcania is associated with tigers.)

124. **nerves:** sinews

126. **desert:** (any) uninhabited place

127. **If trembling I inhabit then:** perhaps, if I then tremble; **protest me:** proclaim me

128. **The baby of a girl:** i.e., **a baby girl**

129. **mock'ry:** illusion (with perhaps the sense, also, of "that which mocks me")

130. **being gone:** i.e., it **being gone**

134. **admired:** amazing

137–38. **strange . . . owe:** i.e., feel like a stranger to my own nature   **owe:** own

146. **Stand not . . . going:** i.e., don't delay your exit by insisting on leaving in ceremonial rank order

154. **Augurs:** i.e., auguries, predictions

155. **By maggot pies and choughs:** i.e., by means of magpies and jackdaws

155–56. **brought forth:** revealed

157. **man of blood:** murderer; **What is the night?:** **what** time of **night** is it?

164. **fee'd:** paid (to spy)

165. **betimes:** early

169. **no more:** no further

171. **will to hand:** demand to be carried out

172. **scanned:** thought about carefully

173. **season:** seasoning (i.e., that which preserves and gives flavor or zest)

174. **strange and self-abuse:** remarkable self-delusion

175. **initiate fear:** i.e., **fear** felt by a beginner, an initiate; **wants:** lacks, needs; **hard use:** practice that hardens one; or, vigorous usage

3.5 The presentation of the witches in this scene differs from their presentation in the rest of the play (except for 4.1.39–43 and 141–48). Most editors and scholars believe that neither this scene nor the passages in 4.1 were written by Shakespeare.

2. **beldams:** hags

7. **close:** secret

15. **Acheron:** a river in the underworld, in Greek mythology

24. **profound:** of deep significance

27. **artificial:** deceitful; skilled in artifice

29. **confusion:** destruction

32. **security:** too much self-confidence

35 SD. **Come away:** This song is from Thomas Middleton's play *The Witch* (Act 3, scene 3). The first two lines read "Come away! Come away! / Hecate, Hecate, come away!" Many scholars think that *Macbeth* 3.5, as well as parts of 4.1, were written by Middleton, perhaps for a revival of the play later in James's reign.

3.6 Lennox and an unnamed lord discuss politics in Scotland. Lennox comments sarcastically upon Macbeth's "official" versions of the many recent violent deaths. The nameless lord responds with news of Macduff's flight to England to seek help in overthrowing Macbeth.

1. **but hit your thoughts:** merely agreed with what you were already thinking

2. **interpret farther:** i.e., go on to draw further conclusions

3. **borne:** managed, conducted

5. **of:** by; **marry:** an interjection, here meaning, loosely, "to be sure" or "indeed"

9. **want the thought:** help thinking

11. **fact:** deed, crime

12. **straight:** immediately

13. **delinquents:** offenders

14. **slaves of drink:** i.e., in a drunken stupor; **thralls:** slaves

20. **an 't:** if it

23. **For from broad words:** as a result of plain speaking

28. **son of Duncan:** i.e., Malcolm

29. **holds:** withholds; **due of birth:** birthright

31. **Of:** by; **Edward:** Edward the Confessor, king of England from 1042 to 1066

32–33. **nothing / Takes:** does not detract

33. **his high respect:** the **high respect** granted Malcolm

34. **upon his aid:** on Malcolm's behalf

37. **ratify:** sanction

40. **free honors:** honors freely given

45. **an absolute . . . I:** i.e., Macduff had answered Macbeth's order to appear with a peremptory "**Sir, not I!**"

46. **cloudy:** unhappy, gloomy; **turns me:** i.e., **turns**

48. **clogs:** burdens

50. **him:** i.e., Macduff

52. **unfold:** reveal

54–55. **our . . . accursed:** i.e., **our country**, **suffering** under an **accursed hand**

4.1 Macbeth approaches the witches to learn how to make his kingship secure. In response they summon for him three apparitions: an armed head, a bloody child, and finally a child crowned, with a tree in his hand. These apparitions instruct Macbeth to beware Macduff but reassure him that no man born of woman can harm him and that he will not be overthrown until Birnam Wood moves to Dunsinane. Macbeth is greatly reassured, but his confidence in the future is shaken when the witches show him a line of kings all in the image of Banquo. After the witches disappear, Macbeth discovers that Macduff has fled to England and decides to kill Macduff's family immediately.

1. **brinded:** brindled, striped
2. **hedge-pig:** hedgehog
3. **Harpier:** perhaps the Third Witch's familiar
6–9. **Toad ... pot:** i.e., **first boil** the **toad** that has sweated **venom** for **thirty-one days** under a **cold stone Sweltered:** exuded
12. **Fillet:** slice; **fenny:** i.e., living in a fen or swamp
17. **howlet:** owlet, small owl
23. **mummy:** mummified human flesh; **maw and gulf:** voracious belly
24. **ravined:** perhaps, ravenous; or, glutted
30. **birth-strangled:** i.e., killed as soon as born
31. **drab:** whore
32. **thick and slab:** viscous
33. **chaudron:** entrails
37. **baboon's:** accented on first syllable
39–43. **O ... in:** These lines (and the stage direction preceding them) are thought by most scholars to be by another author. Since the song that the Witches sing, "Black Spirits," is from Middleton's play _The Witch_, the lines may have been written by Middleton.
54. **yeasty:** foamy, frothy
55. **Confound:** destroy; **navigation:** i.e., ships
56. **bladed corn:** wheat not yet fully ripe; **lodged:** beaten down by wind

58. **warders':** watchmen's

59. **slope:** perhaps, bend; or, perhaps, let fall

62. **nature's germens:** the seeds from which everything springs

63. **sicken:** becomes nauseated (at its own destructiveness)

72. **sweaten:** sweated

76 SD. **Armed Head:** a helmeted head

84. **harped:** sounded, guessed (as in touching the right string on a harp)

95. **take a bond of fate:** bind **fate** by a contract, get a guarantee from **fate** (i.e., make doubly sure that Macbeth will not be harmed)

99. **like the issue of a king:** in the shape of an heir to a throne

100–101. **round / And top:** crown

104. **chafes:** becomes irritated

109. **impress:** conscript, draft, compel into service

110. **his:** its; **bodements:** prophecies

111. **Rebellious dead:** perhaps in reference to Banquo, who rebelled against death by appearing to Macbeth

113. **live the lease of nature:** i.e., **live** out his natural life

114. **mortal custom:** a normal (customary) death

126 SD. **eight kings: eight kings** of Scotland, including James VI (a supposed descendant of Banquo), who in 1603 also became James I of England; **glass:** mirror

129. **other:** i.e., second

131. **Start:** i.e., burst from your sockets

132. **th' crack of doom:** perhaps, the thunder crash of Judgment Day; or, the blast of the archangel's trumpet announcing Judgment Day.

136. **twofold:** double (signifying England and Scotland); **treble:** The reference here is probably to King James's title of "King of Great Britain, France, and Ireland," assumed by him in 1604.

138. **blood-boltered:** i.e., having his hair matted with blood

141–48. **Ay . . . pay:** lines regarded by most scholars as written by another author

142. **amazedly:** as in a trance

143. **sprites:** spirits

146. **antic round:** fantastic dance

150. **aye:** forever

151. **without there:** i.e., you who are outside

159. **horse:** horses or horsemen

164. **anticipat'st:** prevents, forestalls; **dread:** dreadful

165–66. **The flighty purpose . . . with it:** i.e., purposes are so fleeting that they escape unless accompanied by acts that fulfill them

167. **firstlings:** firstborn

171. **surprise:** seize suddenly

174. **trace him in his line:** i.e., are his descendants

176. **sights:** hallucinations

4.2   Ross visits Lady Macduff and tries to justify to her Macduff's flight to England, a flight that leaves his family defenseless. After Ross leaves, a messenger arrives to warn Lady Macduff to flee. Before she can do so, Macbeth's men attack her and her son.

5. **Our fears do make us traitors:** perhaps, (Macduff's) fear, leading to his flight, makes him a traitor (to his family? to his country?)

11. **He wants the natural touch:** i.e., he lacks the **natural** instinct (to protect his children)

13. **Her young ones in her nest:** i.e., when her young are **in** the **nest**

17. **coz:** cousin, kinswoman

18. **school:** control; **for:** as for

20. **The fits o' th' season:** the violent disturbances in (Scotland's political) climate

22–23. we are traitors . . . ourselves: i.e., we are considered traitors while being unaware of our treason

23–24. hold rumor / From what we fear: perhaps, believe what our fears dictate; or judge rumors according to what we fear may happen

27. Shall not be long but: i.e., the time will **not be long** before

32–33. should . . . discomfort: i.e., if **I should stay longer**, (my tears) would disgrace me and make you uncomfortable

37. As birds do: See Matthew 6.26: "Behold the fowls of the air; for they sow not, neither do they reap . . . ; yet your heavenly Father feedeth them."

40–41. the net nor lime, / The pitfall nor the gin: traps for catching birds   **lime:** birdlime   **gin:** snare (literally, "engine")

42–43. Poor birds . . . set for: i.e., people don't **set** traps for *poor* **birds** (**birds** of little worth)

49. wit: intelligence

50. for thee: for a child

54. swears and lies: Lady Macduff defines a traitor as one who **swears** an oath of loyalty to a sovereign and then breaks it; the oath, then, is a lie. Her son seems to take "swearing and lying" as general use of profanity and failing to tell the truth.

72. in your state of honor I am perfect: i.e., I know you well as a noble lady

73. doubt: fear; **nearly:** very soon; very near

74. homely: plain

77. do worse: i.e., physically abuse you; **fell:** terrible

78. Which is too nigh: i.e., such savage cruelty is all too near

4.3   Macduff finds Malcolm at the English court and urges him to attack Macbeth at once. Malcolm suspects that Macduff is Macbeth's agent sent to lure Malcolm to his destruction in Scotland. After Malcolm tests Macduff and finds him sincere, Malcolm reveals that Edward, king of England, has provided a commander (Siward) and ten thousand troops for the invasion of Scotland. Ross then arrives with the news of the slaughter of Macduff's entire household. At first grief-stricken, Macduff follows Malcolm's advice and converts his grief into a desire to avenge himself on Macbeth.

4. **mortal:** deadly; **good men:** i.e., strong fighting **men**

5. **Bestride . . . birthdom:** i.e., fight to protect our prostrated country (The image is that of a soldier straddling a felled comrade and fighting off the comrade's attackers.)

7. **that:** i.e., so that

9. **Like syllable:** the same (or a comparable) sound

12. **the time to friend:** an opportune (friendly) time

14. **sole:** mere

15. **honest:** honorable

18. **and wisdom:** i.e., and consider it **wisdom**

23–24. **recoil / In an imperial charge:** The general sense is "give way under pressure from a king." The image is that of a gun, loaded, or charged, with powder and shot, recoiling upon itself.

26. **That . . . transpose:** i.e., **my thoughts** (no matter how negative) cannot change you into something different from what **you are**

27. **the brightest:** i.e., Lucifer, brightest of the angels, cast from heaven for rebelling against God

28–30. **Though . . . so:** i.e., even **though foul things wear**, when they can, the look of those in a state **of grace**, those really in a state of grace nevertheless continue to look gracious

32. **even there:** in the very place

33. **rawness:** vulnerability, unprotectedness

34. **motives:** incitements (to his protective instinct); arguments (for his protection)

36–37. **Let . . . safeties:** i.e., don't assume that my suspicions cast doubts on your honor, but see them as measures taken for my own safety   **jealousies:** suspicions

37. **rightly just:** perfectly honorable

40. **basis:** foundations; **sure:** securely, safely

41. **check:** restrain, reprove, curb

41–42. **Wear thou thy wrongs:** i.e., carry (as an heraldic device on your shield) that which you have won through your crimes

43. **The title is affeered:** i.e., Macbeth's **title** to the crown is confirmed (**affeered**)

48. **absolute fear:** complete mistrust

51. **withal:** as well, at the same time

53. **gracious England:** the **gracious** king of England

58. **More suffer:** shall **suffer more**

59. **succeed:** i.e., **succeed** to the throne

62. **particulars:** various kinds; **grafted:** implanted, engrafted

63. **opened:** exposed; or, unfolded like a flower

66. **confineless:** unbounded

71. **Luxurious:** lecherous

72. **Sudden:** violent, without warning

77. **continent:** chaste; also, restraining

78. **will:** lust, carnal appetite

83. **yet:** nevertheless

85. **Convey . . . plenty:** secretly conduct **your pleasures** on a large scale   **spacious:** ample

86. **cold:** chaste; or, indifferent

92. **affection:** disposition

93. **stanchless:** insatiable

95. **his jewels:** the **jewels** of one subject

102. **summer-seeming:** i.e., summer-beseeming, suitable for the summer of one's youth; or, summerlike and therefore of short duration

103. **The sword . . . kings:** i.e., the cause of the death **of our slain kings**

104. **foisons:** plentiful supplies

105. **Of your mere own:** from your royal property alone; **portable:** bearable, supportable

106. **With . . . weighed:** balanced against other qualities that are virtuous

108. **As:** such as

109. **lowliness:** humility

111. **relish of:** taste for; trace of

112. **division:** variation, modulation (as if each crime were a piece of music to be played); **several:** distinct

115. **confound:** destroy

122. **untitled:** i.e., unentitled, usurping

124. **truest issue of thy throne:** heir with the most right to the **throne**

125. **interdiction:** i.e., censure

126. **blaspheme his breed:** defame his family line (through his scandalous behavior)

129. **Died . . . lived: died** to the world (mortified her flesh through penances and religious exercises) **every day** of her life

133. **passion:** display of feelings

137. **trains:** wiles, stratagems (such as Macduff's visit seemed to be); **win:** capture, seize

138. **modest wisdom:** wise moderation, prudent caution; **plucks me:** pulls me back

142. **mine own detraction:** my **detraction** of myself

144. **For:** as

145. **Unknown to woman:** i.e., am a virgin (rather than the lascivious beast that I presented myself as being); **never was forsworn:** have **never** deliberately broken my oath

150. **upon:** about

153. **warlike:** equipped for battle

154. **at a point:** in readiness

155–56. **we'll . . . quarrel:** i.e., we will travel together (to join Siward), and may our chance of success be as good as our cause is just **goodness:** success **warranted:** justified **quarrel:** ground for action

159. **forth:** i.e., out of his private rooms

162. **stay:** await

162–63. **convinces . . . art:** conquers (defeats) the efforts of (medical) science

165. **presently:** immediately

168. **the evil:** i.e., scrofula, or "the king's evil," so-called because the king was thought to have the power to heal it with his touch

172. **strangely visited:** i.e., afflicted by this strange disease

174. **mere:** total, utter

175. **stamp:** a coin stamped with a particular impression

177–78. **To the succeeding royalty . . . benediction:** i.e., to the royal line that will succeed him he bequeaths the power of giving this curative blessing

178. **virtue:** power

185. **betimes:** soon

192. **But who:** except someone who; **once:** ever

193. **rent:** rend, tear

194. **made, not marked:** i.e., so common as not to be noted

195. **modern:** ordinary, commonplace; **ecstasy:** frenzy

198. **or ere they:** before they ever

199. **relation:** report; **nice:** precisely spelled out

200. **grief:** wrong, injury

201. **doth hiss the speaker:** i.e., earns the teller of the injury only hisses because it is already an old story

202. **teems:** brings forth

204. **well:** When spoken of the dead, "well" meant "at peace." The proverb ran: "He is **well** since he is in Heaven." See *Antony and Cleopatra* 2.5: "we use / To say the

dead are **well**"; *Romeo and Juliet* 5.1: "she is **well**. . . . / Her body sleeps in Capels' monument."

209. **niggard:** miser

212. **out:** i.e., in arms, in rebellion

213–14. **witnessed the rather / For that:** confirmed the more readily because

214. **power:** forces; **afoot:** mobilized

215. **of:** for; **Your eye:** i.e., Malcolm's person

217. **doff:** put off, get rid of

221–22. **An older . . . gives out:** i.e., there is no one in the Christian world reputed to be a more experienced or **better soldier none:** there is **none   gives out:** proclaims

225. **would:** ought to

226. **latch:** catch the sound of

229–30. **a fee-grief / Due to some single breast:** a grief belonging to one particular person   **fee-grief:** a term modeled on the term *fee-simple*, an estate belonging to one man and his heirs forever   **Due to:** belonging to

240. **surprised:** captured without warning

242. **quarry:** heap

245. **pull . . . brows:** a conventional gesture of deep sorrow

246–47. **The grief . . . break:** Proverb: "**Grief** pent up will **break the heart**." **Whispers: whispers** to   **o'er-fraught:** overburdened

250. **from thence:** away from there

255. **He has no children:** Usually taken to mean that Macbeth's lack of children explains his unspeakable cruelty, the words could mean that *Malcolm*'s lack of children explains his rather callous attempts to cheer up Macduff.

256. **hell-kite:** evil bird of prey

259. **Dispute:** fight against

265. **Naught that I am:** i.e., wicked man **that I am**

270. **play . . . eyes:** i.e., weep

272. **intermission:** delay; **Front to front:** i.e., face to face

278. **Our . . . leave:** we lack nothing now except to take leave (of the king)

280. **Put on:** perhaps, take upon themselves; **instruments:** perhaps, **instruments** of war

5.1 A gentlewoman who waits on Lady Macbeth has seen her walking in her sleep and has asked a doctor's advice. Together they observe Lady Macbeth make the gestures of repeatedly washing her hands as she relives the horrors that she and Macbeth have carried out and experienced. The doctor concludes that she needs spiritual aid rather than a physician.

0 SD. **Physic:** medicine

1. **watched:** stayed awake

3. **walked:** i.e., **walked** in her sleep

5–6. **nightgown:** dressing gown

6. **closet:** cabinet

11–12. **do the effects of watching:** perform the actions of (someone) awake

17. **meet:** proper

21. **very guise:** usual behavior

22. **close:** hidden

30. **accustomed:** customary, usual

37. **One. Two.:** She is presumably remembering the clock striking 2 A.M. just before the murder.

43. **mark:** hear, notice

46. **mar all:** upset everything

47. **this starting:** these starts (i.e., sudden fits)

48. **Go to:** for shame

56–57. **sorely charged:** gravely burdened

59. **dignity:** worth

67. **on 's:** of his

78. **divine:** minister or priest

80. **annoyance:** i.e., injuring herself

82. **mated:** stupefied

5.2 A Scottish force, in rebellion against Macbeth, marches toward Birnam Wood to join Malcolm and his English army.

0 SD. **Drum and Colors:** i.e., a drummer and men carrying banners

3. **dear:** deeply felt; also, grievous, dire

4–5. **Would . . . man:** i.e., would quicken dead men to bloody and desperate attack   **alarm:** call to fight **Excite:** quicken   **mortified:** dead

9. **file:** list

11. **unrough:** unbearded, smooth-faced

12. **Protest:** assert; **their first of manhood:** the beginning of **their manhood**

17. **distempered:** diseased and swollen

21. **minutely:** i.e., every minute; **upbraid:** condemn; **faith-breach:** breach of his oath (to Duncan—or breach of all oaths and vows)

27. **pestered:** infested; obstructed; overcrowded; **to recoil and start:** to flinch in alarm

32. **weal:** state, commonwealth

33–34. **pour . . . us:** i.e., **pour** out every **drop** of our blood in purging (curing) our country

5.3 Reports are brought to Macbeth of the Scottish and English forces massed against him. He seeks assurance in the apparitions' promise of safety for himself. But he is anxious about Lady Macbeth's condition and impatient with her doctor's inability to cure her.

1. **them:** i.e., the deserting thanes

3. **taint:** become tainted

5. **mortal consequences:** that which happens to humanity

9. **English epicures:** a Scottish taunt at English eating habits   **epicures:** gluttons, or those devoted to luxury

10. **sway by:** rule myself by

12. **loon:** fool

18. **lily-livered:** white-livered (because bloodless), cowardly; **patch:** fool

19. **of thy:** on your

20. **Are counselors to fear:** i.e., teach others to be frightened

24. **push:** effort

25. **disseat:** unseat, dethrone

27. **the sere:** the (condition of being) dry and withered

29. **As:** such as

30. **look:** expect

31. **mouth-honor:** honor from the tongue (rather than the heart)

32. **fain:** gladly

42. **Skirr:** search quickly, scour

52. **Raze out:** erase

53. **oblivious:** i.e., causing oblivion

54. **stuffed:** clogged

58. **physic:** medicine

62. **dispatch:** make haste (probably said to one of his attendants who is arming him)

62–63. **cast / The water of my land:** i.e., diagnose the disease from which Scotland is suffering **cast the water:** examine the (patient's) urine to diagnose an illness

69. **them:** i.e., the English

73. **bane:** destruction

5.4 The rebel Scottish forces have joined Malcolm's army at Birnam Wood. Malcolm orders each soldier to cut down and carry a bough from the wood so as to conceal their numbers from Macbeth.

1. **Cousins:** kinsmen

2. **chambers:** i.e., such rooms as bedchambers and dining rooms (see 1.7.31)

3. **nothing:** not at all

7. **shadow:** conceal

8. **host:** army; **discovery:** i.e., Macbeth's scouts or sentinels

11. **no other but:** nothing else but that

12. **Keeps:** remains

12–13. **endure . . . before 't:** not prevent our laying siege to it

15. **where . . . given:** i.e., wherever opportunity offers itself

16. **more and less:** nobles and commoners

19–20. **Let . . . event:** i.e., let us wait to judge until we see the outcome **censures:** judgments **Attend:** await **true event:** actual outcome

24. **owe:** (actually) own, possess

26. **certain issue strokes must arbitrate:** i.e., the definite outcome must be decided by blows

5.5 Macbeth is confident that he can withstand any siege from Malcolm's forces. He is then told of Lady Macbeth's death and of the apparent movement of Birnam Wood toward Dunsinane Castle, where he waits. He desperately resolves to abandon the castle and give battle to Malcolm in the field.

4. **ague:** pestilence (pronounced *a-gue*)

5. **forced:** reinforced; also, perhaps, stuffed ("farced")

5–6. **those that should be ours:** i.e., deserters from our ranks

7. **met them:** i.e., in the field, in open battle; **dareful:** boldly

12. **my . . . cooled:** I would have been chilled

13. **my fell of hair:** i.e., the hair on my scalp

14. **dismal treatise:** dreadful tale

15. **As:** as if

16. **Direness:** horror

17. **start:** startle
18. **Wherefore:** for what reason, why
20. **She should have died hereafter:** i.e., **she** would inevitably **have died** sometime; or, perhaps, **she** ought to **have died** later
22–26. **Tomorrow . . . death:** Behind Macbeth's terrible reflections lie the images of "life as a story" and "life as light" as in Matthew 5.16. See also Psalms 22.15, 39.6, 90.9; Job 14.1–2, 18.6.
23. **petty:** slow, insignificant
24. **recorded time:** i.e., recordable **time**
26. **dusty death:** See Genesis 3.19: "for dust thou art, and unto dust shalt thou return."
27. **shadow:** image without substance; also, actor; **player:** actor
38. **anon:** soon
46. **cling:** wither, shrink; **speech be sooth:** story is true
48. **pull in:** i.e., rein in; **resolution:** determination, steadfastness
49. **doubt:** suspect
54. **nor . . . nor:** neither . . . nor
56. **th' estate o' th' world:** perhaps, the settled order of the universe
57. **undone:** destroyed
58. **alarum bell:** the **bell** that calls to arms; **wrack:** ruin, destruction
59. **harness:** i.e., armor

5.6 Malcolm arrives with his troops before Dunsinane Castle.

2. **uncle:** addressed to Siward
4. **battle:** battalion, main body; **we:** Note that Malcolm here uses the royal "we."
8. **power:** army
11. **harbingers:** announcers, forerunners

5.7 On the battlefield Macbeth kills young Siward, the son of the English commander. After Macbeth exits, Macduff arrives in search of him. Dunsinane Castle has already been surrendered to Malcolm, whose forces have been strengthened by deserters from Macbeth's army.

1–2. **They have ... course:** Macbeth here sees himself as a bear in a bearbaiting, **tied to a stake** and set upon by dogs. **course:** attack, encounter

10. **title:** name

14. **prove:** challenge, test

21. **still:** always

22. **kerns:** i.e., hired soldiers (more specifically, Irish foot soldiers)

23. **staves:** weapons; **Either thou:** i.e., either I find you

25. **undeeded:** i.e., unused

26–27. **one ... bruited:** someone of great reputation is proclaimed

29. **gently rendered:** surrendered without a fight

32. **itself professes:** announces itself

35. **strike beside us:** i.e., fight on our side, side by side

5.8 Macduff finds Macbeth, who is reluctant to fight with him because Macbeth has already killed Macduff's whole family and is sure of killing Macduff too if they fight. When Macduff announces that he is not, strictly speaking, a man born of woman, having been ripped prematurely from his mother's womb, then Macbeth is afraid to fight. He fights with Macduff only when Macduff threatens to capture him and display him as a public spectacle. Macduff kills Macbeth, cuts off his head, and brings it to Malcolm. With Macbeth dead, Malcolm is now king and gives new titles to his loyal supporters.

1. **Roman:** associated here with approval of suicide

2. **lives:** i.e., others living

6. **charged:** burdened

10. **Than terms can give thee out:** i.e., than words can describe you

12. **intrenchant:** invulnerable, unable to be cut

13. **impress:** leave a mark on

18. **angel:** i.e., evil spirit; **still:** always

20. **Untimely:** prematurely

22. **my better part of man:** the **better part of** my manhood (i.e., perhaps, courage)

23. **juggling:** deceiving

24. **palter . . . sense:** trick us by using words ambiguously

28. **gaze:** that which is gazed at; spectacle

30. **Painted upon a pole:** i.e., his picture painted and displayed on **a pole**, as for a sideshow; **underwrit:** written underneath

34. **baited:** attacked from all sides (as the bear is in a bearbaiting)

36. **opposed:** i.e., my opponent

39 SD. **They enter fighting, and Macbeth is slain:** This Folio stage direction is omitted by many editors because they feel that it contradicts the stage direction that immediately precedes it in the Folio: *"Exit fighting. Alarums."* Although early printed texts such as the Folio sometimes include duplicatory or contradictory stage directions, it is certainly possible in this case to perform all the directions printed in the Folio and reprinted here.

40. **miss:** lack

41. **go off:** i.e., die; **by these:** to judge by those present

47. **unshrinking . . . fought:** where **he fought** steadfastly, refusing to give ground

53. **before:** on the front of his body

67. **compassed . . . pearl:** surrounded by the most choice subjects of your kingdom

73–74. **reckon . . . even with you:** make an accounting of (also, take into account) the love each of you has shown, and discharge my debt to you

78. **Which . . . time:** which should be done immediately in this new era

79. **As:** such as

81. **Producing . . . ministers:** bringing forth (to justice) the agents

83. **self and violent hands:** her own **violent hands**

Textual Notes

The reading of the present text appears to the left of the square bracket. The earliest sources of readings not in **F**, the First Folio text, are indicated as follows: **F2** is the Second Folio of 1632; **F3** is the Third Folio of 1663-64; **F4** is the Fourth Folio of 1685; **Ed.** is an earlier editor of Shakespeare, beginning with Rowe in 1709. **SD** means stage direction; **SP** means speech prefix.

1.1	10–11.	SP SECOND WITCH . . . THIRD WITCH] Ed.; *All* F
1.2	0.	SD *King Duncan, Malcolm*] Ed.; *King Malcolme* F
	15.	gallowglasses] F2; Gallowgrosses F
	16.	quarrel] Ed.; Quarry F
	28.	break] Ed.; *omit* F
1.3	40.	Forres] Ed.; Soris F
	102.	Came] Ed.; Can F
1.4	1.	Are] F2; Or F
1.6	5.	martlet] Ed.; Barlet F
	6.	mansionry] Ed.; Mansonry F
	10.	most] Ed.; must F
1.7	6.	shoal] Ed.; Schoole F
	52.	do] Ed.; no F
2.1	67.	strides] Ed.; sides F
	69.	sure] Ed.; sowre F
	70.	way they] Ed.; they may F
2.3	0.	SD *Knocking within. Enter a Porter.*] Ed.; *Enter a Porter. Knocking within.* F
	20.	SD *The . . . Lennox.*] this ed.; *Enter Macduffe and Lenox.* F
	159.	SD *All . . . exit.*] Ed.; *Exeunt.* F
3.1	10.	SD *Lady Macbeth, Lennox*] Ed.; *Lady Lenox* F

	81, 131, 159.	SP MURDERERS] Ed.; *Murth.* F
	162.	SD *He exits.*] Ed.; *Exeunt.* F
3.3	9.	and] F2; end F
3.4	94.	time] Ed.; times F
3.6	28.	son] Ed.; Sonnes F
	42.	the] Ed.; their F
	50.	t' hold] F2; t hold F
4.1	38.	SD *to*] Ed.; *and* F
	62.	germens . . . all together] Ed.; Germaine . . . altogether F
	107.	SD *He descends.*] Ed.; *Descend.* F
	126.	SD *A . . . last.*] this ed.; *A shew of eight Kings, and Banquo last, with a glasse in his hand.* F
4.2	98.	SD *Lady . . . body.*] Ed.; *Exit crying Murther.* F
4.3	5.	downfall'n] Ed.; downfall F
	18.	deserve] Ed.; discerne F
	125.	accursed] F2; accust F
	152.	thy] F2; they F
	183.	not] F2; nor F
	276.	tune] Ed.; time F
5.3	25.	disseat] Ed.; dis-eate F
	49.	her] F2; *omit* F